Counseling and Psychotherapy

Counseling and Psychotherapy

THE PURSUIT OF VALUES

by Charles A. Curran

SHEED AND WARD : NEW YORK

© *Sheed and Ward, Inc., 1968*

Library of Congress Catalog Card Number: 68-9368

Manufactured in the United States of America

DEDICATION:
TO ALL THOSE CLOSE TO ME—
TO WHOM I OWE SO MUCH

Acknowledgements

APPRECIATION and gratitude is, first of all, expressed to all students and others who have aided immeasurably in the clarification of these ideas.

My professional colleagues, particularly at Loyola University, have been both an inspiration and an encouragement. Special appreciation is owed Robert Mulligan, S.J. and Vincent Herr, S.J. as well as Dr. Ronald Walker and Dr. Frank Kobler. I acknowledge also the kindness and valuable comments of Eugene Kennedy, M.M. and Dr. David Bakan.

In the immediate research and production of this manuscript, my gratitude goes to Rosina Mena Gallagher and Jennybelle P. Rardin for constant aid and support. Included here also should be Mary K. Lynch and Mary Gibbons Davis.

For comments on adult and child psychiatric developments, the author owes much to Dr. Mary F. Young and Dr. Norma B. Gutierrez. For special help in initiating the foreign language research project, appreciation is due Mlle Odile Bertrand and the many foreign students who over a number of years have participated in the program.

Recognition should also be given here to my great debt to all at the Menninger Foundation where my associations through the years, proved so instructive and inspiring. To all there and especially to Dr. Paul Pruyser, Dr. Seward Hiltner and Chaplain Thomas Klink, I extend my gratitude.

In a particular way, I owe to Dr. Karl Menninger my deep appreciation for his gracious kindness and friendship.

To Dr. Carl R. Rogers, finally, I must express the debt of a student and friend.

Contents

INTRODUCTION

Toward the Realization of Values

A GENUINE INVESTMENT of self is essential to any authentic relationship and to any purposive life. Of all the basic values that a man searches for and pursues, an authentic and genuine relationship with another person and if possible with many persons, seems to be among the most profound. If and when achieved, it becomes one of the most convalidating of all his personal fulfillments. While this book draws heavily for examples of such authentic relationship from counseling and psychotherapy, a main purpose is to evolve, for more general awareness and use, the conditions of such authenticity.

VALUE COUNSELING AND
PSYCHOTHERAPY

The methods of counseling and therapy illustrated here might be given the general name "Value Counseling and Psychotherapy." By this title we mean to describe a process of self-commitment and involvement that engages counselor or therapist and clients in a dialogue of understanding that strives for more penetrating and effective self-awareness and greater fulfillment of self, toward others. It leads, in other words, to a new "evaluation" and commitment. We have called it "value" to suggest the essential aspect of self-investment on the part of counselor, therapist and clients, if such an authentic relationship and process is to emerge. It is in this sense especially that such relationships can become the models from which to pattern, with necessary modifications, other genuine personal engagements.

Since our focus is on the conditions for authentic relationships and the search for and pursuit of values, we have made no fine

3

distinctions between counseling and psychotherapy, taking these words in their ordinary usage as suggesting broadly the same helping relationship. While *psychotherapy* in its origin, implies a concept of illness, it has come increasingly to signify an ordinary mode of offering skilled psychological assistance at a personal and intimate level. *Counseling,* while it still may suggest simply giving advice and guidance, has also gradually come to mean something of the same kind of intimate, personal and skillful psychological assistance at the unique levels of the self. In this sense, counseling and psychotherapy are often used with a similar connotation, the main difference perhaps now being that counseling tends to refer to an educational, family or pastoral setting and psychotherapy has a more clinical tone. Consequently, throughout this book, we will use the terms *counseling* and *psychotherapy* somewhat interchangeably. Except where clear distinctions are indicated, this interchange will usually be expressed by the term *counseling therapy.* How they differ, and how *guidance* and *education* differ, will be discussed in greater detail in this chapter and elsewhere. Such distinctions, however, do not mean that one excludes the other. On the contrary, a main focus of this book will be to show many instances where they are all intimately related, particularly as regards the requirements for genuine relationships and personal values.

MEANING AND VALUE

As we will also explain later in detail, we are contrasting "value" with "meaning." "Meaning," we propose, is the search for significance, the answer to the perennial "why?" of child and adult. It seeks to order and relate man to the universe. Its aim is also to provide possible areas of personal *orientation*. It affords an option of goals, directions and purposes. "Meanings" give a person his field of options, pointing him to areas of possible choice and self-investment.

"Values" are these self-investments. They are those areas of knowledge out of which each individual makes and shapes—uniquely for himself—his own self-quest and his engagement to others. These are what—in all the aspects of knowledge—he "values" and so considers, in some way, a special good for him. In this sense we could say that a person is what he invests himself in. So also, what he values will indicate what he is.

CONFLICTING VALUES

It is particularly in this area of self-investment and engagement with others that counseling and psychotherapy have their special significance. For it is the maze and crisscross of conflicting personal values—present and past, conscious and unconscious, explicit and implicit, personal, environmental, cultural—that constitute the arena in which the counseling therapeutic dialogue transpires. It is in the facilitating of a more adequate re-sorting and reorganizing of these personal value investments, that the skill of "value counseling and psychotherapy" especially consists.

Since these values are personal and unique, this skill is basically client- or person-centered. Values imply a person who has already committed himself to particular goals, directions or purposes as well as to the persons and particular situations these involve.

What we are stressing here, however, is that the skilled response aims not only at the acceptance and understanding of the person at a basic emotional-instinctive-somatic level but also at the clarification of conflicting self-values. To be sure, the client is usually in a state of negation, conflict and frustration that has a strong emotional component. But behind this and basic to it, is his confusion about and conflict with his own value system—implicit and explicit. His difficulty consists in his being at cross-purposes with himself as value commitments conflict, contradict and impede one another and so throw him into varying degrees of defeat and self-stagnation. The skillfully managed relationship seeks to help a person to re-define himself and so to re-sort his self-invested values. It further seeks to provide him with sufficient integration of his own forces so that he can genuinely give himself to others as well as achieve in greater measure the values he genuinely desires. It is in this sense, then, that we speak of "Value Counseling and Psychotherapy."

THE PROCESS OF CLARIFICATION

A person usually seeks counsel in a state of confusion and conflict, accompanied by a strong emotion or combination of emotions. He may indicate his confusion by saying, for example,

I don't know how to begin, I'm just all mixed up. I simply don't know what's the matter.

He may then go on to say:

I'm just pulled apart . . . I'm in constant tension. I don't know which way to go. I try to move one way and then I'm pulled in another. I can't seem to get clear—what I should do or how I should do it.

This expresses the conflict of various forces or "self-vectors."

With this he might have also said, "I'm just angry and frustrated, I don't know why . . . but I can't seem to get going. I'm just caught and stuck." Or, "I'm just depressed and discouraged a good part of the time."

Upon reflection, one can see that, to be engaged in this confusion-conflict, this depressed or hostile state, implies a deep commitment to a complicated series of values, that is, of self-investments. Otherwise, why would the person be so upset? This is what gives rise to the emotions, and the instinctive and somatic defense mechanisms with which the person is often in such turmoil. We see implied in such intense feelings, even when they are suppressed, an invested person caught up in the conflicting warp and woof of his own personal, environmental and cultural situation. He can be and usually is, "hoist with his own petar."

VALUE PATTERNS

It is the unweaving and disentangling of these conflicting and confused values that constitutes the central achievement of the counseling therapy process. One of the main aims and benefits of counseling therapy, to be sure, is to afford the person a steady and consistent freedom to express and communicate with another who understands and shares in a warm, deep way. But, in addition, this also enables a person to explore and "dig through," as one client put it, these confused conflicting states and their engaged emotions and gradually to uncover the complicated mosaic of present and past values in which the person has consciously or unconsciously invested himself.

Such investments can come from his own earlier life and sometimes be forgotten. They can also come from his environment: from his family value system; from his parents' personal characteristics—particularly the dominating parent in the family structure; from his older brothers and sisters; and from the neighborhood, Church and school environment in which he has been raised. His values also come, in a complicated way, from the whole culture he has inherited.

Such a confused mosaic of values is very complex. A difficult and painful state can result when powerful value vectors from one source—say, a Judaeo-Graeco-Christian culture—are thrown in conflict with vectors of equal value pushing in an opposite direction—like some personal or immediate need. Or, values represented by the mother or father can be in sharp conflict with those adolescent or adult values that have emerged as something which the person himself wants as a fulfillment of his own self-ideal and actualization.

With the aid of skilled, penetrating and understanding responses carried on consistently through a series of interviews, a person usually reveals to himself a complicated overlay of values that are both confused and in conflict. This is precisely the process of both survey and evaluation which counseling therapy affords. In the later stages particularly, it also offers the client an integrating and organizing assistance as he redesigns his life value system and refashions his self-investments and his engagements with other persons and situations. Of the values that implicitly or unconsciously have affected and moved him, he may reject some and choose to retain others. With these latter, counseling through its steady, reflective process, should aid him to a better use of himself and the means at hand to achieve what are now conscious and explicit goals and purposes. In this sense, the unfolding—much as a package might be unfolded or unwrapped—implied in the word "explicit," is itself a helpful description of the process.

Obviously, when the contents of the value package are open and unfolded, one is far more knowledgeable about goals which one wants and how to achieve them. Alternately, by the same process, many previous, hidden and unanalyzed value motives can be discarded as having been useful in childhood, or inherited in some way from the cultural setting or learned from family and childhood environments and yet no longer adequate. In fact, a counseling process may reveal that some of these earlier values are now proven to be impediments and even destructive. Once this is unfolded and clarified, these values can be openly rejected. Previously they may have been somewhat rejected and resisted but often with some measure of self-recrimination and guilt.

Such a counseling therapy process is engaged with values which relate the person to others and to situations beyond himself. It is therefore not simply focussed on his own self-concept and self-actualization. Necessary as these self preoccupations may be, they yet need to be completed by authentic relations to others and to situations beyond the self.

EDUCATION

Each individual person, at birth, may be said to stand on the point of a triangle that extends its broadening base into the past. On this point he is at the existential moment of constant experience, the moment of continual change and, as well, the moment of anxiety that this shifting life encounter brings him. Beyond his primitive infantile endowments usually shared in some way with other animals, a person *learns* to cope with life. This learning mostly comes from others. It comes from those around him who aid him in particular situations—by way of guidance—and from the cultural deposit of his whole civilization—by way of education, formal and informal. In applying this knowledge adequately to himself, he must take counsel with himself, pondering all the aspects of his psychosomatic uniqueness that he can consciously grasp. He may be aided in this by another through counseling or, in a more complex and therapeutic need, through psychotherapy.

Education then, is that broad area of knowledge which the human race has received or acquired through the centuries, the transmission of which in varying degrees is absolutely essential for human survival as well as for the achievement of human meaning, value and ultimate significance and fulfillment. Seen this way, the term *education* has a general quality. It seeks to relate facts and principles together in some kind of orderly and usable fashion.

GUIDANCE

Guidance is more personal. It considers education from the point of view of the personal concerns or involvement of particular groups or individuals receiving it. Like education, guidance is somewhat information-centered. It would be applied, however, to a more immediate and personal need. It is, therefore, likely to be more emotionally charged than educational material since the person receiving guidance would be much more directly concerned and involved.

By analogy with food, education is like the basic raw materials and balanced diet necessary for a stable and adequate growth process, while guidance is the careful cuisine which prepares the food to suit the individual taste.

PERSON-CENTERED

Counseling and *psychotherapy,* by comparison, would be more person-centered and less information-centered. In saying this we do not mean to imply that education and guidance should not also be person-centered. On the contrary, this will be one of our main themes and conclusions, namely that counseling—if only in a "brief encounter" form—is essential to any adequate educational, guidance or other personal relationships which concern values as well as meanings.

In the food analogy, counseling would be aimed at aiding the normal process of mastication, digestion and assimilation. Psychotherapy would be the therapy necessary when serious blockings and impediments to digestion which would endanger health are present.

This implies that everyone must take counsel with himself on any question or decision involving values and personal commitments and that this normal process can sometimes be facilitated by counseling. *Counseling,* in this sense, would be considered a *normal process.* Beyond this, there are obviously blockings and confusions of such a serious nature that they impede the normal functions of personality and so require "therapy," that is, the grave and attentive concern that any illness should receive including, if necessary, hospitalization and custodial care. *Psychotherapy,* then, is at the illness end of a person-centered continuum. *Counseling* would be at the other end of the same continuum, facilitating the resolution of what might be called normal operational confusions and conflicts but where skilled help can still be necessary or advantageous.

MENTAL ILLNESS

Psychotherapy is often associated with the notion of treating "mental illness." One of the difficulties with the model of "mental health," and the contrasting "mental illness," is—as we will later consider—that we may tend to think of these relationships as applicable only to the treatment of "sick" people. This may have impeded us from taking adequate advantage of the richness and depth of modern psychotherapeutic research. This knowledge has too often remained in the arcana of the hospital and the clinic, when, as a matter of fact, it is proving increasingly valuable whenever we use it in human relations.

The same implications can be contained in the emphasis on the word "therapy." This word suggests the cautions, anxieties and dangers surrounding anything having to do with illness. Consequently, those who are not trained as special health "experts," feel reluctant and hesitant to enter and perhaps intrude unwisely in an area that is so concerned with "illness." In this sense, "counseling" is less threatening. It gives some at least, of the positive implications that such psychological understanding implies. Even here, however, much of this understanding could be more generally utilized.

This is not to say that these ideas have not been known popularly. On the contrary, they have been exaggeratedly popularized but often with the notion and implication that they involve application to issues of health and illness similar to those of surgery and complicated medications. While such contentions are obviously true in matters of complicated mental illness, they tend to obscure and remove other applications, to learning, for example, or social relations. Many of the valuable insights that counseling and psychotherapy have brought forward, need to be adapted for more general use particularly in all phases of education, learning and personal relationships.

A further complexity in the use of the word "psychotherapy" and related concepts like "mental illness," is that they contain for many the implicit stigma of possibly being "mentally" sick or even "crazy." This is illustrated by the fact that many soldiers in World War II or after, had a fear of being labeled psychoneurotic (P.N.), even though this meant an honorable discharge. Given an option, they often preferred a dishonorable discharge because at least it did not carry the stigma of this "mental sickness" label. A similar situation can occur in schools where children, through being labeled "mentally sick" or as having "psychological problems," are relegated to some specialized treatment and so isolated from the very forces of normality that could most aid them. From one point of view it could seem a kindness to consider people mentally ill so that, like physical illness, they would be treated with acceptance, sympathy and understanding in place of being rejected as "bad," and "uncooperative" when they need care. Yet what we are now seeing is that the phrase, "mentally sick," can still sometimes contain the same hostility, rejection, condescension and ostracism that expressions like "He's no good!" formerly implied. Given a choice, many people might prefer being "sinners" since this at least offers them the respectful dignity of being considered responsible for what they do, when excused by being labelled "sick," they may feel actually condemned to hopelessness and permanent rejection by others.

COUNSELING AND GUIDANCE

In considering the relationship of counseling and guidance, the counselor's skill may be said to complete the work of guidance. The *skill of the guidance expert* involves being both knowledgeable and able to present the informative material in a way that is palatable and attractive to the individual taste, that is, according to the individual's life condition and various other personal aspects. Being informed in a technical sense, the expert will often give advice on specialized questions for which he has, by way of his training, special competence. Lacking such competence, a person must depend on the specialist for such knowledge and guidance. Because of the expert's respected position, the other person has a particular kind of faith and trust in the expert's knowledge and judgment. But for this relationship to be effective by itself, we must presume the person's having sufficient integration, self-knowledge and control to carry out the detailed series of personal steps necessary to act on this guidance.

The *skill of the counselor,* however, is rather a focus on methods that enable a person to clarify and grow in that highly personal self-knowledge and adequate self-reorganization necessary for the inner strength to act on education, advice and guidance. In this sense the counselor's skill aims at the final development of the person's capacity to act on what he has learned. We see that this will be a person-centered approach. The counselor aids the person to make better choices in the minute details of his personal life. With this help a person can devise better means to his goals. At the same time the counselor's skills help him grow in the ability to integrate his soma, instincts and emotions so that he is in less conflict and division concerning what he can and should do.

Counseling then, does not exclude the necessity of education and guidance. Rather it implies these. Its concern is more the lack of the ability to assimilate such knowledge in the conflict and confusion one finds in daily living. At this point a person may be in no state to act adequately on guidance. Only when such a person, through counseling, has arrived at some measure of assimilation ability, does he seem to have any degree of guidance readiness and the basic inner strength to put such guidance into adequate operation.

RELATIONSHIPS

In the use of these terms we are, moreover, describing *relationships*. That is to say, we are really speaking of educational, guidance, counseling and psychotherapeutic relationships. They are, then, not mutually exclusive. Until recently, the tendency to stress the one-hour counseling or psychotherapy interview, "the therapy hour," implied that no other relationship could interfere or intervene. Lately, however, in what has been called the "ten-minute hour," we are seeing advantages to a relationship of counseling or therapy even for only short periods. In this sense, over a given hour, one might intermingle counseling, guidance and educational relationships with the same person, couple or group. But in recognizing the differing qualities of each relationship, one would know what was intended by each and so could better meet the varying demands they make. This, of course, does not preclude also having the customary thirty or sixty minute "hour" of counseling or psychotherapy.

COUNSELING THERAPY

Because, then, much of the discussion in this book considers issues that are common to both counseling and psychotherapy, we have, as we said, usually simplified this double reference by the use of the term, "counseling therapy." For the same reason, we have commonly used *person* or *client* except where, as in a medical or hospital setting, the designation "patient" is obviously called for.

RELIGIOUS VALUES

Religious values would, of course, necessarily constitute a significant aspect of any treatment of values in all their personal, environmental and cultural forms. This is assumed in our present general consideration of value-search and pursuit. We are concerned here, however, primarily with the way an individual person, in a skilled relationship, searches out and pursues his own personal values, implicit and explicit. Many basic religious values have, moreover, become such a fundamental part of our cultural heritage that everyone is actually affected by them whether he is professedly religious or not. Any treatment of personal values, therefore, by implication, includes this cultural and personal heritage.

A separate book, entitled *Counseling, Psychotherapy and Religion,* will particularly focus on some of the conditions basic to a genuine religious commitment. This would constitute the final value orientation in the life of a believing religious person. For this reason, too, we have implied, rather than directly treated, religious values here.

PLAN OF THIS BOOK

Complicated individual and social factors are bringing about a new sense and restoring an older sense of the "person." We are also again seeing man as a unified being of great subtlety and depth. This involves more than those general life meanings which a man acquires through study, education and guidance. Even more fundamentally it initiates the question of his pursuit of values, those special personal meanings in which he can validly invest himself. So conceived, education, guidance, counseling and psychotherapy are concerned with factors and values that result in personal investment and psychological maturity and not simply intellectual knowledge alone. This is the over-all plan and purpose of the book.

The first section considers these and related issues in separate chapters. The second section discusses aspects of the art and skill of counseling therapy and similar authentic relationships with individuals, couples and small and large groups. The third section considers in detail some educational research on methods and learning apparatus and their implications for both personal values and counseling. The concluding chapter attempts to pull together some general implications for value-investment, authentic involvement and the nature of reality, to which the individual chapters of this book and present developments in psychology and allied fields, seem to lead.

PART ONE
Basic Considerations

1

Value Commitment and Authentic Relationship

VALUE INVESTMENT in the sense of self-commitment, on the part of counselor, therapist and clients or, more generally considered, in other deep personal relationships, runs into some special difficulties that characterize our present milieu. These difficulties are cultural and environmental as well as personal. Our age and perhaps every age since Newton has been characterized by an increasing removal from and the objectifying of experience. In this sense, we all tend to be "scientific" observers of life in ourselves and others, rather than to a spontaneous involvement in experience itself. By watching oneself in action, one really is not acting or knowing or loving, but one is caught between these in anxiety, in being afraid to live. This tendency permeates our culture, as the drama critic, Walter Kerr, has pointed out:

But to recognize something—without having agreed upon it, without even having discussed it—is knowing, too. The mind is stabbed on a spot it did not know was vulnerable. This is knowing by contact, on contact.

We have neglected knowledge by contact in our abstraction-centered lives, have in fact almost persuaded ourselves that it does not exist. . . . When we say "intelligent," or "intellectual," we simply mean "rational," and nothing other than "rational." The mind seems to us to function— validly—by discursive thought alone, as though it possessed but a single power, a single tentacle for searching out truth. Our conviction finally reduces the world about us to the flat lines and empty spaces of the one method we acknowledge.[1]

19

This is especially apparent in any attempt, either through writing or lecturing, to present aspects of counseling and psychotherapy. Our culture tends to make us see things in "flat lines and empty spaces," in a purely intellectualized process according to a mathematical and geometrical model, (developed for us by Descartes, as we will explain later). Here, "rational" has the tone of its use in "rational numbers." It is difficult for people to get engaged in and involved in what they are studying. But such genuine engagement is necessary, if the material studied is to be anything more than "objective" information. This material must somehow catch us at the inner level of our own unique and personal world and really *change* us. This is the kind of learning that is involved in the material presented in this book and this is the main dynamic that relates counseling and psychotherapy to values. Value learning demands personal engagement and change, not simply objective and uninvolved knowing.

Reading about counseling and psychotherapy, then, differs from much other reading insofar as it must involve the reader personally if it is to be really understood. This is similar to the reaction of students who are learning counseling and psychotherapy—they will not really learn until they become engaged and committed themselves. This is usually achieved through hearing recorded interviews, analyzing their content and the art and skill involved, role-playing (simulating actual experiences) and, finally, being in counseling therapy with people, recording this and having their sessions supervised and examined.

TOTAL PERSON INVOLVEMENT

While mere reading cannot do this, the reproduction of interview excerpts can bring the reader much closer to the "feeling with" experience that counseling and psychotherapy demand. In training persons in the art and skill of counseling and psychotherapy, one often observes personal changes in particular individuals while they are learning. This can happen even during a reading assignment. This comes about, evidently, from reading with a committed and engaged attitude. The following written comments illustrate this:

My first response to the material was that it was repetitive and could have been said as effectively in fewer words. Now, however, I feel that in order to get the point across a certain dynamic is also involved in the presentation. By this I mean one has to try and recapture an actual interview, or an experience.

To relate this experience or insight, one has to draw it out, and, just as in the counseling process, the reader has to respond to make it meaningful. Conversely, the reader, and in this case I am speaking about myself, puts himself in the role of client. By doing this I was able to benefit, after several readings, from the experience and awareness communicated.

. . . the material tried so hard to further elucidate the dynamics of a fruitful counseling relationship, that it helped me understand an experience I myself had and thus helped me also to grow in some positive way. . . . it is this level of experiencing or dramatizing that really points out the crucial element. Because I honestly think that unless one has this type of experience, that is, seeing this phenomenon in operation, the material can remain on a cold "scientific" level. Perhaps Teilhard de Chardin captures this same feeling in the *Phenomenon of Man* when he describes the freeing realization of seeing, for "to *see* or to *perish* is the very condition laid upon everything that makes up the universe." This can be hindered if we remain forever the focus of our own perception, thus: "It is tiresome and even humbling for the observer to be thus fettered, to be obliged to carry with him everywhere the centre of the landscape he is crossing. But what happens when chance directs his steps to a point of vantage (a cross-roads, or intersecting valleys) from which not only his vision, but things themselves radiate? In that event the subjective viewpoint coincides with the way things are distributed objectively, and perception reaches its apogee. The landscape lights up and yields its secret. He sees."[2]

This is what I understand by the freeing movement toward insight that a crucial response can open up and help the person to see, through the reflective and precise understanding of another person, whom we call counselor.

What we are speaking of here, then, is a kind of commitment that brings our thought alive not simply intellectually but in an engagement with our total incarnate selves. Speaking of Simone Weil, T. S. Eliot remarks:

It was rather that all her thought was so intensely lived, that the abandonment of any opinion required modifications in her whole being; a process which could not take place painlessly, or in the course of a conversation.[3]

This kind of commitment by no means implies a person obsessionally glued to his own ideas, unable to be fluid and flexible in seeing another view and accepting opposite awarenesses. On the contrary, from greater security in himself, a genuinely committed person may readily give place to the expression of opposition and difference without being aroused to defensiveness and closed resistance. It is rather the person with views that are not integrated but borrowed and external, who is apt to feel very threatened by any disagreement.

SCIENTIFIC KNOWLEDGE

In this emphasis on a total-person involvement, however, we do not mean to impugn the great contributions of the scientific era. These contributions are so vast and their value so all-pervading, one can hardly even begin to question them.

The investigative techniques and detailed precision of the scientific method are also of immense importance. We need scientific knowledge and hypotheses and the precise and accurate methods of observation and validation scientific procedures afford us. In fact, such precision is a necessary antidote to the type of thinking —all too common—that draws sweeping conclusions which, in fact, may be only sophisticated prejudices or unconscious wish-fulfillments. The discipline of scientific design and the careful analysis of data are most helpful and necessary to the serious study of human behavior. The openness to all relevant data implied in the scientific outlook is also paramount for any genuine advance in our understanding. The value of scientific knowledge is clear:

When things *are* so proved out, they are ready to be used; because the knowledge can be demonstrated, on paper or in the laboratory, it can be profitably employed in the strict discipline of all our further work. The method is itself work, and it is the cornerstone of whatever other work we do.[4]

But this kind of scientific knowledge contains serious difficulties. The core of these is that such a method of knowing can lead us to a depersonalized way of relating to life. In such isolation, we may know little of the real value of persons and things. We can be coldly knowledgeable and judgmental of the human condition because we share so little of it. Kerr states:

Abstract knowledge is arrived at by making things as unlike themselves, and as unlike ourselves, as possible: by isolating them from all concreteness and all flesh, by reducing them to disembodied principles . . .[5]

MOSAIC OF LIVING EXPERIENCE

In this book, then, efforts at theory and scientific knowledge will be evident. But the knowledge around which the aim of this book centers is the knowing which pulls us into the vortex of living. This will not leave us with "clear and distinct ideas"—the model of Descartes—but with a complicated and subtle mosaic of ideas, feelings, impressions and reactions. At its best, this kind of knowing, filled with the realities of living as it is, will put us in touch with life, our own and that of others. To quote Kerr again:

It is a knowledge that breeds affection, what Conrad called "the latent feeling of fellowship with all creation." It renews our pleasure in the universe. More than that. As our being touches other being, and lets it flow into us, we are mysteriously aware that our own being has been increased. From having discovered ourselves in a multitude of things we have made ourselves more, or at least have become more amply ourselves. Something like re-creation runs in us like a tide.[6]

People are "hit" by such moments of knowing. Such experiences are personally constructive because the people involved are really "struck" and held fast. The following is a description of such a learning experience from a person in counseling therapy training:

Today I experienced in actuality the "critical response moment" described, in an interview I had with one of my students. I had asked to see her because I felt a certain hostility and resistance on her part to communicate in group conferences, although apparently not due to any lack of intellectual ability.

As the interview progressed, passages from the material flashed across my mind and I was intently aware of their implication and effect on my responses in trying to help her "see" what she was saying. The thing that was totally fascinating to me was actually experiencing the phenomenon by which a person gains some insight into herself. But more than just sharing an insightful experience, I felt we actually developed a relationship wherein we discovered our "selves." The relationship evolved as the interview progressed and the more invested each of us became, the more open and vulnerable we were to each other. When one gets at the heart of the relationship one has with another, one gets at the heart of the issue, the area of the problem. This I experienced as a sudden openness and willingness to trust the other person as she "is." It was a rapport, an empathy which "hits" in a moment of time when one could look the other straight in the eye with no holds barred; when one is aware of the other as a personality, an individual entity. In this moment of truth there is experienced mutually a total giving and a total acceptance of self, a seeing beyond the trappings to the genuine, the real, beneath . . . The interesting thing here is the fact that the subject we discussed throughout the interview remained the same, it was the attitude, the involvement that changed.

The critical response in her case came near the end of the interview when I responded, "You feel that when people don't agree with your ideas they are rejecting you—the you of your inner self." This seemed to produce first a quiet agreement followed by a more violent acceptance wherein she was able to "vomit" forth a seemingly relieving release . . .

At the end of the release she stated "I see now what you saw before and were trying to get me to see too (pause) I feel very peaceful inside—things have kind of slowed down."

One can read the text of interviews, one can intellectualize the "moment of truth" but only when one has actually taken part in the experience, can one really know.

Christopher Fry, commenting on an occasion when he was unexpectedly asked to act as critic of a play he was about to see, says that, throughout the play itself, "I could scarcely hear a word of the play for the noise of my own mind wondering how I should write about it."[7] This is what often happens in a personal encounter. We do not hear what people really say because of the noise of our own mind, "figuring out" a response and answer to them. There is no creative flow and commitment. There is, at best, only objective and impersonal analysis. At worst, there is "games-we-play," trickery, maneuvering or boredom.

SELF-SEARCH AND GIFT

This book is not concerned, then, with people's "problems" and ways of figuring them out and giving answers, like those found in the back of a math book. Insofar as it tries to offer anything except deep sensitivity to the mysteries of life, it rather proposes solutions. But its solutions are not answers, but solvents, ways of loosening and freeing a person to be more truly and genuinely himself; or, in that odd paradox, to both "be" and "become" himself, and to grow in the understanding of, respect for, and love of himself as he is and can be. People sometimes remark, in their most constructive self-description, "You know, I'm really free to become more really myself than I ever was before and I like it." Rogers comments,

What is most personal and unique in each one of us is probably the very element which would, if it were showed or expressed, speak most deeply to others.[8]

In uniquely, genuinely being ourselves we are offering our best gift to others.

REFLECTION

While it is evident that a purely intellectualized process can be a withdrawal and an escape from authentic personal relationships, it is equally evident that such personal relationships can be so intense that one needs time to reflect upon them in order to function adequately in them. How to provide for this reflection is also one of our concerns here, in the section on the art and skill of counseling therapy (cf. Part Two). Reflection on one's own involved state is often necessary in order to make adequate use of oneself. Otherwise, a person can be so taken up with the conditions and demands of the involvement that he confuses, misleads and even deceives himself and others about the intent and purpose of the personal relationship itself. To offer such a means for involved self-reflection is one of the main values of counseling and psychotherapy. It will therefore be one of our main considerations too.

PERSONAL COMMITMENT

It is popular now to consider commitment and engagement in terms of social or political involvement, especially in the current pressing social issues. These questions are related to issues considered here but this is not our main concern. We intend a specially *personal* sense of terms like *involvement* and *commitment*. For all their laudable motives and purpose, social and political issues may not really engage one with persons: they may, like many other "objective" issues, lead away from and displace a truly personal relationship. In any case, in addition to the importance of these issues in themselves, they derive their ultimate significance from persons. It is this personal engagement and concern that makes such social or political involvement finally authentic.

But personal relationship and engagement can also be misleading in another way. There is necessary here a concept of limits, of what has been called "the therapy of limits," to avoid the deceptive and narcissistic maneuvering of people under the appearance of really caring for them and trying to help them. Here a double trap is possible in which one not only maneuvers the other person but is in turn maneuvered by him. Such "being involved with someone" —with its negative implications—is finally "the blind leading the blind."

Narcissus never really saw his own image in the pool. On the contrary, he thought all the time he was genuinely loving another. The difficulty was that when he reached out to embrace and experience love, the object of his love disappeared and Narcissus was convinced he was cursed by the gods.

This kind of narcissistic self-deception is often waiting the un- skilled and untrained person who seeks involvement with others. Here apparently, as in many other human relationships, the sense of "rendering to each one his own" and recognizing the limits of oneself as well as the rights and limits of others, still remains the wisest basis and most solid foundation of personal engagement. For if love is seen as the gift of the self to another, it must imply a right sense of both controlled possession of and the limiting of the self, before one can give oneself. It includes as well the recognition of the mysterious and unique entity of the other that is always beyond me, if I am truly to give myself to *another*. Otherwise the relationship can be simply that kind of narcissistic self-deception which is in the end usually self-defeating. It never reaches anyone but one's self.

AUTHENTIC RELATIONSHIP

Authentic relationship implies and demands a genuine investment of self. Like the word "investment" itself, such an involvement process is value-oriented. It is not enough simply to know the meaning and significance of persons and things, it is necessary to invest oneself in someone and something. This constitutes value: knowing, plus our own degree of self-investment. We are, there- fore, what we value, that in which we invest and involve our- selves.

In this then, counseling and psychotherapy provide us with a model for personal relationship, learning and, in fact, for all situa- tions where meaning and significance of what is represented, have also to become personal values. When a person genuinely invests himself in these meanings and is creatively involved with others in producing their adequate fruition, he has made them personal values. *This bringing of meaning and representation into being so that they become values* is the central process we see evident in counseling and psychotherapy. Such a model of both being and representing constitutes the conditions for authentic relationship and creative commitment to ourselves and others.

By "model" here, we do not mean an ideal or a conceptualization that needs no improvement. We simply mean an operational structure of human relationships that can act as a beginning pattern upon which to establish new and perhaps more adequate designs and fresh ways of thinking. We mean it somewhat in the sense of a hypothetical construct. Models conceived in this manner can be useful means to the organization of our thinking. Moreover, experimental designs may be possible for some aspects of this model as phases emerge for which such designs may later be devised.[9]

Personal relationships to be authentic, should also be creative and produce positive validation from others. The manner in which others respond to and reflect a person, apparently determines how he begins to regard himself. If the attitude of those who are important to him—first, parents, family, then friends, neighbors, school and work associates—adds up to a positive and respectful regard, he will tend to have this regard for himself and be able to give it to others. If, on the contrary, he experiences negation and deadness, little in him can be creative or come to life. So, another measure of the authenticity of relationships is the degree to which they produce creative and constructive self-attitudes and a positive going out to others.

CONFUSION OF LANGUAGE

There is, however, a difficulty in the language that we are employing here. In his discussion of "language and silence," Steiner speaks of the "retreat from the word." In considering the rapid corruption and abuse of the meaning of words in our time, he asks:

What are the relations of language to the murderous falsehoods it has been made to articulate and hallow in certain totalitarian regimes? Or to the great load of vulgarity, imprecision, and greed it is charged with in a mass-consumer democracy? How will language, in the traditional sense of a general idiom of effective relations, react to the increasingly urgent, comprehensive claims of more exact speech such as mathematics and symbolic notation? Are we passing out of an historical era of verbal primacy—out of the classic period of literate expression—into a phase of decayed language, of "post-linguistic" forms, and perhaps of partial silence?[10]

It is particularly the "great load of vulgarity, imprecision and greed" which language must now bear that seriously affects the connotation—conscious and unconscious—of words like "love," "involvement," "commitment," "creative," "authentic," "values" and others used frequently throughout this book. For beyond the rich accumulation of meanings from their Greek, Latin, Norman, Anglo-Saxon and similar origins that the mass of English words carry, and which an educated person understands and recognizes, they now must bear specially corrupted and sometimes crude, ephemeral meanings whose tone and quality are in constant flux. It is therefore difficult to use them with any security that they will not be misleading and alienate the reader or "turn him off." Their use, therefore, must be a calculated risk, with the hope that words will be understood in their basic and original richness and so convey the profoundly positive and constructive forces their heritage represents for man.

VALIDATION AND CREATIVITY

When we speak of a relationship of commitment and the personal validation and sense of creativity that should follow, we mean a relationship with another which, like mercy, blesses him that gives and him that receives. It is a true giving of oneself to another and so ultimately a finding of oneself. Or stated another way, it is a modern extension of the ancient *amor benevolentiae* of which we speak here, a regard for the other, in those things which ultimately and finally are best for him.

This is our core theme and the integrating principle that guides the subject matter and manner of presentation. We are concerned with the conditions necessary to authenticity and genuineness in relationship to the self and in any commitment to others, and with the creative communion and communication these produce. This is quite different from being involved for involvement's sake. This quest to understand the nature of authentic personal relationship and the circumstances which most favor it in counseling, psychotherapy and the related areas of the search for and pursuit of personal values, is the main aim and purpose of this book.

NOTES

[1] Walter Kerr, *The Decline of Pleasure,* New York: Simon and Schuster, 1962, pp. 214–215.

[2] Pierre Teilhard de Chardin, *The Phenomenon of Man,* trans. Bernard Wall, New York: Harper Torchbooks, Harper and Row, 1961, p. 31.

[3] T. S. Eliot, in the Preface to Simone Weil's *The Need for Roots,* Boston: Beacon Press, 1952, p. vii.

[4] Kerr, *op. cit.,* p. 216–217.

[5] *Ibid.,* p. 222.

[6] *Ibid.,* p. 223.

[7] *Ibid.,* p. 234.

[8] Carl R. Rogers, *On Becoming a Person,* Boston: Houghton Mifflin, 1961, p. 26.

[9] Melvin H. Marx, *Hypothesis and Construct in Psychological Theory—Contemporary Readings,* New York: Macmillan Co., 1951, pp. 118–119.

[10] George Steiner, *Language and Silence, Essays on Language, Literature and the Inhuman,* New York: Atheneum Press, 1967, p. vii.

2

The Person in the Human Condition

BASIC TO all conditions for authentic relationship and any search for and pursuit of values, is the person himself. Consequently, the central concern of this book is the *person*—or to avoid a purely abstract consideration of that term—*the person in the human condition.*

Our age seems marked by three major concerns. There is, first of all, the concern for discovering, defining, organizing, integrating and applying areas of knowledge. For an individual to grasp this enormous development of knowledge, even in part, has become by now an almost overwhelming task.

Interwoven with this concern is the pursuit of civilization. The world has become increasingly civilized, but not in the sense that it is one well-organized and ordered city. Rather, it has become a series of *conflicting* organized and even regimented cities within and without, which are in danger of being set on the destruction of themselves and one another. The world is now desperately seeking some kind of living compromise and tolerance between them.

Within these cities, or better city-states, and as part of their struggle with one another, is the growing insistence on social justice, reaching almost the point of a constant cry by a large number of hitherto neglected citizens. They seek and demand a greater share in the goods that modern economy makes possible. They seek this, no longer as the gift or largesse of a feudal manor or paternal hacienda or castle, or from enlightened Management, but as a *right* due their personal dignity as men.

But this alone, for all its importance and pressing necessity, is

31

not enough. Just material fulfillment, even when achieved, will not still the basic discontent of a people more and more lost in large cities, seeing themselves and being seen as a faceless mass, as implements and functionaries of an industrial and civic machine. The answer lies beyond this material goal—necessary as it is—to a re-affirmation, by each person himself and by others in his regard, of his meaning and value as a person. Unless some measure of this self-validation is arrived at, other goals will still be truncated and without final significance. To realize this, one need only consider the mounting symbols of personal conflict—alcoholism, divorce, delinquency for example—among the comparatively affluent, edu- cated and cultured. Obviously more than education, economics and social justice are involved if man is to come into his own. He must search for meanings and pursue values personally significant and dignifying if he is to be genuinely true to himself and others in the process of being and becoming himself.

UNIQUE PERSONAL CONCERN

The third concern therefore, is with the person himself—each per- son. Inside each city, and each city-state, we are seeing a dramatic emergence of each person's claim to some equal recognition for himself. He wants to acquire some fundamental meaning and value that he shares with every other person in the world and that is so recognized everywhere despite obvious differences of color, educa- tion and social status. This characterizes man's third pursuit—his pursuit of self-meaning and of a sense of value in his own unique existence.

This third pursuit is marked by man's concern with himself. Important to modern man is not only the knowledge of the uni- verse and some kind of civilized peaceful, ordered and materially adequate living—essential as these are to his maintenance and well- being. But more centrally and more personally, it is man himself that is of basic concern. He must finally live with himself. He is blessed or condemned by the fact that he must be his own agent and his own implement not only in the process of knowing and civilizing, but also in the process of living. Here especially the concern for the person finally focusses itself. From the macroscopic view of the expanding world of knowledge and the process of civilization, we narrow down microscopically to each man as he views and lives with himself. For by this uniquely personal human agency, he must ultimately relate not only to himself and others but to the whole expanding field of knowledge, to the universe itself and to the city or hamlet in which he lives.

The special character of each man's uniqueness is that, with all his capacity to comprehend and order, as he gropes constructively to both know and govern himself and others, he yet remains an individual. He must always come back to, because he can never get away from, the unique agency of himself. Each man has to live and function through himself.

GENUINE GNOSIS

It is this third concern and pursuit that is the theme of this book. Knowledge alone or even civilization alone can never take the place of the Greek dictum "gnothi seauton," "Know thyself." In the Greek sense, as we will discuss, man is not only in pursuit of *logos* but he is also in pursuit of *gnosis*. He seeks that special kind of self-involving knowledge and understanding which will enable him to live more adequately, more securely and more ingenuously with himself. By so doing, he can best communicate himself as he really is to others. This is our concern, each man's pursuit of *gnosis* as we see it implemented in a variety of interrelated recent developments especially in counseling and psychotherapy.

"Know thyself" in this counseling therapeutic sense, is not simply a "cogito," not simply a reflective logos but it flows out of concrete being. It concerns the actuality of unique living in the person's experience with himself. A man's search for more adequate symbolic self-understanding, is not merely "studying" himself but rather a greater "being" himself. As Ricoeur says:

Now in treating the symbol as a simple revealer of self-awareness, we cut it off from its ontological function; we pretend to believe that "know thyself" is purely reflexive, whereas it is first of all an appeal by which each man is invited to situate himself better in being—in Greek terms, to "be wise."[1]

In attempting to describe one aspect of the counseling therapy relationship, we say, as we will develop later—that the counselor or therapist responds in the *language of cognition* while the person, probing his own momentary self-experience, speaks the *language of affect*. Such a cognitive response aims at gradually giving the person a more adequate symbolization of what is happening to him. By "symbolization" we mean that a person better understands and so can become more integrated within himself. We also mean with Eliade, that

the man who understands a symbol not only opens himself . . . but succeeds in emerging from his personal situation and reaching a comprehension of the universal . . . Symbols explode immediate reality as well as particular situations.[2]

This is so because

symbols are capable of revealing a modality of the real or a condition of the World which is not evident on the plane of immediate experience.[3]

Beyond the cognitive and verbal communication which might be called the personal "dia-logos," there is yet need for "dia-gnosis" in that the person has the option of determining whether this response symbolization fits or does not fit his own sense of himself— his own confused "gnosis." If it fits he may say with enthusiasm or relief, "That's it exactly" or "Yes, that really is the way I feel." If it does not, he may painfully say, "No, you misunderstand. I didn't really mean that—no no, that's not it—it's, it's just awfully difficult to explain to anyone, I guess." One recognizes here a regretful return to isolation and the terrible loneliness of non-understanding.

PERSON IN HUMAN CONDITION

In this counseling therapeutic process especially, we see the human person in an intimate discourse and dynamic with himself. He is

not seen in some ideally rational view—a sort of abstract philosophical man—but in the disordered, confused, conflicting struggle
of his daily reality. Our model of the *person,* then, is not ideal but
real; not his rational promise but his existential, moment-to-
moment, involved self. His animality and rationality and whatever
other abstract names we give him, are, in fact, one, unified, integrated operant as we observe him in his daily existence. This is the
only person we know and experience in ourselves and others.
There is no split-level man.

We can, of course, abstract from this, as did Aristotle, for example, and see an ideally rational "person." Or we can super-
humanize our experience and project this ideal person on God, as
Augustine did, and so see God in personal terms. It still remains,
however, that the person we know and experience is similar to the
person we see revealed in the counseling-therapeutic process—
engaged in living from moment to moment through all levels of
unified being. We are focused, then, on the person as he exists in
all the exaltation and degradation of the human condition. Our
theme is modern man as we find him in ourselves and in those
around us.

PURSUIT OF THE VALUES

Counseling-psychotherapeutic research is making it increasingly
apparent—as we have already indicated—that personality change
is connected with the emergence and clarification of personal
values. As we have said, these values are not necessarily newly
discovered. More often they are really implicit in the person's
earlier self-concept and ideal, in parent figures and in family attitudes, or in the values of neighborhood, school and church. Personal conflicts are due to such hidden personal value conflicts
drawn from some earlier life period and often retained unconsciously.

Personal conflict can result too from basically unresolved conflicts in the value system of our whole civilization. Each of us
inheriting this system, inherits as well its conflicts and confusions.
Our cultural heritage, therefore, like our personal and family history, is not an unmixed blessing. Each man needs consciously to

try to understand these conflicting values and resolve them in whatever degree he can or he may become the victim of them. Lincoln's remark that we cannot escape history, has a personal and cultural, as well as a political significance.

In the consideration of personal values, then, we must think not only of a personal and environmental, but also of a cultural matrix which extends beyond immediate life influences back through the whole history of man.

THE MEANING OF PERSON

To illustrate this, we will trace in some detail the implications of the word "person" itself, from its origin down to its present meaning. The influences of cultural values become evident when we see the comparatively insignificant origin and etymology of the word "person" in contrast to the richness we now give to expressions like, "personality development," "the mature personality," "the fully-functioning" or "the self-actualizing person." *Person* is here seen in a most fecund and profound sense, denoting even the very zenith in the maximizing of human psychological potential.

Concepts like "person" and "personality," then, have special significance and a rich and effulgent meaning far beyond the original meaning of "persona" as a character in a play using a masque "to sound through." In contrast to this empty meaning, the word "person" is now central to the psychological and therapeutic process of becoming mature or integrated. A common way of describing the counseling therapeutic process is to consider it as a transition from a lesser to a greater state of being and becoming a person. Allport, for example, has simply used the word *becoming*.[4] But Rogers carried this idea further with the title, *On Becoming a Person*.[5] The word "person" here signifies the most complete and integrated fulfillment of the self. This "fully functioning person"[6] is seen as the ultimate psychological goal of the self.

This transition from the empty concept of a masque to the rich and full meaning of the modern concept "person," was noticeably aided by the early Christian period and the development of theology. With an astonishingly astute perception and appreciation, these thinkers borrowed the Roman word, "person" and transformed it into a subtle human as well as theological concept.[7] Their respect for the human person and their treasuring of the experience of human relationships could nowhere be more clearly exemplified. These were the finest fruits of their search in the human condition for the worthiest concepts that might, however inadequately, be applied to the Godhead. These ideas of "person" applied to God, were transformed, to be sure, but they nonetheless were drawn from the warm human experience that they knew.

In their efforts to consider God as Persons-in-communion, early Christian thinkers also gave evidence of a subtle understanding of the needs of man. They were not conceptualizing in a vacuum, since they had the tradition of the deep regard for persons in communion and in relation which marked the early Christian communities. This, as we shall discuss later, played an important part in the rapid success and spread of early Christianity especially in large cities where, like today's inner city, people were often only a faceless mass. Early Christian writers were close to this tradition and apparently still sensitive to it. It is understandable, then, how they came to a conceptualization of God as a knowing and loving communion of unified Persons—the Triune God. But this also presented a model for human persons to be in a knowing and loving relationship with one another.

But this awareness of person in the early Christian community must itself be traced to its Jewish origins in the Old Testament where "the relations of God and man are so personal that Jahweh, the Lord of History, appears to be endowed with human qualities, such as wrath, repentance, and jealousy."[8] Cullmann makes this point in his contention that a philosophy of history is a direct result of a Judaeo-Christian view of man.[9]

It is not surprising therefore that when we search for someone who probed himself and the condition of man in a way comparable to the thinking of our age, the name that immediately occurs is St. Augustine. But Augustine, like Freud, did more than probe himself. Henry says:

The philosophical discovery of the person was due mainly, if not exclusively, to the pressure and challenge of the Christian revelation of the Godhead. Under this pressure, directed by Augustine's intuition and genius and by the related doctrine of the Incarnation, he was instrumental in substituting man for the world—*Psyche* for *Kosmos*—as the fundamental analogy whereby to understand and express, so far as possible, the inner life of God.[10]

In his approach, Augustine departed from early nature images and analogies and used concepts drawn from a person's effort to understand and function in integration with himself and others. We are indebted to Sloyan for the following resumé of Augustine's conceptualizations:

Augustine's stress on the ideas of "gift" and "love" . . . is important but it is not what distinguishes him chiefly in the realm of trinitarian theology. He is far better known for his use of analogies to convey the unity of the divine nature and the distinctness of the Three who possess it. He is sympathetic to his predecessors who use the sun's light or a spring's course through a river to a stream to illustrate the mystery. All nature bears the stamp of its Creator in Augustine's view . . .[11]

But Augustine's focus, Sloyan continues, was through studying *man himself* as he looked at himself introspectively and as he related lovingly with others:

God looked within himself ("Let us . . .") in creating man in his image and likeness. Introspection on man's part yields something of what likeness is . . . The tabular representation below will give some idea of the variety of Augustinian usage:

FATHER	*SON*	*HOLY SPIRIT*
1. Lover	Beloved	Their love
2. Being	Knowing	Willing
3. Being	Understanding	Living
4. Memory (i.e., the mind's latent self-knowledge)	Understanding (i.e., the mind's self-apprehension)	Will (i.e., the mind's self-love)
5. Our remembrance of God	Our knowledge of God	Our love for God
6. Mind	(Self-) Knowledge	(Self-) Love
7. Human genius	Indoctrination	Enjoyment

. . . He thought that all the examples above from 2 to 7 conveyed the mutual relations among the equal and coordinate elements of human personality, the first on the left being basic to the other two as the Father is in his role of principle of origin . . .[12]

These awarenesses foreshadowed present psychological concerns that have yielded such a rich vein through this same study of and respect for the person in the human relationship. If we have, therefore, concepts of becoming oneself through adequate "self-actualization," if we now think of "becoming a person," if we use terms like "self-concept" and "fully functioning" person, we are, in a certain sense, continuing a tradition of the value of the human "person" which others and Augustine especially, earlier established for us.

In its origin then, "person" was a dead word, a masque. To arrive at anything like the modern meaning of "person," we must come through Augustine who combined the Greek abstraction of person with a Judaeo-Christian regard for the God-image that he saw in the human condition. Our present respect for the "person" in government and society as well as our goal of personality fulfillment in psychology and psychiatry, is ultimately traceable to these earlier developments in our cultural heritage.

In tracing the evolution of the meaning and value of "person," it is interesting to note that for Aristotle and even for Shakespeare, only the persons of princes and kings were considered worthy subjects of dramatic contemplation. Schiller's *Kabale und Liebe*,[13] produced at approximately the same time as the French Revolution, is said to mark one of the earliest instances in which a commoner—a court musician—is the central character of a classic drama. But even here the involvement of the musician's daughter has to be with the prince, a kind of compromise. We have to come down to our own time, to find those conditions of regard for the dignity of each person which could have produced the *Death of a Salesman*[14] as a serious and significant dramatic presentation. One might say then that the present age is seeing a special fruition of the values attributable to the concept "person." These values are focussed on man as we know and experience him around us, in his real, existent self, not in any idealization or abstract representation.

FROM VERTICAL TO HORIZONTAL

The basic shift that has occurred in our present view of the person and the special value we now give this concept, might be expressed by proposing that we have changed our model of the human condition from a vertical to a horizontal design. In the earlier vertical design, the human condition was seen as a tower extending upward from the poor, the slave and the servant to the master who was rich, powerful and noble. In the Psalms, lightning and thunder suggested the terrible power and mysterious might of God. In Greek conception, as Jove threw his thunderbolts from heaven, lesser gods and goddesses extended down the scale to ordinary people. These were warned to keep their place and not try to rival those above them lest they be punished. For example, Arine, (they were told) for attempting to rival a goddess, was turned into a spider. This might be called the vertical line where both power and the favor or the gods went together.

But modern astronauts are forcing the moon itself and the planets to yield up their secret and their mysteries. One can now easily fly above lightning and thunder. Looking up no longer holds, even for children, the awe and mystery it once did for all mankind. At the same time, the "proud tower," as Tuchman calls it,[15] of social position and prerogative is tumbling. Some common meaning in each man is emerging based on his very own person—not on birth, color, or geography.

Together these shift the model from vertical to horizontal. The heavens indeed still beckon with beauty and allure. But they can be seen, too, in the horizon where heaven and earth meet. This horizontal model has us seeking across the face of the earth and the faces of one another, searching for the vision, beauty, meaning and mystery.

In the model of the horizontal line where the heavens are in the beyond, then, we move toward heaven by moving across the face of the earth, experiencing persons and things. One way we experience the unknown and the mysterious, is by giving ourselves over to and accepting the unique in other persons. In this enigmatic relationship we begin to know and love them. If we trust in them only what is like ourselves and so is familiar and reassuring, we have never really reached them. We have only a narcissistic reflection of ourselves. To reach others is to love and trust them in what is mysterious and unique and therefore unknown. Seen this way, we must trust and love others in order to begin to know them in their unique and special, and so "personal" selves.

This interpretation is by no means foreign to the Judaeo-Christian origins of our idea of "person." Rather it would seem to be its final fulfillment and natural meaning.

One can see an implication of this in the Biblical text: "For he that loves not his brother whom he sees, how can he love God whom he sees not?" (1 Jn. 4:20). Beyond the way a person reflects me and is like me, to love him, I must plunge myself into his uniqueness—that unknown and unresolved part of himself that is totally his. Yet in a certain sense one might say that I have never really known this person; I have only known myself, until I permitted myself this experience of what is unknown, unique and mysterious in him. Only in abandoning myself to this in him can I begin to love him. Through such trusting enigmatic love of another whom I see, I can then begin to have some correspondent love with an ultimate enigmatic and mysterious total Other. This would be a way of seeing and regarding a God-image in each person that I know and reaching God through loving this unique image in him.

VALUE PACKAGE

One point, to be developed later, is worthy of comment here. In this illustration of the value-charged implications in the word "person," it becomes evident that values are often hidden in the use of a particular word, analogy, or example. They can imply value-models. Such models are not only symbols or figures of speech that aid us in reflecting on and coordinating experience, they are also implicit value systems. In accepting and using a model like this, we are, often committing ourselves knowingly or unknowingly, to a set of value norms. In counseling and psychotherapy, for example, crucial self-insights and significant personal changes seem often to hinge on this kind of change in both the symbolic language one uses and the models and personal value systems involved. Values and models are interwoven in linguistic structure and cultural matrices as well as in our personal immediate milieu. These can determine and may even prejudice our approach to any experience.

NEED FOR ROOTS

Since, then, past cultural values intermingle with present ones, we have endeavored in this book to maintain a sense of continuity by drawing on older concepts and attempting to show their present meaning. Modern awarenesses of the human person are brought forward to complement and fulfill rather than to deny older ideas. There is no effort here to break with the past and provide novelty for its own sake. We are seeking freshness of viewpoint and depth of understanding. But if we also recognize a psychological need for roots and continuity, then by unnecessary novelty, we are cutting ourselves off from the past and frustrating this need. What Bernard of Chartres said centuries ago, is still applicable:

we are dwarfs mounted on the shoulders of giants, so that we see more and further than they; yet not by virtue of the keenness of our eyesight, nor through the tallness of our stature, but because we are raised and borne aloft upon that giant mass.[16]

Excessive novelty of expression also removes us from that common language and meaning so necessary to shared understanding and communication with one another. As modern society changes ever more rapidly so that the structure of cities and industrial conditions continue to move more people from place to place, this need for roots—no longer centered in a place—would seem to require this sense of subscribing to the traditional values and of speaking some consistent common cultural language. So, while fresh terminology and viewpoints to meet changing conditions are necessary, yet if such innovation cuts us off from all sense of belonging, it will prove, to that degree, self-defeating. Many of the values we live by and profit from, are not clearly known and recognized. They are implicit in the matrix of our culture. Consequently, in seeking irrelevant changes we may be in the position of the man who was witlessly chopping at the roots of a tree while he was eating its fruits.

New terms and expressions are, of course, intended to produce unstereotyped thinking and force us out of the mental laziness of unanalyzed cliches. We have to think out the significance of these new terms. This may also enable us to investigate again and with renewed respect, areas previously disregarded. The nineteenth century conception of pitch-blende—a source of nuclear energy—as almost worthless, would be an example of this kind of error made so often in the past. A new look can, as in Van Gogh's artistic vision, result in a dramatic and even startling fresh awareness.

But with this same fresh vision we can develop what is already known and accepted. Used this way, rich new insights can emerge from traditional conceptions. We have attempted here, then, this sort of combination of new wine in old bottles and sometimes old wine in new bottles. Our hope is that we have preserved something of the "need for roots" that Simone Weil holds to be so necessary, and yet have been sympathetic to the freshness of vision and fluidity of thought that new theories, terms and awareness about the human conditions have given us.

INCARNATE INTEGRITY

For the last century or so, it has been customary to distinguish somewhat between a learned, theoretical discussion and a practical treatment of any subject. Kant's famous distinction of "pure" from "practical" reason summed up this attitude. The distinction has in fact needlessly dichotomized knowledge. Often, under the guise of theory and abstraction, this distinction encouraged a withdrawal from real experience and the richness it contains. This is especially evident when we are considering the human person. In the abstract concept of person, we are, as we have said, quite removed from the human condition.

As a result of this dichotomy, symbols, concepts, definitions and theories, instead of being anchored in and leading to immediate incarnate experience, became "pure" reasoning tools. This unfortunately often led to irrelevance and unrelatedness. Abstractive definitions and discussions could be maneuvered to rationalize this disincarnate "pure" state into a withdrawal from, rather than engagement with life. They were used not to "explore" and chart immediate experience—in Eliade's exposition of the purpose of symbols—but to protect and reinforce one's state of learned isolation and rational "purity."

Even in talking and writing about authentic experience with the other, we may be in fact escaping and avoiding it. For real experience with another person is a "falling"—a commitment to him in those aspects of himself that are mysterious to us because unique. They are, in themselves, also threatening and anxiety provoking. They are so because, as a result of their mystery and uniqueness, we cannot control or manipulate them and so protect ourselves. The popular phrase, "falling in love," catches well the abandonment and risk which any genuinely personal relationship involves.

The incarnate realism of counseling and psychotherapy has a special kind of integrity that people who tend overmuch to speculation and theory, especially need. For theorizing can be a kind of rationalizing that, in seeing only the ideal and concentrating on the products of "pure reason," not only looks down on the practical but avoids the healthy and chastening discipline of hard facts. This can even become a kind of tyranny of what man "ought to do" in place of what, in his limited personal reality here and now, he really can do. We have therefore tried to include, as much as we can, these hard human realities of man as he is.

Here especially is where the growing experience of counseling and psychotherapy can aid us in establishing other authentic personal relationships, that is, ones that are truly other-centered. For the research in counseling therapy has alerted us to the complexities of achieving any genuinely other-centered regard and of the vast extension and subtle disguises that our own narcissism takes. Relationships that we often call personal can be, for this reason, fraudulent and artificial or, in the slang term, "phony." The essence of such "phoniness" or inauthenticity is to relate to someone and appear to care for him in and for himself, when, in fact, this apparent caring is a disguise for a narcissistic and self-inverted maneuver.

Moreover, if we consider, with Eliade, that any real reach toward the other, is fundamentally religious and a striving toward the Total Other, then this other-centered concern is a major one for all genuinely religious group and individual communications. No real communion of persons is possible without it. All other forms and symbols of communion remain "it" symbols. Even wine, says Aquinas, could not be in itself the repositor or correspondent of friendship. Only a person has this attribute. For "it" objects, like wine, can be manipulated and controlled or "eaten up" by the other. One can really give oneself only to another person.

DETAILED INTERVIEWS

We have included much detailed illustrative material, therefore, primarily to give this sense of authentic personal experience in the struggle toward communion and communication. Simple descriptive material remains too removed and uninvolved. In its printed structure it is dead rather than living. This is so, too, even for recorded printed excerpts but they, at least, contain more of the real conflict and confusion of authentic communication.

Consequently, throughout this book, we have reproduced actual dialogue as it did or would occur to an observer or participant. While this kind of material may make difficult reading—and of course may be skipped—its careful perusal and study will, we are convinced, repay the time and effort spent. Only in this way can we get to man as he laughs and cries, to men who are like ourselves—men in the human condition.

Since the reading of recorded material can be tedious, a resumé and more general analysis would no doubt prove more readable.

But detailed personal material has the advantage of introducing us to the exact verbal experience, which, while uncoordinated and confused, is at the same time often rich, intense and fresh in its spontaneous expression. This is the way human beings really are if we hear them out sensitively and patiently.

Recorded material, too, shows the slow almost imperceptible process by which the counselor's or therapist's responses seek to reach and understand the person. Brief excerpts or descriptions often give the misleading impression that understanding and clarifications are conveyed in a few sharp and clear delineations. This seldom seems to be so. Rather, as we see, by slow and faltering steps together, client and counselor, therapist and patient, mutually struggle to gain some foothold in the morass of confusion and conflict. After a half-hour or so of much plodding and digging, sometimes some kind of solid footing is achieved. One client's comment after an interview suggests that this happened: "Well, I feel now that I have a hold on it . . . I have much more to work with."

By plunging himself into the detailed client statements and forcing himself to concentrate on the exact wording of the responses—even when this may be boring or confusing—the reader is himself experiencing the kind of clinical incarnation through which he really shares the human condition. He "feels with" the person in the Greek sense of sympathy. Speculative and abstract thinking about man, "pure reasoning," often leads to too easy rationalizations rather than to the painfully pursued human wisdoms of suffering and involvement. "He jests at scars who's never felt a wound," might as well also be, "he intellectualizes about problems who's never listened to a wounded heart." The humiliation and even drudgery of the practical—its very "impurity" in the Kantian sense—can indeed be its great significance in aiding us really to understand human incarnation as it is in us. It is not simply to be studied and analyzed from afar, in others. We, too, are "they."

PSYCHOLOGICAL
INCARNATION-REDEMPTION

Central to the changes which an adequate relationship with a counselor or therapist produces, seems to be the growing awareness on the person's part that his body, instincts, emotions as well as his knowing and choice functions are all either conscious or unconscious aspects of himself. He becomes increasingly more aware and accepting of his total incarnate self, and so begins to feel this growth in redemptive self-worth. Part of this growth in self-acceptance—or as it might be called psychologically, this incarnate-redemptive process—is the increasing willingness to admit a belonging to and some responsibility for all aspects of his human incarnate self. He then begins to feel his worth as a total unified person.

Counseling and especially psychotherapy seem often to begin with some manner of self-rejection and removed judgment against the self. One might explain this by saying that man lives in anxiety and fear of his own tenuous hold on meaning and existence. He also rebels against this and his own finitude, by a kind of intellectual and judgmental withdrawal above himself. By criticizing and condemning himself, he is also removing himself in part, from the disorder, transiency, unpredictability and frustration of his own emotional, instinctive, somatic life.

In place of this previous intellectual removal from and rejection of himself, a person in the counseling therapy process grows gradually more respectful of himself and his own uniqueness. In this sense, the counseling therapy process illustrates Santayana's remark:

Let a man once overcome his selfish terror at his own finitude, and his finitude is, in one sense, overcome.[17]

At least, his rejection of his finitude seems to decrease and he comes to have a redeeming sense of his own unique worth and potential and so begins to trust his whole self rather than be constantly at war with some aspects of himself.

By incarnation, in this psychological sense, we mean then, this accepting of self and others as unified persons functioning through all aspects of their emotional, instinctive and somatic selves as well as their more immediately conscious intellectual awareness. By redemption, we mean the feeling of worth and value which a growing sense of unique self-acceptance produces. When it comes from others, such acceptance aids our self-redemptive process by con-validating our worth to ourselves.

In this counseling therapy model of the person in the human condition we see emerging a new kind of humanism. This humanism considers man, not in abstraction or as ideal but as he is, a creature who thinks, loves, works and yet is always waiting for and seeking something in and beyond himself. Eliade also speaks of this new humanism and of a way of approaching and studying man that calls for a whole new "frame of mind."

Now we may anticipate that all these elements are preparing for the growth of a new humanism, which will not be a replica of the old. For what principally concerns us now is to integrate the researches of the orientalists, ethnologists, depth psychologists, and historians of religion in order to arrive at a total knowledge of man. These scholars have untiringly revealed the human interest, the psychological "truth" and the spiritual value of all those symbols, myths, divine figures and practices to be found among the Asiatics and the "primitives." These human documents had hitherto been studied with the detachment and indifference that nineteenth-century naturalists brought to the study of insects. Today we are beginning to observe that they express typical human situations, that they form an integral part of the history of the spirit. Now, the proper frame of mind for discovering the meaning of a typical human situation is not the "objectivity" of the naturalist, but the intelligent sympathy of the exegetist, the interpreter. It is the frame of mind itself that has had to be changed.[18]

Medical, psychological and social sciences are rethinking themselves from such a personalist point of view, so that they may more adequately encompass the results of modern investigation. Religion, too, is examining itself in this same personalist way in order to become truly relevant to man as he really is. Together they are seeking to know, understand and share the concerns of the person, each person. It is this basic aim that relates them and enables them to offer significant insights to one another and to the whole field of human understanding. In this they characterize the "frame of mind" of modern humanism and its concerns for the person in the human condition.

NOTES

[1] Paul Ricoeur, *The Symbolism of Evil,* trans. Emerson Buchanan, New York: Harper & Row, Publishers, 1967, p. 356.

[2] Mircea Eliade, *Mephistopheles and the Androgyne: Studies in Religious Myth and Symbol,* trans. M. Cohen, New York: Sheed and Ward, 1965, p. 207. © in the English translation Harville Press, London, and Sheed and Ward, Inc., New York 1965.

[3] *Ibid.,* p. 201.

[4] Gordon Allport, *Becoming: Basic Considerations for a Psychology of Personality,* New Haven: Yale University Press, 1955.

[5] Rogers, *On Becoming a Person,* Boston: Houghton Mifflin, 1961.

[6] *Ibid.*

[7] Gerard S. Sloyan, *The Three Persons in One God,* Englewood Cliffs, N. J.: Prentice-Hall, Inc., 1964, p. 41. © 1964. Reprinted by permission of Prentice-Hall, Inc., Englewood Cliffs, New Jersey.

Both he (Tertullian) in using *persona* and Hippolytus in using *prosopon* had in mind the manifestations of Son and Spirit in the economy rather than individuals immanent in the eternal godhead. Neither ancient word connoted "person" in its modern sense. The etymological transition had been from face or expression, to a player's mask (per + sonare = to speak through), to an individual who held title to property at law. Tertullian means by the word "the concrete presentation of the individual as such." (J. N. D. Kelly, *Early Chrisian Creeds,* London: Longmans, Green, 1950, p. 115; cf. also *Early Christian Doctrines,* London: Adam and Charles Black, 1958.)

[8] Paul Henry, S.J., *Saint Augustine on Personality: The Saint Augustine Lecture 1959,* New York: Macmillan Co., 1960, p. 7.

[9] Oscar Cullmann, *Christ et le temps: temps et histoire dans le christianisme primitif,* Neuchatel et Paris: Delachaux et Nestle, 1947, especially pp. 38–68. English translation by Floyd V. Filson, *Christ and Time: The Primitive Christian Conception of Time and History,* Philadelphia: The Westminister Press, 1950.

[10] Henry, *op. cit.,* p. 3.

[11] Sloyan, *op. cit.*, pp. 77–79.

[12] *Ibid.*, pp. 77–78. See also St. Augustine, "On the Trinity," *Basic Writings of St. Augustine, II,* ed. W. J. Oates, New York: Random House, 1948, pp. 667–878.

[13] Friedrich Schiller, *Kabale Und Liebe,* Munchen: Wilhelm Goldmann, Verlag, 1960.

[14] Arthur Miller, *Death of a Salesman,* New York: The Viking Press, 1958. See also Erich Auerbach, "Miller the Musician," *Mimesis,* New York: Doubleday and Company, 1953, p. 382–399.

[15] Barbara W. Tuchman, *The Proud Tower,* New York: Macmillan Co., 1962.

[16] *The Flowering of the Middle Ages,* ed. Joan Evans, London: Thames and Hudson, 1966, p. 180.

[17] George Santayana, "Introduction" to *Ethics of Spinoza,* trans. A. Boyle, New York: Dutton, 1950.

[18] Eliade, *op. cit.*, p. 12.

3

The Unity of the Person

WE CAN DESCRIBE the counseling therapeutic relationship, then, as an incarnate-redemptive psychological dialogue leading to self-gnosis and to a sense of greater and more mature personhood and worth. It is a process which is possible through the mutual acceptance by counselor or therapist and client, of both human incarnation and the unity of the person. As a result, a greater personal worth, fulfillment and meaning begins to emerge for the one seeking help. In this intense effort to understand himself, forces are also initiated in a person that make a genuine growth and extension to others possible. In so doing the person arrives at some measure of mature capacity to give himself in love in place of narcissistic self-inversion. What begins, in some aspects at least, with intellectual separation and a resulting dichotomy, conflict and division within the person, slowly moves towards greater unified fulfillment in the self and outward toward others.

These personal changes correspond to changes occurring in our culture. One of the most interesting phenomena of our age is also this movement away from a dichotomized view of man and a return to a more unified view. As a result, there is a new commitment to sharing the total human condition as well as the sense of uniqueness and mystery inherent in the human person.

TWO VIEWS

When one looks at the historical picture of Western man, two profiles stand out. There is the conceptualization of Descartes, and others—dichotomized man whose body, conceived as functioning more or less separately from his psyche, is looked upon fundamentally as a highly complicated machine. In this view the psyche is really seen as man, inhabitating, and controlling but separate from this mechanized soma. Descartes gave this psyche a highly intellectualized form patterned from a mathematical model of knowing. Kant extended this by giving us the basis for a voluntarist, subjectivist and possibly even an authoritarian version of man.

Recent trends have been restoring an earlier image of Western man, that of a unified person who seeks to function with increasing integrity at all levels of the self. Here the older idea of the psyche "animating" man, that is, forming a unity and giving life, integration, direction and purpose to the soma, seems to correspond to this more recent view of man.

In this image, a man is never "pure" reason—in the sense of Kant's *Critique of Pure Reason*—nor a "pure" will whose character depends on having "good" will, nor, in fact, a "pure" anything. He is rather a complicated and partially unfathomable "mixture" of factors, some known, some unknown. Such factors can sometimes reveal themselves in even the most apparently insignificant action such as a momentary stammer or a slip of the tongue. Man has a total response.

Man is also seen as a *mysterium* struggling to know and understand himself. He must believe in and love himself so that he may begin to understand himself. The way he regards himself, his belief in, love of, and struggle to understand himself, largely determines his relationship with others and the world. He is in some measure always an unknown in the midst of unknowns, striving to know and be known and so to love and be loved.

This change to a unified view of man as an incarnate totality is coming about, apparently, from a growing resistance to the mechanized concept of man because of an increasingly convincing amount of research in physics, medicine, psychology, psychiatry and allied fields. This is changing our rigid concept of matter while re-emphasizing the unitary nature of man's reactions to himself and to his environment. We are, in other words, witnessing a change in the image of man as well as a change in our understanding of the physical world. This change is fundamental and equally affects and is affected by counseling and psychotheraphy.

MACHINE MODEL

Psychologically, one effect of industrialism and scientism has been to give us a machine model of man and of the world. Popular discussions emphasizing some of the less favorable aspects of this model are on bookshelves, and phrases like "the organization man" and "the lonely crowd" are already commonplace. It is becoming evident that, with all its benefits, man is not left unscarred by the mechanization of society. These popular books suggest that many are struggling with a complex and disturbing inner world of confusion, loneliness and anxiety. The vast organization of society has dulled our sense of the meaning and value of the person.

That is to say, we see ourselves and one another more as objects, much as we might see machines; and rather than recognizing persons, we now tend to judge ourselves and one another somewhat as we judge machines. If our model of man is a machine, and ideally a smooth-working machine, this kind of judgment is inevitable. For example, we go to our car, turn on the switch, the motor starts, and down the street we go. This is a "good" machine. A "bad" machine is one that does not start immediately or does not run smoothly. But applied to ourselves and other persons, this model often leads to an implicit perfectionism in judgment and an impatience with the much more complex and disordered human process of action.

This mechanized view of the objects and people around us tends to produce a subtle impatience with ourselves as well as with others. By contrast with an automobile, a horse, for example, does "horse around" a good deal; it may take some time to get a bit into his mouth and to saddle or harness him. We recognize, too, though, that such a spirited horse will ultimately give a better ride. If it took one that long to start his automobile, he would quickly decide that it should be turned in for a new one. The basic value here is that something that operates exactly as I want it to, is good, and something else that does not operate promptly and efficiently is bad. As a result, we often begin to see people in the light of machines. In a sense, being so surrounded by these models, it is difficult to avoid doing so. These are the value moulds through which our psychological sensibilities are being formed.

Philosophically, we can trace the origin of this concept to Descartes and his dichotomized view of man. Descartes was faced with the astonishing feats of physics and the model of a mechanical universe as predictable in operation as the planetary system. Since this construct included all matter, man, too, in his bodily constitution was seen in this same mechanical and predictable way. Ampère, in fact, is said to have remarked that if he were given sufficient data he could calculate mathematically the whole history of the human race. Harvey and others were producing evidence of a highly mechanical aspect to the action of the heart and other vital organs. These machine-like models of human physiology were to have profound effects on the history of medicine and to bring tremendous advances, not only in knowledge of bodily functions, but in almost miraculous achievements in surgery and biochemistry.

Descartes felt, in the spirit of his time, that a whole new foundation had to be given to our approach to man. Man's body must be considered as a kind of machine, albeit a most complicated and subtle one. What, then, of man's spirit, his ultimate purpose and being, his real self? These could hardly be reduced to a mere machine, however complicated and mysterious.

Descartes' answer was that man, for all practical purposes, was really his psyche, not his soma.[1] Through this conception, the laws that affected the soma and seemed to demonstrate all its vast and interwoven mechanical properties left the basic spirit of man untouched. Man was in his body, not as simply as expressed by Plato's idea of a rower in a boat, but more like a modern astronaut in a complicated mechanical capsule. Still, this concept left the body basically an "it," a machine with an indwelling intelligence using the body, but actually independent of it.

To relate the psyche to the quantified material world Descartes the mathematician took for his model the disembodied thought process of mathematics. While not material in itself, mathematics was yet quantified and had already proved of extreme value in the predictable and pragmatic aspects of matter. It could thus be used as the link between intelligence and matter. Descartes thought of man as having a purely rational capacity to imitate in his own intellectual operations the clean, uncluttered thought process of mathematics. Mathematical reasoning thus emerged as the ideal kind of reasoning process. Man was conceived as a pure intelligence operating in, but, in a sense, completely above his mechanically constructed body. The ideal logic then became mathematical logic, and the model of human thought and objectivity became the cold exactitude of a mathematical formula.

INHERENT IN PRESENT VALUES

This Cartesian concept was obviously incomplete. It left much unexplained about the human person. But it had the one great advantage of appearing to meet the needs of the time when older philosophical traditions had become sterile and pedantic. This view of man, with additions and changes, has perdured to the present and is inherent in many of our implicit values. All of us, in subtle unexamined ways, are likely to be thinking and feeling in this Cartesian dichotomized vein, even when we least suspect it.

KANTIAN WILL-DUTY

One clear weakness in the Cartesian view of man lay in the operational process. Descartes focused on knowing; he only suggested the process of doing. It remained for Kant to give the final touch to much of our recent view of man by his strong emphasis on the will. Kantian "will" was not, of course, the simple "will-power" idea that, along with body-building exercises, so fascinates the young. Kant, like Descartes, was a most subtle and complicated thinker whose thought was never easily reducible for popular consumption, even for university students. But this popular idea has something of Kantianism in it. Conscience was for Kant a "categorical imperative" that was somehow mysteriously in man as a kind of moral instinct or sense. It was not only like a "still small voice," it could be a demanding, unyielding critic. Freud subsequently clarified this conception of conscience showing how it could become, in a distorted state, a hounding, plaguing, nagging, relentless "superego."

Nonetheless, Kant, with true Cartesian flavor, conceived this moral imperative as unrelated to a complicated but unitary psychosomatic process. Kant's will, like Descartes' intellect was somehow unconnected with man's body in its basic directives. This Kantian concept of an impersonal "duty" as the universal imperative, seems to have been a moral equivalent for the Cartesian mathematical norm of knowledge. It set the stage for the modern concept of ethical values as unrelated to the pursuit of personal values. Ethical values were conceived to be the result of a cold, impersonal "sense of duty," which was later to be variously ascribed to the parental figure, to the conditioning process of the mores of the community, or even to the state itself. Thus ethical values—and with them, religious values seen as duties—were often later regarded not only as being without direct relation to the pursuit of the self and self-excellence but as hindering and even thwarting personal fulfillment.[2]

The mechanical view of man's body, while leaving certain confusions in its wake, was nonetheless accompanied by tremendous gains in the material psychological and particularly the medical world. We do not wish, therefore, to gainsay the vast developments that followed upon mechanism and what might be called mathematicism. Their very yield, which has been a harvest of great benefit to man, may make it seem surprising at first glance that many in the fields of physics, medicine, and psychology should now be doubting or even denying this view. They may appear to be slaying the goose that laid the golden eggs. Why question a source that has proved so fruitful?

The Cartesian view of man has, in a way, reached the point of diminishing returns. Hence it is seriously doubted and even rejected now in many fields, although no one would presume to question its earlier fruitfulness as an operational hypothesis. We cannot dismiss its contributions any more than one would want to turn back to the life of the preindustrial era or return to a period in medical history which lacked the knowledge and skill of today's medical and surgical professions. For, in fact, some of the most important and reliable instruments now in daily use by physicians and surgeons are mechanical devices adapted to basic body mechanisms.

UNIFIED HUMAN PERSON

For all its advantages, however, this mechanical view of man and of matter obscured many aspects of physical reality and of the human person that are now emerging again with far greater force and significance than before. First of all, there is the restoration— or at least insistence upon the need for restoration—of the unified human person and the individual's unique value. This is a reaction against the "organization man" and the "lonely crowd." There is a demand for the restoration of the sense of personhood. Man seeks the "I-thou" world; to use Buber's famous expression.[3] I look for a "thou" in my relations with other men rather than just an "it," and I look for them to regard me as a "thou" rather than as an "it."

At the same time a second insistence is emerging: the need to restore a sense of living things. Mechanism surrounds us all with dead things. Even though a motor runs and moves with far greater efficiency than does a horse, the horse has all the qualities of a living thing, and a motor has not. A motor simply starts and stops. While there is a certain "life" to something that is moving in a magnetic field, it is a fixed kind of movement, and not the movement of a living thing. And so in going from a horse and buggy to an automobile, while we gain advantages in terms of efficiency and speed, we have lost contact with living things. Most of our productive activities now are with machines, which simply move as dead things move. Until a hundred years ago, man had either other men or other living things to aid him in his activities. Now out of the deadness all around us there is rising a need to restore a sense of living things, particularly of the living human person.

But being so surrounded by machines, we have become in some ways more comfortable with non-living than with living things. We have, therefore, an understandable need to catalogue and categorize people, to put them into organizational slots rather than to deal with them in their human freedom and complexity. "Humanness" can, from this view, be seen as threatening and disordering.

Apparently as a result of this Cartesian objectifying of our relations with one another, we tend to use toward one another and toward ourselves what may be called in communication theory, "neutral" language. That is to say, by this "scientifically" objective language we are somehow removed from and uninvolved in the human condition. But the fact is that every human encounter is in some way involved, and its language is not really "neutral." The uninvolved spectator with a neutral language does not succeed in reaching the other person and genuinely sharing with him. He succeeds only in "figuring him out," in solving more or less to his own satisfaction a series of problems or a puzzle.

It is interesting to note the Cartesian mathematical tone of the popular expression, "I've got him figured out." It is also noteworthy that this kind of "figuring out" of another person or the attempt to simplify his complexity and mystery, will seldom make him cooperative. Most commonly it seems to make him quite uncooperative and resentful; however he may mask this attitude by appearing quietly submissive and obedient. In short, when one attempts to "figure out" another, when one tries to "get his number" for the purpose of cataloguing him, one generally ends up by "getting his goat" instead, in the old fashioned phrase. The living being asserts himself in all his conscious and unconscious powers of resistance, attack, escape, withdrawal.

Evidence is now being brought forward to show that man is clearly not a machine nor a dichotomy in the Kantian or Cartesian sense. Recent and extensive research seems to reaffirm that man is not only not a machine, but even somatically he is often a rebellious anti-machine. He is far too complex to operate with the smoothness and efficiency with which a machine can operate. To set up a machine model of man, even though it serves well as an operational hypothesis for some aspects of his physical functions, is to force him into a mould he cannot fit. It is, as Chesterton remarked, "to cut the heads to fit the hats."

UNIQUE INDIVIDUAL PERSON

Medicine, psychology and psychiatry are returning to one of the central tendencies in our Judaeo-Greco-Christian culture: to regard man as a unitary being, caught midway in a complex operational mosaic of spirit and flesh, of knowing and feeling; and to consider the pursuit of self-knowledge in mystery and uniqueness as basic to self-development and personal fulfillment.

We seem to be arriving at an understanding of man that centers again on these aspects that are unique in the individual personality and the conviction that each man has within himself intrinsic powers for personality adjustment and development which he alone can activate. The analysis and diagnosis of personality en masse by mathematical and other group evaluations, are now being reinforced and supported through approaches which focus on the individual person in all his psychosomatic uniqueness.

The field of the physical sciences, especially physics, which, after Newton, has so greatly influenced our Cartesian view of man, has come now to recognize the difference between the laws of mass activity, which Newton studied and understood as the whole of matter, and individual phenomena. Langmuir summarized this new view of physicists:

Just as there are two types of physics, classical physics and quantum physics, which have for nearly 25 years seemed irreconcilable, just so must we recognize two types of natural phenomena. First, those in which the behavior of the system can be determined from the average behavior of its component parts and, second, those in which a single discontinuous event (which may depend upon a single quantum charte) becomes magnified in its effect so that the behavior of the whole aggregate does depend upon something that started from a small beginning. The first class of phenomena I want to call convergent phenomena, because all the fluctuation details of the individual atoms average out, giving a result that converges to a definite state. The second class we may call divergent phenomena, where from a small beginning increasingly large effects are produced. In general then we may say that classical physics applies satisfactorily to convergent phenomena and that they conform well to the older ideas of cause and effect. The divergent phenomena, on the other hand, can best be understood on the basis of quantum theory of modern physics . . .

I can see no justification whatever for teaching that science proves that general causes (convergent phenomena) dominate in human affairs over the results of the individual action (divergent phenomena).

The mistaken overemphasis on convergent phenomena in human

affairs, and the reliance on so-called scientific methods, has been responsible in large degree for much of the cynicism of the past few decades.[4]

The general trends of personality revealed in the analysis of group statistics, and the tests and measurements for personality, intelligence, aptitude, etc., which study individuals *within such a group,* while helpful and revealing, are limited in their mass convergent results. Just as the law of convergent phenomena of mass in physics can be distinguished from individual divergent activity, so we must understand the human person not only by the study of the individual as he relates to mass group statistics but also by an increasing effort to understand aspects that are peculiar to each individual person.

Murphy for example, proposes that we may be over investing in number as a result of a kind of number mysticism:

I would simply ask, as objectively as I know how, and without knowing the answer: "Are we over investing in number?" There is not the slightest doubt that number theory and number preoccupation helps us towards the discovery of many kinds of reality. There is likewise no doubt that number leads into various types of mysticism which become so fascinating, so enriching, as so sustaining that one finds it difficult indeed to come back to the world of plain things and the immediate world to be dealt with. Number mysticism makes us believe that symmetry, order, rhythm have direct predictive power as to what will be actually observed. It has often led us astray.[5]

Since, according to Murphy, this is all carried out in the name of intelligibility and truth, it is difficult to question such data:

The result is, of course, that we force data sometimes profoundly, into channels which are conceived to make them more real, but can only in fact make them less real in the sense of confronting nature as she is.[6]

Such an exaggeration of mathematics can cause us to warp our view of nature's orderliness into a blindness of abstraction:

What we have done, in the light of mathematics since the seventeenth century, is to defy the fundamental sense in Pythagorean number theory and to rely almost wholly upon those higher-order abstractions which make use of continuities, linearities and "normalities" which nature so often contradicts. It is not the mathematics that is intellectually crippling, nor can mathematics ever take the side of one metaphysical proposition against another; but the use of mathematics can become blind, as can any tool revealed by the sociology of knowledge.[7]

Bakan points out a tendency to misuse statistics by failing to recognize the limits of mathematics and that "total" persons are involved as subjects of human research:

That which we have indicated in this paper in connection with the test of significance in psychological research may be taken as an instance of a kind of essential mindlessness in the conduct of research which may be, as the author has suggested elsewhere (Bakan, 1965) related to the presumption of the non-existence of mind in the subjects of psychological research. Karl Pearson once indicated that higher statistics were only common sense reduced to numerical appreciation. However, that base in common sense must be maintained with vigilance. When we reach a point where our statistical procedures are substitutes instead of aids to thought, and we are led to absurdities, then we must return to the common sense basis. Tukey (1962) has very properly pointed out that statistical procedures may take our attention away from the data, which constitute the ultimate base for any inferences which we might make. Robert Schlaifer (1959, p. 654) has dubbed the error of the misapplication of statistical procedures the "error of the third kind," the most serious error which can be made. Berkson has suggested the use of "the interocular traumatic test, you know what the data mean when the conclusion hits you between the eyes. (Edwards et al., *op. cit.,* 1963, p. 217)."

We must overcome the myth that if our treatment of our subject matter is mathematical it is therefore precise and valid. Mathematics can serve to obscure as well as reveal.[8]

This special human element is evident in another way. We are now adapting various mechanical apparatus to human needs such as teaching machines, computers and similar devices. However unusual their results may at first appear, such devices are the products of man and must ultimately depend on him. They are, therefore, revealing man's unique differences from such machines. In so doing, they are also giving us what might be considered a correct use of the term "mechanism." As Whatmough points out,

It is absurd to recoil from the use of the word mechanism here. A machine is a contrivance or artifact made by man, and as such, an extension of mind, and subject to the human mind. What the human mind has done the human mind, *ex hypothesi,* can cope with. Hence meaning may be regarded as activity or expression directed to a goal. As such it is subject to purpose and control (cybernetics), not something to which man is servile, but something by which he may both interpret and modify his environment.[9]

TOTAL RESPONSE

The return to a sense of unity in the human person is affecting not only the development of the psychosomatic approach in medicine, but it also is augmenting the cooperation of religion and medicine. As Royce remarks:

Each of the professions of religion and medicine realizes that neither can be effective alone. The ultimate beneficiary will be . . . the human being whose physical, spiritual, emotional, and social well-being is and always will be the central objective of the total efforts of the physician and minister.[10]

But because a body-mind division is now so ingrained in our culture, it is difficult for us to change this customary divided mode of viewing man. We still tend to view man's reactions in various separated categories which even such a term as "mental health" implies. Reeves has suggested how we must now discard this kind of partitioned view of man and begin to consider what he calls man's "total response" to any given person, situation, or illness:

When we ask how man functions, we find that every moment of life is a moment of total response. Every stimulus that comes to us from the world about us evokes response by the whole of our being. There is no such thing as a purely physical reaction, or a purely emotional, or a purely mental, or a purely spiritual. One or another of these may be the point, the continuum that is marked by "which side is up," but the lines of continuity reach off into all the rest of our being, and there is no part that is not in some degree involved. A particular agent or agency may appear to evoke a particular, and usually a highly specialized, reaction, as when a viral infection brings on a rise in body temperature. Yet this is only the most obvious aspect of the response, the peaking of activity; it is never the whole story. The total response involves much more.

First, in respect to etiology, at any moment of stimulus or challenge the peaking of activity brings into focus all the past lines of our life. Everything—heredity, constitution, early training, parental and sibling influences, education, marital status, job history, habits of eating and sleeping, of work and play, of prayer and church attendance, smoking, drinking, exposure to infection, body chemistry, previous accidents and illnesses—everything that has gone into the shaping of our lives up to this moment figures in some degree in the response we make.[11]

Such a total response is influenced by every significant thing a person *was* as well as *is*. Past and present interweave and relate in every present moment—experiences are not simply past and dead but vividly present and often influencing each immediate reaction.

The future enters here, too. Those persons, goals, and purposes that one invests in, also affect our present state of being. We are, in this sense, always becoming as well as being. As Reeves maintains,

Secondly, this focusing of the lines of our life in any moment of response has reference not only to the past, but also to the future. In addition to etiology, every response has its teleology. Life is always moving on. Every response is not only the effect of what has gone before, but the cause of what is yet to be. We have ideals, values, aims, images of ourselves and of what we wish to become. These all enter into the response, shaping it to get us somewhere, or get something for us, or in some fashion re-define our lives to permit the recovery of equilibrium that has been disturbed.[12]

Moreover, what we are and the way we have been reacting or "responding" to life, seems often to play a significant part in the manner we meet any particular situation. Such reactions, while they may take an obviously physical form such as a particular illness, yet apparently often have other determinants that relate them to our more general life "correspondence."

Reeves proposes that

A third characteristic of the total response is that in any given individual it has a *specificity* that is not accidental. The kind of sickness he comes up with, "mental" or "physical," whether it is a matter of infection or of trauma, the particular organ or organ-system affected— these are not matters of chance. A person's total response always takes a particular form that fulfills the style of his past life and serves to advance his life in the future. We are familiar with the "end-organ" theory, or its more developed statement in the concept of "organ language," or with Gotthard Booth's idea of "symbolic Function." The general drift of these theories is that every person tends to discharge emotion that cannot be expressed acceptably in normal life relationships, through the particular organ or organ-system whose function best symbolizes the dominant trait of his personality.[13]

RESEARCH ILLUSTRATION

In an early research paper, published when this awareness of the unity of the person was just beginning to appear in medical and psychological literature, the author reported on two contrasting aspects of patients with allergic reactions through a method of scoring and evaluating recorded interviews with them. While the findings are now commonplace, the data can still serve to illustrate how this "total response" actually occurs.[14]

We used the term "non-allergic" to designate the group of patients not reacting to the tests for allergy or indicating any apparent physical causes for their illness. These patients had, however, all the symptoms of the same serious illnesses that known allergies could cause. "Allergic" patients were those with the same symptoms but who also responded by positive skin tests to known allergens.

Briefly, the patients' responses on the typescript were divided into four main categories: Negative Emotion, Positive Emotion, Insight and Choice. Each of the main categories were in turn subdivided. The Negative Emotion category, for example, was divided into eight groups: hostility; conflict and confusion; fear and worry; dependency; social maladjustment; escape; rejection of self; and unhappiness. Thus it was possible for the contents of each response to be scored under any of these heads as well as under the Positive Emotion, Insight, and Choice categories. The accompanying chart gives the contrasting scores of the 24 interviews.

The high emotional content of statements of the non-allergic group is quite evident from this chart. Where the allergic cases talked primarily about their precise illness and its effects, the non-allergic group had many more personal factors to bring in. Conflict

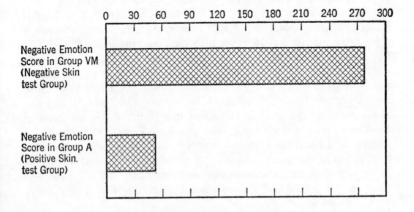

PERSONALITY FACTORS IN VASOMOTOR RHINITIS

Negative Emotion Score
Group VM Contrasted with Group A
24 Cases—Phonographically Recorded History

and confusion statements were highest, hostility scored next, and fear was third. We noticed here that, when they were allowed to talk freely without being directed into physical symptoms, their interview content grew gradually more personal and more openly emotional. It was often their first experience in feeling that they could talk unreservedly about themselves and their disturbances and at the same time receive acceptance in a medical clinic.

We might theorize from this contrast between the allergic and the non-allergic half-hour recorded statements that patients coming to any physical symptoms are often symbolizing their general state of psychological maladjustment rather than giving a clear-cut picture of their illness. Needing emotional release, they are at the same time often constrained to phrase their language in physiological terms, and to make aches and pains the subject of their conflicts and hostilities.

The following excerpt illustrates in personal detail how a variety of factors—physical, psychological, etc.—constitute, in fact, a unified experience for the person undergoing it:

(Mrs. B. comes in gasping for breath—she seems thoroughly exhausted. She lowers her head and closes her eyes.)

I'm just so sick—I can hardly get my breath—you see I just have to pull for every bit of breath I get—I'm just afraid every breath is going to be my last—it's a nervous anxiety, but I just can't do anything about it. I have to pull from way down in here to get my breath. I'm afraid if I don't pull like that I might quit breathing. Ever since I've been a child I've been afraid if anything got wrong with my lungs, I'd get T.B. I've never weighed more than 110 and I've just had fear pounded into me by constant warnings, "Don't get cold—be sure to wear a coat—watch yourself when you get a cold or you'll get T.B." You know, colored people have T.B. so much more than white people and I've always been afraid of it. I do believe that if I had this weakness in some other part of my body besides my chest, I wouldn't be nearly so frightened. I know it's a nervous anxiety condition. I know that's what it is, and yet I just don't have the guts to do anything about it. When I had it the other day, I went to the door and called my neighbor. She came in and fanned and fanned me—that's all my family can do, or anyone else. Then after it was all over, I thought, "Well, my goodness, if I had enough air to go to the door and call her, I must have had enough air to breathe." You see, I just get anxious and want something done right away. I'm afraid others aren't doing enough to help me get my breath . . .

(later in the interview)

Isn't this strange? I'm not breathing as hard now. Talking to you and getting my mind off whether or not I was going to get another breath or not has helped me. I just got my mind off thinking about myself. I was pitying myself and thinking, "Poor Betty—she can't get her breath —and just can't breathe." Well, I quit thinking that way while I was talking and I'm not breathing hard like I was. (pause) This is the most wonderful experience. Now I know I can change my attention from myself to something else and I'll get over this shortness of breath. When I came in here I was so depressed and now I'm breathing all right. It's just because I get my mind off myself when I talked. (pause) Now that I've had this experience, I know I'm just going to have to do something that will get my mind off myself. When I talked to you the other day, remember I said I thought it was my nerves? Now, I know, after this experience that that's what it is. I've discovered it myself that it is a nerve condition just from this experience, that I have had right here, now.

This is something I'm just going to have to work on myself. I like to draw and sketch, and I like dress designing. When I start getting one of these spells, I'm going to get out my pad and pencil and draw and sketch, or anything to get my mind off myself. I like to read and I like to relate the different dress styles with the different historical periods. I can do that and that will be one way of getting my mind off myself. Another thing, I'm so nervous at night. I just roll and toss all night through and I'm up and down all during the night. I was so bad my husband put me in another room. I may think I see something or hear something and I'll call my husband, "Did you hear that?" etc. Usually he's asleep and doesn't pay any attention. I think if I would just wear myself out at night before I go to bed, that maybe I could sleep. I'm going to arrange to do a lot of my work at night, so that I'll just be so worn out I can sleep. I'm going to have to do something. It's terrible to let your nerves get the best of you. I am going to do these things—and I know I have to help myself and I know that I have to do something else besides the treatment the doctor gives. I'll go ahead with the treatment, and then I'll work myself on these other things.[15]

From cases like this, it became clearer why a high negative emotion score seemed to be so characteristic of many of the non-allergic patients. When these emotional conflicts and confusions were expressed and thought through, the intensity of the physical illness often lessened.

One further implication of this unity concept is that neither biochemical, physiological nor psychological factors can be seen as separate but in fact are basically interrelated. Medications can aid the whole person as can psychological aids, each stimulating and affecting the other. Allergies, for example, are often relieved by drugs, even when their basic therapy seem to consist in personality factors. Psychological security, trust, confidence and equilibrium can be, at the same time, significant forces in making medicine and surgery more effective. The same can be said, even more forcibly sometimes, for what might be called spiritual ministration, such as pastoral counseling.

In a more recent medical article, this point of view was summarized thus:

As we think of the work of doctors and nurses in relation to patients and to themselves, we find new and subtle meanings in our knowledge of ourselves as persons and of our relations one to another . . . Striking evidence of this turning is the development of psychosomatic medicine in the past few decades. This development is visible in enormous changes in the relationship between doctor and patient, resulting from the growing awareness on the part of doctors that the patient's whole person, not just his body, is ill. It is interesting to reflect here that old notions of health, wholeness and holiness are expressed in words of Saxon origin, and the ideas of solace and salvation (salus) are embodied in words of Norman-Latin origin. To make a man healthy, we now realize, involves not just his physical, mechanical apparatus, the structure and functions of his body; it involves his whole being. Ultimately, it involves not only his present, but his total future well-being.

We have thus come to a three-dimensional concept of man. We are more and more aware, thanks in large measure to Freud and the development of psychology and psychiatry, that behind the pain and excruciating conflicts in the human body there is perhaps even more pressing and painful anxiety at work in psychosomatic interactions. We now know that in any given illness it is hard to distinguish between the effect of the illness itself and the effect of the anxiety that the illness and its consequences may produce. We are conscious of the fact that, to treat the patient properly, we have to deal with the second dimension—anxiety—as well as with the first dimension—the physical pain and its immediate needs. The third dimension is suggested by the words "holiness" and "wholeness" and "health." Behind the immediate pains and anxieties, is the sense of the passing of years, of the loss of facility of operation, of the diminishing of health with the passage of time, and a growing anxiety about how to handle this inevitable decrease of power. Behind Freud—indeed, behind the concept of human unity of Aristotle and other pre-Cartesian thinkers—there is the wisdom expressed by St. Augustine in his *Confessions:* the concept that God is the goal of man. If we accept this premise, we see that man is not made simply for his achievement, that his health is a passing thing that he cannot hold onto, and that, with the best that medicine, psychology, and psychiatry can do for him, there should emerge out of darkness and sadness of his later years, a realization that none of the material aspects of life can last for long, that life has many boundaries, and that, like water, the more one tries to grip it, the faster it will run off. With what is now increasingly called the existential anxiety of man, comes the third dimension of our human concept: the need of a God . . . Where it will lead us in these fields, we do not know. But it is interesting that we are restoring the notion of holiness and wholeness in health and interweaving the idea of solace and salvation in a unified concept of the human being.[16]

SELF-CONCEPT

Inter-related with this total response sense of the unified person, we are witnessing, too, a return to a sense of the uniqueness of the self and a search for and pursuit of self-values. But this self is intimately related to soma, instinct and emotions in all their unconscious as well as conscious influences and meanings. It is a self in unity with the whole integrated person. This self-quest, in terms of the self-concept, is one of the main aims of counseling and psychotherapy. In allied medical procedures, also, treatment must now consider the "self" of the patient as well as his various physical symptoms and illnesses.

We are made aware through counseling and psychotherapeutic research that the personality is not changed by being forced from the outside like a machine. One does not change a person by some sort of aggressive attack, as one might hit a resistant object with a hammer. We know that such efforts most of the time only marshal the person's resistance and hostility toward change. We are also realizing that education, in the simple sense of telling someone what he ought to do and then explaining it in great detail, does not in itself bring about change.

What we have seen is that a person changes by getting a new view of himself. He comes to see himself in a more fluid, more balanced, and more coordinated way. He comes, then, to act differently both toward himself and in relation to others. While other factors enter into the changes that come about in counseling and psychotherapy, one of the most basic awarenesses we now have is that of the changing self-concept.

This applies too, in our relations with others. We change our relations with other people not just by aiming at something in others; we must also look into ourselves. When we acquire a respectful and valid self-regard, we change our own perceptual field; we change the glasses through which we look at our relations with other people. In this way we can change our actions towards them. They in turn can then change in regard to us.

We all know the conflict between wanting to do something and actually being able to do it. This is what we mean by saying that we are all "normally abnormal." There is no smooth consistency between what we know and what we do. Man is evidently capable of consistent, reasonable action in the various areas of his life, but he must work at it much as he must work to acquire a skill like playing the piano. In a given situation he must struggle to acquire a knowledge of the particular means available to him, a unique individual acting in a unique moment. Then, he must arrive at an integration which permeates the whole psychosomatic system and makes it possible to carry out the action proposed.

This process is a long way from the simple and smooth coordination of a "good" machine. Man is far too subtle and complex for this kind of simple determination of his attitude toward himself and others. With the extensive educational systems and programs we now have, we recognize that there is a great difference between knowing and the actual capacity to carry out knowledge. There is yet a complicated process between learning and the acquiring of the internal coordination and integration of somatic urges, instincts, and emotions that enable a person to carry out a consistently smooth operation. Knowledge is only a first stage of personality change.

UNIQUENESS AND MYSTERY

These recent developments also confirm a return to the sense of mystery, of uniqueness, of the unknown in man. We are no longer sure that we can understand him entirely by "science" in a Newtonian and Cartesian sense. We seem to be returning, too, to that search for the ultimate meaning of man of which Augustine gave us an enduring expression. Man is restless not only at his disordered animal level, but even at the highest level of his rational human fulfillment. The way is open, now, for the reexamination of this most potent awareness.

The restoration of the idea of the unified human person and the self-quest and the reawakening of the sense of human mystery and uniqueness suggests the reappearance of one of the most ancient central tendencies of our culture. It is the burden of the message of the Psalms, of the Greek struggle to "know thyself," and of the Gospel and the Christian seekers. All these ideas have now become excitingly alive and meaningful in science, medicine, psychiatry, psychology, philosophy and theology, as new possibilities for study and research into the nature of man open up. Around this common awareness of the integrated unity of the human person, much of the division of the knowledge of man that has grown up in recent centuries can begin to be healed. Without losing the viewpoint of man that forms and defines their own uniqueness, various disciplines can begin now to come together again in some basic sharing about the meaning of the human person—each from its own view-point.

These different disciplines can meet and function together as they group themselves around the needs of the person. Here disputes and differences, lines of authority and prerogative, abstract and theoretical issues become living, suffering flesh and blood which cry out for help to each of us in our incarnate humanity. Here all can join together to benefit suffering, confused man. Here, in the strange paradox that "he that shall lose his life, shall save it," each can benefit himself and his own field through a profound and renewed human belonging.

Moreover, through the sense of the unity of the person, people of the helping professions and the behavioral sciences can meet and share together with religious people on the level of mutual concerns and involvements with man. Each can learn to speak and understand the language of the other. By so doing, they can throw off suspicions and anxieties and reach some sense of security and belonging together. Each is thus helped and strengthened. The professional can gain in vision, inspiration, and hope, and acquire added respect for and understanding of the ways and means of religious faith and convictions. Religious people can gain in objectivity, precision, realism and in respect, by seeing at first hand the commitment and dedication of the humanistic professions and sciences. Each can be enlarged and deepened through this kind of creative intercommunication. And the ultimate beneficiary is and will be man himself as he seeks to know ever more extensively and profoundly, the meaning and value of human existence.

NOTES

[1] René Descartes, *Discours de la Méthode,* ed. E. Gilson, Paris: Librairie Philosophique J. Vrin, 1935, pp. 114–115. (See also editor's Notes.)

[2] Immanuel Kant, "Fundamental Principles of the Metaphysic of Morals," *Kant's Critique of Practical Reason and Other Works on the Theory of Ethics* (1898). Reprinted as Immanuel Kant, "The Categorical Imperative," *A Modern Introduction to Ethics: Readings from Classical and Contemporary Sources,* ed. M. K. Munitz, trans. Thomas K. Abbot, Glencoe, Ill.: The Free Press of Glencoe, 1958, pp. 259–271.

[3] Martin Buber, *I and Thou,* trans. R. G. Smith, Edinburgh: T. & T. Clark, 1937.

[4] Irving Langmuir, "Langmuir's Address," Presidential Address to American Association for the Advancement of Science, *Science News Letter,* 43, January 2, 1943, pp. 3–12.

[5] Gardner Murphy, "Pythagorean Number Theory and Its Implications for Psychology," *The American Psychologist,* 22 (6), June 1967, p. 428.

[6] *Ibid.,* p. 430.

[7] *Ibid.*

[8] David Bakan, "The Test of Significance in Psychological Research," *Psychological Bulletin,* 66 (6), 1966, pp. 423–437.

See also:

Bakan, D. "The Mystery-Mastery Complex in Contemporary Psychology," *American Psychologist,* 20, 1965, pp. 186–191.

Pearson, K. S., "Statistical Concepts in Their Relation to Reality," *Journal of the Royal Statistical Society* (B), 17, 1955, pp. 204–207.

Tukey, J. W., "The Future of Data Analysis," *Annals of Mathematical Statistics,* 33, 1962, pp. 1–67.

Schlaifer, R. *Probability and Statistics for Business Decisions,* New York: McGraw-Hill, 1959.

Edwards, W., Lindman, H., & Savage, L. J., "Bayesian Statistical Inference for Psychological Research," *Psychological Review,* 70, 1963, pp. 193–242.

Berkson, J., "Tests of Significance Considered as Evidence," *Journal of the American Statistical Association,* 37, 1942, pp. 325–335.

[9] J. Whatmough, *Language: A Modern Synthesis,* New York: The New York American Library of World Literature, 1956, p. 68.

[10] From an address, "Caring for the Whole Patient," by Dr. Milford O. Royce—President-elect, 1967, of the American Medical Association, Chicago, Palmer House Banquet, Anderson Foundation, November 10, 1966.

[11] Robert B. Reeves, Jr., "The Total Response," *Journal of Religion and Health,* 4, April 1965, pp. 247–248.

[12] *Ibid.*

[13] *Ibid.*

[14] Charles A. Curran, "Nondirective Counseling in Allergic Complaints," *Journal of Abnormal and Social Psychology,* 43 (4), October 1948, pp. 446–449.

[15] C. A. Curran, et al, "Personality Factors in 'Allergic Disorders,'" *Journal of Allergy,* 18, 1947, pp. 337–340.

[16] C. A. Curran, "The Physician's Understanding Heart," *The Journal of the American Medical Association,* 188, April 13, 1964, pp. 140–142.

4
Meaning and Values

A UNIFIED VIEW of man, then, sees human action as a composite result of a complicated and subtle dynamism. So, while we may and often must distinguish modes, such as psychic and somatic, intellectual and voluntary, conscious and unconscious, these are never really seen in isolation, or as separate from other aspects of man's human condition. But these and other distinctions can give evidence of varying degrees of self-involvement. For, in certain types of knowing—in degrees of abstraction, for example—the self seems less totally engaged than in the kind of conscious commitment that certain actions imply. The knowing that involves immediate personal action seems a different sort of knowing than the one which concerns knowledge as such. We have previously classified this under the distinction of "logos" and "gnosis." But we can also think of it as a difference between *meaning* and *value*.

MEANING QUEST AND VALUE PURSUIT

We might then speak of a quest for meaning and the search and pursuit of values. By contrasting "quest" with "pursuit," we are also contrasting "meaning" and "values." To repeat what was said earlier, we can distinguish between the quest for meaning and the pursuit of values by saying that "meaning" here stands for the intellectual search to understand the significance of reality and experience. Values would imply a further step whereby, having acquired some measure of significant meanings, a person may then search out special areas in which to invest himself. In this way values become personal norms, goals, and purposes in proportion as we have committed ourselves to them. So we may quest for

74

meanings but we genuinely pursue values. The personal significance of any educative process then, becomes finally oriented and
integrated in values. Such a pursuit of values and not simply the
quest for meaning would designate the purpose of counseling and
psychotherapy. For these demand not only an intellectual understanding but a deep and involved self-commitment.

Without question, one of the strongest urges in man is to inquire
into the significance of experience. Insofar as he is human, then, he
not only consciously experiences but he also strives for some answer to the question "why?" Piaget points out:

But its very abundance leads us to look upon the "why" as the maid-of-
all work among questions, as an undifferentiated question, which in
reality has several heterogeneous meanings . . .

There are three big groups of children's "why"—the "why" of causal
explanation (including *finalistic* explanation), those of *motivation,* and
those of *justification.* Inside each group further shades of difference
may be distinguished. After a certain age (from 7 to 8 onwards) there
are also the whys of *logical justification* . . . they can be included in the
"whys" of justification in general.[1]

To aid in answering these "why's," education and guidance are
necessary. Such information helps the child and adult profit by the
learning and awareness of mankind as well as the experience and
training of particular individuals. He obviously cannot begin to
answer all these basic questions by himself.

In this quest for meaning, each person takes to himself and
makes part of his own existence some aspects of the concepts and
awareness that the education and guidance of others have given
him. Without values, in this sense, the most adequate education
could still lead to frustration and disillusionment.

Frankl asks the basic question—

What happens if one's will-to-meaning remains unfulfilled? What if the
person finds himself frustrated in this most human demand for a
meaning to his existence? What if he fails in his striving to give his life
a meaning worth living for? What we can observe in the majority of
people is not so much the feeling of being less valuable than others, but

the feeling that life no longer has any meaning. What threatens contemporary man is that which I call "the existential vacuum" within him. What we have to deal with, then, is, as it were, a "living nihilism," characterized, as is each sort of nihilism, by the denial that Being has a meaning.[2]

Man's "why?" is not only a quest for meaning; it is also an effort to stave off the anxiety with which the constant change of daily living threatens him. "This too shall pass away" stands above every human achievement and purpose. Not only the passing fulfillment of the moment, but the most secure of human accomplishments are subject to the threat of final dissolution and loss.

Living as each man does, in a world of constant change, there is a striving for consistency and some manner of predictability as a protection against the anxiety of this constant change. There is a seeking for the "raison d'être" of things, for law, principle and whatever in each experience can be found to be common to other similar experiences. In this way, uniqueness can begin to be coped with. Life gains in meaning if one can see in new experiences, elements that are not totally unfamiliar and strange and which have, at least, some aspects of more enduring significance. Each unique experience becomes less threatening and anxiety-charged. This seeking for commonality, consistency and for what endures in each unique experience seems to constitute the core of man's search for meaning.

Since education is the basic way a man is helped to find meaning in existence and the sources of those values to which he can give himself and which give goals and purpose to his achievements, it is a basic means of self delineation. A person is what he invests himself in.

NECESSITY OF EDUCATION

We can also see in this concept of meaning and value both the intellectual process of knowing and the total-person process of doing. Both are essential to any final achievement and fulfillment. Without education, a man's scope of values is curtailed and he is forced to be dependent on and directed by others. The man of limited education is less likely to have as many options from which to chose as the better educated man. As a result, his views tend to be stereotyped and narrow. He has a narrower margin of freedom in making his personal life-choices. This denies him the wider range of life values that a greater education affords.

Such a man can often be the victim of mass emotional persuasion. His lack of knowledge can make him especially prone to this kind of external and passive motivation. The following description suggests the way this phenomenon can and did operate:

It lies in the nature of an organization that it can only exist in a broad mass, where a more emotional attitude serves a high, intellectual leadership. A company of 200 men of equal intellectual ability would in the long run be harder to discipline than a company of 190 intellectually less capable men and 10 with higher education . . . The new movement rejects in general and in its own inner structure, a principle of majority rule in which the leader is degraded to the level of a mere execution of other people's will and opinion. In little as well as big things we advocate the principle of conditional authority of the leader coupled with the highest responsibility.[3]

By extending to each the widest possible information education makes possible a broader, deeper and more extensive grasp of life issues. Only such a person can be said to be really educated. Education at its best, then, should aim at giving the most complete grasp of the meaning and significance of life in proportion to each person's capacity to absorb and understand.

STUDIES NOT SUFFICIENT

But, as we have seen, more than knowledge is necessary for commitment and fulfillment. The whole person must be engaged. Not only his intellectual understanding is involved, but in some significant areas at least, he must also engage and invest his entire self. Such value awareness would characterize a responsible person who is genuinely committed—an inner-directed person—not one who

waits for the impulse from outside, swaying often between changing moods and fashions of thought and feeling.

Commenting on the widespread belief and trust that the study of
classical literature and culture can, of itself, produce a deeply
human person, Steiner says:

The simple yet appalling fact is that we have very little solid evidence
that literary studies do very much to enrich or stabilize moral perception, that they *humanize*. We have little proof that a tradition of
literary studies in fact makes a man more humane. What is worse—a
certain body of evidence points the other way. When barbarism came
to twentieth century Europe, the arts faculties in more than one university offered very little moral resistance, and this is not a trivial or
local accident. In a disturbing number of cases the literary imagination
gave servile or ecstatic welcome to political bestiality. That bestiality
was at times enforced and refined by individuals educated in the culture of traditional humanism. Knowledge of Goethe, a delight in the
poetry of Rilke, seemed no bar to personal and institutionalized
sadism. Literary values and the utmost of hideous inhumanity could
coexist in the same community, in the same individual sensibility; and
let us not take the easy way out and say "the man who did these things
in a concentration camp just said he was reading Rilke. He was not
reading him well." That is an evasion. He may *have been* reading him
very well indeed . . .[4]

Rather, without some deeper kind of value engagement of the
whole person, such intellectualized and removed imaginative study
can heighten indifference and inhumanity. Such artificial engagement can minimize genuine relationship to the real condition of
man.

Because we are trained to give psychological and moral credence to the
imaginary, to the character in a play or a novel, to the condition of
spirit we gather from a poem, we may find it more difficult to identify
with the real world, to take the world of actual experience to heart—
"to heart" is a suggestive phrase. The capacity for imaginative reflex,
for moral risk in any human being is not limitless; on the contrary, it
can be rapidly absorbed by fictions, and thus the cry in the poem may
come to sound louder, more urgent, more real than the cry in the street

outside. The death in the novel may move us more potently than the death in the next room. Thus there may be a covert, betraying link between the cultivation of aesthetic response and the potential of personal inhumanity . . .[5]

In our present culture, as we have discussed, intellectual awareness has become separated from the whole knowing person, in a kind of neutrality. We have placed a premium on objectivity, on distance, on removal in proportion as we can get far away from people. We are "distant" people and we get increasingly threatened as we find ourselves intimately related. The educative process has been infected by this kind of intellectual distance.

RECOGNITION OF AUTHENTIC VALUES

Counseling and psychotherapy by contrast to this neutral distance relationship, have gotten people involved not only through intellectual awareness but also by a total psychosomatic engagement. If we say that values are meanings plus self-investment, then counseling and psychotherapy have indeed been value-oriented experiences.

When people change in counseling and psychotherapy, it appears to be not simply because someone has educated them but because they have come to what is often a rediscovery of basic values. What Heinz Hartmann applies to psychoanalysis can be said of all effective counseling and psychotherapy. By this process a person is somehow engaged in a growing sense of personal responsibility and in an internalization of an authentic value system:

But let us return to the factor of self-knowledge, so intimately connected with the process of analysis . . . Despite what the great Plato thought about it, we do not believe in a simple correlation between the steps toward insight and the steps to moral improvement. A remark of Freud's is to the point here. It is from the same letter from which I quoted before: "I do not agree with Socrates and Putnam that all our faults arise from confusion and ignorance." Still, we cannot write off the cases in which increased self-awareness does have an effect on the moral codes. Broadening of self-knowledge, including also motivations which are commonly unconscious, can lead to a broadening also of the sense of responsibility, the avoidance of easy rationalizations, and so on. Furthermore, it seems likely that a clearer and more objective awareness of motivation and of one's actual value structures also allows a more subtle form of control, which is certainly one of the factors with which we are concerned in considering moral conduct.[6]

This "more subtle form of control" is made possible not by simple "will-power" or by more education but rather by a growing discrimination and clarification of one's "authentic values."

The recognition of one's authentic values, and their distinction from those which are not authentic, is not infrequently sharpened in the course of the analytic process. This will not change a "bad" person into a "good" person, or only rarely. What it means is that the codes can become less distorted, often less one-sided, expressions of the moral aspect of personality. The individual can learn to see more clearly the moral aims, ideals, imperatives he actually adheres to and to understand them in the context of his personality, and as his own. You know how carefully we avoid, in analysis, imposing ethical demands on our patients. But what often does happen as a consequence of analysis is that the patient's own authentic moral values become dominant in his codes.[7]

This is the unfolding of and growth in the realization of an inner value system. But it is not simply solipsistic. Rather it enables a person to relate better with others and with the life situations in which, here and now, he finds himself.

INNER VALUE SYSTEM

We see in the counseling therapy process, then, an unfolding of an inner value system that is yet objectively effective in producing a better operational fulfillment and achievement. Operational reality, by implication, has apparently some kind of reasonable substructure (granting all its apparent disorder) into which the client's own reasonable process penetrates. The counseling therapy process ultimately facilitates not only a more rational integration and control of the personality, but also somehow a better, more adequate way of living.

SOURCES OF VALUES

There are moreover a variety of factors that determine a person's pursuit of values. These consciously or unconsciously influence the goals a person has and the choices he makes. There is, as we have said, the self in its known and hidden present and past life experiences. There is the environment, which determines the immediate milieu from which many self-values are absorbed. But, in addition, there are the values hidden in the matrix of the culture itself—values often dormant as well as active and sometimes in conflict. Yet the person himself may be only partially aware or even completely unaware of this. But these values can influence him even more than those that seem more personal and immediate. For in his final existential anxiety, it is to these values that, explicitly or implicitly, he often turns.

The counseling psychotherapeutic process is in this sense, then, a search for basic values as well as a striving for immediate self-awareness. But it is a personal pursuit of values which are uniquely meaningful. Yet this independent pursuit does not finally produce rebellion or anarchy. Rather, the opposite seems most often to happen. When a person, with integrity and security, probes himself through the searching realtionship with the counselor, he tends finally to retrace the steps by which many of the basic values of our civilization have been determined. At the end he often finds and grows to accept concepts and guidelines that have proved fundamental to the process by which civilization itself has been formed.

What happens in the counseling therapeutic process might be symbolized by the illustration used earlier—a triangle. The client begins at its peak, with unique and personal events, situations, feelings, and reactions that seem peculiarly to happen only to him. Slowly he moves down to the discovery that others share many of these things—that he is not as different or unique as he thought. He begins to adapt himself to others and to learn from others but in a way most interestingly personal and self-determined. In counseling, where the counselor struggles to understand him and thus he is helped to understand himself, he studies and investigates himself in an intense search which the counselor's responses keep objective and in a sense impersonal.

This mutual process of the client's reasonable self-search leads down the triangle to issues and values that are increasingly more universal and more fundamental. It can lead—it does not always—to the most basic questions of all, the meaning of life itself and to a struggle with all these final anxieties and concerns which one would call philosophical and theological.

But even when the basic and universal issues of life, symbolized by the broad base of the triangle, are not questioned by the client, they seem contained and implied in the values by which he questions and changes in more immediate personal situations.

Some years ago Rogers wrote (discussing a case) that insight tends to move through the "difficult and painful . . . not for its immediate but for its long-time satisfaction."[8]

This awareness might be carried to further conclusions. The analysis of the counseling therapy process demonstrates that increased insight and a broader understanding of his personal values, aims, and purposes, enable a person to direct himself toward and eventually to reach goals that are more permanently satisfying. But since no transient, material thing can, upon analysis, produce the permanent security, peace, and lasting happiness that each one seeks, the fear of loss seems always to be the other side of every human possession and security.

Each man seems therefore to be in a state of both being and becoming for which no transient goal or value—however immediately satisfying—can offer any final longtime fulfillment. We seem to have implicit here a profound core of existential anxiety in each person, an essential dissatisfaction that is both unique and yet shared by mankind.

From what emerges in the counseling therapeutic process, then, a person's self-knowledge seems often incomplete and inadequate unless he grasps something of the basic cultural values that have, until now, implicitly guided many of his choices and goals. It

seems apparent that a person often seeks not only personal integration but he also seeks in some way an integration with the values
of the civilization that produced him and still affect him. He needs
to know not only his relationship to his parents, family and
immediate environment but also to those older peoples whose
thoughts and values have influenced him with equal, if unknown,
potency. As he grows in self-understanding, he grows to see that
many of the hidden reasons he had for doing things, were in fact
absorbed from the implicit traditions around him. In recognizing
this, he may consciously reject some of these values especially
when they are in some way, in conflict. Often, however, he seeks
more adequate and effective ways, unique to himself, of achieving
these life-goals.

INDEPENDENT RESPONSIBLE PROCESS

This process of self-evaluation often frees a person from the
Kantian concept that all personal values are imposed on him by a
kind of categorical imperative—which has come to mean either by
parents, society or the state. Rather it opens a person to the stimulating pursuit of himself in an independent search for reasonable
self-values. Yet, this independent and personal process allows for
the possibility that one can ultimately come not to rebellion and
anarchy against his culture but to the acceptance of many of those
values which have established and maintained it. Such a realization
often helps a person feel restored to the civilization that produced
him and is basically responsible for his democratic tradition. But
such a sense of belonging to traditional values in no way impinges
on his freedom to be unsparingly honest and sincere with himself
in his own self-determined pursuit, through counseling, psychotherapy, or by other educational and social means.

Moral conduct may be seen, therefore, not simply as something
emerging from a sense of duty and coming from parents, the
neighborhood, the culture, society, or even from the state. All
these influences do occur in the process of growth and education.
But basically moral conduct is the result of mature responsibility
for the self. This results not simply from educationally-acquired

insights but from a profound and intense self-search and understanding. Only in this way does a person seem to begin to unfold
the mystery of self, and of self-responsibility.

GUILT AND VALUES

Psychological guilt then could be considered the failure to achieve
fulfillment in some aspect of one's own basic value system. It
would therefore be a form of self-attack and rejection—a kind of
surrogate or dichotomized blaming of the self for this failure as in
the expression, "I am disgusted with myself." If the values involved are not clearly evident and thus less consciously recognized,
this might result in states of depression or anger whose cause
would seem to be unknown. But such depression or anger could be
the consequence of a self-rejection or self-attack that is suppressed. As values become recognized and move out from their
hidden position behind these emotions, one might then experience
more direct and conscious guilt. Such guilt, however, could also
begin to become constructive when—through the counseling process particularly—one could consciously direct the self to better
achievement of these heretofore hidden values or one might clearly
decide no longer to invest in them. In either case, a main source of
guilt would be removed.

The nature of guilt would then follow from and be determined
by the nature of those things to which one has committed oneself,
or which one's family, neighborhood, religion and culture stand
for. A conscious process through counseling therapy would not
remove guilt necessarily. Often it would rather make such guilt
more positively constructive in furthering the achievement of the
projects and goals to which the person's values direct him. Failure
to achieve these would be a basic source of this kind of psychological guilt.

There is, further, an existential quality which would follow from
the necessity of always choosing a particular situation as the
means of value fulfillment in place of the ideal goal or image one
may have abstractly. Much as if for example, I choose to go
North, I can always question and later attack myself for failing to

achieve whatever going South, East or West might have brought me, so, no choice can be without the possibility of self-attack and guilt. I can never really know what would have resulted, had I chosen something else in the actual limits of the operational situation.

Here counseling therapy often results in a more peaceful acquiescence with what a person's existential choices have brought him and a greater fruition and investment of self in these, in contrast to his earlier plaguing himself with the loss of what he never had or really could have. This can be seen, for example, in marriage counseling. As people grow realistically to accept one another they also accept each one's limitations and potentialities. They then are less apt to project hostility and blame for unfulfilled ideals and goals that neither could really ever give the other. They also dream less of what marriage to a different person might have been. They can begin again to commit themselves to actually realizable fulfillments in one another and in their children.

The concept of sin, added to that of psychological guilt would, of course, more directly connote a faith-commitment to religious values. In our presentation we have assumed religious values to be contained in the whole question of values. So, as we said earlier, we have not treated them separately. But one might say that sin, as it relates to guilt, connotes a dimension of offense against not only oneself and others, but more basically, against God. Sin connotes not simply a barrier between oneself and one's self-ideal which produces a psychological guilt and self-attack; it is more than an impediment between oneself and another human person whom one loves. It involves a relationship with a personal God. We must add a third dimension here, coming from a commitment by faith and hope to divine love and affiliation. Sin, in the traditional sense of "grave" sin, constitutes a barrier to this relationship. Sorrow for sin and forgiveness given and accepted can only follow upon some formal, conscious repentence for one's sin against God, and the acceptance, in religious faith, of the restoration of the divine love relationship. In this way, by sorrow and forgiveness, one recommunes with God.

The word "atonement," with its suggestion of being "at one" and being in the same "tone" together, connotes the living quality by which genuine sorrow heals the rupture of the bond of love between God and man. Sorrow would then be "atoning" oneself and relating again with God in faith, hope and love. Such consideration invokes, in addition to psychological guilt, a more extensive relation to divine faith and religious conviction. It would therefore be more fittingly treated in detail under religious values, which, as we have suggested, we have reserved for another volume.

A NORMAL PROCESS

It is becoming clear in present psychological research that a vast number of people need help not in knowing what to do—as they already know much from personal guidance and education—but in taking counsel with themselves in light of this knowledge. They need greater integration around what may be called their disordered appetites: their conflicting psychological and somatic, instinctive and emotional urges. They need to bring these disordered appetites into an ordered line with what they reasonably know they should do. This is the way growth toward psychological maturity seems to be brought about.

This is applicable not simply to "disturbed" people with "problems," but rather to us all. While we may not be pathologically disturbed, we cannot claim any smooth coordination of our instincts and emotions as they relate to thought and action. We cannot control them as we are normally able to control our muscles: e.g., I tell my hand to move and it moves. Emotions and instincts, unlike my hand, do not move by simple command; they have a kind of will of their own. They can be brought under control only by what may be called a "gentle persuasion." That is to say, this kind of coordination results not simply through aggressive willing, but rather through a whole-person process. A person achieves this by taking counsel with himself about the particular situation and persons involved, making a proper and careful judgment of the best way for *him* to bring about desired goals, and finally by an insightful integrating of his emotions, instincts and soma, carrying out the act. In this way, a person's appetites are brought into an ordered, smooth-flowing, operational balance with his own reason-ableness. This, of course, is no easy process but difficult, complex and demands time, as we are seeing.

NEW AWARENESS OF CULTURE VALUES

The counseling therapeutic process, then, seems to confirm views of man which, while they are in some ways new, are yet also fundamental in the tradition of Western civilization. Many of the things this process is revealing, in a fresh and pragmatically effective way, are not so completely new that these older conceptions cannot support and even clarify them. To be sure, much underbrush and debris have gathered here that must be swept away. Much misunderstanding, confusion and misinterpretation must be clarified. These concepts must be adapted to what we now know of personality dynamics and the therapeutic process. Yet, new awarenesses still can be linked up with an older tradition and value scheme without warping either.

But to achieve this we have to recognize the distortions these terms have acquired and so seek to grasp these conceptions with something of the freshness and clarity they really originally had. We need to rediscover the origins of many of those common concepts which we have implicitly accepted in Western democratic society and which most of us want to preserve. But we can take these values too much for granted. So, in a kind of cultural self-defeating mechanism we are in danger of jeopardizing their sources while we yet enjoy and treasure many of their present effects and advantages.

Consequently, questions are being raised now about the assumption that a value-free attitude is a true scientific attitude. On the contrary, what seems to be increasingly evident is that such an attitude can be a "head-in-sand" withdrawal and escape from basic issues and thus not a scientific attitude at all. Odegard points out that

unfortunately this value-free posture tends to blind the so-called hard-nosed social scientist to the really great problems of man and society and often focuses his attention upon relatively unimportant issues. It helps to explain the monumental accumulation of trivia and the ponderous elaboration of platitudes that characterize so much contemporary social science. And it tends to make social science a more or less sophisticated servant of any power elite that may seek its services in the manipulation of human behavior, regardless of goal or purpose.[9]

Rather, science is quite the contrary of this. It neither pretends hardness nor softness but sees itself invested in the human condition. As Odegard continues,

A value-free science is of course absurd in any strict sense since science has its own norms, standards, or values, by which its statements are tested and/or evaluated. Nor is it enough to say that scientific values are merely methodological or procedural, concerned with means and not ends, except only as they aid in the objective pursuit of truth. For truth wears many faces, and to discover what is true or false is not unrelated to the discovery of what is good or bad. A scientific concept can be true or false in the degree to which it corresponds to the norms or standards of science itself—i.e., to meter readings—and it may be good or bad in the degree that it contributes to, or corresponds with, the basic needs and goals of human life. Unless science is merely random behavior or idle curiosity without purpose, it has a responsibility to discover and to serve these basic needs and goals.[10]

This kind of investment is in a special way the burden of the social sciences. They, even more than the physical sciences, directly concern themselves with factors which introduce change and betterment. They assume man to be goal-directed and responsibility-oriented. Odegard insists that

this lays a special obligation on the social sciences because they are by definition concerned with man and society. So-called behavioral science, whether hard-nosed or soft-nosed, assumes that human behavior is goal-directed, and that in striving for these goals, men choose among alternative modes of conduct. It assumes also that in choosing, they are conditioned not merely by the physical world and the pressures of appetite and instinct but by formal education in rational modes of thought and behavior. Rationally induced changes in human behavior thus become as reasonable—as scientific—as rationally induced changes in the physical environment. There is nothing unscientific in social scientists seeking to change those conditions of character and environment that impair man's ability to make rational choices among alternative modes of behavior.[11]

However much scientists may wish to retain a neutral or aloof attitude, in an age of science they are in fact highly admired by others and their opinions are invested with a special significance. Consequently,

scientists are not immune from the responsibilities of other citizens. They need to be reminded that attitudes of Olympian indifference or cynicism toward moral and ethical problems in a society that has all but canonized the scientist can issue in apathy and cynicism among others, attitudes dangerous alike to science and a good society.[12]

We need to reconsider and evaluate afresh therefore, all aspects of our culture that contribute to a respect for and understanding of human dignity. At the same time we need to devise more adequate means of inculcating these values and transmitting them. To know is not enough. As Carmichael has pointed out,

the present known facts in heredity already make it seem foolish in religious, moral, or esthetic fields to believe that each new generation can disregard all the painfully evolved experience and wisdom of the past . . .

The methods of learning about values in art, literature, philosophy and religion are not in all respects the same as those of science. In some of these studies, emotions and attitudes of appreciation and feeling, as well as logic, must be exercised. Thus, at least some of the perceptive members of each generation will gain, as in no other way, an inner enlightened understanding of the personal and social values that have always characterized man at his best and noblest.[13]

When Carmichael reminds us of the "painfully evolved experience and wisdom of the past" and urges us not to thoughtlessly "disregard" it, he is equivalently saying that civilization itself, by what in some ways may be thought of as a kind of social counseling process, slowly comes to its own wisdom and system of values. This process does not perhaps differ fundamentally from what each person must, in some measure, pursue for himself. Consequently, the two processes can coincide, at significant points, and yet be genuinely independent too. In fact it is this very personal and independent self-evaluation that is the most secure guarantee against passive acceptance of abuse and corruption in the civilization itself. Such a process of self-evaluation around cultural values most assures that a civilization remain genuinely true to its "best and noblest" expression of man in place of producing a personless mass with perhaps indifferent or cynical observers studying, analyzing and calculating them in the name of "science" or of some new image.

What we are seeing in counseling and psychotherapy tends to confirm this view of the need for an "inner enlightened understanding." We are witnessing evidence which re-confirms the value of personal gnosis in place of mere intellectual and "scientific" logos. The emphasis is again on evaluative and integrated self-knowing through feeling and action, in place of Cartesian calculated objectivity and distance or the Kantian categorical imperative of "must do" and "ought to do." This brings us closer to the Biblical and religious sense of "knowing," which can mean to "become part of," "to enter into"—even in the sexual sense—and to "share burdens" rather than simply to weigh and consider from afar.

The end effect of the counseling therapy process seems to lead a person to see and love himself and others in a more incarnate and more trusting way. Religious faith, in a sense, supports this by moving a person less to try to figure people out than to trust the mystery of life and to commit himself to others in faith and love. To do this adequately a person must seek to know himself and others in such a way as to further positive self-regard and regard of others, and thus enlarge the capacity for self-gift which would constitute genuine love of others.

EDUCATION: MEANING AND VALUE

Looked at in this way, we could say that an education which concerns itself with meanings only—especially in a purely Cartesian intellectualism, would be inadequate. If we relate to others only in meanings, we have only intellectual awareness. Unless the meanings of education offer people some option of self-investment, it is a truncated presentation. Under certain conditions it may only increase guilt without any constructive means to relieve it. Such guilt, as we will consider later, can be fostered, for example, by an unrealistic self-ideal that is often the result of a too idealistic educational process. If, however, education also presents material that gives people true options for realistic self-investment, they can make this self-investment if they so desire and begin to operate constructively.

Each person hears what is said in unique ways. To be personally effective, the matter of education must reach a person at the point of this uniqueness. Such an educative process has to go beyond the intellectual logic to the unified man who operates through his whole person. The real forces for self-investment are as much his somatic-instinctive emotional structure as his intellectual awarenesses.

We do not intend to imply here that education, which concerns itself only with meaning, is, as such, unimportant. On the contrary, intellectual learning, in the sense of acquiring a grasp of the meaning and significance of a wide variety of facts, laws and principles, obviously adds immensely to the breadth of options open to a person. In this respect, the less education one has, the more foreshortened one's view, and the more limited one's field of options in which to invest oneself. One's life values, therefore, are very dependent on the breadth, depth and wisdom of one's education in meaning. One might say that the water of value choices cannot rise above the level of one's educational advantages. Consequently, educational relationships, providing as they do the basic stuff and source of value choices, play a fundamental part in personality growth and development. In some ways with genetic endowment and other environmental factors, they set the limits to the potential of each person's ordinary life fulfillment.

LEARNING INTEGRATION

But in a personal sense, in proportion to the self-investment I make in a meaning, that meaning assumes a different operational form for me. Stating it another way, I may say that I can grasp many meanings in the educative process that do not engage, involve or commit me. They are simply things I know. They broaden the option of my possible commitments, but do not of themselves involve me. A person may learn many facts and rules such as those of a foreign language grammar, for example, simply to defend himself against the threat of humiliation and failure. He may, however, as we will see, remain hostile and resistant to speaking such a language. Or he may acquire knowledge that is of so little personal concern that he never reverts to it again, after his study is completed. Such depersonalized knowledge seems wasted in contrast to those areas of knowledge that are of deep personal significance and concern. The following comment of Montaigne is still apropos:

To return to our mutton, there is nothing like whetting the appetite. Otherwise, in education, you turn out asses loaded with books. By dint of lashes we give our pupils a schoolbag full of knowledge to take home with them. Whereas, to do well, learning must not be merely installed in the house, but married . . .

In the choice between a teacher who had a well-turned rather than a well-filled head we need a man with both, but preferably with manners and understanding than with learning. And we want him to do his work in a new way . . .

In plain truth, our education, its pains and expenses, aim at nothing but to stuff our heads with facts—of judgment, prudence, and virtue, no word. And it has succeeded altogether too well. Instead of teaching us prudence and virtue, it gives us their etymology. We learn how to decline Virtue, but not to live it. If we don't know what Prudence is in effect and by experience, we know it by jargon and rote . . .

It is not a mind we are educating, nor a body; it is a man. And we must not split him in two.[14]

Since neither the necessity of personal values in education nor their neglect in the educational process are recent discoveries, the issues Montaigne raised are still as relevant now as they were in the Sixteenth century.

COUNSELING IN LEARNING

What we can add now to aid this process, however, are counseling therapy skills. These are especially important in this transition phase where meanings are to become values. Since meanings alone do not engage a person, one can learn a great deal about the world and still be uninvolved as a human being. A person makes his own investment in a particular area of meaning either by taking counsel with himself and putting his whole psychosomatic self into the commitment, or by entering a group or individual counseling relationship. The more he could do this as he learns, the more likely what he learns would become a personal value and not simply a meaning.

To make a personal commitment is a more profound, anxious and even angry experience than simply to absorb meaning. The nature of the classroom experience would change in proportion as we think of values, rather than meanings, as the end purpose of education. Once we free ourselves from Cartesian and Kantian concepts which separate intellectual and voluntary experience from somatic involvements, we can accept the fact that all aspects of the person are inextricably interwoven in any moment of learning. A main aim of the educative process then would be not just to impart meaning, but to enable the person to comprehend values. The educative process would in this way be much more concerned with methods, skills and relationships that promote value investment than with simply having the student learn the meanings in the courses he has taken.

Significant personal learning might be heightened by the increased combination of counseling relationships and learning experiences. Rather than counseling and personality change being seen as something separate from or at least secondary to the intellectual aspects of learning, we might begin to devise more ways of incorporating them directly into the learning experience. This far more fits the psychosomatic unity that we now understand the human personality to be than methods still laboring under an exaggerated intellectual and dichotomized view of man. This process of learning would be more personal, more value-centered rather than simply measured by the meaning content alone. Its aim would be to produce self-involved learning rather than learning only for a grade, or utility, or simply for the acquisition of impersonal knowledge. In this way, learning and the process of maturity would not be separate but interwoven, mutually strengthening and supportive of personal growth and value commitment.

NOTES

[1] Jean Piaget, "The Language and Thought of the Child," *Classics in Psychology,* ed. Thorne Shipley, New York: Philosophy Library, 1961, pp. 995–998.

[2] Viktor E. Frankl, *From Death-Camp to Existentialism,* Boston: Beacon Press, 1959, pp. 98–99.

[3] Adolf Hitler, *Mein Kampf,* trans. R. Manheim, Boston: Houghton Mifflin Co., 1943, pp. 436 and 344.

[4] Steiner, *op. cit.,* p. 61.

[5] *Ibid.*

[6] Heinz Hartman, *Psychoanalysis and Moral Values,* New York: International Universities Press, Inc., 1960, pp. 91–92.

[7] *Ibid.*

[8] Carl Rogers, *Counseling and Psychotherapy,* Boston: Houghton Mifflin Co., 1942, p. 210.

[9] Editorial, "The Social Sciences and Society," *Science,* 145 (3637), September 11, 1964; taken from Peter H. Odegard, *The Educational Record,* 45, (190), 1964.

[10] *Ibid.*

[11] *Ibid.*

[12] *Ibid.*

[13] Leonard Carmichael, "Science and Social Conservatism," *Scientific Monthly,* 78, June 1954, pp. 372–379.

[14] *The Autobiography of Michel de Montaigne,* ed. Marvin Lowenthal, New York: Vintage Books, 1956, pp. 18, 23, 24, 27.

5
The Process of Maturity

MATURITY, seen as the goal that emerges in counseling therapy, might be defined as the capacity to respect, possess, and at the same time give the self. The person apparently slowly achieves this through the experience of being genuinely respected, regarded, and understood by the counselor or therapist. But the counselor and therapist also, must, in some measure, have acquired such knowledge of his own needs and tendencies that he can truly give himself over to the person in the counseling therapeutic relationship. To be effective, he too must have acquired a similar kind of maturity.

But the maturity we speak of here, is not simply some abstract "reasonableness" or some ideal norm. These, in fact, can be misleading if not rightly understood. Maturity must be grounded in each one's unique and incarnate awareness of himself, his capacities and his limits.

This has been one of the great contributions not only of clinical psychology and psychiatry but of Kiergaard and modern existentialist thought: it has made us conscious of the being of man in existence; of man in a state of "happening." In so doing, it has forced us to precise and detailed observation of the actual condition of man, so that we can "tell it like it is," as the current phrase expresses it.

In this chapter we will pursue further some of these aspects of the counseling therapy process as they regard the goal of achieving greater maturity or more adequate mental health.

SELF AFFIRMATION AND CONTAINMENT

Maturity and mental health, as revealed in counseling therapy, seem to involve both the love of self and the courage to be, that is, to pursue one's own excellence. But it also involves the capacity to temper and contain the self in those narcissistic urges which would tend to defeat oneself or to control and manipulate others and so rob them of meaning. It therefore implies a basic sense of "to each his own", allowing others their own unique pursuit of excellence. Only in this balanced way does one really seem to come to a genuine love of self and others.

In the process of counseling therapy, people often grow to see that they are attributing exaggerated values and meanings to many pursuits which, upon counseling analysis, turn out to have far less significance. The importance that they had originally given these pursuits scales itself down so that they can finally discard them. Or they may continue them but see them now in a more limited perception. Consequently they expect less from them and are not disappointed when this more restricted yield turns out to be theirs. A person can now anticipate with a fair degree of accuracy just about what the action will mean to him and so invest in it only the limited value that such a project has. Previously having tended to hope for a reward that the activity could not possibly have given him, he felt forced, in frustration and need for compensative relief, to continue this exaggerated investment, and so continue on a self-defeating treadmill.

We have seen that counseling concerns itself with the search for those meanings which, invested in, result in a pursuit of values. It is this self-investment and pursuit that constitute the highly personal aspect of counseling. Such pursuit involves a courageous self-affirmation and a tempering self-containment as well as a sense of other persons. What one sees is that the urge to self-excellence is both encouraged and stimulated and at the same time cylindered and contained. Otherwise it looses itself in ineffectiveness, in compensatory drives that are self-deluding and often self-defeating, and in the manipulation maneuvering of other persons. Obviously such a description of self-affirmation and self-containment is not new. But counseling therapy extends in depth and subtlety the dimensions of this process and facilitates its more adequate realization.

POSITIVE SELF-INVESTMENT

What people seem to arrive at, as we have seen, is that in learning to love themselves and give themselves to others, they first need a sense of self-worth. In proportion then, as I consider myself worthless, I have nothing worth giving; hence, love is impossible, or possible only at an extremely low level. For love to have dignity, meaning and worth, I must see myself as having value. This kind of positive self-regard appears necessary for any genuine relationship with another person. This confirms what Aristotle proposed:

The characteristic element in our friendship for our neighbors, and the points which distinguish and delimit the various forms of friendship, seem to have their origin in the sympathetic feelings with which we regard ourselves.[1]

Summing up all the reasons for this kind of respectful self-regard and contrasting it with the self-indulgence that impedes friendship and so defeats a person, Aristotle concluded:

In this sense then it is, as I have said before, right that he should be self-loving. But in the vulgar sense, no one should be.[2]

The Biblical tradition sums this up in the concept that one should love both self and neighbor—with the love of self the model of our love of others.

Here we see a basic way in which psychological "redemption"— the gaining of a sense of worth, and meaning and security—operates. Various states of anxiety dominate infancy. These suggest that a child apparently feels himself on the verge of annihilation. Such existential anxiety is visible in the child's fear of darkness, catastrophic feelings he sometimes has about a simple event, or the panic he may experience at the loss of a little fetish doll that he carries with him for security.[3] As we grow older, we apparently may simply acquire more adult things in exchange for the fetishistic objects that were our childhood protections against anxiety. We look to our accomplishments for reassurance in moments of anxiety. We invest in external things, a car, a house, etc., in a way perhaps not really different from the child, if more sophisticated and expensive. We have not then ever entirely put away the security symbols of childhood.

Anxiety and the feeling of worthlessness seem to be interrelated. Perhaps they are two sides of the same coin. One might say that because man is born out of nothing, he is always on the edge of nothing. He is pushed toward feelings of worthlessness and anxiety because he has nothing that is finally his. Disorder and the tendency in nature to disorganization also point in this direction. In man this tendency seems to lead him toward the threat of personal disorganization. Lillie has remarked:

Unless counteracted by directive action the casual or random element in nature tends to increase. If things are left to chance, not only does organization of any high degree of complexity fail to develop, but what organization there is tends to lapse or disappear.[4]

Anxiety is furthered by the constant threat of these tendencies toward disorder and stagnation. People can feel a kind of threatening catastrophic disorder for which the only solution seems to be to "drive" themselves into activity and achievement, even if these goals prove to have little or no genuine value for them.

The text "perfect love casts out fear," suggests the continuum between the fear of disorder and annihilation, at the one end and love at the other. If then, in gaining maturity, we are to move toward knowing how to love, we shall have to move away from the basic existential sense of worthlessness and anxiety, in the direction of the sense of being redeemed in the freedom to love.

What seems to happen, however, as we earlier proposed, is that we do not escape from the state of worthlessness until someone loves us. In this sense we are first "redeemed" or given a sense of worth through someone else and his concern for us. When we are loved, we begin to build up capital, so to speak, in our own values. We can then start to give some of this in love to others.

This seems to be one basic norm of maturity. The more mature person, because he is secure in being loved, can plunge into life, whereas the less mature, feeling himself to have little value or meaning, feels threatened, defensive and so withdraws, or approaches life negatively. One might be said to feel himself "redeemed," the other "unredeemed." Applied to a theology of human belonging this would mean that somebody must redeem us in a purely human way by loving us and so giving us a feeling of self-meaning and worth, before we can feel loved enough to participate fully in a belief in divine Redemption.[5] Unless we can love and be loved, we apparently are handicapped in the way we understand, feel and cooperate with love.

GENUINE SELF POSSESSION

If love is considered the capacity to give the self, then a core impediment to giving oneself is the lack of self-possession. Plato described man as a driver of wild as well as tame horses, in the sense that the degree to which he became a mature person was the degree to which he tamed and so achieved possession and control of basic, primitive and disordered urges in himself. If, in addition to feeling myself worthless and being anxious in a world I see only as hostile and threatening, I have no control over myself. To offer myself as a gift would be only an empty gesture. In proportion as I lack self-possession, such a gift of self would be meaningless. Unless I have attained some measure of understanding and control over the primitive urges in myself, my basic anxieties, and my compensatory needs, I really do not possess myself enough to give myself. I can give only the appearance of loving; I cannot make a genuine gift of myself.

In this state, a person's apparent love for another may really be only a kind of subtle manipulation. This can be like selling something on time-payments: in the course of years, the recipient will pay back the actual worth of the "gift" many times over. So, in the name of love, a person may do a sincere service but the demands he finally makes on the other person over months or years, may far outweigh the initial act of kindness.

Seen this way, it seems difficult indeed to really love. Primitive forces, unconscious needs, emotional satisfactions can stultify and weaken our intent. We may then discover that the purpose was not love at all, but a subtle and clever use of others for our own needs. This often comes about because we become personally identified with something we have made an investment in and we find it difficult to separate ourselves from our investment. Our invested identification with others, as a parent might be invested in a child, for example, makes it hard to disentangle ourselves and regard them separately, in their own unique persons.

OVERSIMPLIFIED PERCEPTION

Moreover, there is evidently a basic impetuosity in everyone, a kind of nervous resistance to evaluation before action that results in the quick stereotyped reaction and answer. Because of an exaggerated desire for simplicity, clarity and precision, we are evidently unwilling to lower ourselves to the human condition of seeing things in a mirror darkly instead of face to face. We are not willing to struggle through the complexity of personal issues. We seek the immediate solution, the simple answer.

One reason for this seems to be that under certain kinds of surprise or stress, we tend to react first as simple animals. An experiment illlustrates this. If, without prior warning, I quickly wave my hand in front of a volunteer subject's face, his head will move back and he will blink. If I continue the motion, his head will finally stop moving back and he will stop blinking. When we ask people to tell us what happened, they say that they just saw a narrow object, that they were not really conscious of what was coming toward their eyes, and their heads went back automatically. In other words, a built-in defense-reaction takes possession. The person must make an effort to reach a cortical awareness that he is taking part in an experiment and that the thing in front of his face is not going to hurt his eyes. As he begins to think, he recognizes the experiment he volunteered for. At about that moment, his eyes will stop blinking, and he may smile a little.

INSIGHT AND CONTROL

This illustrates the process and struggle for insight and control over primitive defense reactions. The primitive reaction may still be in possession again, however, because if the motion is repeated, the person will often again blink and pull back his head. So one reacts often as a defensive animal, as well as a rational being. Consistent operational rationality is a difficult process of self-knowledge and control which is only slowly acquired and must be continually renewed to be maintained even in a particular action.

In other words, we can be primitive, infantile and adult at the same time. In moments of sudden insecurity we are at first apt to be primitively infantile, even though we generally try to mask this even from ourselves. One aim of counseling-therapy is to aid a person in the struggle to become more totally human and mature. This is not easy when people are seemingly enslaved by these primitive and childish reactions. But the moment of freedom is that kind of awareness which frees a person from the bind of these reactions. He can begin to exercise control because he has operational insight and can act on it. This is not abstract intellectual awareness but an inner, somatic, instinctive, emotional insight that is operationally effective in guiding the self. It furthers self-possession, and so enables one to give himself to another. Only in this way can one truly love.

Getting to know and possess the self then can be attained only by a long and often painful struggle. Moreover, we cannot really know ourselves in the present unless we look back on all the aspects of the psychological matrix that made us what we are; all the coping mechanisms, all the childhood needs and fulfillments that affect us in the present moment of any choice. People often grow to see that many present judgments have been influenced by things that happened to them much earlier in life.

PHRONETIC PROCESS

A first aspect of maturity, then, is the ability to take adequate counsel with the self. Out of this comes the second phase which is the judgment or evaluation of the self. In the process of growth, this judgment may result in the rejection of past attitudes or values, and so set up new ideals or goals. In this sense, it might also be called the evaluation phase.

This process resembles that which Aristotle called "phronesis." His term, long since a part of English usage, has been variously translated. It was originally translated as "prudence." This is the meaning Montaigne has in mind when he laments that, through education, "If we don't know what Prudence is in effect and by experience, we know it by jargon and rote."[6]

Unfortunately, however, the English word, "prudence" has undergone such a great change in its connotation and meaning that it now suggests a cautious, perhaps grudging or legalistic attitude. Obviously this is not the meaning that it had for Aristotle.

McKeon gets around this by translating "phronesis" as "practical wisdom."[7] But here we run into the Kantian implication that the opposite of "practical" would be "pure." This involves us in the issues between "practical" and "pure" that we discussed earlier. To avoid both of these perhaps the term "operational integration" might better combine the modern psychological implications of the word "operational" with the necessity of seeing things in integration.

One might add to this the connotation of the German translation of "phronesis" as "sittliche Einsicht," ("practical insight") to suggest the inner self-awareness such an operational integration demands.[8] Stated this way, then, the aim of this phronetic process would be to arrive at a state of personal integration sufficient to enable a person to proceed with smoothness and dispatch into the desired operation and fulfill it.

Aristotle added to this process the concepts of "euboulia" ("good deliberation") which required adequate self-research and evaluation; and "eusunesis" ("perspicacity") which described the necessary penetration and perspicacity of the self and its situation in order that the process of "phronesis" be adequately determined since "its end is what ought to be done or not to be done."[9]

REASONABLE OPERATION

In this light it is interesting to note that the word "counseling" itself, is apparently drawn from this Graeco-Christian tradition. Aquinas, following Aristotle, defines the virtue of counsel as the first stage in the prudential or phronetic process—the "euboulia" of self-research and inquiry into present and past personal factors. Counseling in this sense could be defined, as we have seen, as that skill by which the counselor enables the other person to take more reasonable and profound counsel about himself and others, and so to arrive at greater "euboulia." In this "taking counsel with himself" he is also helped to make better use of the information that personal guidance and education have given him.

If we understand "virtue" here as meaning a developed capacity for reasonable operational consistency, then counseling therapy, in the modern sense, could be directly related to phronesis and the development of the virtues of "counsel" and "prudence," as the sources of greater operational integration.

Rogers would seem to be implying this when he says, commenting on his observation of the therapeutic process:

I have little sympathy with the rather prevalent concept that man is basically irrational, and that his impulses, if not controlled, will lead to destruction of others and self. Man's behavior is exquisitely rational, moving with subtle and ordered complexity toward the goals his organism is endeavoring to achieve. The tragedy for most of us is that our defenses keep us from being aware of this rationality, so that consciously we are moving in one direction while organismically we are moving in another.[10]

This would not mean that man is incapable of great viciousness and disorder—the daily news report alone would show the contrary. It would, however, support Aristotle's contention that a person can seek and project anything, even something cruel, vicious or self-defeating, as an apparent good because he makes it appear as satisfying one or the other of his immediate short-term needs even when it is actually contrary to the over-all good of his whole person. Conflicts arise, apparently, because an individual's craving for particular personal, emotional, or sensual satisfactions are leading him away from the reasonable goals which he basically seeks. A man is, therefore, capable of a most complex self-deception. He can allow himself to be misled by particular urges to objects and goals which he knows will not really satisfy him or finally be good for him.

The focus of counseling therapy then, would be to enable the person to get a more reasonable view of himself and others. Through this increase in inner self-knowledge, he is able to take advantage of his knowledge of what is good to do and actually to carry it out with more coordinated consistency. In this process he grows in maturity. As he restrains and modulates his aggressive urges, he is developing *self-containment;* as he spurs himself on away from his fearful withdrawing urges, he develops *courage*. As he comes to have a more *balanced regard* and love for others, he is more able to impose limits on his own exaggerated self-impulses.

This illustrates Augustine's comment that, "Prudence is love choosing wisely between the things that help and those that hinder" the self. This can be done by oneself. Aristotle, Augustine and others in the past have indicated this. What is added in the counseling therapeutic process, is a person with skill in a special kind of sensitive and regarding understanding.

UNREALIZABLE IDEAL

But while what people experience in counseling therapy is in some ways similar to these earlier Greco-Christian concepts of Aristotle, Augustine, Aquinas and others, yet there is a difficulty in the way in which these concepts often appear only in ideal, and therefore, unrealistic forms. This can result in defeating a person rather than in helping him to realistic psychological maturity.

One of the difficulties, for example, with Aristotelian ethics is that it is an ideal ethic. Its ideal presumes an absolutely rational man at every moment. But in the human condition, one must face failure, limits and sinfulness. One can feel terribly let down, when he fails to achieve the ideal unless he had acquired a realistic sense of his own human limitations. In this way an ideal may become a tyranny of what one "ought" to do, a nagging super-ego, which impedes rather than aids adequate achievement.

Here we might argue that the religious view of man as a "sinner" is more clinically and existentially the condition of man than the abstract view of some ideal "reasonableness." This can, at best, be only an abstract norm—at worst it can be a rejection of man's real state.

In some things, it is easy to see the difference between the human condition and the norm, or ideal. It is obvious in bowling, for example, that the ideal is a strike each time and a three hundred score; in baseball one should bat one thousand—a hit each time. These are the ideal goals for each effort. But, in fact, we know the human condition produces much lower than this. One is a significant success with two hundred in bowling and three hundred in baseball. We need to recognize similar limits in human performance. Without this we can often be defeated by a psycho-logical guilt structure built up by the false ideals projected upon us by forces outside ourselves. Such a structure of guilt is often not really moral guilt and it may not be clearly conscious. We may not recognize its source but just carry it around with us as a kind of depressive self-criticizing voice.

Such an inability to attain an ideal can lead to a failure and frustration stage. The person may then give up. This can be dem-onstrated readily in animals who, after being subjected to intense frustration, run aimlessly about or withdraw in total defeat. Con-sequently, such a person must lower his self-ideal in order to arrive at some measure of realistic self-achievement. Here, genuine self-knowledge leads him to appreciate himself for what he is and to stop condemning himself for failing to achieve an impossible self-ideal.

Sometimes, however, personal reevaluation may bring a person to a greater sense of his own potentialities. Here, then, he begins to aim at higher and more demanding achievements and goals, as his confidence and reasonable self-regard increase. In this, his goals move away from "pusillanimity" or "inferiority complex," to a more courageous self-commitment.

POSITIVE SELF-REGARD

In this process as we see it in counseling therapy, a reorganization of the self is brought about by the establishment of a more self-respecting concept of what the person is and what he can do. He learns to judge in relation to his personal limitations and capacities and to feel satisfaction in achieving as much as he can and in trying to do better. He experiences a positive recognition of his self in relation to others and a deeper sense of self-regard.

This path from negation to self-regard can be said to begin with the sentence, "I am disgusted with myself." It then moves toward an attitude of ambivalence in which the person says: "I am still disgusted with myself in some ways, but in other things I feel better about myself." In some significant areas, the process reaches the stage when the person can say: "I am pleased with myself."

In this final stage a person's growing self-understanding and evaluation fuses into the planning of new and better solutions and the making of more significant choices according to these new life plans. These choices may be small and hesitant at first because the person is insecure and has to grow in confidence and hope. Gradually, the solutions that are planned are acted upon. These actions, because they have been carefully thought out and organized, usually prove more adequate and successful than previous life plans. If they still fail somewhat, the causes of failure can be examined. Here especially takes place the evaluation in action necessary to the tactics or strategies for adequate living—the "epitactiche," as Aristotle called it.[11] As a person's plans begin to succeed, he gains confidence in his tactical self-judgments and so often takes more rapid strides in acquiring new ways of acting.

REASONABLE PURSUIT OF EXCELLENCE

One basic aspect that emerges is the gradual self-affirmation that is concomitant with growing and respectful self-regard. We have called this the courage to invest in and pursue one's own excellence. Tillich has called it "the courage to be." Explaining this he says:

Life has many aspects, it is ambiguous. Nietzsche has described its ambiguity most typically in the last fragment of the collection of fragments which is called the *Will to Power*. Courage is the power of life to affirm itself in spite of this ambiguity, while the negation of life because of its negativity is an expression of cowardice. . . . Virtue for Nietzsche as for Spinoza, is self-affirmation.[12]

Aquinas following Aristotle, saw this ambiguity as tied up with contingency and as implying both rationality and freedom. One has to posit or affirm oneself in a judgment and make a commitment in a choice of a particular goal since, "particular objects of activity are contingent and consequently the reason may judge in either way about them and is not determined to one side or the other."[13]

We have seen, however, that unbounded self-affirmation becomes finally alienating and self-defeating. One must therefore balance and channel such will to power-affirmation by what Alfred Adler has called "will to community." It is in the gift of self to others, after the self is in some measure possessed, that such self-affirmation is most adequately fulfilled—if we can judge by the path that counseling therapy seems finally to take.

GOAL-DIRECTED COURAGE

What we have seen, too, is that the counseling therapeutic process is goal-directed. People not only may change goals as they see themselves and their situation more clearly; they also may devise better means to surmount barriers to those existing goals they still desire. In any barrier or conflict situation there is a recoil-urge to avoid and escape the conflict. This reaction may be readily seen in animals. Unless conditioned otherwise, at the continued encounter with pain or serious discomfort, an animal will simply pull away, and stop trying. A similar recoil urge in man must be controlled by mature courage. Maturity at times demands a special kind of magnanimity, when the goal or tasks involved are unusual and particularly demanding.

TRUST SELF-AGENCY

Essential to such courage is confidence in the self. This is so because, if the self is to be the instrument for these significant achievements, it is necessary for a person to trust himself. Just as the workman must have confidence in his tools and the musician in his instrument, so a mature man seems to grow in confidence in the implementation of himself. At the same time, he grows in his trust in others to aid him. The initial act of audacity—in trusting somebody else—can be difficult. To trust myself to another is threatening and can arouse instincts of defense and escape. In giving myself to another I risk primitively a kind of removal from the herd. Thus I risk the rejection of others. I must initially give up my state of introverted comfort and security as I move out into what may be a cold and difficult relationship. There is the possibility that the person may turn on me and attack me in some way. Recall the situation of the man in our psychological experiment, who, not protecting himself, gets slapped in the face. In this sense, having been slapped once, it would be psychologically quite difficult to turn the other cheek and run the risk of being slapped again. This is the risk we take when we proffer love. We have no assurance that the other person will not turn on us. If I see a situation as psychologically threatening to me and yet offer a defenseless acceptance of another person, I make a difficult act of self-gift and engagement.

We are speaking here, of course, not of issues of basic injustice where reasonable defense and attack may be necessary and even obligatory. We are rather trying to catch the idea of a primitive defense drive that—animal-like—can impede and even thwart a genuine acceptance of and commitment to another person where he, at first, appears resistant or hostile to me.

These kinds of anxiety that make it so hard to give ourselves are most often exaggerations. Situations seldom present the extreme dangers we are apt to project on them. But in a certain sense we seem required to risk ourselves, somewhat as a shepherd must if he remains to face a wolf. Also, people can sometimes be astonishingly gentle and reciprocating. We see this in the way the world took Pope John to its heart, in responding to this loving gift of the self. People everywhere were touched by his gentle openness and gently loved him in return.

COMPENSATORY SATISFACTIONS

But there is yet an opposite kind of situation that, by its allure of appearing both easy and rewarding, can lead us away from our real commitment and gift of ourselves. In addition to goals with anxieties and barriers, there is another kind of goal which, being *easy to achieve,* often acts as a compensation mechanism deceptively leading us away from barriers we must overcome. This non-barrier goal is disorientating not for what it gives but for what we can falsely assure and promise ourselves it will give. Compensatory needs come forward so that we crowd into something easy, an allure and meaning beyond its necessarily limited content and reward. Since a vast number of tasks which daily face us are comparatively easy to do, there is almost no limit to the extent to which we can make these situations or actions appear significant and fulfilling. We give them this significance, however, only because we are really using them as escapes from more difficult and often frustrating tasks to which we are already committed. It is around these kinds of excessive escape urges that we must temper and modulate ourselves through self-knowledge and limits if we are to make a true gift of ourselves to what really matters. Otherwise we remain bound-up in an unending chain of escapism that can lead us nowhere. To arrive at these self-limits is to acquire the capacity of self-containment in a particular situation.

SELF-CONTAINMENT

This tempering process is in fact a containment and the cylindering of the self. We mean this somewhat in the way that a cylinder contains the explosive force of a combustion or steam engine, and so channels and directs this force constructively. In much the same way, the explosive force of the soma, instincts and the emotions need such containment and directionality if they are to be effective in aiding the person to arrive at the goals he really seeks. Otherwise these energies tend to disperse themselves and weaken their constructive force through inadequate compensatory fulfillments. These then either lead away from the more courageous goals of personal respect and excellence or at best they simply afford a respite from these more intense and demanding projects and efforts. As such they may be valid diversions or recreations but often little more. The containment of the self-forces then, somewhat in the analogy of a cylinder, is basically necessary if courage in the pursuit of one's own excellence is to be finally effective.

TEMPERING OF SELF

Few words in the English language cause as much difficulty in its variety of meanings as the different forms of the verb, "to temper." Used as a participle "tempering" retains something of the original meaning of refining and strengthening. This is obvious when we speak of "tempered steel" for example. The noun "temper," however, means anger. One can guess that it acquired this meaning from the original idea that one should temper anger and so moderate one's irritations. This is still contained in the phrase "to lose one's temper."

We have used the phrase, "the tempering of the self" to catch something of the refining and strengthening quality that seems necessary for maturity. A person in pursuit of his own excellence seems often to bounce between difficult barriers that impede certain desired goals, and easy goals and achievements from which he seeks far more than they can give. He must, therefore, temper and restrain himself in these compensatory drives toward what the popular and somewhat paradoxical phrase would call "too much of a good thing."

However, temperance, while still vaguely suggesting the general meaning of tempering the self, is usually immediately understood by most people in the context of alcoholic beverages. Interestingly, one recent research on alcoholism points out its relationship to the person's self-concept and lack of a sense of value:

The test results, however, were possibly more valuable as aids in understanding certain dynamics of the alcoholic personality. The collective results of all the testings would seem to suggest the following:

(1) The alcoholic has a poor self-concept when he is sober. (2) Two factors, among others, prompt him to drink; namely, (a) to escape from his own feelings of loneliness, inadequacy and lack of personal and social worth, and (b) to help him overcome certain psychological inhibitory forces within his personality structure so that he can affect and project a more positive self-image to others. (3) Even when he is drinking, however, the alcoholic does not feel more positive about himself. On the contrary, when he drinks he tends to confirm and aggravate within himself his already low evaluation of himself.

If the conclusions suggested above are correct, it would seem that therapy for the alcoholic should include efforts to assist the patient to an understanding of his personal worth and value with emphasis on who he is rather than on what he has done, or not done, in the past. Of necessity the testing procedures obscured the unique personality structure and self concept of the individual alcoholic. However, the test results, particularly those obtained from the analyses of variance, suggest uniqueness existed between test performances of individual subjects. It would seem, therefore, that any therapeutic program for treatment of an alcoholic should seek to help the patient not only toward a feeling of personal worth but also toward the acceptance and understanding of his worth and value as an unique human person.[14]

The courage to be and to become means then, not only to plunge into the difficult and threatening when one might tend to hold back or escape but it also demands, on the other side, a corresponding tempering of these escape compensatory urges. Otherwise one may lose oneself in an inadequate and self-defeating pursuit of persons and things both too easy to achieve, and disappointing and frustrating in their value once they are achieved. One must temper one's urges to overvalue and overpursue easy goals which tend both to deceive and defeat one and so lead one away from mature progress and genuine achievement.

INTERRELATED PROCESS

Courage to really be oneself and the tempering of these deceptive and self-defeating urges are not separate but rather interrelated processes that mutually support and channel the self into constructive fulfillment. While the use of temperance in the context of alcoholic drinking is only one limited example of what we mean by this process of the tempering of self-urges, it yet offers us a convenient illustration of aspects of the self that can and must be applied more generally in the process of maturing.

Like alcohol, sexuality seems also a common instance in which basic personality needs may show themselves in conflict. A person's desire for some control and restraint, as often seen, for example, in marriage counseling, may be in deep conflict with impulses to have "affairs." If so, one often observes a growing containment of these urges as the therapy process continues.

Sexual conflicts like alcoholism, are basic problems in our culture for which no clear solutions have as yet been determined. The novelist, J. B. Priestley, has pointed out the tendency in our society toward exaggerated sexuality which he calls eroticism, and he has noted the self-defeating system this involves:

Now for various reasons, some of them obviously commercial, eroticism flourishes in our society on a scale never known before, not even before the decadence of Imperial Rome. One reason for this is that eroticism is a shortcut to masculine interest and curiosity. It is a safe and easy card to play. Eroticism, unlike sex and love (and these two are also to be distinguished) apparently offers something for nothing. It is sexual pleasure without sexual responsibility. It is having your cake and eating it. Unlike sex it is not completely natural and it is at the furtherest possible remove from love which is extremely personal. Eroticism is impersonal which explains why women may lend themselves to it but never believe in it and it is artificial, man-made, belonging to a technically advanced but very confused civilization. Eroticism we might say is the twanging of a single nerve concentrating on a certain kind of excitement and pleasure to the exclusion of everything else. It is solitary and self-regarding, other persons involved in it being treated as instruments, things. Nothing worth calling a relationship can be created by it. One sex cannot do the other sex any good in eroticism. The opposite sex is not really there, so to speak, in its true complementary character . . . it must be clearly understood that on this level we are discussing there is no relationship between the sexes as sexes, not this man and that woman but man and woman; when we come to persons we arrive at love.

Eroticism, closing in on itself, wanting a sensation and not another person bars out love.[15]

Such a description of eroticism would see it as part of a compensation mechanism that leads away from rather than to, a genuine love relationship. This is another of a wide variety of ways by which a person can defeat himself by giving special significance to actions, goals or relationships when they are really forms of compensation for personal emptiness or insecurity. It is the old adage in different dress—the grass on the other side of the fence can always be made to seem greener if we cannot get to it or if we cannot accept the simple reality of life limitations.

When this is the case, the self-knowledge people gain in the counseling therapy process acts to restrain such compensatory urges and so keep them pointed to the difficult and hard goals that make for growth in psychological maturity.

Steiner points out a further complication in this regard, in the untempered code of total sexual statement in novels, plays and literature. These may fail in the delicate respect and privacy due the realm of deep and intimate feelings. At the same time they may let loose in unrestraint the hidden sadisms of basic impulse. Speaking of this lack of fineness and respect in recent writing, he says,

And there is none for the sanctity of autonomous life in the characters of the novel, for that tenacious integrity of existence which makes a Stendhal, a Tolstoy, a Henry James tread warily around their own creations. The novels being produced under the new code of total statement shout at their personages: strip, fornicate, perform this or that act of sexual perversion. So did the S. S. guards in rows of living men and women. The total attitudes are not, I think, entirely distinct. There may be deeper affinities than we as yet understand between the "total freedom" of the uncensored erotic imagination and the total freedom of the sadist. That these two freedoms have emerged in close historical proximity may not be coincidence. Both are exercised at the expense of someone else's humanity, of someone else's most precious right—the right to a private life of feeling.[16]

MATURITY OF LIMITS

Another consideration that aids in genuine love of another and that one often sees emerging in counseling therapy, is the sense of the limits of the self. The definition that justice is the giving to each one that which is *really his own,* has psychological significance here. This idea of justice is obviously quite different from the Kantian categorical imperative that justice usually suggests today. But unless one can truly recognize and accept another as a person in his own right, one cannot genuinely give oneself in love to him. Alfred Adler, as we have said, caught the essential issue when he proposed that there are within us two wills that are in conflict with one another. The first, the will to power over another, can be described as self-centered satisfaction in controlling another. The opposite of this is the will to community—the urge to give oneself to another and to the need of others. Control of my will to power leads to community since it involves a sense of the limits of myself and the recognition of the other. In this light, we can see how this concept of justice is essential to love. I cannot give myself to another unless I first have respect for the limits of our respective two selves.

We actually have to restrain our urge to control and manipulate, in order to move out of ourselves into a communion with another person. In order to really love him, I must give him his meaning as a person. Often one of the chief values in acquiring counseling skills is that they enable us to control our own willfulness toward others, to repress our urges toward assertion of power over them where we have no purpose intruding. Such intervention may weaken a person's own urge to the self-affirmation of maturity by making him more dependent. But by recognizing my own limits as a counselor or therapist, I am giving the other person his place. Only then can I make him the object of a genuine love.

In gaining a respectful regard of others and limiting ourselves in their regard, we control compensatory urges by moderating exaggerated self-centeredness and aggression. This kind of selfishness, because it is not authentic self-love and genuine self-regard but a narcissistic self-inversion, can not only encroach on and impede others but also defeat ourselves in their regard.

SHARED REGARD

We can see why moderating this tendency to exaggerated self-regard is also basic to a just regard of others. In this one seeks to arrive at the "reasonable pursuit of one's own excellence." Such a definition well delineates a core therapeutic goal and basic value scheme. While immediately applicable to counseling and psychotherapy, this broad goal could also be applied to education and society itself. With such a basic goal, the rights of society and personal values could be preserved. But this would not distort or frustrate each person's need of integrity, responsibility and basic independence.

Such a goal of growing self-regard seems essential not only to one's own adequate self-love but as well to the right kind of regard or love for others. In counseling and psychotherapy both client and counselor are struggling to achieve this kind of mutually respectful and reasonably fulfilling love. Through having acquired a right sense of self-love, each will have an equally just and loving regard of the other's right to pursue his own excellence with help perhaps, but in a way that is genuinely independent.

Counseling therapy, then, seems to lead through a process of phronesis, to both self-affirmation and self-containment. This results in the cylindering of the self and its forces and energies, in the direction of a respectful and constructive pursuit of one's own excellence and that of the other. This discussion is, of course, intended only to give the broad outlines of how this phronetic process toward maturity occurs. In subsequent chapters, we will attempt to demonstrate this in greater detail as well as the skill which facilitates this process.

MENTAL HEALTH

One further concept can, however, be briefly considered. It is customary now, to consider a discussion of psychological maturity under the general category of mental health and mental illness. While this concept has been undoubtedly beneficial, yet the term "mental health" is still, in certain ways, an analogy. Carstairs has pointed out that:

One seldom encounters articles, and still more rarely monographs, addressed to the definition of physical health, but those concerned with mental health are numerous indeed . . .

Today, it is generally accepted that the etiology of disease is multi-factorial and that not only trauma and infection, but also factors in the patient's physique and personality and in his environment, have to be taken into account. Medicine is still predominantly concerned with the study of disease; if fitness is discussed (as John Ryle, the first Professor of Social Medicine, pointed out) one has to ask: "Fitness for what?" A Welsh coal miner and an Olympic sprinter may each be well adapted to their tasks, and yet unless they were first made sick by a series of immunizing shots both might prove a liability on a tropical expedition.

Physical medicine, then, has evaded the trap of trying to define "positive health" by thinking in terms of specific challenges to the human organism and the degree of success with which they are met. There is no such uniformity on the side of mental health. Here it seems at times as if every writer on the subject has put forward his own personal definition . . .[17]

To avoid this confusion, Menninger, Pruyser and Mayman use the term: "The Vital Balance." They include, in a chapter called "The Intangibles," love, faith, and hope, considering that these are, "crucial determinants of effective healing; indeed that they are sublime expressions of the life instinct."[18]

Szasz[19] and others[20] have questioned the value of the concept of "mental health" and even suggested that its effect may be more pernicious than helpful. Unquestionably, like all other "mental" terms, it suggests a dichotomy—basically Cartesian—which goes against our more recent concepts of the unity of the human person.

Pruyser answers the question: "Is mental health possible?" by saying that

. . . mental health should be seen not as a state of rest nor as homeostatic return to a previous condition, but as a realization of values which can only be achieved through becoming as opposed to "being." Earlier we spoke of "heterostasis" and indicated how strained the traditional language of science becomes when it tries to deal with goals, strivings, purposes, expectations and the realization of potentialities. Yet we cannot evade the issue that, psychologically speaking, living is worth its cost only when it entails progressive order; increased awareness of the complexities of reality, deepened wisdom and enlarged experience. And these, we submit, may well be the produce of the suffering and temporary defeat represented by a phase of illness.[21]

We cannot however, entirely disregard the final possibility that some aspects of mental illness may be and probably are, a true disease, in the biological sense. Bailey points out:

It is relatively easy to persuade oneself that neurotic patients do not suffer from a disease but it is not so easy with schizophrenic patients. The greatest of the psychogeneticists (Janet, Freud, Jung) did not believe that the symptoms of schizophrenic patients could be explained adequately by psychological factors; biological factors were of primary importance. Whitehorn says of the elaborate psychological studies of such patients that the results speak neither for nor against psychogenesis. Under these circumstances it behooves us to search earnestly for possible biological causative factors.[22]

Therefore, we do not yet know all the issues involved in mental health. But all seem increasingly to agree that people are aided most, whatever the treatment, by some kind of understanding love. Whether it occurs in psychotherapy or counseling or any kind of medical or psychiatric encounter, or more fundamentally, in any real friendship, some gift of self seems basic.

To focus too closely on sickness, however, is to suggest and encourage our urge to cure others. But often the urge to change a person under the guise of curing him, succeeds only in pushing his negative will farther toward resisting us and defensively opposing us and not changing. In addition then to the concept of mental illness, we need also to think of simply "bearing of one another's burdens." To love first and to be willing to spend time in genuine understanding, is itself a fundamental kind of sharing the burdens of the human condition as well as one of the most effective types of personal aid we have yet discovered.

NOTES

[1] Aristotle, *The Ethics of Aristotle,* trans. J. A. K. Thomson, Maryland: The Penguin Classics, Penguin Books, Inc., 1953, p. 266.

[2] *Ibid.,* p. 276.

[3] Melilla Sperling, "Fetishism in Children," *The Psychoanalytic Quarterly,* 32 (3), 1963, pp. 374–392.

[4] Ralph S. Lillie, *General Biology and Philosophy of Organism,* Chicago: University of Chicago Press, 1945, p. 85.

[5] Charles A. Curran, "Towards a Theology of Human Belonging," *Journal of Religion and Health,* 4, (3), April 1965, pp. 227–242.

[6] Montaigne, *op. cit.,* p. 24.

[7] *Introduction to Aristotle,* ed. Richard McKeon, New York: Random House, Modern Library, 1947.

[8] *Aristoteles: Nikomachische Ethik,* trans. Franz Dirlmeier, Frankfurt am Main und Hamburg: Fischer Bucherei KG, 1957.

[9] Aristotle, *op. cit.,* p. 436.

[10] Carl R. Rogers, a note on "The Nature of Man," *Journal of Counseling Psychology,* 4, (3), 1957, p. 202.

[11] Jean Voilquin, *Aristote: Ethique de Nicomaque,* Paris: Librairie Garnier Freres, 1950, p. 276.

[12] Paul Tillich, *The Courage to Be,* New Haven: Yale University Press, 1952, pp. 27–28.

[13] Thomas Aquinas, *Summa Theologica,* trans. Fathers of the English Dominican Province, New York: Benziger Brothers, Inc., 1947, I, Q. 83., A. 1., p. 418.

[14] James A. Vanderpool, "Self Concept Differences in the Alcoholic Under Varying Conditions of Drinking and Sobriety." (Unpublished Doctoral Dissertation, Dept. of Psychology, Loyola University, 1967, p. 110.)

[15] J. B. Priestley, "Eroticism, Sex and Love," *Saturday Evening Post,* April 29, 1963. Copyright 1963 by J. B. Priestly. Reprinted by permission of Harold Matson Co., Inc.

[16] Steiner, *op. cit.*, p. 76.

[17] G. M. Carstairs: Review of "Normality: Theoretical and Clinical Concepts of Mental Health" by Daniel Offer and Melvin Sabskin, *Science,* September 23, 1966, 153, p. 1513. Copyright 1966 by the American Association for the Advancement of Science.

[18] Karl Menninger, et. al., *The Vital Balance,* New York: The Viking Press, 1963, pp. 357–400.

[19] Thomas Szasz, *The Myth of Mental Illness,* New York: Hoeber-Harper, 1960.

[20] Ernest Becker, et. al., *The Revolution in Psychiatry,* New York: The Free Press, A Division of the Macmillan Co., 1964, pp. 206–209.

William Glasser, *Reality Therapy,* New York: Harper and Row, 1965.

——, *Mental Health or Mental Illness,* New York: Harper and Row, 1961.

For an alternate view, see: *Biological Treatment of Mental Illness,* ed. Max Rinkel, New York: Farrar, Straus and Giroux, 1966.

[21] Paul Pruyser, "Is Mental Health Possible?" *Bull. Menninger Clin.* 22, 1958, pp. 58–66. Also in *The Vital Balance,* p. 414.

[22] Percival Bailey. M.D. "Introduction" to *Biological Treatment of Mental Illness,* ed. Max Rinkel, M.D., New York: Farrar, Straus and Giroux, 1966, p. vi.

PART TWO

Art and Skill

6

The Art of Understanding

BECAUSE OF the difficulty of gaining self-knowledge, it is evident that this process is often made more effective by the help of another person. A moment's probing of our own memories may reveal that those times when we gained self-knowledge were often occasions when we felt deeply understood as we tried to express ourselves to someone. Such moments usually occur because we trust someone and the other person has penetrated beneath the surface and has really reached us. These moments of deep awareness can determine our later life. In retrospect, the details of the occasion—the time, the place, what we were doing, the very words of the conversation—may come back to us with startling clarity.

There is too, often, a subtle, existential aspect to such happenings. Suppose the other person had not cared enough to have made the incident possible. One may say that someone else would have, and that subsequent events would have turned out the same. But it is even more likely that not having been repeatedly understood in this way, by people who genuinely cared for us, our lives might have been quite different.

There is a significant difference between the type of human encounter in which one clearly listens with concentration to what the other person has to say, and that in which one expects to give some answer—whether of agreement or disagreement, of guidance, of judgment, or whatever. So often in the latter kind of relationship, it is hard for us really to hear what the person is saying because our mind is divided. We are half hearing him and half working out what we are going to answer as soon as he stops. In this relationship it seems, people say, "I want you to talk to me." But what they often really say is, "I want to talk to you." There is quite a difference. When a person says, "I want to talk to you," this suggests the relationship we now call counseling. If someone says, on the other hand, "I want you to talk to me; I want you to explain something to me," and he really means it, then he is suggesting a relationship of education, guidance or information.

It is becoming increasingly clear that to be understood by another can be an end in itself and does not have to lead to anything further. That is, there is a growth in understanding myself, once I have been truly understood by someone else. The most striking memories that come from early childhood, are not necessarily of educational relationships with people. These may not be nearly so sharp as the memories of someone who was willing to listen. These are often the encounters that most deeply affect one's life, even though this same person may have been in a number of other roles such as pastor, teacher or tutor. As we said, one often recalls most vividly those particular moments in time when this person was really trying to understand, when both his words and manner conveyed that somehow something deep had gotten through. We are referring to this kind of experience when we say that to be deeply understood by someone is an end in itself. Such an experience carries with it subtle after-effects that can often significantly affect a person's entire life.

TEACHABLE SKILL AND ENGAGEMENT

It is obvious, therefore, that we must do more than trust to chance or impulse or to some special endowed unique quality for such an "understanding" experience to occur. We must think rather in terms of "skill" that can both be studied and taught. One may well ask what is the nature of the skill that makes this kind of self-understanding and growth possible and whether it really is teachable. Certainly it is teachable, but one learns it by reflecting on himself and how he relates to others as well as by studying examples of such skill. For, we are concerned with achieving in ourselves and others that special kind of understanding that we have said is a combination of both "logos" and "gnosis."

Two aspects must here be considered. There is, first, a precise and definite understanding skill that is linguistic and cognitive. That is, it hinges on a detailed and exact grasp of the feelings and meanings behind not only a person's words but his tone, his body movements, his face, his hands—even the meaning of his silences. This skill—like any other "savoir faire"—can be taught and learned by practice, especially under skilled supervision.

But behind this skill there is an intangible and delicate quality that constitutes a deeply human engagement with openness to another person. Without this "heart-felt" element, skill can be helpful no doubt, but at a more superficial level. It never really elicits the genuine trust and commitment of the other person. Its results at best remain immediate and on the surface—they never arrive at the profundity of a real relationship. This kind of skill remains coldly "professional," it never becomes really personal.

By deep personal openness and engagement, we do not mean sentimentality or emotionalism. These can be both artificial and manipulatory unless they are authentic and spontaneous responses —uncalculated expressions of the counselor or therapist's honest transparency. Such moments are rare.

UNDERSTANDING HEART

We mean rather a kind of personal quality which, while often readily apparent in an experience, is extremely difficult to put into words. Somewhat like squeezing water, the effort to get hold of it, loses it. We will try, however, in various ways to describe and interrelate both this quality and the skill that seems to further relationships that are fruitful and helpful to others. Before discussing "skill" as such, however, we will first consider the less tangible but essential element of the "art" of understanding.

To understand another at the deepest level of his feelings and reactions is an immeasurably more profound, complex and delicate kind of understanding than simply to know the meaning of the words he uses. Yet this is what another person really means when he says after an interview, "You know, he really understood me." The counselor's striving to understand him intensifies the person's own efforts to understand himself and to share with the counselor what he slowly and sometimes tortuously is discovering about himself. As one person put it, "Because you are trying so hard to understand me, I'm urged all the more to want to explain myself clearly to you and to myself."

We may get a further clue here from the familiar Bible story of Solomon who prayed for and was given "an understanding heart." The "heart" suggests in a poetic way the emotions, the qualities of love, of inner peace and sincerity as well as the level of man's suffering, his pain with himself, his discomfort and discontent. Heart speaks to heart when this kind of communication takes place. This is the significance of the slang phrase: "He really digs me." It suggests not just understanding the meaning of words in the linguistic sense, but a "digging down" to a deeper level of communication, a level of all the common problems of human beings, the joy and sadness, the strengths and weaknesses we all share. Such understanding is rare. It "stands-under" the level of "problems," and helps a person arrive at their source.

The man who sees another man simply as an object, say, as "good" or "bad," as one might view a machine according to the promptness with which he does what one wants him to do, soon becomes impatient and irritated with the other's failures and weaknesses. But when another person speaks from his heart, then his voice is really the voice of the "I" in the relationship and he speaks of "my" sufferings, fears and insecurities as well as his own. When I have let him know that I understand at the level of myself, even if only with my eyes, with my quiet listening to him or a little phrase I have used, there is a chance he will leave feeling, if nothing else, that his burden has been shared, that he is no longer alienated and alone.

BRIEF ENCOUNTER

In this context of the value of even a momentary understanding between people, one might ask if we are not too concerned with the hour-long interview and the long series, with its expense, its elaborate skills and setting, and so overlook the moment when a person just needs someone who can give himself in a "heart-felt" relationship.

AUXILIARY REASONING POWER

We have seen, moreover, that the skill of the counselor or therapist is not aimed at achieving something dramatically new. It aims at helping the client to take counsel with himself and finally to acquire the integrated command over his soma, instincts and emotions that will enable him to perform the acts counseled. The counselor or therapist in this sense acts as a kind of auxiliary reasoning power, but not in any cold, objective, impersonal way. His skill involves a deeply empathetic and sympathetic attitude toward the person who tries to objectify and interrelate all the myriad confusions and disorders inside himself. Counseling therapy may be called a kind of rational mirroring relationship in which the client is helped to gain a new view of himself that he could not have achieved unaided. Its intent is to aid the person to *reflect* on himself and his actions—somewhat as a mirror reflects his external aspects.

This is one of the main aims of all forms of psychotherapy, even when additional measures such as medication, occupational therapy, custodial or supportive care are needed. Counseling therapy does not take the place of such measures nor does it supplant education, guidance or forms of persuasion, encouragement, confrontation or advice. Rather its purpose is to afford a person this special kind of understanding encounter.

INTENSE AND SUBTLE RELATIONSHIP

While it is easy to describe the counseling therapeutic process in these succinct terms, no description can catch the intense and difficult pursuit of self-knowledge and integration which the client or patient undergoes in seeking to acquire even the beginnings of integrated self-awareness and mature self-direction.

Nor can one catch in simple description the subtle and complex relationship that must exist between counselor and client, therapist and patient. Here the necessity of mutual involvement in the human condition is most strikingly demonstrated. The counselor or therapist cannot stand apart in an "objective," intellectualized Cartesian way. He must be a complete person, psychosomatically committed to a sensitive and intense personal communion in a true giving of self. The counselor is first to give himself. Then, more slowly but just as surely, the person coming for help gains the confidence in turn to make a genuine commitment of himself. The counselor-therapist relationship is one in which he tries to give himself and so to be at the disposal of the other. He seeks no personal return except the other's best fulfillment of himself.

We can see that this kind of intense commitment is a long way from a cool "scientific" analysis or from trying to "figure someone out" or "get his number." Indeed, there is reasoned objectivity here, but of no impersonal sort. On the contrary, this objectivity is suffused with a regard and respect for the unique meaning of the other person. It seems to involve a friendship totally for the other, which the Greeks held to be the very zenith of all friendship. Aquinas, borrowing this, makes it the model by which we can somehow approach the idea of Divine friendship. Such friendship involves both a profound sharing of the human condition and a new commitment of human beings to one another, often at the deepest level of their loneliness and weakness. It signifies one of our most ancient Judaeo-Graeco-Christian concepts of personal relationship, the concept of the "understanding heart" that was for Solomon himself the epitome of all his wisdom.

EXPERIENCED KNOWLEDGE

This "art of living," as Augustine called the right use of counsel and prudence, has, by reason of its being such an art, a quality of incommunicability about it. No one learns to play the piano or to drive an automobile simply by listening to lectures on these subjects. In this conception, the "doing" abilities are contrasted with the "knowing" abilities. The latter remain in themselves theoretical, speculative and removed. They become "doing" abilities only as they move through the arts, the skills, the capacity of the individual person to carry them out in the unique integration of himself and his own particular environment. It is evident why such integrating ability, as well as particular arts, must always have elements that are unique and therefore incommunicable. These cannot be acquired simply through the knowledge that comes from education, but only through that which comes from experience. In our terms, the art of living involves not only meaning but values.

BEING UNDERSTOOD

We use the English word "understanding" in a number of ways. But we have one peculiar use of it which we immediately recognize and yet would have difficulty defining in any other words. We know immediately what is meant when someone says, "I saw him and he was very understanding." It somehow conveys the idea that the person was trying to understand me and my values—not simply attempting to instruct me.

In a sense this is a strange use of the word "understanding." It does not mean that the person was particularly learned or knowledgeable. Used this way, the word "understanding" does not seem to apply to the area of knowledge at all. It seems to imply that the manner and attitude of one person enabled the other to feel secure that he was communicating himself and being accepted as he was. This kind of understanding acceptance also implies something positive, respectful and complimentary to both the one understanding and the one understood. We know that in the speaker's mind, the other person is now seen as someone sensitive, warm and to be trusted. All this is contained in the adjective "understanding."

A person may say something like, "You really can talk to him. You can get through to him. He comes down to your level; he really listens." In this context these expressions need no further explanation.

But suppose someone says: "Well, I am pretty disappointed. You told me to go over to see this person and I did. But he just didn't understand. I couldn't get through to him, he didn't seem to know what I was talking about. He just isn't the kind of person that I think anybody could talk to—or at least I couldn't talk to him." Here again, what does this strange lack of "understanding" mean? Why this feeling of being disappointed, blocked and frustrated? A human encounter got nowhere. There was no movement of one to the other. There was no communion and therefore no communication.

It is this special kind of communication between two or more persons that we are talking about. In this sense, counseling and psychotherapy are not something new, but simply a refinement of the way in which we all often try to listen to people. We endeavor to hear them in such a way as truly to understand them and to convey this understanding back to them in language that lets them feel and know that they have been accepted and respected in themselves. Such an understanding of others and ourselves involves a patience with the long process between simply knowing "what were good to do" and acquiring the self-knowledge and integration that enables a person, sometimes step by feeble step, to move steadily forward to the point where he can do what he has known all along he should have done.

In commenting on the experience of ten minutes as a client, one student observed:

You know, you were trying so hard to understand me, that it sort of forced me to concentrate my powers in trying to understand myself and in trying to explain myself more and more clearly to you.

He then added:

I don't know if I would even have tried this without you. But you were there so sincerely in your efforts to understand, that I was forced to use these ten minutes for a maximum understanding of myself. And as a result, I understand myself better.

As a person is moved to deeper understanding of himself, he seems to develop a greater and more reasonable respect and regard for himself. This follows from the fact that as more aspects of the self emerge, the person recognizes himself as a more worthwhile person than he had thought he was. According to our incarnation-redemption model, as he becomes more respectful and less fearful of aspects of his incarnate self, he grows more truly respectful of and loving toward himself. He begins more to love himself loving, rather than love himself hating, as Aquinas phrased it.

OPEN COMMITMENT

While we have seemed to stress the listening aspect, counseling-therapy consists in more than simply being a good listener, even though this is an important and necessary first step. There are many different ways in which we can listen to a person. One may immediately have the impulse to give advice without really questioning whether the advice is valid or likely to be accepted and acted upon. He may decide what he will say on the spur of the moment while the person is yet speaking. A person often begins such advice with what is, in fact, an impossibility: "If I were you . . ." In a phrase like this, it is obvious that we are not leaving ourselves—not really moving over to the other person with a real understanding concern. Consequently, what we say will likely be ineffective and even meaningless to the other person. It is too concentrated on ourselves.

Often too, we can offer advice not so much because we expect that it will be effective, but rather as a subtle form of self-defense. That is, if an issue is later raised about this person's conduct we can clear ourselves with, "Well, I talked to him before about that a number of times. I told him he had to stop it." Advice and even reprimand, as we will later see, are not without value. People can be helped to change this way. But usually more than this is needed. And being in such a position can so involve us in complicated attitudes in ourselves that we cannot give genuine understanding to the other person.

The basic urge to self-defense and the subtle unconscious ways it can affect our relations with others in any personal situation of stress, has implications for any position in which a person is teaching, advising or directing others. Selye cautions about the complexity of vengeful feelings which, under stress, can emerge and control our actions. These feelings can be, he says, "a savage distortion of the natural wish to teach others not to hurt us."[1] In other words, at a basic primitive personality level we apparently have an impulse to see others as "inimical" to us, our goals and personal security. Unless understood and controlled, these "inimical" feelings of self-defense, can, in a displaced form, impede a genuinely understanding relationship. When another appears as a primitive threat to a person's security, the person may really be protecting himself by manipulating and controlling the other through giving him advice and direction. He may be fundamentally afraid of him and so unwilling to open himself in a genuine attempt to understand.

If we ask what the Biblical expression about loving my "enemies," means psychologically, perhaps it could be thought to have reference to the need to control these displaced urges to self-defense in any encounter with others. In fact, it may be the confused awareness of this that often causes other people to remain silent, for fear of "bothering" us, and so appearing foolish or arousing hostility in us. If at a basic level any personal relationship with another is threatening, and so arouses self-defense, then any expression of personal difficulties would be "bothersome" and "a nuisance." Having so perceived them as "enemies," a person's immediate primitive urges may be to get rid of them—either by escaping from them or, blocked in this, by attacking them in disguised ways. These reactions would need to be made conscious, be understood and controlled, in order for real understanding to be conveyed to another.

A comment sometimes made by clergymen, for example, as a result of counseling training, is that, for the first time, parlor calls and telephone calls no longer are seen as negative—as nuisances, irritations and interruptions. Physicians too, receiving counseling training, have noted the same changes in attitude towards calls of patients or discussions about fees. This is a way of saying that these encounters are no longer seen as "inimical"—arousing urges of self-defense. They become occasions rather, for a constructive and positive communication.

We then love our "enemies" psychologically in such a way as to make them friends. This would be one way of applying Roger's concept of "unconditional positive regard." I move toward a person with all my own defenses down. I have, in other words, a conscious positive regard toward him in my respect for his unique meaning as a person. We are not, therefore, two enemies facing each other and perhaps even attacking each other in subtle psychological ways. We break through this state of mutual self-defense by a genuine love of our "enemy," by being open to him and so controlling our defense and attack urges.

A primitive urge that counteracts defensiveness is empathy. In a photograph used to illustrate empathy, a pole-vaulter is poised in mid-air on the point of pulling his leg over the bar. The picture also shows some of the spectators with one leg up in the air. These people are obviously unaware of their own reaction. But they are so identified with the athlete's struggle to get over the bar, they are unconsciously trying to help him. This empathetic reaction can be raised to a conscious, deliberate, human level. Then it becomes sympathy, in the original Greek sense, where we "feel with" the other person as we try to understand the verbal components of his communication.

FEAR OF COMMITMENT

Unconscious and therefore unanalyzed cultural values can also impede genuinely understanding relationships. We have already discussed the way our culture tends to depersonalize relationships —for example, by turning them into the form of "problems" or "puzzles" and so avoiding any deep human relationship. Such values put distance between us and others and lead us to relate to "it" objects, rather than to persons, in a remote, impersonal and neutral way. So conceived, the best, because most protective, human relationship would be the one furthest removed from commitment. But this can have the effect of arousing basic negative reactions in the other person in an "indignation" that—like the word's original meaning—is a defense of his own personal dignity. When somebody is cataloguing a person as if he were a crossword puzzle, it tends to arouse all his own primitive defensive resistance and hostility. He is then impelled to attack or escape.

The Gospel parables, such as those of the lost sheep and of the fisherman going out into the deep waters, seem to imply that a person must take the risk of entering a place of danger—the wilderness or the stormy sea—before he can open himself or be opened to the warmth and security of genuine love. And on the other hand, the story of the Prodigal Son gives us the mysterious theme that a man may have to know sin, degradation and even complete humiliation—"hit bottom" as the Alcoholics Anonymous might say—before he can make the return of love.

The New Testament parable of the talents (ancient money) is often interpreted in an intellectual manner as relating to the way we use or hide our "talents." To be talented is, in this sense, often meant to indicate a high I.Q. or scholastic achievement ability. On more careful scrutiny of the Scriptural parable, one sees that this is not the main point. The man with one talent, in his anxiety and fear of risk, buries that talent; he does not lose it, but he protects it with great care; he withdraws, in his anxiety to keep distance between himself and his "fearful" master, (at least as he sees him). Here we might, in a modern version, see the master as his projected father-figure. In his suppression of anxiety by encrustation and withdrawal, the man "buried" his one talent. The story rejects this man—the only one of the three who is rejected—for his fear of taking a risk, of making an investment and commitment.

We are afraid to love apparently because we fear to run the risk of losing some valuable part of ourselves. It is much safer to keep distance and avoid getting close to others so as not to risk the danger of jeopardizing ourselves. But this is a self-defeating paradox, like that of the person who is afraid to enter water until he learns to swim. This is expressed with the penetrating statement, "He that shall save his life shall lose it, and he that shall lose his life shall save it" (cf. Mt. 10:39). By giving in to my protective urges to avoid risk, I never can know open human communion. To account for this conflict, Adler, as we have observed previously, suggests two wills in man: the will to power, which concentrates on control and so on determining the actions of others and of ourselves: and the will to community, which demands a sacrificing of power in order to gain community, communion and communication.

In the training of people for the practice of counseling and psychotherapy, and in the research in learning reported later, there is repeated evidence of the threat inherent in the prospect of any kind of personal commitment or involvement. This is so apparently because, in attempting to give ourselves to someone, we take off a mask and relinquish many of our defenses. If we were simply primitive animals, we would be urged to protect ourselves from being attacked, injured or devoured by our natural enemies. Our first fear, then, is a result of our primitive anxiety about what the other person or the group will do to us, what we may lose in the relationship. To enter into any involvement with another, we have to be willing to take this chance.

ENGAGED WISDOM

A person can also "rationalize" basic fears by seeming to withdraw above and beyond the human condition and to look down upon it as a purely intellectualized being might be thought to look upon mere men. This distance is then masked as "objectivity" to cover and displace an anxiety and fear of involvement one cannot consciously handle. One popular idea of Solomon's wisdom is apparently due to this kind of rationalized intellectualism. He is seen as a great judge who stands calmly apart. But in his dream, Solomon did not ask for wisdom in the sense of knowledge greater than that of other men. The Hebrew text says he asked for "a listening heart."

A client, a psychology graduate student, struck by this idea, wrote the following after a counseling session:

To offer someone "an understanding heart"—or "a listening heart," as the Hebrew might also be rendered—is to give oneself over to mirroring this person in depth. One does not merely hold up to him the flat-surfaced mirror of an auxiliary reasoning power—one gives oneself wholly to his self-creative struggle in a kind of real intercourse. It is whole-person intercourse, of which sexual intercourse might be a limited type, in which two people engage themselves to bring forth new life.

Such engagements have as their *raison d'être* the human drive or "will to meaning," to use Frankl's expression. Their meaning is meaning itself, in the intellectual order. And in the personal order, their value is to be found at the very core of human values. For if "value" may be defined as "meaning plus involvement" or "meaning plus self-investment," in taking respectful counsel with himself a man commits himself to his own self-worth. And when he does this in and through the person of another, his commitment is existentially richer and fuller. He is not now just himself, alone with his intentions—however potent he may feel himself in these—but in this very moment he has actualized his intention in speech and so has really thrust himself into the other person. The counselor represents indeed a feminine principle, penetrated and impregnated—through hearing—with this very delicate thing, scarcely more than a breath, that hopefully now would take a hold on life. How interesting, in this light, the idea of the counselor's warm acceptance.

Thus, for the client, that moment of change—of passing from some particular potency to a certain act—is intensely "actual." In and through this other, the counselor, he is more closely at one with himself; and he is true to himself in a more extensive way than he could be alone.

In "an understanding heart" the more emphatic word is "heart." The person is in trouble, he cannot understand himself because he has locked himself out of his own heart. Even some "mis-understanding" on the counselor's part often will not impede seriously the communication. But a counselor's failure to commit himself, or even a momentary withdrawal of his commitment—frigidity or anxious defensiveness in the feminine principle—is always a very painful experience for the client. It can be terribly so, and terribly destructive—both of the counseling relationship and of those seeds of new life that the client is perhaps beginning to germinate within himself. The analogy to castration seems not out of place here.

Communication, then, while it is a matter of linguistics and the meaning of words, is also something more. Genuine communication is based on understanding in the deepest meaning of that word's usage. One might personalize it this way: At the moment when I feel the response of your listening-understanding heart, I know the risk I took in attempting to communicate myself to you, was not in vain. I have taken the chance of the human encounter with you; I have given my defenseless self to you and you have not betrayed me; you have penetrated the depth of my human weakness, have loved me in the deepest sense of the gift of self. In giving myself in this way, I have received from you something that was far beyond what I had before. I have been healed because, with your understanding and sharing you have given my life back to me as a fuller, more resplendent thing than what I took the risk of giving to you.

Love is not words; it is experience. We must offer to others the experience of lowering our defenses, taking the risk of loving them, even when we see them as inimical to us, for only when they have encountered love from us can they be given the chance to love us in return. Aristotle said that it is a greater thing to love than to be loved. This is the heart, too, of the Psalms and the Christian Gospel. It is also the core of counseling therapy and of any authentic relationship.

NOTES

[1] Hans Selye, M.D., *The Stress of Life,* New York: McGraw-Hill, 1956, p. 286.

7

The Skilled Response

THROUGHOUT this book, we have stressed the point that the counselor's cognitive and verbal precision greatly influence counseling effectiveness. This is somewhat different from those points of view which emphasize either the counselor's theoretical orientation or his warmth, acceptance, sympathy, permissiveness, yet minimize or even disregard the exact formulation of his responses.

We do not wish to downgrade these other factors. We see counseling therapy, however, as an existential relationship of *communication*. From moment to moment, the high and low points of this communication are determined, not simply by the client's feelings and reactions or the depth or shallowness of the relationship. The communication is greatly affected by the degree to which the counselor or therapist cognitively understands the client's verbal struggle to express how he feels. Effectiveness depends on the way the counselor or therapist can put this into language which, when heard by the client, furthers the client's ability to recognize his own affects (feelings).

PRODUCTIVITY OF LANGUAGE

In our previous consideration of the importance of basic theoretical issues or the quality of the relationship, we have not wished to minimize, then, the importance of accurate verbal communication. Language too is basic to the client's moment-to-moment striving to free himself from rigid emotional bind and narrow defeating self-concepts and so become more creative and open with himself and others.

Recent studies on language and cognition such as those of Lantz and Stefflre which stress the "productivity of language," suggest research areas on the significance and nature of the verbalizations which most effectively implement client self-understanding.[1]

Studies in association and creativity also offer research possibilities here. If the associations available to a person are "an important factor in creative ability,"[2] then we might theorize that client creativity is furthered by the way the counselor's responses free the client from narrow association bonds and so stimulate him to become more creative in his reactions and affects.

This stress on the importance of actual verbal formulations of client and counselor reinforce the importance of the careful study of verbatim interview reports. Fortunately this is made possible now by easily available electronic apparatus.

Guardini remarks that language is the very realm of consciousness in which every man lives, not a product, but a presupposition of human life. He stresses the basic verbal character of the world and relates it to the concept that, "language is not only the means by which we communicate conclusions, but mental life and activity are carried on in the process of speech."[3]

Studying a series of interview excerpts with these observations of Guardini in mind, one person wrote:

Through the more adequate cognitive language of the counselor, the existential truth of the client became objectified. *The word became incarnate* for the client. Realization dawned. The significance of verbal interplay in moving the client's insightfulness forward, had been focused in the verbal "trying on" of symbolizations by client and counselor.

To bring this deep self-realization about demands a special kind of skilled understanding and verbalization on the part of the counselor or therapist. We will therefore examine further some aspects of this special skill.

LANGUAGE OF AFFECT

The ancient phrase, "heart speaks to heart", and expressions like a "heartfelt talk" convey the idea that when one speaks "from the heart," one communicates at a profound self-level. Emotions, instincts and soma all combine in this kind of heartfelt communication. A person "opens up" his heart when he unrestrainedly speaks out his deepest feelings and pains. Such a language might be called the language of the heart or more technically, the *language of affect*. This is usually the language a person speaks at the beginning of the counseling therapeutic dialogue.

But by such language, one simply "feels" and says what he feels. He has little or no reflective awareness of the meaning of these "feelings"—they are just happening to him and he is describing what is happening. They are, in this sense, "happenings." They have not yet acquired real significance. So he is somewhat the victim of them when he cannot act on them in place of their acting on him. In this state he is "reacting" to these happenings in him—he is not able to assert himself over them.

LANGUAGE OF COGNITION

The counselor's help here is, among other things, to provide the person with a means of grasping the significance of these feelings or happenings within him. The counselor, we say, recognizes these "feelings" through the client's communication and responds to them. In this response, the counselor speaks the *language of cognition*—he recognizes what he heard in the language of affect—the "happenings"—and gives them significance by enabling the client now to begin to "re-cognize" himself—or cognize—what he has been feeling. He then is no longer merely passively affected and moved by these happenings. He can now begin actively to penetrate their meaning and value for him, see the hidden goals and purposes they represent and so begin to disentangle himself from those states of cross-purpose in which he found himself. He now begins to "see" more clearly the personal significance of these emotional, instinctive and somatic happenings instead of being victimized by them. In place of his earlier confusion and conflict, clarifications, evaluations and resolutions of this conflict are now possible. His real goals emerge as he discards as unnecessary and impeding, opposite values and goals carried about perhaps for many years in an "unrecognized" form but until now still unconsciously motivating and controlling him.

As this kind of personal meaning begins to appear, the person grows to recognize with increasing clarity, relationships between and within his various actions and motives. In place of a segmented and truncated self-view, configurations gradually appear. Out of these "gestalts" of himself and his situation, better self-evaluations occur as the counselor follows, recognizes and helps him integrate his emerging self-insights. Slowly a more coordinated picture of himself, his needs and his present values come forward. He develops a more authentic self in the sense that he can now reflect and choose those values of which he is, in a measure, the author, in place of being in a constant state of cross-purposes.

In such fashion, then, the counselor's language of cognition aids the person to greater cognition of himself. In place of reacting to happenings within and around him, he begins to be able to act on himself and his situation. By such reflective dialogue through another, the person comes to be more self-reflective himself, more self-recognizing and so gradually grows less in need of the counselor's aid. At some point he can feel himself sufficiently non-segmented, sufficiently integrated in soma, instincts and emotions to be able to recognize, on his own, both his conflicts and their causes and the real goals and purposes he now wishes for himself. He can then say he no longer needs the counselor's help. He can actively speak a language of cognition to himself as a result of his own self-reflection and conscious awareness of his personal value system. He has arrived, therefore, at a state of self-evaluation adequate at least for his present circumstances.

DISCRIMINATING AWARENESS

For some years now we have been attempting to evaluate the client's reaction after counseling by asking three questions. These questions are asked by the counselor immediately after the counseling interview has finished. These three questions are: first, a vague, indefinite question worded usually like this: "What were your reactions or feelings, or have you any comments about the interview just finished?" The purpose here is to get the client's comments with as little effort to direct the answer as possible. As the client answered, the counselor responded, as in counseling, until the points seemed adequately expressed. The second question was: "Would you comment on the counselor—his manner, responses, etc?" Again this train of thought and feeling was followed until its end. The third question was a miscellaneous one such as: "Would you care to comment on any other aspects of this particular interview?"

Our purpose here was to get information on the client's immediate reaction. Taking advantage of the intense dynamism between counselor and client at the end of an interview seemed a good way to do this. While, as we shall see, comments were often positive, clients sometimes expressed hostility to a counselor. They therefore felt free to do this. Their comments sometimes included a variety of negations, either about the interview just finished or ranging more generally.

When we examined the results of this kind of questioning of a variety of clients, characteristic statements like the following were repeated in a similar form many times:

I've never been listened to so well—no one before ever cared so much about what I was saying. I have confidence in speaking, even if what I say is stupid. I trusted the counselor to hold what I said and not to let it slip or become blurred. In such a situation I can react to myself and my own thoughts and feelings much as I might react to those of someone else. There is an objectivity about the counselor's responses that is freeing.

As this excerpt demonstrates, the clients seemed to focus their positive comments on the counselor's capacity for discriminating, listening and careful understanding. This does not mean that the warmth, the sense of commitment between counselor and client and similar aspects of the relationship were unimportant. They were, rather, apparently taken for granted. Had these been seriously lacking they would more likely have been the source of client comment. In their comments, clients often discussed how the counselor's *exact wording* in the precise formulation of a response was of special help to them.

ADEQUATE SELF SYMBOLIZATION

Using our earlier concept of meaning and values here, we might propose that the dialogue in counseling therapy is, then, first, a means through which a person can begin to understand and get some grasp of the significance of his actions. The response tries to reach and symbolize the basic feelings, goals and values that "stand-under" the particular incidents recited. The client signifies that the response fits by his reflective "Yes, that's it," and similar remarks much as a person might say to a tailor, "That fits." He has equated the words of the counselor—not just with what he said but with the way he felt. This, in fact, really caused him to speak as he did. His recognition of himself, therefore, was aided by the words he heard. They could then become symbols of his feeling state and lead to his grasp of the values they stood for.

Consequently, the precise choice of words on the part of the counselor or therapist plays an important part in this self-clarification. Such cognitive discourse produces a more adequate self-symbolization of all that is happening in one's "inner-view." Such symbolization then enables the person to begin to get a better "hold" on himself and "to pull himself together", as popular expressions describe it, and so arrive at a better integration and more adequate use of himself. He becomes, in this sense, more self-directive.

PENETRATING RESPONSES

There is, of course, no quick way of acquiring skill in this kind of counselor or therapist sensitivity. One could no more do this than one could learn in a few easy lessons how to play the piano. But for the purpose of further clarification, let us consider a familiar counseling situation.

A married man is talking about his difficulties with his mother-in-law:

Well, I don't know what to say, but the trouble is . . . let me explain it this way. We haven't any children and my mother-in-law lives with us.

We've been married five years now and we have this new house. And everything that we try to do together, she is always in on it. I mean, she just seems to be in everything.

For example, if my wife irons my shirts she has some comment. She doesn't do it right. Always there is something wrong. Or for example, when she prepares the meals—again she's right there to comment. I don't think there has been a single meal that's served that she hasn't made some negative remark.

And the same thing goes on when we have guests, young couples that we know. Now you'd think she would go back to her room and stay there—but no, she doesn't. She's right in the center of the front room and she's entertaining. I just . . . I don't know, but my wife's so discouraged and so depressed. I just can't stand it. But when I bring it up to her, this is the worst of all. When I bring it up to her she just won't hear about it. She says we agreed to have her mother.

We bought the house under those conditions, she helped us financially when we were first married. We agreed to this, she says, and now I've just got to put up with it. But I just can't put up with this, that's all. I've reached the end. I don't feel I belong in my own house.

There are a number of ways we can respond to a statement like this. The first possibility is that of agreeing or disagreeing. Here we might say something like, "Well look Tom, you know how mother and daughter are. Your wife is her daughter after all. It's hard for her mother to give her up—to see her as an adult married woman." Even though this is true, we can guess that if Tom were defensive before, he might be even more so after this. Or we might choose to give sympathy and at the same time encourage him to continue doing his duty as a husband. Such a response would probably be acceptable, but it would still stay on the surface. What deeper meaning can we penetrate here from the incidents and feelings described?

We can start by picking out the basic feeling-tone or hub, as it were, that is connecting these individual spokes or incidents apparently arranged together in the man's memory-stream. The central feeling-tone is evidently made up of discouragement, frustration and conflict. All three are interwoven. If we ask ourselves what is the cause of these feelings, it seems to be centered on his mother-in-law's taking over his wife's role in the home and leaving him with a feeling of non-belonging both to his wife and the home.

We seek then *to penetrate the core of this man's communication by catching and symbolizing in words the basic emotions and their cause.* The incidents he gave were intended to make us understand this. If we fail to understand at this deep level, he may feel forced to add more incidents in his painful effort to be understood. However many incidents he gives, they will all be efforts to communicate these basic feelings of frustration, discouragement and conflict. Even his wife has failed to understand his resistance to her mother's taking over her place. One response might be:

You're discouraged at the way your mother-in-law has taken over your home and even affected and discouraged your wife, as you see it—but she can't seem to see it. So it's just very frustrating. You're pulled two ways. You want to fulfill your agreement and yet you feel that it's impossible now.

BASIC FEELINGS AND CAUSES

Responding in this fashion to a basic feeling and its cause seems the best way to give a person the initial feeling of being truly understood. He will usually indicate this by saying something like, "Yes, that's it exactly. That's exactly the way I feel." His whole manner will often show relief and appreciation. There are other factors also necessary to a good counseling communication, but this point of understanding at a basic emotional level seems fundamental.

We remarked earlier that to be understood is an end in itself. This man did not ask to be told what to do. He just asked to be understood and for this understanding to be communicated in words that would have personal meaning. If we understand a person in this way from the moment he starts to communicate, we initiate a dynamism by which he begins to take counsel with himself through us. Its intent, as we have said, is to enable a person to grow more knowledgeable about himself and, as a result he can start to make better judgments about himself and gain a more integrated, better coordinated command of himself. The person also acquires greater courage to face difficulties rather than to seek to escape them as he understands his situation better.

This emerges apparently from the existential experience of being understood—not just in one or another statement but warmly and consistently through the half-hour or hour of the interview period. But this does not necessarily always have to take a long time. This counseling dynamism can sometimes be initiated even in moments of genuine understanding.

PERSONAL VALUES

Personal values enter here when the basic causes behind particular actions begin to emerge. Usually part of the person's conflict is the head-on collision of opposite values in which he has invested or made an unconscious commitment. This often has the person, "right in the middle—I can't go either way," as he will say. This conflict is resolved through gaining sufficient self-insight to discard one set of values without guilt and carry out the other. Sometimes as a result of acquiring vision and release from emotional constriction, a person may finally arrive at the complicated means of fulfilling both sets of values in turn.

We can now examine the merging value conflict as we continue our interview:

Well, I must explain that we promised my mother-in-law that she could live with us after we had our own home because she gave us money earlier so we could marry while I was still in school. And I really want to keep that promise but, now that she's been with us for two years, I just can't stand it any longer. My wife keeps insisting we made a promise and this about drives me nuts too—we're always quarreling over it now. She never even tries to see my point. I'm just fed up, that's all—promise or no promise!

In contrast to the values of gratitude and appreciation involved in his original promise, he now finds that this commitment is in conflict with his personal values of self-esteem, wanting his own home and a desire for positive relationship with his wife in place of constant quarrels.

Catching this conflict of values or self-investments and at the same time understanding the resulting suffering, the counselor might respond:

You're caught because you want to keep your promise but in fact you just can't see how you can do it—after two years experience with your mother-in-law. What adds to the conflict and pain is that your wife can't seem to see this and you keep quarreling about it. But you've just had about all you can take. It's got you very disturbed.

SYMBOLS AND INSIGHT

Earlier we quoted Eliade as saying that

symbols are capable of revealing a modality of the real or a condition of the World which is not evident on the plane of immediate experience.[4]

This is so because immediate experience as we see in this illustration, is a complex interweaving of impulses and impressions from all levels of a person's being. At the moment of experience then, one is hit or struck by experience and often "the mind is stabbed on a spot it did not know was vulnerable."[5]

Some kind of reflection is therefore necessary if experience is to have significant personal meaning. To aid and intensify this reflection is the purpose of the skilled response. This reflective self-awareness is achieved through this process of symbolization or linguistic exchange. By such adequate symbolization of himself, a person is opened up beyond himself and his own narrowed experience. By definition, "understanding" should move him from the unique aspect of his own individuation to that which he has in common with other persons and things. Such symbolic communication should "explode immediate reality as well as particular situations."[6]

As a result, the person gropes slowly to move out of the narrowed and sometimes imprisoning aspects of his uniqueness, to an understanding of himself in a more abstractive and symbolic light. He "opens himself" and "succeeds in emerging from his personal situation and reaching a comprehension of the universal."[7]

"Insight" in counseling therapy therefore is not simply abstractive understanding—as it might be generally understood—but a *special kind of symbolization which is drawn out of and has particular pertinence to the person's own emotion-somatic charged situations.* Nicholas Hobbes points out, in reference to a young man with authority conflicts:

The task of the therapist is not to help the client gain insight into the fact that he has trouble with authority because of his unfortunate experiences with his own father. This is far too abstract a formulation to be of help. He has got to be helped to identify and use comfortably the *specific symbols that are elicited in him* by authority figures. The symbols must be divested of their anxiety producing potential.[8]

CONDITIONS FOR EFFECTIVENESS

Hobbes sums up his own view by saying that the effectiveness of counseling therapy relationships

will depend on the extent to which they provide an opportunity for the client to experience closeness to another human being without getting hurt, to divest symbols associated with traumatic experiences of their anxiety producing potential, to use the transference situation to learn not to need neurotic distortions, to practice being responsible for himself, and to clarify an old or learn a new cognitive system for ordering his world.[9]

This groping for "specific symbols" adequate to a person's immediate emotion-charged situation is therefore one of the main aspects of the counselor's or therapist's skill. But this is, in fact, a triple process, consisting in:

1) the client's own confused and "mixed up" effort to express himself in the emotion-charged language of affect

2) the counselor-therapist's striving to understand this language

and to respond in a more adequately symbolic or cognitive form

3) the client's hearing this, analyzing it in relation to his own affect-cognitive state and allowing that it either does or does not "fit".

It is evident then that responses have a kind of tailor-made quality in this sense that they must not simply be "stock" responses but have an exact fit from moment to moment. They must coincide precisely with the changing self-awareness of the person's individual communications.

To look more carefully at the way precise responses can be formulated and to examine counseling therapy from the point of view of this symbolic process and its precision, we have devised the following Emotion-Insight-Choice Diagram.

In this cross diagram, areas of understanding are assigned to each line. The bottom of the vertical line indicates "negative emotions"—i.e., the expressions of such feelings as anxiety, hostility, depression, etc.; and their "somatic overtones" such as "not feeling well," or "having a hard time physically," or "feeling fatigued," etc. In the beginning of counseling therapy, people's statements tend to be predominantly negative insofar as they are discouraged, depressed, upset, without knowing why. So confusion and conflict statements are related to negative emotions at the left of the horizontal line.

Mixed with negations and conflict and confusions are usually some positive feelings, indicated by the next arrow pointing to the top of the vertical line. These tend to lead to the first stages of insight to the right of the horizontal line, which leads to new and finally more adequate choices as the next arrow shows. As we see, as new areas of conflict are examined, other negations and confusions are expressed and explored. So the counseling-therapy process might be seen as the swirling motion mounted on the E-I-C Cross—the motion itself suggesting the dynamic, existential moment-to-moment quality of the person's changing feelings, attitudes and communications during counseling therapy.

DEGREE OF INTENSITY

When the counselor hears negative statements, he tries to determine the type of negative emotion and also its strength. A person, for example, says, "I feel just a little bit irritated by what she did." A "little bit" irritated would characterize this as a minor negative emotion. On our diagram, one might score it *two*. It is important that the counselor catch not only the irritation but the degree of intensity. If the counselor says, "You are really upset by her," this will be rejected. The counselor responded to about a point *seven* of negation and irritation, and the client really stated only about a

E-I-C CROSS

(Emotion-Insight-Choice)

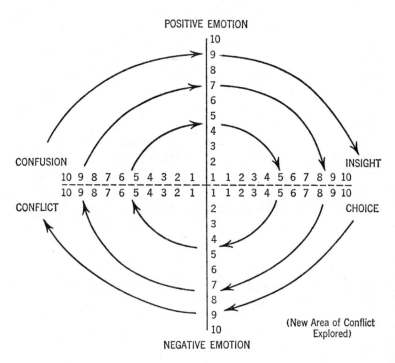

point *two,* or a minor feeling of irritation. This misunderstanding usually forces the client to explain again—sometimes now showing some irritation with the counselor—that he had only a mild hostility feeling. The numbers here are, of course, not important in themselves, they are simply to indicate that some discrimination is necessary in the degree of emotional intensity if the person is to feel understood. This kind of precision can be overlooked in a too loosely worded response.

If the counselor misses the irritation altogether, the client may feel unfulfilled and rejected, as if the counselor has in effect said, "I don't want to hear about this." The client is then often forced into an artificial communication as a kind of protective coverup because he was left feeling that he was not understood.

For the same reason, when a person communicates a strong negative emotion, it too should be exactly shared and understood by the counselor. Negative emotions usually diminish in intensity when they can be completely explored by the client and are genuinely accepted by the counselor. The client is thus helped to get a more reasonable understanding and control over them. If he cannot explain them to the counselor, they usually get worse because he was forced to bottle them up. But when one deeply understands a person who is fearful or discouraged, for example, the end effect seems to be that he will begin to see some of the brighter side of his position. At a certain point, after a period of being understood in a negative mood toward someone's failings, the person may say, "Well there really are some things that are good about him. He is a good manager and he is orderly."

When a person can drain off a negative emotion by speaking about it in this fashion, it often loses its compulsive drive and narrow focus. He can see the broader picture. He can begin himself to disapprove some exaggerated aspects of these negations as he objectifies them. The result is that a person will then say to himself what one might have wanted earlier to say to him; but he will say it more effectively. Moreover, he no longer "feels" so negative and he can therefore begin to talk and act more positively.

The top line of our figure refers to "positive emotions." Within the framework of a highly negative-emotion statement, a counselor can usually catch at least a small element of positive emotion or attitude. In marriage counseling, for instance, after there has been much talk of unhappiness, a wife may say, "I do have a nice home, and he is a good worker—I can be thankful for that."

These positive attitudes should also be reflected by the counselor. But they can easily be missed, especially if they are surrounded by a great number of negative expressions. Postive emotion is like a small flame which gradually starts a fire. If it is clarified, it can grow to be a source of unfolding in a person—one which increasingly disperses negative emotions.

INNER VIEW

Counseling therapy is a looking at the "inner-view" of a person as the client describes himself. As the counselor puts this into words, he turns the "inner-view" into the "interview," so to speak. The person then measures what the counselor says, in relation to his inner-view of himself. If the counselor consistently misses or distorts the client's description of positive and negative feelings and attitudes, a detour can occur which may delay or impede the process. The client may feel he must explain himself over and over again. This can gradually cause him to become defensive and lash out at the counselor or at himself.

If the counselor recognizes he has not understood the client's description of some basic feeling, he may say to the client, "Perhaps you could say that again and I'll try to get it." In a good relationship where the two people are working together, the person will repeat what he was trying to describe and explain it at greater length and so help the counselor in the struggle to understand. The counselor is usually given a number of opportunities to hear again complex feelings and reactions. If, however, his responses consistently fail to reach the level of intensity of the client's feelings and adequately symbolize them, then the client will become increasingly defensive or grow cautious and less communicative. Or, he may simply turn the relationship into an information-interview by getting the counselor to answer questions.

CONFUSION-INSIGHT

On the horizontal line of the above diagram, we have the statements of greater or lesser insight. People usually begin with little insight, describing themselves as confused or not knowing what to do. A person may say, "I just don't know what's the matter. I'm all mixed up." "All mixed up," is a strong negative-type statement. The counselor therefore ought to catch this at about *eight* or *nine* —that is, at a high degree of non-insight. He might respond, "You're just pretty confused and you don't know what to do or where to go." The client may then go on to say, "No, I don't. I've struggled with this for a long time."

A woman in this state may cry. But a woman can communicate even minor negations and discouragements by crying. Crying, particularly in women, is not necessarily negative—it can be sometimes also positive, or it can be simply a frustration reaction in a woman where a man might be more openly aggressive.

A person might go on to say, while crying, "This is my third change in three years and I don't think I'm going to get along here either and I don't know why. I don't know what's the matter; I'm so discouraged. I'm sure I'm getting a bad reputation. Everybody knows that a person shouldn't be sent around like this. . . ."

This is obviously a somewhat strong negative confusion statement. One catches both confusion and discouragement in the response: "You're quite discouraged, and one of the things that adds to your discouragement is that you're pretty confused about it— you don't know why you can't succeed; it isn't clear to you and you're afraid of what may happen."

There is an important difference between a person's general state of confusion and confusion in one particular area only. A person may say, "In general I know what to do. But I just don't know what to do about this one person." This is a limited confusion. The counselor then must hold up this distinction in his response. "As far as the whole job is concerned you're pretty clear about what to do. Your particular difficulty, at the moment, is with this one person."

CONFLICT-CHOICE

The conflict line is the opposite of choice, to indicate that vectors of emotions and values of equal strength tend to produce indecision. They impede choosing one series of goals and rejecting the opposite. This holds the person suspended painfully "in the middle." As his confusions clear, he can gain positive confidence in reorganizing these conflicting forces. This tends to diminish the force of some of them so that he can take an option on one course of action and have sufficient integration to begin to follow it.

The line in our diagram that is opposite to confusion and conflict represents "insight and choice." It includes new awarenesses, plans and achievements. It is also important for the counselor to learn to recognize and respond to these, especially at the later stages of the counseling process. Sometimes a counselor learns to respond well to the negative attitudes and confusions, but he gets uncomfortable when insights and the area of new plans are discussed. One reason for this could be that most of us have heard more of people's negative expressions and less of their positive communications, since people tend to release negations to us. In ordinary relationships they more often keep positive feelings to themselves, having less need to tell us about them. Or, when we hear them, we do not feel any need to help them.

A common type of insight expression concerns responsible independence, for example: "Well, I know I must see this myself—I can't just be a little child and expect other people to do this for me all the time." Insight statements like this are, therefore, a movement toward assuming responsibility. For the insights are about relationships with other persons or situations: "Well, I've always more or less been this way and even my mother used to tell me that I was. I never realized this before, but I see now that I'm acting toward the supervisor, here, just about the way I used to act toward my mother at home—I guess I never really worked that out." We notice here a dawning self-insight which related a past and a present state.

NEW PLANS OF ACTION

Sometimes, usually toward the latter part of an interview, insights fuse into new plans or achievements: "After our talk the last time, I was thinking over the things we talked about and I tried to act a little differently. You know, it worked out better. I realize now that this way is better than before and I feel better too." Here, the new plan resulted in new achievements. This needs to be clearly caught by the response and held up to the person, so as to reinforce it, "As a result of this awareness the last time, you did set up this new plan and it has proved to be better for you."

The counselor can be so anxious to have success that he might respond, "Well, things are fine now and everything is all set, isn't it?" The person has not said that—he merely stated that he tried something, and it seemed better than the old way; and he feels better. Consequently, he may feel resistant and be forced into negation again since he was not truly understood. The counselor must let the person grow slowly into security with these newly acquired awarenesses and new plans. The ultimate effectiveness of counseling therapy for a person may demand fundamental changes in his self-concept and changes in his attitude toward others as well. If this is so, attempting to hurry it up by artificially positive responses, seems only to delay and even to impede it.

It is evident that the counselor is not just responding in an echoing way. This, in fact, will soon cause people to become resistant. He is really trying to understand, through the intercommunication of words, a person's deepest inner-views or awarenesses of himself and to symbolize them adequately. The counselor's reasoning process couples into the reasoning of the client. Together they slowly work their way out of the client's confusion, conflicts and negations, into a constructive self-awareness, insight and better way of acting—on the cross-design diagram, from bottom to top and from left to right.

As we suggested, examples from visual perception can sometimes aid in demonstrating how insight develops. Usually the beginning of an interview is similar to a film-slide in a projector before it is focused. At first you can hardly see it. Let us say it is a picture of Leonardo da Vinci's "Last Supper," with only vague contours or masses evident. The process of insight is like the adjusting of the lens until finally one sees that Christ is in the center and John is here and Peter is there. It is always the same picture; but as it focuses, it becomes clearer.

DIALOGICAL GNOSIS

With the clarification of this insight "gestalt" or configuration, there is, at the same time, the slow emergence of personal values, often in conflict. With a broader and more integrated self-view, comes either the freedom to discard some conflicting values or the insight into how to gain a more adequate realization of these values. As we have seen, these values may sometimes be hidden in one's psychological matrix and carried over from early childhood or they may be in the culture itself. Until now, such values have been only implicitly accepted by the person. But they could be governing his life even though he never consciously recognized or "evaluated" them. The counseling therapy insight process aims at both self-evaluation and coordination of thought, desire and action. In this way the counseling therapy dialogue becomes also a dia-gnosis, that is a gain in inner operational knowledge and self-actualization.

NOTES

[1] D. Lantz and V. Steffire, "Language and Cognition Revisited," *Journal of Abnormal and Social Psychology*, 69 (5), November 1964, p. 472.

[2] M. Mednick, S. Mednick and C. Jung, "Continual Association as a Function of Level of Creativity and Type of Verbal Stimulus," *Journal of Abnormal and Social Psychology*, 69 (5), November 1964, p. 515.

[3] Romano Guardini, *The World and the Person*, Chicago: Henry Regnery Co., 1965, pp. 130–138. (First published as *Welt und Person*, copyright 1939 by Werkbund-Verlag, Würzburg.)

[4] Eliade, *op. cit.*, p. 201.

[5] Kerr, *op. cit.*, p. 214.

[6] Eliade, *op. cit.*, p. 207.

[7] *Ibid.*

[8] Nicholas Hobbes, "Sources of Gain in Psychotherapy," *The American Psychologist,* 17 (11), November 1962, p. 744. (Italics mine)

[9] *Ibid.,* p. 747.

8

The Clarification of Conflicting Values

IT IS EVIDENT that the personal situations brought up in counseling therapy are emotion-charged and the conflict and confusion accompanying these feelings seem to be value-laden in some manner. By "values" we mean here the special significance and investment discussed earlier. When the person begins to "understand" or "see" as he may say, instead of simply "feel," this seems to involve the uncovering of some sort of value conflict. Adequate choices are impeded because somehow what one wants to do and often feels guilty for not having done, runs contrary to some other basic life plan or operational value system. An important aspect of the skill of counseling therapy is, then, the manner in which this affect-cognitive value conflict is clarified.

Cole and Miller, for example, in a study of the relationship of values to academic performance, conclude that

logical support may be given to the idea that values, to be meaningful, must be tied to behaviors which provide need satisfactions. That is, if a value is to have relevance as a determiner of behavior, it must encompass behavioral preferences . . .[1]

GOAL INVOLVEMENT

If we examine the nature of the emotions themselves, it becomes evident that they contain explicit or implicit values and personal goals and needs. In a way that has not been sufficiently investigated in counseling and psychotherapy, any complicated emotional reaction seems to be the result of some already committed goal involvement and need. One of the main things the counseling therapy process does then, is *to disentangle* and help the person *clarify the nature of this goal or need,* its *present value* to him and *pose the issue* of whether he wishes *to continue its pursuit.* This is the path that personal evaluation in counseling therapy takes.

PERSONAL PERCEPTUAL FIELD

If a person is strongly moved, it seems apparent that he both wants, likes or loves something or someone and that, at the same-time, he will be hostile to or, at least, opposed to and frustrated by anything or anyone that prevents his achieving what he desires. In other words, a person creates a personal perceptual field around anything he wants by saying, equivalently, this is "a good thing for me," meaning, "this should bring me some kind of happiness." Anything in the way is a "bad thing for me and so I will try to avoid it."[2]

Such fields, however, can become unconscious and unrecognized even though they still motivate the person. As we have seen, they may be carried over from earlier periods in life, they may be contained in family or neighborhood values or they may be in the value system of the culture itself.

Thus in counseling therapy there is a melange of confusion-conflict statements mixing together negative emotions of hostility, resentment, frustration, anxiety, resistance and similar negations with some kind of positive emotions and even insights. These all represent certain known or unknown value goals.

As counseling therapy unfolds these various present and past personal values, hope is stimulated, courage grows, self-confidence emerges and a person begins to gain satisfaction in even small achievements. But negations like depression and anxieties appear whenever impediments to these value goals arise. Anger and hostility are part of the effort to surmount these barriers. Impulses to deep discouragement are strongest when it seems the barriers cannot be overcome. Here, as we have seen, urges to compensation through the achieving of substitute but inadequate satisfactions from easy goals are apt to be most intense.

From this, one can see that the presence of these strong emotions already imply a variety of goals. Often when goals that were previously hidden are uncovered, the person can choose different goals and so diminish the emotional forces toward these goals after he has traced their origin back to its sources. Somehow, once this evaluation process is carried out, the emotions are often far less demanding and the person can begin to act on his alternate choice instead of being in the "caught-in-the-middle" conflict.

CLARIFICATION AND INTEGRATION

One of the main things the skilled response achieves, therefore, is that it offers a person clarification of and gradual operational integration in this kind of emotional conflict, and the hidden goals, needs and values such conflict implies.

A client's comments, made immediately after a half-hour of actual counseling, may help explain further the process we are describing. This is part of the research to which we referred earlier. This young woman was a college graduate, unmarried, now employed. The general content of the interview concerned a relationship with another woman with whom she worked. At the beginning of the interview, as she explained later, she knew only that she felt guilty about this woman's leaving the position, but the client did not know clearly why she felt so guilty. The interview was primarily concerned with exploring the reason for this guilt. This produced what she considered a profound new insight about herself. This insight fitted into a pattern of conduct that she had never clearly seen before or faced in herself. The following is the client's comment on the counselor's responses:

I found it especially helpful when you started by saying that you saw two pictures, or when you pointed up a contrast in what I was saying. That helped me much—it just immediately lined up so many stray factors . . .

As soon as you said there was a contrast, I was prepared right away to classify, to distinguish and relate.

I felt freed almost instantaneously from a lot of cluttered awarenesses, a lot of hazy, half-defined ideas. I could just see a straight way with two sides, I could easily look to right or to left and see each thing fall into its place.

This was apparent to me in this interview. My initial awareness was about this girl and the relief that I felt about not being in her position, along with the other image of her as a person. Well, just to be able to distinguish this much made me much less guilty.

I had just about half as much to be guilty about, because I could understand and readily forgive myself for that much anyway. These other things were mixed in and were just elements of the whole picture. To see even this much I found encouraging in itself. I felt much more ready to face the real issue. It was less complicated, once I understood it at least partially. It was so quick. You said it in maybe a quarter of the words that I used, but it took care of it right away. Even in one response.

The following continues her after-counseling comment:

It (the interview) has been most valuable—very revealing to me. The incident that started this whole insight process was bothering me but I didn't see where it would fit. I just saw it as the most negative thing in my life this last month—the one unresolved, the one that I had put away as far as I knew because I didn't know quite what to do with it . . .

The comment continues:

I was for the most part thinking of positive things. Well, maybe this whole switch in feeling from gaiety to seriousness just threw up these other things that were serious to me. Anyway I see it now in relation to these other things that I had never faced before. I was forced to face this, even if I couldn't resolve it. But the other implications I had never faced . . .

A much bigger thing, volume-wise and importance-wise, came with it, and something that is more generally my role. I see this more often—I don't have so many instances of the other to observe, but this I can.

I feel now that I have a hold on it. Your linking these for me, or at least showing me how I have linked them, has helped wonderfully. I have much more to work with. I have much more to examine and see clearly, whereas before I was lost, really. I mean this one little thing was just a rare species, I thought.

After a pause, she then said:

I feel positive about it now. As a matter of fact, this surprises me.

This interview has been tremendously helpful for that . . .

If I could guess about it, I would say that this has been much more satisfying than, say an interview on some positive thing—where I would just reassure myself some more and perhaps bury this a little deeper . . .

I see that the other things are still there, but now this is taken care of in a way that I hadn't hoped it would be . . .

I thought of it as a lost experience—at least until I'd see something like it again that I could compare it with . . .

Now I feel hope for it—a kind of a coming to life that I associate with a flicker of something constructive. Although it's very very ugly in itself, I can recognize that although I do ugly things, I don't have to do them all the time—but can take care of this, for instance.

Some details of the client's earlier counseling experience may be helpful here. Three years before she had participated in counseling as a client over a six month period. The reason she asked for counseling at that time was both a sense of personal conflict and inadequacy, and poorer, although not failing, school performance. Her scholastic achievement in the honors program, which until then had been the focal point of her self-regard, had become jeopardized. Her lowering grades had forced her out of the program and she was missing more classes. In addition, she had gained 20-30 pounds from overeating. She felt "discouraged all the time," and this state was complicated by, if not causing, abdominal upsets for which she was receiving medication.

We have in this picture of the client before she came for counseling, a negation toward self which was attacking her at three basic levels of personal value: 1) her school achievement, 2) her personal appearance and 3) her physical health. In this we have the complicated interweaving of psychological and physical factors that so often mark this self-rejecting picture. Over a twenty-interview series, she worked through her conflicts sufficiently to improve her grades, she lost weight, and achieved a more general feeling of positive regard.

The present interview occurred about two and a half years after the ending of the counseling series. She had graduated the previous spring but had returned for a visit. She telephoned the counselor partly simply to "see" him and tell him how well things were going—as she said on the phone.

VALUE-BASED GUILT

Since the client emphasized the importance of this one response as being the highpoint of the whole interview, it should be revealing to look at this response as it actually occurred. It appeared about the first ten minutes of the interview. Up to this point there were a number of pauses. The client, after saying some vaguely positive things about her work, found it hard to continue. This is indicated by a pause of some duration. The following is the actual client statement made during the interview:

I find that my new experiences with these people (in the office) are fresh and different. (Pause) There is one in particular that I have never been able to forget—I feel guilty about it.

What happened with this girl has happened many times before in my life, I'm sure, but I would not have noticed it. There was a girl who started work in the office shortly after I did. She was full-time and she started taking over little things that I had been doing. I saw in her so many of the things I wanted to overcome in myself and that I had overcome to a degree. I found that I was despising her. I would respond only superficially in our conversation. I would just go about my work. Then I noticed she got herself in trouble. I watched her go through the troubles I would go through; she wouldn't show up—the way I used not to show up for things; she did sloppy work. I found her in the position that I used to be in, of giving excuses and laughing things off. I never saw all that so objectively before.

I felt strange about it. I felt a relief that I wasn't going through this; and I felt very safe, very secure—just relieved that I wasn't in this. And then I thought: "Well, this is no way to feel. This is a person and she is in a place I was in; and I should care." I don't know, I felt when she failed I would succeed; when she fell down, I would pick up—this horrible thing, that I was succeeding in her failure. Then I was gay and I was functioning just perfectly and I was just exact about everything.

It seemed to be almost proportionately as she was not showing up and not doing things right, I was kind of falling into it. I realized that, after a while, and I was terribly ashamed. I resolved that I would care for this girl and would really try to experience something with her. Then she didn't come anymore. She quit, or she just didn't show up. And it was over. And I had never rectified it with her—on the level of experience, where I had been guilty in all these series of relationships. And she was gone and I was left with this ugliness. I could just intellectualize around it but I just couldn't do anything about it. I don't know how I ever would have resolved it. It's just come and gone.

In the context of the interview itself, it is intriguing to note how the client's guilt about this one relationship was introduced. For the first few minutes of this counseling interview she had been talking about the contrast of her new experience with the old. The new job was making her more practical. She was trying to carry out the things she had acquired from her previous counseling. All this indicated her satisfaction at the ability to see things herself in new situations. Then, after a long pause, "There is one in particular that I . . . feel guilty about." It was like the perception of a small dot or spot which gradually became larger and larger until it was the center of focus. In this excerpt we see this incident grow and assume a position of central importance to her. It became so important that it was the centerpiece of the rest of the interview.

We notice that she immediately comments that her guilt is partly due to the greater sensitivity that she now has. As a result of the previous counseling series, she is apparently more observant of herself and more open and aware of her own feelings toward herself and others. She is at the same time more reflective and even self-critical. This type of self-criticism, while often guilt-producing, is more discriminating and more finely delineating. It therefore seems closer to producing constructive results as one grows to see its value sources more clearly.

People at the beginning of counseling are often feeling guilty. This guilt, however, seems rather to be associated with self-disregard and rejection. The sentence, "I am disgusted with myself" is more broadly negative than a particular feeling of guilt directed at some action or relationship. Guilt expressed at the later stages of the counseling process seems to result from a person's having discriminated more finely in assessing particular emotions and attitudes. He is therefore less generally self-rejecting, even though he may be sharply guilty about a particular situation.

CONFLICTING VALUE SYSTEMS

One notices here the projection of two conflicting value systems on the other woman. From one value perception, she represents the client herself in a way of acting which is now no longer acceptable to the client. Hostility and resistance to this person, then, followed from and was in fact a normal result of her present change in operational values as a result of the counseling interview series. The same structure that had gone into being hostile to and resisting these ways of acting in herself were understandably triggering negative emotions toward the other person. In a way, one might say she had never left herself in these negative feelings.

On the other hand, however, this person was obviously someone who had a claim to some kind of regard and respect from her, even if this respect followed simply from her own gratitude—as she expressed later in the interview—at the changes she had experienced in herself as a result of someone else's concern for her. In this sense, her hostile and resisting feelings to the other woman were a kind of a betrayal and ingratitude for all that she herself felt she had received.

It is not difficult then to see how the guilt which was the conscious feeling that caused her to start talking about this situation, was also the result of two strong personal value systems in conflict. On the one side, her present view of herself and her achievement in improving her own manner of acting contained hostility and resistance to anyone representing her previous operational system of carelessness, neglect, procrastination and tardiness. On the other side, having gained so much from someone's concern for her, gratitude now strongly moved her toward openness and sensitive consideration for others in imitation of what she herself had received. What stood in the way, apparently, was the wall of negative feelings for the woman's conduct as symbolizing an operational self she was anxious to discard. In this sense, then, the woman's actions, like her own at an earlier period, could only be resented and resisted. Her rejecting conduct seemed to follow from this "caught-in-the middle state."

Since she had not adequately clarified these feelings and the personal values they contained, the positive, open regard for the woman, which she genuinely wanted to have, would confusedly appear to be an approval of a past self which she now strongly resisted. It is evident how the precipitating feeling of guilt which started her talking about this incident, was itself the result of this painful personality value conflict. We can see how, as she said, being able to distinguish these attitudes in herself made her feel less guilty.

A RE-COGNIZING RESPONSE

Let us now look at the counselor's response to this somewhat involved and complicated client statement:

Your perception is that this girl was really two persons: she was herself, and then she was your "old self." These two got elaborately combined and it was a tremendous relief to see that you weren't this "old self," in seeing her do all the things that you would readily have done. It was your freedom to do all the better as she did all the worse. Insofar as you were fighting yourself, it was extremely satisfying to see that you weren't this person at all anymore and could, in a sense, be spurred on to be the exact opposite. In this "old new self" struggle you lost touch with her as a person and you never did anything, really, to help her. You just almost delighted, in a sense, in your freedom from this same "old self" that she symbolized and, in a sense, was. And what is bad, now, is that you have come to this realization.

(Client breaks in: "Uh-huh.")

... that this girl isn't there anymore and there isn't any way you can make contact with her. This leaves you both guilty and blocked. She needed help just as you did and you didn't offer her any such help.

(Client interrupts with: "I think that I'm shocked that I did this.")

This is a new phase of yourself. It may have been something you did before in the past but you didn't know you did it. But certainly now this is clearly seeing you did it and it is very shocking to you.

(Client interrupts again: "I can't see anything else except that it is equivalent to hating her, to despising her; and that's about as selfish as it can be.")

Yes, you did despise her; and you are shocked now with the realization of how selfish it is.

If we compare this response with what the client herself said in the interview, we notice that the response extends out to both the experience the client was talking about and the client's own verbalization of it. *Basic feelings,* the *reason for these feelings,* and *sharper discrimination* and *symbolizations of the values* they contain are *extended* and *delineated* in the *counselor's response.* Compared with what the client originally said, *the picture is clearer though not different.* We can see how the counselor's response clarified the value conflict. This made it possible for the client, through the remainder of the interview, to spell out with greater precision what her present values were. In other words, she was able to turn destructive guilt into constructive guilt. At the end of the half-hour interview, she was not without guilt, but it was a guilt which, as she said, in her comments, contained hope. It did not leave her in a frustrated *cul de sac* for which she could see no solution. The "ugly" feeling she had at the beginning of the interview was one of the reasons why she was reluctant to face herself by discussing the incident. Without the counselor's help, perhaps she would have tended, as she said, just to suppress these feelings in trying consciously to forget them.

Another point is the way the counselor responded to the client's final statement of intense hostility both to the other woman and to herself for having this feeling. "You did despise her, and you are shocked now with the realization of how selfish it is."

When we see the subtle personal value system which this hostile feeling toward the other woman contained, we also see how basically misleading and disrespectful would be any attempt by the counselor to tone down the intensity of negation which the client was expressing. Not only would this run the risk of being misunderstanding and therefore rejecting, but it also could have blocked the client from further exploration of the positive operational values which were at the other side of this intense negation. It is for these reasons especially that the counselor tries to respond to the exact intensity level of the client's communication—as we discussed earlier.

When we see the capital importance which the client places on this one response of the counselor, it is interesting to speculate what might have happened had the counselor's response been less sensitive and accurate in its understanding. Possibly the interview would have bogged down and taken a negative turn. Or it might have regained the superficially positive tone it had in the beginning. But a basic area of guilt and discouragement might have been left unexplored. The client might even, to use her own terms, "perhaps bury this a little deeper" and by such repression delay further the therapy process.

PROCESS PICTURE

The following diagram (cf. below) may further clarify the "inner-view" process that the client was describing about herself. *View I* is her generally positive self-perception at the beginning of the interview. After a short time, a black spot labeled "One (experience) I feel guilty about" appears. As she is free to unfold this guilt and relate it, it ends in a negative self-picture which is now central in her inner-view: "She was gone and I was left with this ugliness" (View II).

Comparing this now with her comments at the end of the interview about what the half hour had brought her in self-awareness, we have *View III*. The black spot has become white and developed

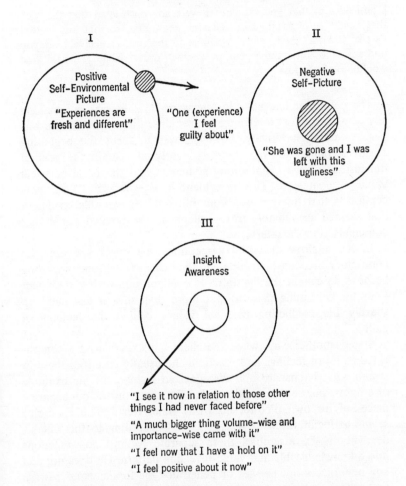

into a sense of positive self-awareness about a basic conduct pattern in herself that she had never faced before: "I see it now in relation to those other things I had never faced before . . . A much bigger thing volume-wise and important-wise came with it . . . I feel now that I have a hold on it . . . I feel positive about it now."

In her final comment the client says:

I noticed also that your responses were so constructed that the part that would be clarifying and relieving came first, so that just in that part of it I was made more receptive to the rest. Conceivably if you had said the same thing, but in another order, what you said first would have been lost.

The counselor himself said afterwards that he was not making any conscious effort to arrange his response this way. What he was perhaps doing intuitively, however, was to focus the beginning of his response on what seemed clearly to contain the general dimensions of the client's long statement and the basic personal values it contained. This is evident in the phrase: "Your perception is that this girl was your old self." It was this statement that seemed so valuable to the client, as she pointed out in her comments after the interview.

In the analogy of visual perception, one might say that the counselor's response facilitated the client's self-understanding because he caught the "gestalt" or configuration of her statement —its total meaning pattern. But more than this, it also held up sharply the conflicting personal values behind the feelings of guilt.

Stated another way, when the client has experienced a complicated series of feelings and reactions, he usually describes these in a somewhat haphazard and disorganized fashion. In the example of a jigsaw puzzle, we could say that the client throws out separate pieces of his own picture, his own "inner-view." The counselor seems to facilitate client insight when—according to this client's description—he assembles these separate feelings and reactions into a knowledgeable and value-revealing pattern. He does not add any new pieces but he sees or penetrates the fundamental pattern that relates and gives meaning to the client's recital of his separate reactions. It is somewhat as if he were to say, after the client has handed him a number of separate jigsaw pieces, "Doesn't this perhaps make an ear?" or "Now it seems we have Lincoln's face," etc. These are what the actual pieces fit together to make, but in looking only at separate pieces—one after another—the client apparently could not see this. We notice this suggested in the client's

comment: "I felt freed almost instantaneously from a lot of cluttered awarenesses, a lot of hazy, half-defined ideas. I could easily
look to right or to left and see each thing fall into its place."

But the pieces fitting together according to a perceptual field is
not all that is important. What gives significance to the way the
pieces fit, is that, in some manner, they are part of an operational
value system which the person now wants, or in wanting something
else, now has rejected. This is obviously different from simply
seeing pieces related visually.

PRECISE SENSITIVE DISCRIMINATION

According to this client's explanation, she apparently *did not*
clearly understand what she had said to the counselor. Even after
she had spoken of herself at such length, her idea of the meaning
of this lengthy description was still vague and undefined. It was
the counselor's response, according to her, that sharpened the
focus and gave her a clear delineation of both sides as well as the
foreground and background features and the underlying values. As
a result, she could begin to see and understand herself and the
situation. She could now see herself in central vision, so to speak.
She no longer saw this aspect of herself, as a person might see an
object bothering him on the periphery of his vision, as a threatening unknown. It no longer needed to be feared, avoided and suppressed and looked on as the source of undefined guilt. She said
she was immediately less guilty as a result of even this one response. She then later began to experience hope and positive self-
reference.

In addition to other basic elements in a constructive counseling
therapy process, of capital importance for this client then, was the
counselor's precise, sensitive and discriminating understanding,
and the words he used to communicate this. According to the
client's own evaluation, core insights and progress seemed to
center around this.

To summarize this process in terms of a linguistic concept of a
double language exchange, we could say that the client attempted
to communicate complicated somatic, instinctive and emotional

reactions by trying to put these into words. Behind these reactions were hidden basic operational values, present and past. The counselor's skill consisted in understanding this affect language—somewhat as one might understand a foreign language—and in giving back his response in the "language of cognition." That is, he recognized and reorganized the confused feelings into their basic personal value significance. In a sense we might say that he "translates" this affect language into a "recognizable" form—as German might be translated into English. The client can then analyze with less emotion and confusion what he has been feeling and so begin to "see" himself more clearly and "get a better hold on himself." This apparently results from a better recognition of himself through his own affect expression and the counselor's more cognitive-value translation which he feels really "fits."

Seen this way, we must think not only of ways of establishing a warm and deep "understanding heart" relationship between client and counselor but also of the counselor's precise analysis and verbalization of the client's affective language, since the client apparently often does not clearly understand what he has said until he hears it back, in cognitive form, from the counselor. It is because of this, apparently, that the counselor's response plays such an important part in facilitating the client's self-reorganization.

AUXILIARY REASON AID

This counselor response—in contrast to a less adequate one that might have been made—also furthered and facilitated the client's own reasoning about herself. It did so by sharpening and clarifying the client's dialogue with herself. As she said, "I felt more ready to face the real issue. It was less complicated." In addition to sympathy and empathy, the counselor was also a genuinely understanding auxiliary reasoning self. This intensely concentrated effort to understand, furthered the reasoning dynamics in the client.

The client pointed up this process in her remarks: "As soon as you said there was a contrast, I was prepared right away to classify, to distinguish and relate." To "classify, distinguish and relate" are logical states in the reasoning process. The counselor furthered progress then, in this client's view, by a kind of pump-priming reasoning, particularly in one crucial response. This response, formulated in the fashion that it was, seemed to free, encourage and stimulate the client's ability to reason with herself about this particular situation and its implications and the basic personal values it contains. She was then able, with the counselor's help, to continue, during the rest of the interview, to reason about herself and the patterns of conduct and values of long duration which this incident highlighted for her.

Earlier we spoke of how the client has a hand in his own redemption—that is, his own growth in self-worth, and respectful self-love. We see here how this person's positive self-regard, in contrast to an "ugly" self-image, was correlated with broadening self-insight and an open willingness to face hitherto hidden aspects of herself. Somehow with the courage to face herself through the counselor's skill, she could come to a more loving self-regard even though this also involved facing some painfully negative aspects of herself. But in facing them this way and regretting them, as foreign to her genuine self-ideal or conscious value system, she somehow was freed from her negative feeling bind and was able to view herself positively and constructively. By becoming more positively accepting of her total incarnate self, she gained in a sense of genuine self-worth. It was the counselor's skilled and sensitive understanding, however, that made her sufficiently cognitive of herself to be able to make these gains. She could not, apparently, have done this alone.

SYMBOLIC SELF FREEDOM

We have previously indicated how the exchange between client and counselor often appears to represent the client's creative struggle for a conscious symbolic awareness of what he is feeling. When, over a period of verbal exchange, such a symbolic awareness is achieved, the client seems relieved and freed to go on to other and sometimes new associations and self-identifications.

In the following situation, a client struggled to explain to a counselor-in-training his pain at the counselor's failure to understand the feelings he was trying to communicate. Then came an impasse, with the client staring angrily at the counselor and both unable to speak. The client was made mute because of his mounting anger and pain at not being understood, and the counselor was paralyzed by the intensity of the client's resentment. The supervisory counselor then intervened by making a counseling response to the client's anger. In the process of four or five exchanges, the client was now discussing this frustration of trying so hard and with such embarrassment to tell the previous counselor his feelings and yet not being at all understood by the counselor. At this point the supervisory counselor responded that he just felt "half-in and half-out."

The client picked up the phrase with, "Yes, that's it, half-in and half-out (pause) . . . Yes, that's exactly the way I feel, half-in and half-out—and you just feel a damn fool!" Yet, simultaneously his face and his manner became that of a freed person. He smiled, laughed a little, paused, looked at the counselor-in-training warmly, and then said, "Let's try again, shall we? You know, I feel better toward you now. The odd thing is that I really felt from the beginning that you would be someone I could talk this thing over with and I kind of feel like that again now."

While other things are certainly involved here, yet the freeing moment seemed to come with the verbalization, "half-in and half-out," a verbalization that came from the cognitive struggle, over five or six exchanges. They finally arrived at a precise and satisfactory verbal cognitive clue or symbol for what had been so deeply disturbing and impeding in the client's communication with the other counselor.

In this sense we may have tended to over-simplify when we previously considered such a process "insightful" in the perceptual or logical sense. What happens here is more than the fitting together of pieces like a jigsaw puzzle picture—even though this helps catch some aspects. Rather *a different kind of client cognition* was achieved that was *more symbolic* and yet able to free him from his temporary emotional block. This resulted from the verbal formulation of the counselor, apparently. It was this formulation, digested and assimilated, that seemed to free the client for continued creative striving to understand himself.

KEY CONCEPT

Following are excerpts from the beginning and end of a ten-minute recorded interview in which one sees this joint effort of counselor and client in a struggle to find adequate symbolic communication. This ends with one word, "audience," as the key-concept. Upon analysis, we can see how this word ties up the conflicting operational value systems that impede the client in his own counseling and in his other relationships.

He had just heard another recorded counseling interview. The experience of listening to this short interview affected him so deeply that he asked the counselor for a ten-minute interview. Here we notice the conflict centers directly on being unable to listen to people even though, when he does, he is convinced it is an effective and satisfying way of relating to others.

Counselor: Good, let's set it up for ten minutes, give or take a minute or so and we can discuss whatever you like.

Client: I was just struck listening to that tape that—ah—of my own experience, first as a teacher in high school, that I couldn't talk to kids. I could get along with them, I could run a class, and I would take the time, but it always wound up me doing the talking, and I could not seem to get the barrier down. It bothered me then and to some extent it still does. (Pause) It just seems some way or other dishonest—this business of being sneaky. A person would think I was sort of a peculiar guy who would do this. I mean he'd say, "O.K. Doc, you want me to talk about this business, this psychology jazz."

We can already see why listening to the other ten-minute tape was so painful for this client. On that tape he heard the client talk about feeling uncomfortable and dishonest in just listening to people, and seeming a "phony" instead of just bluntly disagreeing with them. This person, appearing to share the same kind of operational self-attitude and values with the other client, found in this an explanation and even a justification for his own difficulties in trying to counsel high school students. It seemed to him, also, that he felt dishonest in just listening to people and consequently he was motivated to talk to them.

The counselor responds as the interview continues:

Counselor: A parallel here, in this heightening your feelings, is, as I get it, that you feel if you were to do this this way or in some similar way, the other person would react as thinking this is very odd. You would feel reflected by them as very odd—that they must certainly see you in an uncomfortable way.

Client: Yes, I would immediately want to fill that time up with talking as the easy way out.

Counselor: Yes, so you did talk because you did not know what else to do. The tape has brought this up sharply and you are living through this again.

Client: (Pause) I might say that I did not have the courage to be quiet. I used to sometimes—working at the school—count to ten. I would bring myself to do that and just concentrate on that because I trusted it enough to go that far. I was even surprised—sometimes it worked! Still I felt very uncomfortable.

Counselor: Again, there's enough evidence here if you could just even control yourself on a mechanism of ten that something did happen, didn't it. So you did have a conviction that it did happen and were surprised.

Client: Yes.

Counselor: And so the conflict is—if you could do this it might be a good thing, but your problem is that it is even a real difficulty to try it.

Client: Yes, that's it.

The interview continues in this vein with the client telling of one experience of really understanding a classmate by truly forcing himself, and how rewarding it was and how much his classmate appreciated it. He then returns to a discussion of the previous tape relating how similar his own reactions were to those of the person on the other tape. The counselor responds to this:

Counselor: What the two of you are saying, as I get it, one (the person on the previous tape) to the other, is the pain and discomfort of really trying to understand what another person is saying, in contrast to the much easier and simpler and more relieving "just letting them have it," in a more superficial forcing something of yourself on them. It is far more complicated and painful and self-limiting to genuinely try to understand.

Client: What bothers me is that I can see the good and yet I find it very difficult to catch myself and to be able to make that decision and hang on to it even for a relatively short amount of time.

Counselor: Yes, you see this, you are convinced, and this is the painfulness of it as I get it, that when it seems to work in the rare instances when you can do it, why is it so difficult to carry it out?

The conflicting values at this point seem to be a feeling of dishonesty and artificiality in trying to listen to people on the one hand and yet an emerging awareness that he would like to do more of this. This new value, reluctantly accepted, is reinforced by his observation that when he tries to listen to people and control himself enough to understand them, even for a short period, this appears to work. He is convinced enough by this that he would like to do more of it but he seems unable to do it.

He is beginning to face, too, that the feeling of "artificiality" may really have been a rationalization. What he now admits to himself is the difficulty of really doing this kind of understanding listening in place of an easier and simpler "taking over." The interview continues:

Client: Why do you always try to sell something yourself, or to tell someone something that you have done, and that you have found successful rather than to sort of prescind from that, from your own enthusiasms and joys and sort of gather what somebody else is thinking?

Counselor: Why do you always need, as you see yourself, why do I always need to project myself over on others: *to force them to sort of be an audience* and appreciator of me, rather than some reverse of giving myself to them, so to speak, to appreciate them, to understand them.

One notices here an interesting exchange of pronouns. This often occurs. The client, speaking of his own operational plan in a somewhat negative way, uses the pronoun "you," but he is describing what he sees himself doing. The counselor starts with the same pronoun, "you," and switches to "I," but he is responding in the person of the client. One way of explaining this would be that the client, accepting perhaps for the first time a different view of why it is hard to listen to people, cannot quite say "I" but must project it out with the pronoun "you." The counselor in turn, starting with "you," may have felt this was too strong and direct for the client, and so he simply turned it into an inner-view relationship by the use of "I." In any event, it seemed acceptable to the client as we will see in the next response.

CORE VALUE AWARENESS

The word "audience" not only describes his personal situation, and integrates the feelings and needs expressed, it also very exactly sums up the personal value system involved. The client is struck by this word:

Client: That audience thing . . . you . . . well, sometimes I like to perform, I like to be clever. This is immediately satisfying if you think you're fairly good at it.

Counselor: So you see the other person as an audience to reward your performance. This is the impulse to take over the stage kind of thing. The reward is to get the audience's applause, to get the audience's approval. It is this that takes priority in value over being an audience to them and appreciating them. (Pause) Well, our ten minutes is about up.

The counselor has obviously summarized as well as responded to what he feels are the client's awarenesses at the end of the ten minutes. To have an audience is rewarding and it is this and not simply the feeling of dishonesty and artificiality that impedes the client in his efforts to listen to others.

The conflict of personal values here seems to be the client's self-concept of being clever, wanting to perform and needing appreciation. This is so rewarding that in most relationships he prefers this.

The opposite would be to try to become an understanding and sensitive receptor of the other person's communication. This choice, however, does not leave him without insecurity and even guilt. It was this conflict which the hearing of the previous tape triggered and so motivated him to ask for the ten-minute interview.

MOTIVATION TO COUNSELING

This short interview and the fact that hearing another tape initiated it, gives us a clue as to how some people apparently come for counseling. They can, it seems, go for a rather long time in a state of conflict until some particular incident or experience so heightens the conflict that they must do something about it. But, as in the situation here, someone who seems understanding and to whom they feel able to speak, would need to be available. In this we are reminded of the old saying applied to significant periods of history: "Two things are necessary the man and the moment: the moment is not enough without the man; and the man is not enough without the moment." Adapting this we might say that both the precipitating moment and the availability of the understanding person are equally necessary.

DIGGING TOGETHER

Since we followed the procedure of asking the client to make an immediate comment, we now have an opportunity to explore further, through his observations, what he felt he received from the ten minutes.

Counselor: I wonder if I might ask you to comment on your experience here?

Client: Well, I don't think I've thought about the audience end of it in which we got into at the end . . . I thought *we sort of dug through to that*. It was a little bit scarey. It's the same sort of thing to be able to do something like this about yourself as it is to try to listen to somebody else.

Counselor: Same risk.

Client: Yes.

Counselor: The same engagement, the same commitment . . . Anything about the counselor's response?

Client: Well, that word "audience" came out loud and clear. I wasn't expecting it.

Counselor: Any other reaction to the counselor?

Client: Well, I knew I was being listened to. This would go without saying, you know. I felt that, you know, when you are on the other end of one of these things you realize how hard it is not only for the counselor but for me. You, well, it's sort of a unique feeling that you don't have very often, like you're on the spot and you're working.

Counselor: It's hard work.

Client: Yes.

Counselor: It's a real taking counsel with yourself through another in that sense, it's a hard self-digging process with somebody right there with you.

Client: That's right.

It is evident not only that the "audience" need was a new awareness but also that the process itself was almost like two people digging through a tunnel until they reached some element of daylight.

Counselor: Any other comments?

Client: Well, maybe the obvious one is that you do feel that this kind of work is rewarding.

Counselor: It seems worthwhile either way. It seems also worthwhile as a client. You realize that it has helped you.

Client: It's not something sensational but still you feel like you're reaching in the right direction—it's not like sitting in your room, alone.

Counselor: Yes, this kind of concentrated cylinder through another does work in a way that doing it alone probably wouldn't.

The supportive assurance of another's sharing concentrates and intensifies the person's own efforts at self-awareness. Obvious as this is in itself, the comments of this client call attention to what might still be overlooked. We are back again at the sense of communion and belonging that a "listening heart" brings us.

GROUP COMMITMENT AND CONVALIDATION

Since this occurred in a small seminar, the other members of the seminar then commented at some length, asking questions and sharing many of the client's same feelings, reactions and difficulties. The client later commented to the counselor and the group:

Client: One of the things I thought of was the fear of being labeled as one who is always trying to get into the act.

Counselor: Thinking you were again doing the same kind of thing you were talking about.

Client: It struck me, as you were all talking, my own hating people who do show off and not wanting to be that way, and yet knowing very well that in some sense I am in this category.

Counselor: Paradoxical.

Client: Yes. It's a little bit hard even here to assume the other men here would go along with my being sincere.

Counselor: Your relationship to the group was insecure because there was an ambiguity about how you felt they felt. You were not sure on which side of the ambiguity they may interpret this. But there was real help in hearing their reactions.

Client: I was just going to say that I didn't feel that they had reacted this way in that sense, because there was real frankness that everyone who did talk, said what they were thinking. This is reassuring. I really feel very close to them now in a way—closer than before.

Here as we see, the others members' open and frank response to the client, filled out the counselor's acceptance by extending it into a group response and shared communication. This brought the client added reassurance and a sense of closeness. He knew now they had many of his same feelings and difficulties. Through sharing with the client his effort to understand himself and be understood, each one in the group was brought to a greater commitment and involvement with him and with one another.

At the end of Thomas Mann's novel, *Dr. Faustus,* after the main character had publicly revealed himself in an intensely personal release,

he spread out his arms, bending over the instrument and seeming about to embrace it, when suddenly, as though smitten by a blow, he fell sidewise from his seat and to the floor.

Frau Schweigestill, though she had stood farther off, was by him sooner than the rest of us, who, I know not why, wavered a second before we moved. She lifted the head of the unconscious man and holding him in her motherly arms she cried to those still in the room, standing anigh and gaping; "Let me see the backs of ye, all and sundry! City folk all, with not a smitch of understanding, and there's need of that here! Talked about th'everlasting mercy, poor soul, I don't know if it goes's far's that, but human understanding, believe me, that doos!"[3]

NOTES

[1] Charles W. Cole and C. Dean Miller, "Relevance of Expressed Values to Academic Performance," *Counseling Psychology,* 14 (3), May 1967, p. 275.

[2] See Magda B. Arnold, *Emotion and Personality,* II, New York: Columbia University Press, 1960, pp. 275–278.

[3] Thomas Mann, *Dr. Faustus: The Life of the German Composer Adrian Leverkühn as Told by a Friend,* trans. H. T. Lowe-Porter, New York: Alfred Knopf, 1948, p. 503.

9

Counseling and Guidance

GUIDANCE, as defined earlier, is personal information for an immediate situation and need. Obviously such guidance has to come from another whom we will call an expert. The expert is considered, by training or experience or a combination of both, to have special qualifications and a particular kind of knowledge. Such a relationship is obvious between physician and patient, lawyer and client and in similar traditionally established relationships. In fact, one of the confusions between guidance and counseling has been the tradition by which, as for example in the title "counselor-at-law," such a knowledgeable expert was often thought of as a counselor and his giving of expert guidance was considered counseling. Even now we have not entirely separated these two. In our present discussion we will see that they need not be absolutely separated. On the contrary, we propose that the assimilation of expert guidance can often be facilitated if the expert also has counseling awareness. But counseling, in itself, we consider a special and distinct skill and understanding. So while counseling and guidance need not be completely separated, they need to be clearly distinguished or confusions may result.

DISTINCTIONS

The relationship of counseling and guidance can also be seen in an educational context. To review for a moment, the concept of meanings in their most universal form—the kind of basic traditional awarenesses that our civilization has arrived at—are given in general education. In other forms these conceptions of education become more personalized and are for a more immediate application. A person is usually in a state of specific personal need when he seeks guidance. Guidance in this sense, even more than general education, would be involved in values.

Thus, a class in sociology, philosophy, religion or psychology may discuss marriage. If it is discussed in terms of its meaning, this is education. Particular attitudes toward marriage, for example, may be shown to be related in varying ways to value systems, ethics and personality, and so reveal the sources of our concept of marriage—philosophical, theological, sociological, legal, etc.

But assuming that there is an engaged couple in the group plus a number of couples "going steady," much of the educational material may be filtering through to them as guidance. For them, the lecture is personalized; they may ask questions in class or even consult the lecturer afterwards, not because of the educational material but because of their personal involvement.

General education tends, then, to be *intellectually* oriented toward principles, facts and general information; guidance is oriented more toward the whole emotionally committed person. In other words, two people engaged to be married are emotionally, instinctively and somatically involved in a topic like marriage. It is obviously more than an intellectual issue for them. This distinction is the basis of *guidance*. Here we might distinguish, too, between general education—as intellectually centered—and the whole-person *educative process*.

Both general education and that which would educate "the whole man," however, are related to giving information, whereas counseling would not be information-centered *or* meaning-centered but person-centered. Consequently, a counseling relationship would be intended to enable a person not only to *accept* a particular set of values but to be able to *operate* from them. A couple wanting to marry already has a value investment. They may need more personal information. If we suppose, however, that whatever came up in the class involved something they have been discussing or even quarrelling about, this could constitute a barrier to their sense of security and fulfillment in one another. Such anxiety would then, as we have seen, tend to cause them to need to take counsel. Most likely, a positive personal discussion with the professor after class will provide not only more detailed knowledge but also a counseling relationship. So, even though this is an educational setting, it is, in fact, also a guidance and counseling situation.

There are a variety of factors to be considered whenever we consider a relationship in which an expert is giving someone personal information. There is, first of all, the implication that this information should further the person's growth in maturity. The manner of presentation should be such that it aids the person's assimilation and use of the information. If increasing his knowledge also increases his dependency, it may only feed his infantile need of the supportive expert. For guidance to be effective, it should implement and not retard the person's maturing process. Other factors related to the nature of the relationship with the expert are the quality of faith and confidence involved in consulting an expert for guidance and personal information, and the responsibility this entails on the part of the expert. There are, moreover, a variety of instances when the expert may assume, the need to fix limits for the relationship and to judge how effective the chosen role and limits may reasonably be expected to be.

Consequently in this chapter we will discuss guidance and counseling together, exploring some of the means by which counseling can aid relationships that exist between a person seeking guidance and the expert who gives it. Even a limited counseling process may aid in the acceptance of personal information and the limits which such information may impose.

DIRECTIVES-CONTROL

More recently, the consideration of counseling has gradually become separated from the idea of guidance largely through issues involved in what came to be called "directive" counseling. The difficulty with directive counseling was not so much the directions given—this obviously is necessary on the part of any expert—as the fact that they often appeared to take away from the client his legitimate area of option and so leave the responsibility entirely with the expert, counselor or therapist. In this sense they illustrated Bakan's concept of mystery-mastery complex.

Explaining this Bakan says:

. . . the mystery-mastery complex . . . consists in the simultaneous pursuit of two objectives: (a) to keep the nature of human personality from being understood, to preserve it under a cloak of mystery; and (b) to master, or predict and control, the behavior of human beings.[1]

Later Bakan concludes:

The value of understanding of human functioning does not inhere in its application in the usual sense, but in its possession. This is one of the most significant results of the clinical enterprise. In order to help a person who is in psychological difficulties we work to enhance his understanding of himself, and of his relationships to others.[2]

We can see here a possible relationship between the traditional mathematical Cartesian model and the concept of "experts" who are to be considered masters and so are needed to "solve problems" and then give the "answers" to others who are in mystery. The main function of the latter then would be—as Kant later maintained—to follow the dictates of their "sense of duty", and its "categorical imperative", and carry out the directives given. Clearly the only requisite in this kind of model, would be the client's "good will" in doing what he is directed to do.

Summing up his discussion of contrasting viewpoints in counseling, Arbuckle concludes:

On the one hand the counselor might see his function and the purpose of his relationship much the same as would the behavioral engineer, but the significant variable would be the human relationship. His purpose would be to change the individual into some predetermined "better" pattern, and this would likely be in terms of someone else's decision as to what a member of a society should be like. . . .

On the other hand, the counselor might see the purpose of his human relationship as the enhancement of the individual, the development and the flowering of the individual as a free human being, one who is able to live the life of the human, one who does not need certainty, one who does not have to have guarantees of happiness and joy. Man would be the determiner of his direction, and the counselor would be one who would help the client, as a free individual, to accept the responsibility for his own determination of the direction his life might take.[3]

While the term "non-directive" has been in large measure discarded, it at least called attention to the difficulties involved in simply advising others and not aiding them further. Giving expert guidance to people without recognizing that this could further their own dependent and escapist tendencies would not really be helping them.

TASK-ORIENTED COUNSELING

We do not mean here to minimize the value of intellectual achievement, a learning project or other operational task as a focal point for coordinating the forces of personality in the direction of positive integration. On the contrary, this is one of the main values of the educational process or, in fact, any task that genuinely engages a person.

Later in this chapter we will consider some positive effects of counseling as an aid to hope and courage in continued successful achievement. This involves, too, the advantages of what we have called "operational counseling." In any task-oriented operation, such as learning a foreign language, one can be helped by counseling to resolve the personal conflicts that are triggered off by the difficulties of the learning process itself.

That such task-oriented activities can also facilitate psychotherapy is obvious from various forms of occupational therapy used in psychiatric treatment. The assumption however, that information or direction is all that is necessary, implies sufficient integration on the person's part to carry out the knowledge given. But in many instances the task itself, and the directions, limits and demands which the guidance imposes are so difficult and confronting that the person also needs counseling aid. It is this kind of interrelationship of counseling and guidance of which we speak here.

DEPENDENCY-RESPONSIBILITY PROCESS

The child, understandably, is proportionately dependent on an older person or an adult and so needs guidance and direction. But, this may gradually become a form of regression and infantilism when such dependency leads away from rather than toward growth in mature and responsible independence. Such a dependent client seeks to be constantly reassured and helped by proposing that the counselor answer all his questions. Guidance thoughtlessly given here only serves to reinforce this regressive infantile dependency and is therefore self-defeating for the client. Rather than leading him to the internal assimilation of the information and a genuine growth toward maturity, it may only further his parent-figure dependency.

People in this kind of dependency system are in a complicated self-defeating bind. They constantly seek information and guidance from others. But, in what may be a kind of basic self-understanding, they seem to realize that such supine dependency only holds them in childish attitudes and so they may obey the directives in such a way as to cause them to return again and be even more dependent. Often they may blame the expert when, because of their half-hearted cooperation, apparently, the information did not prove effective. Without cooperative and responsible self-direction, even the most expert and accurate knowledge received from another will usually prove ineffective and inadequate. Such people end up in the bind of going from one expert to another and being unable to profit from the advice of any of them. Counseling is obviously needed here and not simply more guidance.

In the following excerpt a person seems at first to be caught up in this inability to take any direct responsibility for himself or his situation. We notice how the counselor's responses, rather than giving more advice by answering his questions, gradually enable him to begin to take some responsibility for himself and to start a counseling process. In this way he can hope to arrive at some self-directiveness and internalization of the expert knowledge he has already received. As a result he may be able to profit maturely from this or further information that he might then fittingly be given.

Client: Well, I was down at student personnel and they were talking to me about my grades and some other things and they suggested I come up here to the psychology department and talk to somebody up here. I don't think there is anything special, I just need some advice, or something like that, uh, sort of, I don't know what courses to take and I'm having trouble with my grades and evidently I'm bright enough from these tests and so on, I know that, they told me that in high school. But I seem to have a hard time concentrating and studying and I guess I run around a little too much and things like that, so I just thought if you'd give me a little advice, tell me something to read or anything like that, that might help me out a little bit, just what do you think? What should I do?

Counselor: You're wondering about what you could do in terms of reading or whatever help you might get. You have difficulty studying. You're basically capable in terms of intelligence but you have a hard time concentrating and there are a series of distractions of that sort and you are wondering what you can do about it.

Client: Yes, I mean, I don't know what you do up here but maybe I suppose, advise students, I guess kind of tell them or kind of straighten them out. Oh, I've talked with a number of people and they all tell me, of course, to study more and not to run around so much, get more serious—I clown around quite a bit—but I don't quite know how to do that. I guess I really want to do that all right, I mean I would like to get through school but you know, tell me how do you do it, how do you just change like that, how do you become a better student?

Counselor: Other people have told you and you see this yourself in a way, that you need to spend more time with your studies and become more serious. It is clear to you and you really want to do this. The difficulty for you is just how do you do this?

Client: Yes, yes, that's it. I suppose anybody who goes to school, if they have any sense, want to pass and get good grades if they could. To tell you the truth I'm getting fed up hearing all through high school and now after a year in college, that I'm really bright and I ought to do a lot better. Well I suppose I am and I guess the more I think about it I'm getting kind of tired of hearing people tell me that and still getting low grades. Even in high school while I never flunked anything I was always on the edge of one or two courses and all I heard from the first day I talked to a teacher about my class work, I heard that I was bright and that I shouldn't get low grades like that. So I'm kind of tired of hearing it.

Counselor: You're sort of tired of having it pressured on you that you are bright and capable. You're willing to admit that it's so after all these years of emphasis, and, as I get it, you'd really like to do something about it. You'd like to start functioning more at the level of your real ability and you're fed up with always being on the edge of flunking and always having people call you in and talk to you about your low grades.

Client: Yes, I . . . that's about right, I guess, I—I *am* tired of it and I wish I could do something about it and maybe you could help me.

Counselor: Yes, it's something you'd really like to change, isn't it?

Client: It sure is!

Counselor: And you'd like to get help here to do this.

Client: That's really what I want, I guess. That's something funny about myself. I guess I've always been the kind of guy that never really lives up to what others think he ought to do. I don't know why but I guess there's something there.

Counselor: Some blocking between you're doing what others think you ought to be able to do and what you actually do.

Client: Blocking's about right, I guess. There's something odd there. I get an urge to go in the opposite direction or something.

We notice that this person has already begun to look at himself and what *he* really wants and is—in contrast to simply receiving information *about* himself from someone else. He is, as we see, beginning to take counsel with himself through the counselor and so move toward the "possession" of understanding in himself, as Bakan described.

EMOTIONAL DEFENSE-RESISTANCE

The need for personal information, even when it is not accompanied by dependency or escape from responsibility, usually finds the person in a somewhat complicated emotional state. In such a condition, people can be rather narrowed in their view and fixed on immediate solutions. They can be defensive, resistant and urged to escape if the information differs from what they expected.

In the process of receiving personal information, then, the person may become negative and hostile, particularly if the information restricts him in some way. Such relationships can, without directly intending it, also be confronting. Much of the same type of personal conflict that one experiences in any kind of limits can also be present.

A person's resistant, defensive or escapist state can become especially evident as the information begins to imply these personal restrictions and limits, or appears to be demanding some change in a person's attitudes or actions. Issues that might be clear and limits that would be readily accepted in a less involved condition can cause people in emotionally charged situations to become openly hostile and personally attacking or, alternately, to remain coldly silent and basically uncooperative and rejecting.

In such an emotionalized state, the person is apt to be focussed and constricted, and thus easily made resistant by information which, on the face of it, might appear innocuous. Consequently, for guidance to be effective, not only counseling relationships may be necessary, but a certain sensitivity peculiar to the guidance relationship itself seems necessary.

GUIDANCE-READINESS

To begin with, there should be some hope of effectiveness, evidence of a possibility at least, that the person can make constructive use of the guidance to be given. There is no point in giving information at a time when it will only make the person more resistant or discouraged. Rather, there should be some indication that the person can assimilate this guidance and act on it.

This seems best accomplished by attempting to establish a state of what might be called "guidance readiness" before any effort is made to offer such guidance. This is often achieved when there has been some counseling exchange that makes a person feel his "inner-view" and reactions are truly understood. Moreover, if one can have even a short counseling session with a person and then see him later, one can meanwhile think over and more adequately plan the information interview.

EXPERT SELF-AWARENESS AND SKILL

There are, however, certain aspects involving the expert himself that can help or hinder the acceptance and assimilation of the information he gives. Often, when a person seeks information from another whom he considers an expert, he has actually triggered off an anxiety in the expert as well as in himself. The expert may feel himself "put on the spot" without consciously realizing his anxiety.

Such anxiety can be aroused even when someone simply asks a question. As a result, the person to whom the question is directed may be quickly moved in self-defense to supply an answer. The focus here is on the expert's defending himself, rather than a recognition that the questioner may not really want an answer. He may really have "grabbed at" a question simply, in his own confusion, to say something in order to begin a relationship—somewhat as a passenger, made anxious by a lurching bus, "grabs" a strap.

We seem somehow to have inherited an image of the expert which implies that he is fraudulent if he does not immediately have an answer. This resembles the way some people used to think of the "best" physician as the one who diagnosed the patient's trouble the quickest. But quick diagnosticians are almost non-existent in medicine now. In a vast number of personal issues too, it is quite evident that no one has the answers for someone else. A person can get help, information and support from someone, but the final decisions must come ultimately from himself.

Valid information that is really pertinent to a person usually demands time to prepare or, if one finds that he lacks adequate knowledge, to consider what other resources are available and what referrals can be made. This delay can be achieved simply by saying something like: "Would you give me a little time to get some material together? Could I see you tomorrow? Perhaps now you'd like to talk for five minutes or so about yourself and your side of this?" In this way, a limited counseling relationship which may or may not continue later, has been established.

Such delaying of guidance avoids a too quick solution. It affords an opportunity to check on source material, prepare more carefully the information or directions to be given, and allows as well some time for thought on the manner of presentation. Such striving to tailor personal information to fit the person's state of "guidance readiness," will, with counseling aid, more readily enable him to accept and assimilate the guidance given.

Sometimes, however, in such a situation the person comes to the next interview, not for the guidance information but for counseling. He may appear to ignore the fact that the expert, having agreed to give guidance material, has gone to some trouble to prepare it. Frustrating as this can be, the expert has a clear clue that much as he thought this was a guidance need and prepared for it, the person is in greater immediate need for counseling understanding from him. Such a person has realized that, for the present at least, he needs to continue to think out his side. He now has seen, apparently, that this would be of more value to him than guidance information, even though he appeared to seek this in the earlier introductory meeting.

INFORMATION-GUIDANCE NEED

While people feel rejected when they are not understood, they seem also to feel rejected when the person from whom they expect a particular kind of guidance or information fails to give it to them. In research with physicians, for example, we found that when physicians delayed too long in giving the person a medical diagnosis, this actually was a source of resistance and anxiety for the patient. Obviously, this was the kind of information the patient legitimately expected, considering his feeling of insecurity and threat. Some even began to imagine various kinds of serious illness that, supposedly, the physician was afraid to tell them. People expect certain precise and determined functions, as well as definite kinds of guidance information; they can, therefore, be disappointed and feel rejected if they do not receive the response they are really seeking.

Since guidance information, too, can appear as a kind of confrontation of the person, it can have threatening tones and so produce resistance. This resistance can be directed to the person giving the guidance. This is especially true if the guidance appears to be merely a personal opinion or attitude. One way of preventing this is to present guidance information or material in a somewhat impersonal way. If possible, for example, a passage could be read from a guidance manual. Or, one might begin with: "Generally the opinion of experts in this matter seems to be . . .", or, "The regulations of the school are . . ."; "The findings of the research are . . ."; "The results of the tests seem to indicate . . ."; "Our Church teaches . . ." "Impersonal" in this sense, does not mean cold or indifferent. Rather, the intent here is to prevent the relationship from seeming to be merely a personal submission to the expert's opinion, with no other authoritative support.

Another advantage of this is that since the expert is not personally involved in this information, he can then assume the immediate or even long-time role of counselor. The person can then unfold his feelings of resistance to the information or his discouragement and fear that he cannot carry out the guidance. In this, he can feel assured of the counselor's sensitive understanding of these negative emotions. This can, even in a short period of time, make it possible for the person to begin to assimilate this material and gain confidence and courage that he can act on what he has received.

INCARNATION VS. DISGUISED CONDESCENSION

When it is also clearly evident that the expert is subject to the same authority as the person who is receiving direction, this often removes the personal sting of superiority. When both are subject to the same conditions, this makes it clearer that the expert is not merely speaking out of personal dominance or his own whims. But if a tone of either condescension or aggressive dominance is given, it is much harder for the person to control his negative emotions. He then may resist the information as a vicarious way of resisting the person giving the information.

In our later discussion of a learning research project, we will see how anger and resentment were aroused in the learner by the expert's condescension. Since the expert was aware of mistakes and the learner's foreign language handicap, it was often difficult for the expert to permit the learner to struggle to use knowledge he really had. But the learner delighted in and fought for this independence, and it aided him in his learning growth process.

In a similar way an adolescent or an adult receiving guidance may appear inadequate and dependent. Nevertheless, the person receiving guidance is still seeking to be considered an adult. While he may lack information in a particular area, or while he may be subject to others in some way, from the point of view of his position in a school or wherever it may be, he or she nonetheless remains a person striving for maturity. In handicapped people such as amputees, one sees sharply this distinction between the need for help in a particular action and yet the sensitive reaction of an adult. Any handicap invites the tendency to condescend to the handicapped person and to "baby" him. Actually, such a manner is often violently resented by the handicapped adult, who wants very much to tell us that while he may have lost his legs, he is still a grown man. Blind people, for example, contrary to the popular tendency of leading them across the street by the arm, prefer to hold the arm of the other person and so guide themselves. Similarly in the presentation of guidance information, it is important that the child or adult be left with the feeling that he is a person and is still respected by the expert. The expert must therefore consciously control this tendency to "baby," especially a child or a young person who may be in need of information, guidance or direction.

Thus, condescension, even when it appears to be supportive, can often produce resistance. Sometimes this is easily recognized. One can say to a young man, for example, "Oh, after all, Jim, you know we've all had to put up with various things and this is not unusual in going through school. We all have troubles, you know." Such a statement may arouse in the person hearing it the question: "Well, what did I come here for if I didn't hope to receive some help or information to aid me to resolve this? It does not help me simply to tell me that others have troubles or difficulties." Condescending reassurance of this sort is apt only to add to his burden the further resentment that he was treated as a child.

But condescending attitudes and needs in oneself, in the role of expert, can be difficult to uncover and not easily apparent. They can be buried in suppressed attitudes and resentment toward others. Often the expert himself may need to undergo counseling himself before he can really arrive at a sense of the meaning and value of others, reflected in a manner of presenting guidance that is suffused with this sense of the dignity and the responsibility of the client.

As we have said earlier, such condescension can also produce exaggerated dependency. The immature often feed on such a parental manner. This encourages their own regressive needs. On the other hand, such people can begin to grow more mature when they encounter someone who avoids encouraging such immaturity and who rather sets up conditions which further the person's own responsibility. There is need, therefore, for conscious regulation of unconscious urges to treat people as if they were children, simply because they happen to be in a position of seeking information or direction.

COMMITTED CONFIDENCE

The nature of guidance also implies a respect for and a faith in the expert who is giving the information or direction. This has an important consequence. Insofar as one is given valid information by such an expert, he holds confidence and faith in such direction and guidance. On the contrary, there is a serious pitfall here if a person is misdirected by someone in whom he places implicit faith. The expert's assuming a guidance role for which he is not equipped can cause a person to lose this faith. If the information presented proves inadequate or inaccurate, this often makes it difficult for a person to return and accept any further information or direction. This may even impede going to anyone else. This is the gist of the old saying, "Fool me once, shame on you; fool me twice, shame on me." We are reluctant to trust another, even when such a person should be trusted, if, in a previous experience, that person has misled us or made us feel humiliated and resistant.

Whenever the expert is expressing what is clearly a personal opinion, then, it seems best that he say so. In this way, the ordinary symbolization a client might attach to the expert's direction or information is not involved. The person has been alerted to the fact that the expert is simply presenting an opinion. This may, in fact, be a valuable opinion—one that comes from expert knowledge and experience—yet it can still be recognized as simply a personal view. This allows the person receiving such an opinion to feel free to differ with it, or at least question it, without incurring a sense of guilt. This would be especially applicable, for example, in religious guidance and similar authoritative relationships. The realization that these are simply matters of opinion, even though they be expert opinions, is often freeing for the one receiving such information or direction. It allows him to take maximum advantage of the wisdom of such opinions. At the same time he has freedom to analyze and discriminate in a way he would not if such opinions were presented with the full authority of a religious tradition or similar directive.

Sometimes it is important for the expert simply to be able to say, "I don't know." In this he is freeing himself and the other person from the mystery-mastery bind. He is saying, in effect, "There are no God-figures—I'm human too." This may, in fact, be precisely what the client needs to help him face the mystery of himself and to learn to live with his own mystery as well as that of others. This could be a maturing process for him.

EXPERIENCED EXPERT

One can be an expert by training, knowledge and study. One can also be an expert as a result of experience. This suggests the knowledge and experience of the mountain "guide" who has passed many times over the same dangerous climbs. This kind of wise, experienced guide is a demonstration of the phrase, "What you are shouts so loud I cannot hear what you say." Since he stands for what he really is, such a person is especially valuable to those less experienced, not only because he is trusted to give helpful information and direction, but also as one holding up a realistic ideal with which they can genuinely identify themselves. They are able to have confidence through him that they themselves can attain a similar goal.

One difficulty in "experience guidance," however, is the tendency to write a romance of the past. Since "distance lends enchantment," actual experiences can often become part of an autobiographical fiction. After incidents have been retold a number of times, it may be difficult to separate what is imaginary from what really happened. If this is simply interesting story-telling, it does not matter. But when one is drawing from one's experience as an expert to give guidance to others, such romanticizing may in fact prove misleading. Consequently, while the experienced guide has valuable wisdom and knowledge to offer, it is important that he carefully delineate the facts and the situation as they really were— being aware of the tendency to change, distort, or exaggerate when he is recounting personal experiences. Careful and objective self-criticism is necessary here to distinguish fact from fiction.

The effectiveness of such guidance can be furthered by what might be called a "smorgasbord" method or presentation. People seem in a better position to assimilate personal material if they are left free to accept or reject the conclusions of these experiences. Time does, in fact, change the value of an experience, opinion or judgment. Aquinas uses the expression, "As long as a man sits, he is sitting." By this he means to point out that as long as conditions and circumstances remain basically the same, then the value of the experience and the counsel resolutions would still hold. It is only when the same sort of conditions still exist, that the experienced expert's opinions and reminiscences are of value. Communicating experiences with the circumstances of the past honestly detailed, better allows persons hearing them to make their own applications in the present.

EN-COURAGEMENT

An important contribution of the experienced expert is that of giving encouragement. Encouragement is not courage. Courage seems to come rather from the person's taking counsel with himself. Courage mounts much as bricks put together make a wall or a building. By deciding something and then carrying it out, successfully and repeatedly, one builds up inner strength. With each new achievement there is an increase of courage and confidence to continue. The word encouragement, however, suggests that it comes from another. This is not at all the same as flattery. Flattery would be dishonest praise, which, like a false coin, is ultimately valueless if not self-defeating. Real encouragement strives to be honest so that the one receiving it can rely on it. Such encouragement is of particular help at the insecure and hesitant stages in the beginning of a function or process, where the performer genuinely needs the reassurance of an experienced observer to continue and improve performance.

Helpful as encouragement can be, it is also easy to forget to give it—particularly if the expert is seeing a number of people each day. One can fail to realize that, for each person, the interview has been a unique experience. Understandably, the expert, from his side, may see only a brief relationship with another—one of many people he must see that week. This does not change the effect the meeting has for each one seen. Here especially it is important for the expert, or person in any role of prestige or authority, to remind himself to encourage each one, if such encouragement can be validly given. This can significantly further the recipient's confidence and courage to continue. A difficult and hard chore can be lightened by such understanding and encouragement.

THE IMPORTANCE OF HOPE

The fact that such encouragement runs the risk of transference and dependency must be considered and recognized, but it should not cause the neglect of the positive effects of encouragement. It is one

of the fundamental ways by which a person is helped to grow into
an achieving and responsible adult. It aids learning and is one of
the main sources of hope.

In focussing on counseling as related to anxiety and conflict, we
may overlook the fact that a counseling relationship can also result
from hope. There is, in fact, an interesting cultural background to
our modern concept of hope. Menninger shows how the Greeks
fatalistically considered hope an evil.[4] whereas the Old and New
Testaments made it that central positive force which our culture
now sees.

What, then, is the modern notion about hope? Are we Greeks or are
we Jews? Or do we ignore hope altogether? Our shelves hold many
books on the place of *faith* in science and psychiatry, and on the
vicissitudes of man's efforts to *love* and to be loved. But when it comes
to hope, our shelves are nearly empty, and our scientific journals are
silent. The Encyclopaedia Britannica devotes many columns to the
topic of love, and many more to faith. But poor little hope! She is not
even listed!

The cupboard is not entirely bare. Much has been written by Chris-
tians on hope and on Messianic hope. Hope still plays a prominent role
in Judaism, dramatized by the Nazi holocaust on the one hand and the
Israeli triumph on the other. We are using the word "hope" in a
broader sense, describing less an aspect of religious faith than the
character of a certain mental set. What is the scientific view of
hope?

In his three-volume examination of psychoanalytic treatment
Thomas French deals extensively with hope as the activating force of
the ego's integrative function. He believes that hope is an essential part
of the recovery drive: "Hope is based on present opportunity and on
memories of recent success."[5]

After giving detailed accounts of the therapeutic importance of
hope not only in psychiatric but in all medical care, Menninger
points out its neglect in some scientific circles. The Cartesian
mathematical prediction hypothesis, if accepted literally, would
leave no room for hope.

Richter comments on the data of death in humans that seem to

result from hopelessness and the similarity of research on the
death of rats in hopeless experimental situations:

This sudden-death phenomenon may however be considered also as a
reaction at a much higher level of integration. The situation of these
rats is not one that can be resolved by either fight or flight—it is rather
one of hopelessness: being restrained in the hand or in the swimming
jar with no chance of escape is a situation against which the rat has no
defense. Actually, such a reaction of apparent hopelessness is shown
by some wild rats very soon after being grasped in the hand and
prevented from moving. They seem literally to give up.
   Interesting evidence showing that the phenomenon of sudden death
may depend on emotional reactions to restraint or confinement in glass
jars comes from the observation that after elimination of the hopelessness the rats do not die. On several occasions we have immersed rats in
water and promptly removed them. The animals quickly learned that
the situation was not actually hopeless and so became aggressive and
tried to free themselves or escape and showed no signs of giving up.
Such conditioned rats swam on the average of 40 to 60 hours or more.
Once freed from restraint in the hand or confinement in the glass jar,
speed of recovery is remarkable. A rat that would quite certainly have
died in another minute or two becomes normally active and aggressive
in only a few minutes.[6]

   Marcel, moreover, has developed in detail the sense of abandonment to the other and to mystery which hope implies.[7] Encouragement can be the beginning of this positive hopeful state,
when a person proposes to himself that he can really achieve this
previously inconceivable goal. Basically, it is the encouraging convalidation of someone he trusts, respects and who he feels has adequate knowledge which often leads a person to begin to hope for a
particular achievement, goal or relationship.

POSITIVE COUNSELING

In this sense, hope can be a source of counseling because—being
hopeful and encouraged—a person may then begin to take counsel
about how he might achieve his desired goal. Counseling inter-

views can be just as constructive in this positive sense, if not more so, as in resolving confusions and conflicts.

From this positive view of counseling, many relationships might be reconsidered, such as pre-marital guidance and counseling. People may undergo a counseling process, for example, not because they are in conflict but because they are encouraged and hopeful, and wish to make the most creative use of their married life together. In our focus on personal "problems" as the reason for counseling, we have neglected these constructive and significant aspects of the counseling potential. Counseling, from this viewpoint, needs to be seen positively in relation to encouragement and hope, not simply negatively, as a means of resolving confusion and conflict.

The following excerpt from an interview with a woman married two years, demonstrates the effects that such a pre-marital counseling relationship has produced. It seems evident to this person that without the constructive gains in knowledge of herself and her husband which she acquired from *this positive kind of counseling* before marriage, their relationship would have been less fulfilling and supportive:

Client: I think your phrase of his being sure about me is good because he's sure about me, but then he's also sure about himself. I think that probably more than he could ever have been by himself. I think through me he has gained a kind of, well, self-confidence, or independence, that I don't think he could have gotten otherwise.

Counselor: So, because you've been treating him in an open, accepting way, that is to say, you've been opening yourself up to him, and because this manner of his hasn't made you resist him since you've had ways of understanding him, and accepting him in it, this in turn has opened him up more and enabled him to be more confident in himself. If I understand you, he sees himself succeeding with you, so to speak, whereas he might have otherwise failed.

Client: Yes, he certainly does see himself succeeding with me in that sense, it's as though we're quite different and yet not so much, you know, as though in our limited way we can relate to one another in a sincere way, and I think in a trustful way, too. At least I think that without the counseling relationship that I had I am sure that this would not be, I am sure that we might not even be together now . . . uh, because of my tyrannical way, I think, and his passivity and . . . uh, and now that I look back at two years, it's amazing that it has worked so well, and never either of us feeling undignified.

Here we see an example of how the repeated experience of openness and transparency in individual and group pre-marital counseling sessions, has made it possible for this person to arrive at the same openness and trust in herself and her husband in their marriage. Similarly, experiencing this from her, her husband, in her view, is also more sure and at ease with himself and her.

Client: At least I'm not afraid to be aggressive or to make a decision when I have to, and I don't blame him if he can't, you know, make the decision sometimes, or if he's too passive about it. I can accept this more readily I think. I'm not afraid of being aggressive when it seems sensible to be so, and to make the decision when it seems I should.

Counselor: Yes, a real acceptance of yourself as you really are, the more aggressive and the more decisive of the two, yet there's a real acceptance of him as he is in his passivity and hesitancy, and, uh, you see a real dignity between you in this, in contrast to what might have been just a tyrannical domination of him if you had not taken this much more respectful attitude toward yourself and him. You're both more truly really yourselves, and respectful of one another. . . . We have about a minute or so in our time.

Client: Yes, I, uh, I think the result of this is because I respect myself more that I can respect him more, and because I can respect what I am, whatever it may be, and be at ease in it, and accept that I can be respectful of him and whatever he is, not try to change him or anything, but just accept him.

Counselor: The core of this is, as you see it now, a genuine respect for yourself, a genuine acceptance and appreciation of what you are, not trying to change falsely views of yourself, and correspondingly a genuine regard and respect for him as he is, not trying to make him something else.

The issue of mutual respect which is basic particularly to early marriage relationships, is here highlighted. Having acquired respect for herself, she has conveyed this to her young husband. This is in sharp contrast to what might have happened. Her aggression and his passivity might have triggered them both into increasingly greater distance from one another and simply reinforced these differences. Had this happened, their marriage might have already been in serious difficulty in her view. What has actually happened was a respectful and mutual acceptance of one another.

COUNSELING REFERRAL

Another related situation here is what might be called a counseling referral. It is a sustaining counseling relationship shared with another expert or counselor until the person has gained confidence in, and is at ease with, the new relationship.

Simply telling a person he "should go to see . . ." is often ineffective and even rejecting. It can seem like a "brush-off." A person who has taken the risk of communicating himself once at an intimate level is often too insecure and threatened to readily try it again. So a simple referral to someone else rarely works. A more sustaining and supportive relationship is necessary with the person in whom he has originally placed his confidence.

This can be accomplished by a joint session with the other expert or counselor. The session begins with the new expert or counselor in an observer role. But gradually the relationship moves over to him as he begins to respond. The original counselor then recedes into the role of observer.

Gradually, rapport is built up with the new expert or counselor. This can happen in one interview. Given a choice, the person may say he is now secure with the new counselor. If more than one interview is necessary, this three-way relationship can be maintained as long as the person needs it.

This supportive counseling position can be especially effective for the religious pastoral counselor. Here, particularly, people are often strengthened in their therapy with a psychiatrist or psychologist when they have, sharing their sessions, the presence of the pastoral counselor who made the referral.

In the case of expert information, such as the results of medical examinations or psychological tests, the counselor's presence and skill can aid the person to a constructive use of this new and perhaps threatening information.

Much greater and more effective use could be made of this kind of "team" relationship—for example with the pastoral counselor, in the case of serious illness or incurable disease, as against leaving the person with no counseling or personal resource.[8] But it also could help many other people profit by referrals. They would feel supported and strengthened rather than feeling, as they so often do, that the person making the referral was merely uninterested and "didn't want to be bothered."

AUTHORITY FIGURE

The function of giving personal information can be especially complicated for a person in a position of authority. Here the difficulties may be compounded by the fact that the information may impose direct and even painful limits on the other person's conduct. In such a situation, it is important that the person in authority have a positive and constructive self-image. We have discussed the importance of the self-image in the counseling process. It is also important in authority guidance. A person's image of himself can be a basic factor in the way he carries out his authority functions. If he sees himself in a constructive light and is convinced that his function is truly helpful to others, he has a greater chance of being really helpful. But if he sees his position in a negative and distasteful light, he can communicate this by often appearing to be uninterested, inconsiderate, or even harsh at times. Our image of ourselves as the model of the way we treat others, applies here too. Consequently, if a person is at peace with his own self-image, he has a good chance of communicating this peacefulness to the atmosphere which surrounds him.

By this phrase, "at peace with his own self-image," we do not mean taking delight in dominating others. In our culture this is an ugly stereotype of those in authority. The fear of being considered domineering could make one uncomfortable and ill-at-ease in his authority position.

It is difficult to trace the source of these various negative images of authority in our society. One possible source would be the image of "the Prussian" after World War I and of Hitler, later. This image may have become somewhat generally associated with people in authority. It may also be tied up with an exaggerated notion of "freedom," which regards all authority as oppressive. In any event, such a negative stereotype is the exact opposite of that Western cultural tradition which envisages that the person in authority represents "reasonableness." He is seen as a valuable and constructive aid in helping another person achieve what that person really wants. Anyone in authority functions best if he sees himself in this constructive light—as helping and benefitting others rather than as a deterrent to freedom and happiness.

We do not mean here that the person in authority should expect to be popular. This can bring disappointment and may end only in making him or her feel rejected and bitter. Rather, there must be a genuine acceptance of the burden of authority. But by trusting to the other person's capacity for reasonable acceptance of such authority as a basic benefit to himself, one is, in fact, genuinely respecting oneself and the other.

IMPOSITION OF AUTHORITY

In observing the training of traffic policemen some years ago, it was interesting to note that in a certain state, a traffic officer was trained to treat the driver with extreme courtesy, even when he was giving him a traffic ticket. The policeman was reminded that as a taxpayer, the driver was, in fact, his employer, and that the citizen's violation of a traffic law was in no sense a justification for humiliating him or treating him as an inferior. In other words, the driver remained an adult worthy of the policeman's polite consideration. Another point stressed in the training was that, when explaining the traffic ticket for speeding, for example, he should place emphasis on his role of saving the driver from a serious accident. That is to say, the policeman presented himself in the light of an authority cooperating to promote the safety and welfare of the driver himself, as of the other citizens on the highway.

This training reveals certain psychological awareness that apply to the imposition of any authority. A child or adult does not lose his claim to be respected simply because he has broken a regulation. And further, the fact that one is commissioned by the state, as a policeman, or by a school system as a teacher or counselor, does not imply that there is a personal affront involved in a violation. On the contrary, it rather implies that the role of authority is one of cooperation in promoting what the person himself also really wants, which is to drive safely and to return home safely and not end in a hospital.

Many regulations, moreover, are simply practical solutions with a variety of interpretations. These can sometimes be reasonably at variance. A person in authority who tends to identify himself with the regulation will often make even a minor violation appear to be a rejection of himself. Involvement like this, rather than furthering the observance of subsequent regulations, seems only to confuse personal insult with the minor violation. Rather than conform, a person may be urged to repeat the violation out of resentment, as a symbolic protest against the undignified and affronting encounter with the person in authority.

Attributing motives or implying reasons why a person has broken a particular regulation may cause further negative complications. A student, for example, might readily have accepted a teacher's report that he or she broke a rule. But when, in addition to the report, the teacher or others attribute motives that are untrue, this condition may add a greater burden to the relationship and color it with a negativism that it would not otherwise have had.

UNDERSTANDING EXCHANGE

When a person has had a chance to make clear the cause of a violation, it may become reasonable. Explanations, though, are not always reasonable. Often they are defensive reactions. Such a series of rationalizations and self-justifications may not square with the facts. Here a counseling relationship seems a better way of helping the person work through his own self-justification to a more constructive and cooperative attitude about the regulation and the necessity of following it in the future.

If one simply says, for example: "The teacher who is in charge of this has reported. . . ." and then stops, the other person has now the responsibility of reacting in some way. This may arouse defenses, and he may at first give voice to these defenses. But assuming that the observation was true, one is often already in the midst of a deep interior struggle. The person now can be helped by counseling—even if it is only for five minutes—to renew his desire to submit to the other regulations to which as a high school or college student he has committed himself, and to face the personal weakness that caused him to break this regulation. This kind of understanding communication does not diminish the importance of the regulation or question the accuracy of the observer's report, but at the same time, it gives the person an opportunity to reexamine and reevaluate his own motivational pattern. It may lead to a series of counseling interviews.

A position of authority, therefore, need not be concerned only with carrying out rules or depend mainly on fear and punishment. It may, through the aid of a counseling relationship, become a constructive growth process. This can result in better and more cooperative behavior. But, even more importantly, it can be the occasion of a new emergent of self-awareness and positive self-regard. This, in turn, seems the most adequate way of assuring some kind of stable and consistent respect and regard for the rights of others. And such a positive attitude, in a democratic society, constitutes the core reason for supporting law and order.

This leads us to a direct consideration of how limits on one's actions are a part of the maturing process. Controls, coming at first from others, must be internalized if a person is to be genuinely self-directive. But such self-control and self-limitation is not easily come by. We will therefore consider and illustrate in the next chapter some further complexities in this process of the maturity and therapy of limits.

NOTES

[1] Bakan, "The Mystery-Mastery Complex in Contemporary Psychology," *The American Psychologist,* March 1965, 20 (3), p. 186.

[2] *Ibid.,* p. 191.

[3] Dugald S. Arbuckle, "Kinds of Counseling: Meaningful or Meaningless," *Journal of Counseling Pschology,* 14 (3), 1967, p. 224.

[4] Menninger, *The Vital Balance,* pp. 381–382.

[5] T. M. French, *The Integration of Behavior,* Chicago: University of Chicago Press, 1952, as quoted in Menninger, *ibid.,* p. 382.

[6] C. F. Richter, "Sudden Death Phenomenon in Animals and Humans," *The Meaning of Death,* ed. Herman Feifel, New York: McGraw Hill, 1959, pp. 308–309. Used by permission of McGraw-Hill Book Company.

[7] Gabriel Marcel, *Homo Viator: Introduction to a Metaphysics of Hope,* New York: Harper, 1962.

[8] *The Meaning of Death,* ed. Herman Feifel, New York: McGraw-Hill, 1959, pp. 308–309.

10

The Maturity and Therapy of Limits

ANY PERSONAL CHANGE brought about through counseling therapy or by any other means includes the imposition of self-limits. The process of therapy involves the gradual restricting of oneself in regard to immediate but misleading satisfactions, and guiding oneself to longer and more adequately fulfilling goals. The ability to impose limits on oneself and to conform oneself to these limits is basic to this process, as to any process of maturity.

Life, somewhat like the white lines and open spaces marking the dimensions of a playing field, is both freedom and limits. Limits at times have to be invoked in life as in a game, making the ensuing encounter sometimes both difficult and painful. But this is, in itself, a process of maturing. This maturity and therapy of limits, therefore, also relates counseling and psychotherapy to values. The invoking of such limits can be evidence of a genuine relationship of caring for another. In treating "fraternal correction," Aquinas, for example, following an ancient tradition, considers this a part of love. Shakespeare conveys this unaltering and sometimes confronting quality of love:

> Love is not love
> Which alters when it alteration finds,
> Or bends with the remover to remove[1]

It is quite evident too that values are not only accepting and reassuring but also confronting. In this sense values often do not bring "peace but the sword." Peace of mind, however expressed, is not secure and fixed like the peace of the dead. It is rather an intensely living peace that comes only after risk, pain, struggle and conflict. It is a peace made possible only by deep self-investment. It must, in our terms, result from the fulfillment of personal value.

GROUP PROCESS

Until now, for the most part, we have concentrated on the relationship of two people in counseling therapy. We have also been exploring ways in which this relationship might be used as a model from which to pattern other kinds of authentic involvements. But there is increasing emphasis now on group therapy and the general advantages of the dynamic process that the group itself creates for each member. There are, of course, many similarities and a number of significant differences between group and individual counseling therapy. We will subsequently consider these in some detail. At the moment, our particular concern is the manner in which the presence of even one other, as in marriage counseling, or of a group of people, involves each one in what is sometimes the difficult process of recognizing the limits of oneself and the unique existence of the other.

As we shall see, one of the advantages of any type of group process, such as marriage counseling, group therapy or discussion, or a counseling-model kind of learning, is this very presence of others. For it directly imposes limits on each one. Such consciousness of the limits of the self and the rights of others is perhaps the central dynamism of group experience, and one of its most constructive potentials for facilitating mature growth in each.

LIFE CONFRONTATIONS

People usually come for individual counseling only after some form of difficult and conflicting self-awareness has penetrated them. Life is, in this sense, already threatening them, i.e., they are getting poor grades, they are in danger of losing their wife or husband; their job is in jeopardy, their children are failing in school, etc. In other words, they are already faced with certain issues which they must resolve. The client, then, is often painfully aware of the need for help. Such life confrontations are important in initiating counseling.

In psychotherapy, too, some kind of therapy of limits is usually necessary. Mayman comments:

A permissive atmosphere and a sincere respect for the worth of the individual are essential ingredients of good psychotherapy, but there are times when the most respectful and accepting thing to do for a sick person is to insist on his being confined to a closed ward, or put to work in a full activity program, or treated with a variety of more subtle therapeutic modes. One needs more than kindness and good will to be an effective therapist. . . . We must know how to bring to bear our knowledge and skills in such a way as to help the person come to grips with his intrinsic resistance to growth and change in a delicate art.[2]

This "delicate art" of a therapy of limits needs more exploration and research if we are to know how to make it most effective. We are only beginning to understand how to present confronting knowledge in a constructive way. Unless this is done with sensitivity and skill, it so threatens a person that either he defensively withdraws and closes himself off from change, or he attacks and resists in hostility and rebellion. In neither state is he able to acquire that self-awareness of the need for new knowledge and change which would further personal learning, counseling or psychotherapy. He must be helped to "come to grips with his intrinsic resistance to growth" which his conflict with limits involves.

MATURITY: SELF-INVOKED LIMITS

One necessary aspect of the developmental process as a person grows from infancy to adulthood, is, then, a corresponding growth in this sense of, and ability to relate to, limits. As we have seen, any loving act of giving oneself to another is only possible when one has arrived at a sufficient degree of knowledge of oneself and of the area of oneself and of the other. This must be combined with the capacity to limit oneself, and thus give independent meaning and value to the other.

This growth away from narcissism can be demonstrated by the way any expert performance, even in sports, finally demands careful conformity to limits, i.e., self-discipline and control. Maturity, in this sense, is to the whole of life what conforming to the rules is to a sport: a highly developed particular skill. The process of maturity is revealed in the child's development through the social activity of play, as he grows in the ability to internalize limits and controls.

In their demand for disciplined skill in conformity to complex rules, sports have something in common with every fine human performance. This applies to any truly artistic work as well. In this sense, such activities are models of this aspect of the maturing process.

St. Paul used athletics as a type for religious dedication. When the rigorous self-discipline demonstrated in running, boxing or other athletic performance is carried to a higher level, the same psychological principles of maturity are involved. Value and achievement are proportionate to the way the limits in a performance force us to demonstrate a high degree of ability and self-control. Skill consists, then, in both conformity to these limits and in the ability to overcome the inherent difficulties of the game or task.

There is, then, an ascending scale of self-commitment, from the self-centered child who refuses to participate, to the point in self-understanding where one finally desires to give himself to a task or game and to others in a maturity of limits. This involves a complex self-operation that is finally a disciplined and artistic gift of self.

LEARNING CONFRONTATION

Later we will examine some of the subtleties and complexities of a learning experience when it incorporates doing as well as knowing. Learning that engages a person in self-investment and action can be difficult and frustrating even when, intellectually, one knows what one ought to do and wants to do it. Genuine learning implies a similar kind of painful confrontation with the self and the imposing of limits before it reaches any fulfillment.

An old folklore expression says that, "He who does not know that he does not know, is unteachable." To be teachable, the learner must at least "know that he does not know." This usually requires a process of self-confrontation and self-awareness.

But often before the person faces himself and what he does not know, and so becomes teachable, others must somehow show this to him. And when a person is the object of such a confrontation, his defenses are apt to be aroused. He may feel indignant. His basic self-esteem may be threatened. In this defensive state, he can close himself off and so resist the knowledge and self-awareness he needs.

In the light of relating this kind of self-confrontation to learning—in the sense that the learner needs really to accept that he does not know if he is genuinely to learn—one recognizes a special significance in the word "discipline." This word which now tends to connote limits and confrontation, originally referred to that which is learned. As such it makes a person who learns, a "disciple." Interestingly too, the words "docile" and "docility", which now suggest a passive submissiveness, originally meant, "teachable"—an essential prerequisite for learning. This quality is not simple passivity but an active reaching out and grasping of the matter of learning.

In a direct learning experience, e.g., learning a foreign language, the limits, with their confronting and disciplining effect on the learner, are evident. He must adapt his ear, tongue, eye and comprehension to words and grammar that are not only strange but very uncomfortable. Here the nature of the learning process itself makes this confrontation and invokes its own necessary limits, restrictions and demands.

AGENT OF LIMITS

In many personal relationships, however, the other person often becomes the agent who imposes limits. In so doing, whether as teacher, supervisor, superior, etc., he often attracts to himself the hostility, resentment and negation the other person has towards the invoked limits. The person thus restricted usually feels personally affronted and transfers his conflicting feelings to the other person. A complicated and painful emotional impasse can arise.

A counselor's awareness, as we have seen, can help by understanding the painful state of the person, thus assisting him to begin to look at himself more constructively. Rather than simply increasing his resentment and resistance against the one voicing the limits and restrictions, counseling responses can aid a person to begin to distinguish his negative reaction and conflict from the person who is, in fact, only the occasion and voice of necessary limits.

SIMULATED EXPERIENCE

In the following recorded excerpt, we present a simulated confronting experience, with comments upon what occurs. In so doing, we can gather some clues through which the delicate art of the invoking of limits can be observed.

The main point illustrated here is the manner in which the person invoking limits is also a counselor who understands the pain limits can cause and the need for release and negation. We see this happening in the process which the invoking of limits initiates. To say something finally constructive to a person about his excess anger and his lack of cooperation is a complex and difficult task. Yet this can happen with the help of counseling awareness. The following involves such a situation—in this case a simulated interview between a school superintendent and teacher (Bill), both men.

The term "simulation" here describes a technique like that by which astronauts are trained to "simulate" the actual experience they are later to encounter in the atmosphere. (The psychological simulation process through which people *experience* what is being discussed theoretically, can frequently be helpful not only in the training of counselors and therapists but in teaching generally, by illustrating, with taped recordings and commentary, what is being analyzed.) It has many advantages. Different ways of reacting can be contrasted and compared. The people simulating the confronting experience can then be asked to comment on their reactions in a way not otherwise possible. As we shall see (below), their feelings are quite real and their reactions similar to those of persons in a non-simulated encounter. In this way, too, contrasting procedures can be tried, with the advantage of comparing the corresponding reactions.

Superintendent: I just want to talk to you for a short time, Bill, maybe ten minutes or so—I know you have to get to class. But I wonder if we might not think about something. I suppose this is not entirely new to you, but I feel that I should bring it to your attention and I suppose honestly compliment you by saying it to you directly. This has been said to me a number of times and I want to honestly say it to you.

There are real difficulties in your classes, Bill. I suppose you probably know this, but the director of studies is worried about the fits of anger that you have. Now, we all get angry. You know I do and everyone else does, but he feels from the remarks of the students and even more seriously from the complaints of some of the parents that these are more complicated situations; and he feels maybe that if you knew this and understood this you might be able to do something about it.

This lines up, Bill, with a number of other things and I thought I might just more or less present them all to you. Some of the teachers think that you just avoid them, that you don't really care to work with them on committees and so forth. You know we've been trying ways of the faculty working together in teams and committees on particular projects. They feel you're uncooperative. They feel this very strongly—and that's my reason for saying it to you. Some actually feel hurt by this and they wonder what's the matter, why you seem, in their view, to avoid them so much.

Now I suppose that another thing that interrelates with this is that there is a general report—and I've seen this myself—that you are seldom at any of the faculty meetings or the weekly committees. I know there are reasons for missing and I appreciate that you have work to prepare, and other things that can justify this. Our general feeling, however, is that if something is calling a teacher away continually and constantly from faculty and committee meetings it should be brought up. My view is, and I'm sure you've heard me say it repeatedly, that a teacher should be freed from tasks which continually keep him away from faculty and committee meetings.

So I think that in bringing this up to you directly, Bill, I'm complimenting you, honestly. I know that you will understand this in the way that I mean it. I want to bring this to your attention and give you a chance to think about it and to do something about it. (Pause) Well, do you want to comment on any of this, Bill?

Bill: I get the worse classes in this school, and then I do my best to try to teach them. I get these lugs and I try to discipline them and I try to do what their parents should do for them and what do I get for it—complaints, teachers talk about me behind my back, they even make snide remarks when I'm around and they wonder why I don't stay around them, why I go off, they talk about me not being around for meetings. I don't feel like being around. I just know they're all thinking: "Look at him, what a lousy teacher, why doesn't he do his work, why does he have to be a problem to us, why do I have to follow him into the class?" I just don't get any satisfaction out of going to a meeting with an atmosphere of hostility like that. Everybody blames me. You never hear a kind word around here. You call me in and say you're being complimentary to me by telling me this. I don't exactly feel that you are being complimentary if it's a case that you've been forced into this by the others, with them on your back, there is no other way out. You either have to say this to me or have them on your back all the time. I guess you just had to have it out, I don't feel very complimented at all . . .

Superintendent: What I get Bill is a feeling of hurt that, first of all, my statement of honest respect for you isn't true. You think I'm doing this because I was forced into this by the others. You're hurt because you feel you are really acting as a disciplinarian for these boys, trying to give them a sense of order, and its all backfiring and you're being criticized and rejected by them. This is why you don't feel like going to meetings or really being around them very much. You feel hurt by this because in your own mind you're doing a good job in your struggle to discipline these boys and bring some order into their lives.

Bill: Not exactly. I don't really feel I'm doing a good job. I really think that I'm failing in this, that I'm trying but that the results are usually bad. This makes it worse. If I felt that I were doing a good job, I wouldn't care what these guys thought. I feel I'm doing a lousy job, and they know it's lousy. They say it, and this is what hurts.

Superintendent: What is really hurtful, so painful, is that you're really trying very hard, but not succeeding. You have a sense of failure in this whole thing, and the criticism of the group just mounts your sense of failure. You know what you're trying to do, but you're pretty convinced it's not coming off. They're only mounting your own sense of failure and criticism of yourself. Does that catch it better?*

Bill: Yes, I think that's more the idea. One keeps trying, and one just seems to be going in sort of a vicious circle. I guess it's just a case that I just don't know how to solve this problem. I just don't know which way to turn. I try everything I hear about how to handle a class and I think I prepare my lessons and I think I've got the right approaches to the boys and I just don't get the right reaction. I go into class and I feel that they're waiting there, just waiting for a chance to do something to get my goat. Then I pass a teacher in the corridor and he looks away, as if to say "You, why are you around here, anyway?" So in the next class I'm madder than I was in the previous one, and things go from bad to worse, day after day.

Superintendent: Yes, we both have to get to class in a minute or two. You're discouraged in this, aren't you? And you're at the point of being very low, hopeless; this is mounted by the feeling of the students in the class towards you. They're very negative. You feel the teachers are too, so you're surrounded by discouragement. I might suggest, Bill, that perhaps we can talk about it again next week. Are you free on Monday usually, after lunch?

Bill: I have one class after lunch, and then my time is free.

Superintendent: Well, why don't I set it up for, say from 2:00 to about 2:30? I'll be free next Monday at this time and I'll be here. We'll then have more time to talk this over together.

CONSTRUCTIVE PROCESS

The following comments, in answer to questions, were then made by the person in the teacher's position.

Question: What was your reaction to the overall experience?

Bill: I got some of this bad feeling out of me, simmering down toward the end. I had worked up a good mad, and it gradually tapered off, whereas you kept very calm about the whole thing.

---

* We notice the clear re-tailoring of the response so that it includes Bill's sense of failure.

Question: What would you say helped you to disperse your negative feelings? What helped you to become less angry and less defensive?

Bill: Well, I think when you took that accepting attitude there, by stating, "Well, you feel that all of this tends to increase your feeling of frustration and your isolation," and so on, and I sort-a said to myself, "Well, I guess this is true." About that time I felt a relaxing of the tensions.

Question: Would you have come the following Monday?

Bill: Yes, I guess I would have. I was admitting that there is a problem here and I needed help with it.

What we have here is the simulation of an encounter painful for both persons—an encounter that understandably might be put off as long as possible—much as we may tend to delay going to a dentist. The information, as we would expect, made the person both angry and defensive. One might even say that a person has a right to anger and defense in such a situation. The other person here recognized this and, instead of being defensive in return, tried to understand in a counseling way.

One notices that once the anger was understood, expressions of discouragement quickly emerged. The person no longer appeared hostile and defensive but now seemed a lonely and discouraged man, and seen in this way, he was more appealing. With the relaxing of his tension, he seemed to be able to face his inadequacy better and to resolve to talk it over on another occasion.

Two key counseling responses were fundamental here—the one accepting the person's anger and resentment, and the other expressing concern for his discouragement and loneliness. One can see how much easier it might have been for the principal to give in to his own needs for self-justification and defense, but this would likely have only produced greater hostility and resistance in return. Little cooperation would then be possible.

DEFENSIVE ENCOUNTER

We see this happen in the following. Because the superintendent reacts defensively, a different series of emotions are experienced

and both parties continue to be negative. Bill, as teacher, responds
to the superintendent's initial list of complaints against him:

You've got me pretty well pegged. You've got all the information.
According to you, I'm no good in class; I'm not around for meetings—
I can't stand to be around them, that's why. Nobody hardly ever talks
to me but everybody is talking about me behind my back. You want to
know why I don't come to meetings? This is supposed to be a teaching
community. I'm supposed to go there feeling I'm part of the community. But I don't feel any of the satisfaction that's supposed to come
from going to these meetings.

Superintendent: Well, now, that's one way of seeing it, but to me, it's
not a matter of having you pegged. That's not the point. After all, it's
my job here to do what I'm trying to do, and if you had this job you'd
be doing the same thing. I'm just attempting to present to you what has
been presented to me. Some of it I must truthfully say I don't know.
Some of it I do know but it's not a matter of pegging you. No, it's a
sincere effort on my part and I think, well I think we have a good
faculty and a good school. Really I don't think they're as bad as you
feel they are.

Bill: You say it's a sincere attempt on your part to—I suppose, the
implication is, to help me out. But they're all after me. They've just
pushed you. They said to you, "You've got to talk to him," and you
know, really, that unless you talk to me, unless you face me with this,
you're not going to be able to get along with them. They've just pushed
you into this. You're really not too much interested in me.

Superintendent: Well, you know I said that we just had a few minutes
here, Bill, and I'm very conscious of the time. Well, you see it your
way and that's the way it is. But, if I may say so, Bill, that is the
trouble. You always see things just your way. That's the point with
many of these other teachers. You say that they don't speak to you in
the corridor. They tell me that they've tried to say this to you fifty
times and you won't listen. You see it's the same thing. Now, I've tried
to say it to you but we just don't seem to be communicating at all.

This discussion seems to get nowhere except to make each person more defensive and confirmed in his original position. There is
no "moving forward," as there was in the previous encounter.

Rather, the teacher seems only to have been made more negative. The following comment was made by the person in the simulated role of Bill:

My reaction would not have been that I was placated or anything else. It was, "Yeah, that's right. Sure you've judged me, my reasons and so forth. You don't give me a chance when right away you say—'You're making this up or you're imagining it.' " I simply could notice the difference that I wouldn't be seeing my problem at all, or moving forward with it. Certainly I would not have had the diminution of anger that was typical of the previous experience. Instead I would have probably gotten madder because you were attacking me further.

TRANSPARENCY

Another situation in which such confrontation can occur is when the spontaneous expression of feelings of one person involves others. Rogers speaks of "transparency" as that quality of a relationship through which the counselor can express emotions or attitudes that he feels may impede genuinity and communication. We can have this also in a group either with the leader or between group members. It can contain the same type of spontaneous transparency.

Having examined contrasting reactions in a simulated encounter of limits, we can now consider recorded comments on a real situation where conflicting feelings involving others were openly communicated. In this instance, two persons came late and their entrance so disturbed the speaker in a psychological seminar, that he got confused and blocked. He openly expressed his conflict and disturbance—not as directed hostility toward the two late-comers, but simply to release his negative emotional block. He then was able to continue his presentation.

The leader's presentation has just begun. It is to take ten minutes. He is concentrated on the sense of isolation experienced, in the Scriptural parable, by the Prodigal Son, and the way it symbolizes the alienation of man. The couple coming late have to interrupt, with a shifting of chairs and confusion, in order to find seats. The leader had to stop his presentation and find seats for

them. As he tries to start again, he has lost his thought, and with it
the involvement and intensity of the relationship that he had with
the group before the two people arrived. As he stands there struggling with these conflicting emotions, he openly shares his feelings
with the group. It is important to notice that he is not blaming or
attacking anyone. He is simply talking about his own inner world
of feelings and how, at the moment, these conflicting feelings
impede him from continuing what he was doing. While this may
appear confronting, it is at the same time trusting the group and
the two people who came late, to understand as he openly, "trans-
parently," conveys his feelings. The alternate here would be to suppress the feelings, displace them and continue the presentation,
but run the risk of its now being artificial, covertly negative and
even vengeful because of unexpressed resentment and conflict.

Speaker: His (the Prodigal's) money is gone and he is alone, isolated,
bitter and hostile toward himself, toward his own foolishness and the
ridiculousness of what he did. He is caught in the terrible struggle of
whether he's worth anything or not, the painfulness of this, in his
bitterness toward himself, his . . . (Pause) . . .

(As the two late-comers, after some noise, stand confusedly looking
for places.)

There are two empty seats down here . . .

(Pause . . . he attempts to go on and cannot. He just stands there,
feeling confused, with a surging of other undefined feelings rising in
him.)

I'm sorry but I think I better say this. I'm just confused myself now. I
really did not expect an interruption. I deliberately came late myself to
assure that everyone coming would be here when we began. I'm kind
of thrown now . . . (pause) . . . well, to go on—his bitterness toward
himself and his loneliness . . . (pause) . . . I must apologize for these
feelings of mine at the moment but I believe I better get them out if I
am to continue this in the right mood. I wonder, if anyone else comes,
could you ask them to stay outside till we've finished this ten-minute
presentation. I'm sorry but—I just seem to be irritated—I know you'll
understand the feeling. In an attempt at an intense group relationship
such as this, I believe it would have to have a seminar quality with all

the members present before anyone begins to speak. This would seem to be necessary for this kind of group.

Well, let's go on. The bitterness and loneliness of this young man might symbolize us all in one form or another. . . .

The leader has made an open expression of his feelings, much as a client might do in an interview where he expects an adequate understanding from the counselor. In this case the leader presumes such an understanding without anyone in the group needing to say it.

REACTION

During the discussion that followed the ten-minute presentation, no one except the two late-comers commented on this interruption, the others seeming to have forgotten it, as the presentation and discussion absorbed them again. After some time, first the man, then the woman, did comment. The trustfulness and openness of the leader's communication of his feelings helped them rather than hindered them, and really aided them to become a part of the group. Without this they could have continued to feel isolated throughout the whole discussion.

The following are recorded comments made afterwards by the two people. We notice how helped they felt by the leader's spontaneous negative expression and how fundamentally constructive it was. This, we see, is quite different from what would likely result, had the leader directly attacked them. What he did rather, was to speak openly of his own conflict and blocking, trusting them and the group to understand and accept this.

The first to comment was the man:

Comment 1: Initially as I walked in, the inappropriateness of my entrance made me feel very isolated from the group. I could sense the intense concentration and involvement of the group in what was going on, so I felt as if I were actually kicking furniture around or something —I felt such estrangement from the group. I could not get out of it. I literally almost couldn't listen to what was being said because of my feeling of having stumbled into such an intense group experience.

Two things helped me greatly. The fact that you immediately made a comment and cleanly brought it out in the open. You accepted my guilt or whatever you might call it. You did it cleanly. There wasn't anything phony about it. This helped me and brought me closer to the group. After listening awhile I felt myself come into the group again and find myself. This period of isolation or alienation ended as I was again within the group. I think this, to me, made this discussion very much more poignant. The whole message was in essence the alienation one can feel and the need to resolve to come back to the group, back to feeling whole and healed.

Leader: In a literal way you were the Prodigal and somehow the cleanness with which this was recognized and your guilt, if you want to put it that way, was openly stated—this helped you begin to feel differently. Finally this seemed to be complete when the group started to unfold. Your alienation was somehow healed, the distance was diminished.

Comment: This experience highlights the fact that people are so seldomly challenged in their guilts, that they are just left hanging, left to have the guilt within themselves but given no way to expurgate it. You could have just let it do, but you had enough respect for me that you were willing to confront me with this, and it meant a great deal to me.

Leader: It was helpful to have just some clean statement of fault. Maybe it was offering you a point of repentance but the fact that I, as the symbol of the group or righteousness or whatever symbol I was, gave you something to encounter in yourself and in me and in the group, seemed to be helpful in contrast to some vague undefined sort of cloud or mist that might hang over you and the group and wouldn't get you this clean healed feeling. The clean encounter seemed very helpful.

The comment of the second person, a young woman, follows:

Comment II: I also felt more accepted by the statement. I also felt more drawn in after you had spoken than before. Before, I felt apart. But soon after this I felt extremely involved in everyone's recollections of what this meant to them . . . I think tonight's experience was extremely helpful because I'm the type of person, I'm hard on myself when I feel I've been guilty and especially if it's with people I feel mean something to me or who are very close to me. I have a hard time forgiving myself. I think this is more of a loneliness, you know, apparent in yourself than even being in a far-off place because you can leave that place, but you can't leave yourself. This is what I felt.

Leader: What you're really saying then is that the Prodigal is in each of us, but certainly it's in you and your loneliness and your alienation is in some way basically within yourself as well as in other people. The inability to forgive yourself when this thing happened was a kind of condemning of yourself. I might comment, in return, that I was not trying to rebuke you. I honestly couldn't go on. That's really what it was about. I had reached a point of such a kind of dichotomized feeling with myself, it was beyond politeness or beyond just good manners. It had reached the point where it had me so caught that I was unsure that I could go on with the thing I was trying to do. I think this was the reality which would have been communicated . . . that it wasn't intended to be a rebuke. I just was in pain at this oddly dichotomized series of double feelings I was suddenly caught up in. Somehow I had the feeling that you people can share this. If there is some kind of real feeling that is genuine in one person, he can trust the group to say this. It would be almost like kicking someone in the shins without being sure; it would be sort of a relief and helpful if the person would just state his pain. I think if this were an attempt to really confront or rebuke people, it could have been artificial and false. It did seem to come off because I was just saying something spontaneously that I was really deeply feeling at the moment, almost as if a person might yell "ouch."

Comment II: Yes, I really felt the honesty of the communication, the righteous indignation which you felt; I think, as you said, if you tried to rebuke me and said, "Well, get out; you're breaking up the group," or something like that, it really wouldn't have seemed as clean. But this did seem clean; it seemed justified at the time. This is what I ought to do for myself instead of holding something inside of me and not letting it go, and then some other time use this venom in some other situation when it is not really relevant. I should actually confront myself or the other person at the time with an honest feeling.

Leader: I think that I simply was saying how I felt. It really did not go out to you, granting that you maybe were the cause of it, as one might be the cause of someone's shin being sore. He has a right to tell you that it's hurting, distinct from what someone did or what they intended to do.

What we see here, on the part of the two people, is a process similar to any kind of learning that involves self-control and limits. There is the same difficulty of adapting. But this is different from masquing oneself and yet continuing to be hostile through suppressing resentful and vengeful feelings. This was helped by the transparency and honesty of the leader and by his effort to understand them.

LIMITS AND COUNSELING

The invoking of limits can also be used constructively as the beginning of a counseling process, in a wide variety of circumstances that we may not ordinarily think of as counseling situations. To demonstrate this further, we can consider a project in a large boys' high school. Disciplinary issues were conceived as a process of invoking limits in such a way that they led to personalized family counseling.

The procedure followed here was to notify a student's parents— or if a small group were involved, all the parents together—that they must come to the school for a joint interview, to include the Dean of Discipline, the student (or students), and the parents and that more than one interview might be necessary.

The interview began with the Dean saying simply something like "John, will you explain to your parents what this is about?" Obviously much more than this simple sentence was involved. This is given merely to indicate how responsibility was immediately left with the student and his parents. The Dean could then act as catalytic agent and emotional "clarifier" as the group process emerged. It rapidly became group counseling therapy. Some aspects of this type of group counseling discussion will be considered later.

The following chart shows the contrast with the previous year, when this approach was not used.

While each class shows a noticeable decrease, it is most marked among juniors and seniors. This may suggest that a counseling relationship was more effective in proportion to the age of the student and his relative independence.

Resumé and Comparison of Suspensions
During the School Years of 1959-60 and 1960-61

1959-60		*1960-61*	
Freshmen		*Freshmen*	
1st Suspension	72	1st Suspension	60
2nd Suspension	17	2nd Suspension	24
3rd	5	3rd	9
4th	1	4th	2
5th	4		
6th	3		
Sophomores		*Sophomores*	
1st Suspension	124	1st Suspension	97
2nd	64	2nd	30
3rd	18	3rd	5
4th	7		
5th	1		
Juniors		*Juniors*	
1st Suspension	114	1st Suspension	78
2nd	46	2nd	22
3rd	17	3rd	2
4th	5		
Seniors		*Seniors*	
1st Suspension	151	1st Suspension	64
2nd	57	2nd	8
3rd	23	3rd	1
4th	2		
Actual Suspensions	731	Actual Suspensions	402
Distinct Individuals Involved	461	Distinct Individuals Involved	294

Training in counseling was necessary in order to enable the leader to handle the ensuing process. Reactions ranged from silent uncooperative resistance to explosive negative attack and defensiveness. But, whatever happened, a constructive dynamism had started which could begin to bring parents and students together in a common confrontation of the school-issue and themselves.

The acceptance of silence, resistance, hostility, defensiveness and similar negative feelings and the sensitive counseling clarifications that slowly came as each one began to feel he would be accepted and understood could, as we can see, effect not only better school cooperation but significant changes in the entire family attitude and relationship. Where a group of students and their parents were involved, a whole "milieu" could be effected and perhaps significantly reached and influenced in a way not otherwise possible.

In the light of the probability that many of the students had strong mothers and weak fathers, one can see, too, the importance of this kind of experience with a masculine symbol of discipline who is strong and unyielding, yet warm and understanding. A rich relationship often followed these encounters, as the students accepted both the Dean's right and determination to invoke necessary limits and his willingness and ability—in an incarnate redemptive way—to reach and understand them at the level of their own human weakness. They could begin to feel worth and self-regard, and to identify constructively with this image of masculine strength. Obviously more than better discipline was involved in a kind of deep constructive personality growth that such encounters make possible.

TUTOR-COUNSELING

A personality factor that can impede the initiating or effectiveness of a counseling relationship is a person's anxiety about what others may think. This is especially true for adolescents who may be unwilling to come for "counseling" since it may imply to their acquaintances that they have "personal problems." Such student difficulties, however, are often associated with poor study habits and failing grades. Consequently, a tutoring and study-skill program and the limits these may involve, can be combined with personal counseling. The two can be interwoven either by alloting a separate time for counseling as part of the tutoring period or by using counseling—even for five or ten minutes—when personal conflicts and confusions seem to be impeding the immediate learning process.

This can be done with small groups of students—somewhat

homogeneous, particularly in age and study difficulties—as well as with individual students. The fact that it is focussed on tutoring and on school study and classroom difficulties often make it less threatening than a direct counseling or therapy interview might be.

This kind of tutoring-counseling relationship seems often not only to improve learning and school achievement but it can bring about significant changes in the person. In this sense, it might also be called "operational counseling therapy," in that it is centered on a particular learning operation, such as learning a foreign language or mathematics, as the immediate norm and measurement of the changes that may occur.

Such a tutoring-counseling concern can be more precise, relevant and significant, particularly for adolescents and college students, than the more vague, undefined and threatening area of "personal problems." It can also involve a therapy of limits, since lack of study discipline is usually a part of the student's difficulties.

The following report illustrates how, (under the heading of "tutoring"), learning, counseling, invoking limits, and encouragement went together to aid a particular student in a study, classroom, and home conflict:

TUTORING REPORT

Tutoring (in a high school Spanish deficiency): One-hour sessions, twice a week, over a ten-week period.

Results: June passed the required examination, receiving full senior high school status. She also spoke Spanish. Previously she had never spoken Spanish during the class conversation periods, according to the teacher.

June is a "C" student in most subjects at high school. She had three years of Spanish but failed it in her Junior year and also in a summer course following this. After twenty sessions using a combined technique of counseling and tutoring she passed the required examination. Her teacher remarked how surprised she was with June's progress and when she made mistakes now, they were "intelligent."

After the third session, June's mother commented how much June liked the tutoring sessions. Previously she had resisted any special help.

I believe this was partly because I encouraged her by reinforcing the idea that there were not so many verbs to be learned since verbs were her main block. It was also, I believe, because she gradually began to trust me in my attempts to understand her.

At each session, but especially the first, she interrupted the lesson with negations toward her Spanish teacher. She frequently referred to her as a mean, unreasonable woman. But June kept emphasizing that it was not that she did not like her teacher and that the teacher did not like her. On the contrary, they seemed to like one another very much. The teacher was just "ridiculously perfectionistic," according to June. June felt the teacher did not consider her limitation but, in fact, she could do more than she was doing. I responded to these comments with counseling responses and then we came back to the exercise. We followed this procedure until about the tenth session.

At this point she began making foolish mistakes. "Funny" mistakes, as she called them, like "you" for "I," plural for singular, wrong verb tenses, etc., took up the next two sessions. I decided to confront her. I told her that I felt she was being unfair to herself by this sort of conduct which usually resulted in a clever wrong answer, just the opposite of the correct answer. I proposed it seemed a kind of "trick" to me. She agreed saying she had decided to do this about the fourth grade. She decided then that there were two Junes and the funny, fat, fun-loving, class entertainer was the one she chose. The other June was a June who knew the right answers but did not know how to let others know she knew. A counseling response to this led her to say that *now* nothing was real for her because nobody understood her; she felt differently from everyone else, her mind worked differently. A response to this sense of uniqueness and isolation brought tears. We both sat in silence for a short while and then I broke the silence saying, "Let's think about it." So we finished the exercise, the tears dried up in the process and we ended the session.

The foolish guessing continued for another session and then she became anxious. She asked me if I could call up and postpone the examination. When I responded to this by considering her request, she backed down and informed me that she knew I could not have the exam postponed. Both parents asked me what I thought. Would she pass: When I said she would if she really studied this last week both parents chimed in with "We know you can do it, June." This brought the response from June to her father, "Oh, Dad, you've never studied a language, you don't know what you're talking about."

June started the sixteenth session with some negative comments about her father. I responded with counseling responses. She finally said she had decided to find some other way to get even with the "old monster" because she really did want to pass this test.

However, at the same session she began to be anxious again saying she did not think she could do it. She stressed how afraid she was. I responded to her fear. She also began again complaining about her teacher, the headmaster, her mother and father. At this point I became stern, telling her that we had spent over a month reviewing most of the material in the text and that from the tests I had given her she knew the material well enough to pass. Secondly, I told her to stop whining and review the material once again herself, and that at the next session she was to present any material she did not understand. I reinforced the idea that there was no time for foolishness. I told her she could call me anytime during this last week if she had any difficulty. She called only twice, both times asking intelligent questions. I gave her an explanation and she continued her own study at home. During these last sessions, she knew what she did not understand; we discussed it and covered about twice as much material as we had in the other sessions. She took the examination and passed.

Interestingly, this report demonstrates something of the same change in self-concept as basic to learning which we will see in the learning project reported later. June had to reject her fourth grade view of herself as the "funny, fat, fun-loving, class entertainer," to become June who not only "knew the right answers" but knew how "to let others know she knew."

This parallels the therapeutic insight awareness of the person who had two "selves"—a previous fat, careless self, now projected on someone else and so causing her to reject that person—and a more recent self she approved of, accepted and wanted to continue to be.*

For June, some self growth was apparently interrelated with and necessary to, her successful language learning achievement. Learning then, even in a classroom, seems intimately related to many value factors beyond those that contribute to knowing or not knowing. While on the surface this was simply a series of Spanish

* See "The Clarification of Conflicting Values," p. 185.

words or phrases by which June either passed or failed an examination, it was in reality much more. To achieve success in the examination required a change in June's outlook on herself, parents, teacher and the whole of her personal world.

We notice, too, that invoking limits seemed to help June marshal her own constructive forces and cylinder her anxiety to a positive outcome. But basic here, in addition to the tutoring, was the warm, genuine acceptance and understanding recognition produced by the counseling relationship achieved in these brief moments of time. This seemed to be fundamental in affording June a new foothold to bring into constructive use what she knew. It helped her, too, to the positive and respectful acceptance of herself that was necessary to her succeeding in the examination.

Earlier, we commented on how *group* relationships, especially, invoked limits on each member. We will now consider this further in marriage counseling, in group counseling and discussion, and in a community learning project where the group becomes deeply engaged together in the learning process. Many of the concepts of the maturing process of limits as well as aspects of counseling understanding and skill which we have already considered, will be evident. New elements, however, are involved, particularly how to arrive at genuine communication and mutual understanding and support, in place of each one's competing from his own will to power, and suppressing or masquing those hostile and vengeful feelings which impede true trust and real communication.

NOTES

[1] Sonnet 116, *Shakespeare, The Complete Works,* ed. G. B. Harrison, New York: Harcourt, Brace and Co., 1952.

[2] Martin Mayman, "Toward a Positive Definition of Mental Health," American Psychological Association Symposium, September 1955. Quoted in Karl Menninger, *et al, The Vital Balance, op. cit.*

11
Marriage Counseling: Communication toward Mutual Values

MARRIAGE and the family obviously are major concerns of counseling and psychotherapy. Here psychological and social forces meet with religion in an effort to shore up and sustain the marriage and family structure. The issues involved are extensive, so extensive in fact that a vast array of psychological, sociological, medical, educational, guidance and counseling services are, in varying ways, seeking solutions and offering aid. To consider these, even in small part, would be certainly beyond our scope. Even to consider marriage guidance or the aspects this might include together with counseling, would involve an extended discussion. Our treatment will focus, therefore, on means of restoring communication between married people and the uncovering of values which they share together as persons or because of their common investment in the marriage. Here especially, children can also play a basic role.

LACK OF COMMUNICATION

A study of men and women of the upper middle class concludes:

If there is a core problem in handling the world of men and women, the nub of it is the impasse in communication between the married or otherwise related man and woman who would be presumed *a priori*, because intimate, to be in good rapport. These impasses persist despite

233

the fact that this is a highly educated, articulate group, highly adept in social skills . . . Viewing the matter qualitatively, the evidence forces us to an extremely depressing conclusion: there are very few qualitatively good man-woman relationships at this age in this class . . . This is meant to include the narrowly sexual as well as the more diffuse companionship and intellectual aspects of relationships.[1]

These findings correspond to what appears to be a central issue in marriage counseling, the lack of any genuine communication between the married people themselves. Since this seems basic to marriage conflict, one can say that one of the main aims of marriage counseling is the restoration of mutual respect and genuine communication, as well as the rediscovery of the personal values that caused the two people to invest in one another originally in so fundamental a way as marriage. To arrive at this, conflicting issues and values impeding communication and relationship, must be mutually uncovered and removed. In the light of these aims, we would have to place marriage counseling somewhere between individual counseling and group counseling.

MARRIAGE RELATIONSHIP

Marriage counseling then, does not simply mean the counseling of a married person—this could be simply personal counseling, even though some issues of married life might arise. Marriage counseling would more directly center on difficulties between husband and wife. From this point of view, it obviously seems better for the counselor to see them together whenever possible. Seeing husband and wife together, and sometimes even with the children, gives marriage counseling its peculiar milieu and place, midway between individual and group counseling.

There is also individual counseling with married people, in which the counseling process is not different from that used for the single. This is taken for granted in most of the literature, where a client is not ordinarily identified as married or single when he comes for personal counseling.

By marriage counseling we mean a counseling relationship, even with one partner, whose main presenting concern centers in some form around the marriage relationship itself. These distinctions can, of course, sometimes fuse into one another as when a couple coming for marriage counseling slowly grow to realize that the marriage issues are incidental to much more personal psychological conflict in one or both of them. Conversely, a married person may come for personal counseling and grow to recognize that major personal issues concern husband or wife, and cannot be adequately resolved without the other person also coming for counseling.

JOINT COUNSELING

We have said that marriage counseling, as such, seeks to restore and facilitate communication and the sharing of mutual values between the married partners. This leads to a procedural point that seems to be of capital importance if the marriage counseling relationship is to be preserved: every effort should be made to keep the couple together in the counseling relationship and to separate them only when, by common option, it seems clear to both that the issues are unique and personal and do not directly concern the marriage. Obviously marriage does not eliminate a person's sense and need of his own uniqueness. It should not, therefore, deprive him of a uniquely personal counseling relationship if he so desires.

One of the great advantages of marriage counseling, however, is that it allows marriage partners, sometimes for the first time, to see one another at levels of awareness that ordinary ways of marriage communication never seem to permit. To counsel them separately would be to rob them of one of the richest aspects of the marriage counseling relationship. An important facet basic to the value of marriage counseling is the fact that emotional involvement is often so great that married people can rarely communicate sensitively or point out difficulties without becoming quarrelsome and abusive, or simply escaping and avoiding discussion. Marriage counseling allows them, often for the first time, through the skilled sensitivity of the counselor, to treat of painful common areas and yet retain, or regain, mutual respect and dignity. Simply to see married people in individual counseling interviews, while it may and often does help their marriage, fails to provide this profound and rich mutual experience, where they can see one another in a way never before apparent to them.

In the light of this special aim of marriage counseling, every effort should be made from the beginning to keep the couple related together in their common marriage concern. This applies even to the original phone call or casual encounter when the counseling appointment is made. In fact, this often overlooked aspect of the marriage counseling—the beginning conversation—can be far more crucial for the success or failure of subsequent interviews than usually appears.

HEARING EACH PERSON

Generally speaking, the person who is in genuine conflict or in obvious suffering is the one who makes the initial approach to the counselor. By telephone or personal encounter this married partner has an evident need not only to make the appointment but immediately to begin to release some of the pain and conflict he or she feels. This is all quite understandable when one considers the emotional state the person is likely to be in. To counsel this party alone runs the danger, however, of an immediate difficulty for the marriage counseling process. It can give the impression to the other partner that the counselor has already heard one side and is now biased and prejudiced in favor of that side.

When we consider that one of the counselor's main roles is to communicate his warmth and understanding to both partners so as to convince both that he will genuinely appreciate and respond to all their negative and positive feelings, the implication of a biased attitude can seriously jeopardize his function. This can be heightened by the fact that the partner making the appointment may, wittingly or unwittingly, convey this notion of the counselor's taking one side when reporting the call about the appointment to the other person. It is easy to see that, already, the other partner is given grounds to feel left out and misunderstood. His or her hostility against even keeping an appointment which someone else has made is quite understandable, especially if this person already feels that the other side has been heard and that the counselor is therefore now prejudiced against him or her. The more both people can anticipate that each person's view will be fairly heard and understood by the counselor, the more both seem to feel sure of the counselor's regard and respect.

AVOID PREJUDICE

To achieve this and avoid a biased beginning, a number of procedures seem to be helpful. If possible, it would seem preferable for someone other than the counselor to arrange his counseling appointments. Secretaries can politely block off the caller's tendencies to want to communicate elaborate reasons and feelings in explaining the need for marriage counseling. Rather, the appointment should be made with as few details as possible, leaving these for the opening counseling interview itself.

If the counselor is the one making the appointments, he needs to be especially conscious of not prejudicing his position with the other partner by too lengthy conversation with the person making the appointment. Generally, as we have said, one partner first approaches or calls. Immediately the counselor should suggest talking to both partners, together, as soon as possible. Even though the person calling may want to release his or her side, it seems preferable not to hear him out at this time. One method that has worked effectively, is to request the phone number, then call back when both parties are at home. The counselor can then talk to both, simultaneously (in a two-telephone home) or consecutively, allowing both parties to feel a part in making the initial appointment.

EACH ACCEPTED

Whatever the procedure, however, its main purpose is to help the married couple feel that each is accepted for himself, and that the counselor is genuinely striving to understand, accept and clarify each one's position, viewpoint and feelings. Only with this kind of beginning can effective marriage counseling result.

When the two people come for the interview, the procedure and skill involved is fundamentally the same as in individual counseling. Conflicts, confusions, negative feelings released, investigated and clarified produce insights, new self-evaluations and, often, different and more adequate solutions, in a manner similar to that occurring in individual counseling.

DYNAMIC TENSION

One basic difference, however, is the dynamic tension produced by their being together and speaking not only to the counselor but through him to one another. Moreover, in a way usually not possible when they are talking without the counselor, they can see aspects of one another unfolding that they never knew or understood before. It is, in fact, this new view of one another—of seeing one another in depth—that brings about many of the changes that occur. Usually such penetrating views of one another are not possible when they are by themselves, either because they quickly end up quarrelling or because they cannot get beyond purely surface discussions of themselves and their differences.

SPECIAL SKILLS

Consequently, marriage counseling demands special skills in addition to those necessary for individual counseling. First of all, the counselor has the obvious complexity of understanding two people, rather than one. Moreover, he must do this in such a way that neither feels rejected and misunderstood while he is trying to understand the other. This is clearly no easy task; it makes maximum demands on the counselor's alertness and delicate choice of words, so that each client feels he is genuinely getting through to the counselor. The counselor must carefully control his attitudes and his words so that his effort to share the feelings, insights and reactions of one, does not cause him to distort his understanding of the other's communications.

Gradually, as each client experiences the counselor's sincere efforts at real communication with him, he grows increasingly able to trust the counselor and himself to deeper self-penetration. Being more sure of the counselor's understanding, each can risk misunderstanding and rejection by his marriage partner in a way not possible to either without the counselor. This makes possible, too, a whole new view of themselves in relation to one another. This new view can then bring with it a respect and regard much deeper than they originally brought to their marriage. It is this kind of mutual renewal and restoration of marriage purpose and shared values that is the main aim of marriage counseling, distinguishing it from other forms of individual and group counseling.

FAIRNESS AND CONCERN

As we have emphasized, a key point in the counselor's skill is his scrupulous fairness and honesty in catching and reflecting, in his responses, the emotional content and self-awareness of each partner's expression. The counselor must trust to all the hidden, unexamined forces in their marriage that brought them together in the first place, and have kept them together up to this point. They have already invested something of themselves—and often a great deal of themselves—in one another. This will be undiscernible at first, both to themselves and to the counselor, as the more painfully negative aspects of their relationship force themselves forward. But as these are drained off, each can begin to see his own and the other's inner world brought out and reflected in the counselor's cleanly filtered but genuinely fair responses. They then start to look on one another differently, and to appreciate the hitherto hidden or obscured values they represent to one another. The counselor trusts for this process to emerge, just as he trusts a similar process from negation to positive self-reference and more adequate choices, in his experience with individual counseling.

SEPARATE RELATIONSHIP

In the process of marriage counseling, there may unfold, as we have said, material that the client feels is too personal or not related enough to be discussed as part of the marriage counseling relationship. This could be, for example, material from a work relationship for the husband or for the wife, complications between mother and daughter dating back to the wife's early childhood. In such instances, if the married couple are given a chance to discuss this, they can decide, as in any other counseling decision, whether they might gain further understanding of one another by sharing even these more personal areas together. It seems better here, as in so many other phases of counseling, for the counselor to trust to the couple's own option. They usually know one another's reactions, often quite subtly. This knowledge will come forward to aid them if they can think out such options together in counseling before they make their decisions. While married people may choose to share intimate self-awarenesses, they sometimes may also choose, for reasons that are peculiarly their own, to work some things out separately and they may, in fact, not actually wish to reveal them to one another. The counselor should be willing to accept this decision and offer individual counseling interviews if the partners so desire.

MARRIAGE COUNSELING PROCESS

As in group counseling, the counselor in marriage counseling tries to respond to each person and hold up, in a cognitive, understanding way, both contrasting viewpoints and the associated emotions. In addition to aiding growth in self-awareness, as in individual counseling, this also helps the couple to see one another's side. In this way, they can begin slowly to change their own view. Moreover, through the counselor's respect and understanding, each person can begin to grow again in respect and understanding for himself and his partner.

Often, especially at the beginning, a couple will break in on one another in their need to argue or contradict what the other is saying. Since this kind of disagreement will trigger them into a heated quarrel, it seems preferable for the counselor to intevene by giving his response before the other answers. This lets the person speaking, feel understood by the counselor. The counselor then recognizes the other person's urge to answer and disagree, responding then, in turn, to this.

At first this may be somewhat surprising for both, but soon they recognize the counselor's fairness and sincerity, and they wait until he speaks before responding themselves. Already a kind of therapy of limits has been established that distinguishes this from a quarrel. This helps them to begin to struggle together for mutual understanding and respect, as they start to listen to each other's reactions and differing viewpoints.

The following excerpt is an illustration of marriage counseling with both husband and wife. It begins in a way that is typical when one partner feels a grave need and the other does not see anything particularly serious. It takes only a short time, however, for both to become involved in a constructive effort to explore the barriers that impede them from the creative relationship they both still desire.

Counselor: As I mentioned to you when you called, I just have fifteen minutes, but then we can conceivably go on from there. I hope that you will excuse me for calling it off then, but you understand the reasons I gave you. (Pause)

Husband: This all seems kind of silly . . . She can tell you why we came down . . . go ahead . . . you talk.

Wife: I think our marriage is breaking up—I really do! I do not see him anymore. I just may as well be living alone—that's all!

Counselor: So, John, as I get your view of it, *you don't see what the point is.* Mary, you see it as an extremely serious thing and see it *reaching a crisis.*

Wife: I . . . I can't believe it. I thought I had all the answers to a perfect marriage . . . My parents had a nice relationship . . . and I thought we could too—but it is just impossible if you never see your husband. He is always busy at work or school.

Counselor: What is *disillusioning* here is that John seemed like a perfect partner and you felt that perfect fulfillment that you saw or felt you saw in your parents. A great *disillusionment.*

Wife: Yes.

Husband: Well, she doesn't get the thing. When we were undergrads, everything was nice and we had a good time and everything looked nice. She did not realize that when we got married . . . that I am going to work during the day at the agency . . . going to school at night . . . she always wants me to stay home and study. I can't study at home, you know, the only place I can study is in the library for an hour. Then on Saturday I go over to the library and have Mrs. Cronin type my papers. And . . . this is the situation that we have and I think we just have to accept it. If she can't accept it, then there is something wrong with her, but this has to be this way. I have to work and I have to get through school.

Counselor: So, what you see here, John, is a very simple *limited reality.* You can't do it any other way. You have to go to school, you have to work, you can't study at home. These are just facts and if you can't be with Mary the way she wants, you feel there is just something wrong with her and her *inability to face this and accept it.*

Husband: That's right.

The counselor stated the time limit and then let the interview immediately begin. We notice that he does not go into an elaborate explanation or series of apologies that might only serve to delay the interview.

In a situation where limits of time and other circumstances necessitate a short initial contact, the counselor needs to control his own tendency to guilt feelings. Unless controlled, these may cause him to go into excessive apologies or explanations which absorb the time and focus of the interview—time that should be quickly turned over to the two people themselves. The counselor must be in control of himself here. If he gives in to his need to have his own feelings understood, he is in fact making the clients *his* counselor—that is, he is forcing them to understand him. This can end in confusing rather than helping the relationship.

UNDERSTANDING CONFLICTS

We have italicized what we consider to be key counselor phrases. We notice that at the end of this excerpt both John and Mary have had their conflicting positions understood by the counselor. They are, therefore, already more secure in the counseling relationship even though they remain at odds with one another.

Mary: Yes, but he won't let me work, and I have been willing to let him stay at the library . . . Really, I have even prepared late meals for him and he comes home late and what does he tell me—he met Joe and he had a hamburger, so there's a lovely meal.

John: Well, I just . . .

Counselor: Excuse me, John. Mary, as I get it, you are deeply hurt. You are really willing to accept this situation if he would go along with your side, which would mean that he comes home when he is finished studying and when you have prepared a meal for him. Or that he let you work. Or . . . as I get it, you want *some give on his part* to see your side of it.

Mary: Yes, yes, I do.

John: Well, that sounds pretty reasonable. You got to study. I come home and I try to study . . . and she starts to give the story of why I should be . . . Well, her dad gave me some golfclubs and a gift subscription to a membership in the country club. But I haven't got time to play golf. He wants me to go over there and meet all his friends and all that sort of stuff . . . and I come and try to start to study. She's all the time telling me why I should be more active in the country club and I get tired of hearing that sort of thing. I can study better in the library, and if I am going to make it in school, I just can't stay home and listen to her and all this bunk about the country club and her dad.

Mary: He just doesn't appreciate . . .

Counselor: Excuse me, Mary. Let me see if I can get this . . . On your side, John, there is a pretty deep feeling that she does not catch at all the *reality of your life*. That she is, in a sense, with the country club, *putting you in a way of life you can't accept.* You don't feel comfortable in that country club existence . . . you want to go to school *and make it on your own.* So you feel that she doesn't *share* what you want to do. She is trying to *force* this other way of life on you which you resist very strongly—it is just something you want to *push away.*

John: That's right. I've got some work to do and I want to do it.

Counselor: Yes, you're *determined* that this is what you want to do and you are going to do it, you are going to push it through.

COUNSELOR INTERVENTION

In this excerpt the counselor has intervened both to respond to Mary and again to respond to John. In their comments after the interview both John and Mary remarked that this helped them because it kept them from quarrelling with one another. Even before this, however, both Mary and John really felt understood by the counselor. Had they not felt this way, the probabilities are that they might have been resistant to the counselor's interventions.

Stated another way, it seems the counselor may invoke limits and intervene when the client feels he is genuinely being understood. By such intervention, the counselor prevents quarrelling and furthers the couple's constructive efforts to reestablish their relationship with one another through him.

As the couple continue to explore their differences, what begins to emerge is John's resentment of Mary's attachment to and dependence on her father. Mary in turn feels he is indifferent to his family, and so considers any family closeness as excessive.

Toward the end of the fifteen-minute interview, the counselor, in the following response, is holding two points of view and contrasting and comparing them:

Counselor: As I get it here, John, you see that there ought to be a kind of separate relationship between your father and yourself, well as two adults. He wouldn't always be showing you his things and you wouldn't either. Now as you see this, Mary, he just neglects his family . . . It isn't any virtue at all—you see it as indifference to his family and you don't want to do that.

Mary: No, I don't want that. I think that's terrible!

Counselor: Uh-huh . . .

John: Come off it! Look, my dad lives his life. I live my life!

Counselor: Uh-huh . . .

John: That's . . . your situation, your dad's leading your life for you and you are trying to lead your dad's life or something. I don't know . . . I think that people should stick to themselves. That's the way to be and you can't be a success in life unless you stick to what you want.

Counselor: There are really two sets of values here, aren't there? I mean at this point. Your value as you see it, John, is to be independent, be on your own . . . It is not that you see yourself indifferent to your parents or as neglecting them, it is just that you see yourself separated as an adult and you want to keep it that way. Now, Mary, as you see it, this is indifference and this is just coldness and you can't accept that value. You see yourself as married but not as totally unrelated to your parents, your father and mother. You want to keep an attachment to them. And you see this, John, on her side as it were, that she is just being taken over by them. That she isn't a person in her own right, and this is, as I get it, what you resent.

John: She likes that whole deal, the country club kind of life. Sometimes I don't think she wants to be *my* wife. I think she wants to be some kind of a social gal . . . she does not want to be a wife and be at home . . . she wants to be out all the time, in the country club playing cards and all that kind of stuff—she doesn't want to have anything to do with my life.

Counselor: Yes, so what you are saying is that her values are not the values that you would need in a wife. These take her in another direction.

John: Yes, that's right . . . she wants something else . . . I don't really know what she wants.

Mary: I wouldn't have married you . . . I could have had it anyway . . . I had it before I married you . . . I married you because . . . I married you because I wanted to.

Counselor: Yes, as you see this Mary, this isn't so . . . the way John is stating it. You wouldn't have married him if you didn't want what he represents, in that sense, you had these other things and you could have stayed with them. So you don't feel this is true, the way he is stating it. This doesn't really represent what you want.

Mary: But I did not want to live alone either.

Counselor: Yes, you don't want to give up what he represents but what you feel forced into is a completely isolated life.

CONTRASTING VALUE SYSTEMS

Here we see again the way counseling often results in a comparison of personal value systems. Two people are looking at the same reactions in one another, and in contrasting them, each is frustrated. But through the counseling process they have been able to ventilate and so expose and explore more deeply, exactly what each one wants from the other. While the communication is made directly to the understanding counselor, it is witnessed by and can, to some degree, be understood by the other partner also. We notice this being suggested by John as the interview ends.

Counselor: We have a minute or so in our time . . . I'm sorry I have to leave.

John: I'm willing . . . I'm willing to go along with trying to stay home . . . But I don't think she would . . . I don't think she wants to give up that country club stuff . . . she wants everything her way and I don't want to stay in the library and study all the time either, but I have to do it because I am not going to be successful unless I keep going to school . . . so

Counselor: Yes, you feel you are willing to give in on this and try to spend more time studying at home and be with her. You feel that this isn't really what she wants but she really wants this sort of symbolization of her father and the family and . . . well . . . you can't go along with that.

Mary: Well, if you're willing to stay home, I'm willing . . . well, I'm just willing to . . . to try . . . to try to change.

John: I don't think you're going to quit harping about the old man . . . I think that you're just going to keep on with all that sort of bunk.

Mary: You don't even give me a chance!

Counselor: You are sort of saying something here, Mary, as I gather. You're weighing something—it would suggest that you would try to give in on this and to be more cooperative. Your reaction, John, is that she can say that but she won't really do it . . . This makes you feel, Mary, that the cards are stacked against you—he won't even let you try.

John: Well, I'll . . . sure . . . I'm willing to try . . . to make an effort.

Counselor: You are opening up the possibility for her. Our time is about up and as I said I have to attend this meeting. I would be very pleased to see you both again. Would next Monday evening be convenient?

John: I have class on Monday . . . but I could come after 7:30.

Counselor: Well, let's make it about 8:00 to 8:30. O.K. Mary?

Mary: Oh, yes . . . I have the time.

DIRECT ATTACK

Another common complication especially evident in marriage counseling is that the two people begin immediately to attack one another somewhat heatedly. This can prove disconcerting for the counselor and throw him into confusion. In addition, some circumstances may be suggested that cause the counselor to inquire for more information. Both of these common situations can disorganize the counseling relationship and the counselor. In the following recorded excerpt one sees this illustrated.

Husband: We've been having a little trouble, by "little" I mean the fact that we're separated.

Counselor: You're separated at the moment.

Husband: Yes, we've been separated since we've been married. In fact, this is the second one. She uh—I went through this once before. It cost me about six hundred bucks. I was down at the Notre Dame game with her and went out to dinner, and thought we had a wonderful evening. But the next day I get a summons and she's with these two lawyers. This is going to cost me more, so I'm willing to call this thing quits. I've had it.

Counselor: You've said you've gone through this once before.

Husband: Yes.

Counselor: You got a formal separation, did you?

INFORMATION SIDETRACK

This counselor's question could be a seeking of information he feels is necessary. But if it is necessary, it would be better left until the end of the counseling session. During the counseling interview, people of their own accord often bring forward all necessary information. The counselor needs only to be patient. This counselor, cannot quite get into the counseling role because that word, "separation" has him threatened. But, his need for information at this stage impedes his understanding the husband's deep feelings. This impulse, (particularly in the beginning of an interview) to ask a question to gain additional information is a common difficulty in counseling. Here, the question was really of little or no value. This situation was already finished. The counselor is not helping them at this point.

Let us consider the feelings which the counselor in his preoccupation with the word, "separation," failed to clarify. The client is expressing deep disappointment. He thought things were going all right with his wife and suddenly he is faced with divorce papers.

The counselor might have shown his understanding of these feelings with a response like: "You felt deeply let down, didn't you, when it happened before? You thought things were going all right—there was the game and the dinner the day before. Then suddenly it had all switched. This and the expense made it pretty rough on you." The interview continues:

Husband: No actually we didn't.

Wife: I couldn't stand to be with him any longer. This had come to the breaking point and I didn't wait for a formal separation. I just left.

Counselor: I see. The last time you had trouble you just took it upon yourself—

Wife: That's right. I found it unbearable.

Counselor: Thought you just couldn't be with him any longer.

Wife: Not at all! Can't stand the sight of him.

Husband: That's what I mean. Let's end this thing. I'm holding down two jobs now. I bought her a new house and she got herself a car, and

I'm paying the insurance on that. And I tried to tell her, "I can't get you a car yet." Then, we were just married a couple months. She thinks I've got scads of dough. She was discontented, so I gave in. The little car which I got her was fairly nice, too. Then after we got the car, she wanted a new house. I don't know what else I can do for her.

Wife: I think he's married to his job. He's always at work. He has two jobs—and if he could get two more, he'd get those too.

Husband: She knew that when we got married.

Wife: I thought you'd have a little more time with me, though. I never see you any more.

UNDERSTANDING INTERVENTION

When feelings are strong, as in this case, a rapid emotional cross-fire is likely to develop. To prevent this, the counselor must intervene and hold off the second remark until he had responded to the first. After a short time, as we said, both parties get used to the fact of the counselor's "sandwiched" response and each one more often delays his rebuttal until the counselor had responded.

The great advantage of this process is that each person can feel his point of view was understood by the counselor, even though it was rejected by the other party. Consequently, an exchange that would quickly have led to another bitter quarrel, through the counselor's calm, sensitive responses, gradually becomes a sharing of differing points of view. They can begin to see how each other feels and reacts to the same situation because the counselor's presence and responses tend to keep both more reasonable. When they are alone, their feelings are soon too intense for these exchanges to produce any such understanding.

Another advantage of the counselor's presence is that people slowly disperse their emotions through his responses, as in individual counseling. They are then more able to begin reasoning constructively together, with the auxiliary reasoning and understanding of the counselor, in contrast to simply mounting attacks on one another—which previously produced only more anger, hurt, and resultant bitterness.

We see that this counselor is much too slow and hesitant. He seems somewhat overcome by the immediate emotional blast. In his next response, however, the counselor does more effectively reflect an understanding of both sides. The interview continues:

Counselor: Well, it seems right from the start there was a difficulty of your working at two jobs, and you said it was the thought of trying to provide for Joan as well as you possibly could. But now she definitely feels that it kept you out of the house too much.

Husband: Yes, and she knew the score.

Counselor: She knew you were working that much when you got married. And you don't feel she . . .

Husband: She doesn't appreciate any of my problems.

Wife: I should have married a much younger man. He's twenty years older than I am. He just can't see things the way I see them.

Counselor: So right from the start you have had a considerable amount of difficulty. You don't seem able to see eye-to-eye on . . .

Husband: I see. She's the one that doesn't see.

Wife: The only one you see is yourself.

Husband: Somebody ought to tell her what it means to be a mother, what it means to be a homemaker. She doesn't know. Nobody ever told her.

Wife: I don't see how you'd know. You're never there to find out.

Counselor: So, Mike, you feel that she just hasn't been all that you would expect a real good wife and mother ought to be. Of course, you feel that you could be, Joan, if he had given you the proper opportunity. But with this constant work, you don't feel that you have enough time to spend with him.

In this last response, the counselor is beginning to reflect both sides in a sincere and balanced way. As he intervenes this way and calmly understands both, each feels accepted and respected as a person and each is helped to be less emotional and more reasonable. Slowly, by this process, deeply divided couples can begin to see the other's side—sometimes for the first time since they began their many quarrels.

Buried resentments, long since hidden or only expressed to

wound, can emerge again, to be mutually shared and gradually understood and lessened. The more fundamental and positive reasons why they married in the first place, can then reassert themselves, giving new dignity and respect to their exchange through the counselor. By such a process one can hope that the basic personal values still inherent in their marriage, will begin again to restore them to a positive relationship and genuine communication.

FURTHER ISSUES

Some further questions might be raised here—questions which, while generally applicable to any form of group or individual counseling or psychotherapy, are especially relevant to marriage counseling.

First of all, there is the basic question whether the person really wants counseling at all; perhaps he simply wishes some kind of guidance information about marriage. This is complicated by the fact that people often begin with a question or a series of questions, not so much because they want answers as because they do not know how else to start. If the questions are answered, the relationship may end before counseling even began.

One clue concerns the question itself, as we saw in our discussion of guidance. If it is somewhat vague and undefined, often confusedly related to another person, a counseling need could be suggested. But the more direct and clear the question, the more likely it is to be really an "information" question.

If the counselor chooses to answer such a question, he should be as brief as possible, allowing the person then to make the more personal application if he so chooses.

A vague question which also contains the person's anxiety or disturbance, may be directly responded to in a counseling way, such as, "You're somewhat anxious and disturbed about that, aren't you?" Often, such simple clarification of feeling can free the person to make a direct statement of counseling need, such as, "Well, it's really about my husband and myself—I think we need help."

Marriage counseling seems clearly indicated when a person talks directly about himself and his partner. Sometimes, what begins as marriage counseling may develop into individual counseling for one or both—sometimes with the partner as an observer if this is mutually agreeable.

It can also happen that what begins as personal counseling, for example, about a man taking a new position, can gradually unfold to reveal some basic issues that concern both himself and his wife. At this point, with the wife's participation, it becomes marriage counseling.

SPECIAL RESISTANCE

Because of the complication of small children, particularly, and the difficulty of getting baby sitters, the question might be raised about conducting marriage counseling in the couple's home. This is possible and can be effective if a clear time limit is set and those social involvements avoided which would impede a clean counseling relationship.

It must be recognized, however, that the counselor's coming to the home may be somewhat confronting, for at least one of the partners. The counselor has to be prepared to accept this and to accept as well this ensuing hostility or coldness as a part of the beginning counseling relationship. If he is patiently and genuinely understanding of these resistances, the relationship has a good chance of becoming positive for both partners.

Similarly, resistance can be evident through one or both remaining silent and appearing uncooperative. Silence, as we have said elsewhere, is a form of language too. While it may be resistance, the counselor can hold to the realization that at least both have come and that this in itself is an important positive step. Slowly, sometimes imperceptibly, each begins to communicate more openly as he grows secure and trustful of the counselor's relationship with him.

Such trust is furthered, as we have seen, not so much by anything the counselor does directly to elicit it as by his genuine integrity in going out to the two married people in a deep and honest effort to respect and understand the differing viewpoints and feelings of each. Getting this kind of "consensual validation" from the counselor is basic to their slowly regaining some of the respect and regard they once had for one another. Hope grows and with hope comes renewed efforts on the part of both. This is the best married counseling can accomplish—it must depend finally on the strength of the original forces that attracted these two people to marry and has, until now, kept them in some, even remote, relationship to one another. The core of marriage counseling, then, seems to be the restoration of some sense of mutual understanding and some joint feeling of working together, in place of constant conflict.

The following excerpt, a beginning interview, illustrates how, at first, the two people speak with no relation to one another, appearing to ignore what the other has said. At this point the husband pays no attention to his wife's interruptions.

Counselor: As you see it, Marge, it's just a kind of a pile-up of things and Don is sort of avoiding you and your mother is somewhere in it, too, as far as you can figure it out.

Marge: Mother is not in it at all, but I think you're right about his avoiding her. He works in this Army program teaching kids and he's got all the time in the world to devote to them and he's got none to devote to us. And mother, well I just don't know how she is tied up in it but somehow she just keeps coming up as a block between us all the time. And yet there is nothing else we can do. I just have to live with her, there is just no place for her to go. She does help out and she does mean well, but Don does not see this. She is just in the way and mother is this and she is that. I just can't take it anymore.

Counselor: Perhaps your mother comes in it, it's not clear. But what you see is a contrast in the way Don is dedicated to these kids at his work and yet you have a feeling he neglects his own family. And this is one phase of it that leaves you hurt, that leaves you rejected in a sense by him, that he prefers the children at his work rather than his family.

Don: Well, you've hit it right on the head—it *is* her mother. We've been married four years and prior to the time we got married we talked this over and we realized there was this mother problem—that we would have to keep her with us.

Marge: (breaks in) Yes, but you know it is always mother—that's all you ever complain about.

Don: (continues quietly) I knew it would be somewhat of a burden that I was willing to put up with at that time. And it did work out fairly well the first couple of years. She was liveable then.

Marge: (interrupts angrily) She is liveable now, if you would only be liveable.

Don: (continues quietly) She realized that we were a young married couple and she would absent herself from the house and give us the privacy that we needed. She has her sisters living and I would not mind driving her out once and sometimes twice or even three times a week.

Marge: Mom does not like it over there and you know it.

Don: This would leave us alone for two or three hours and we would have the relaxation my wife and I needed. But now she doesn't go any place and I come home tired and she is always imposing herself in the conversation and making the meals. She just seems like she's taking Marge over and taken over our lives. She is just domineering and domineering.

Marge: She is no more domineering than you are. She is just trying to help out the situation. She knows what you are doing, you're gone all the time.

Counselor: As I get it, Marge, you don't quite agree with this, but Don, your feeling is that the situation was workable at the beginning but it doesn't seem to be anymore. You just can't get this person out of your hair, sort of thing. She could go over to visit people but she doesn't do that. She is just there now in a sort of negative way all the time. And Marge, you feel this is not true at all and that she is really very helpful. The stubbornness is not on your mother's part but on Don's part.

Marge: It certainly is. She was so good to us to begin with and she is still but he just won't cooperate. Now she must want to move away and . . .

Don: That is not true! This woman will never move except into our bed! I love my wife. We had a good relationship for three or four years. But it's changed. I have taken up the hobby of building. I put in a workshop in the basement just so I can get away and be alone. I have a hard job. I work with children all day and I come home and I need an atmosphere where I can relax and . . .

Marge: You're not the only one. I'm home twenty-four hours a day. I never get out of there.

Counselor: Again, there is a kind of a double view of the same situation, isn't there. As you see it, Marge, your mother is not stubborn and is not doing the sort of interfering that Don says she is. But Don you feel that she definitely is and that your work has you involved with kids all day long and so you go down to the workshop just to get away from this. Marge, you're involved with two kids twenty-four hours a day, too, on the other side. You want Don to give some consideration to you and the kids at home.

Marge: That's right, that's right.

At this point, it seems evident that Marge is relieved because she is finally really understood. We notice, in the next response, she addressed Don for the first time in a somewhat conciliatory tone.

Don: I realize that there was going to be certain sacrifices to be made when we got married. We did not get married early in life. I had a chance to see other young people and friends get married. I was aware enough to know that there would have to be sacrifices on my part— like having her mother living with us. It just seemed that Mary's mother was aware of this too. She realized perhaps that I did not know her too well. She was going slower then, easier. In other words, I think she was holding back, she was aware that we needed privacy and that we did not want someone else interfering in the decisions that should be made by just the two of us. But it seems that now every decision that is made in the house, she has to make it. She does the cooking, she wants to give all the advice. I just stay away.

Marge: She does not mean to do this, Don. She has done this all her life. She's getting pretty old now and it's just more noticeable.

At this early stage, the focus is on each one telling his or her "side". As each feels his view is understood by the counselor, he

starts to relax and become less aggressive. They then can begin to
regard and consider one another again. By such slow steps, communication between them is gradually restored—first through the
counselor's response to one as the other listens. Later, they can
begin again directly to listen to and respond to one another.

INVOLVING THIRD PERSON

In the following excerpt, at the close of a later interview, the
question is raised of a third person, the wife's mother, coming for
counseling:

Counselor: What I get here—our time is about up—what you are
raising, as I see it, is the question of whether Marge's mother shouldn't
be here, too, since so much of your discussion has hinged around her
and she isn't here. What about the possibility of your mother and
mother-in-law coming with you the next time?

Don: I think she might. I haven't quite made up in my own mind
whether the first years we were married, she was just holding back
what she really was like. And now, a few years later, she has just let go
with both barrels. I don't know whether she just needs to be made
aware that she's infringing on our marriage and causing this animosity
on my part or whether she—ah—or what she's doing. I think she
should be made aware that she's doing this.

Marge: Well, I . . .

Counselor: (breaking in) Excuse me, Marge, as I get it, Don, you'd
like to see her here because she's definitely part of it. Marge, you were
going to say something and I interrupted you.

Marge: Mother's not going to like this. Her idea is it's our job to take
care of ourselves. It might help her. I don't think she's going to do it.
Why don't you (turning to Don) tell her to do it, you ask her to come
along:

Counselor: You're raising the question, Marge, not whether it couldn't
help her or not but whether she will come. As you see her, she sees
marriage as your affair so you want Don to take the responsibility of
getting her here.

Marge: I think he can do it better than I can. She knows how to tell
me no! Maybe if she realized it was important to him she'd listen to
him because she still does.

Don: Listen! that's your mother and . . . boy! You two stick together and you two fight this thing out together. I'm not going to have anything to do with her until she straightens herself out. That's just the way I feel.

Counselor: Again, here there is a double view of the mother, isn't there? Marge, you feel Don would have more influence since she's your mother and can control you. As you see it, Don, these two stick together and you don't feel any part of that. So you feel it's Marge's job to fight it out with her mother and get her here.

Marge: I know this sort of thing bothers mother—it sort of threatens her. I just don't know how to talk her into it. It took me a long time to get this far.

Counselor: It's hard enough for you to come, so you're pretty sure it's going to be difficult to persuade her to come.

Don: I think she might be aware of what she's doing. I think she knows that in some way she's taking over our lives. Sure it'll threaten her, but so what? She needs to know the facts of life of our marriage and you (Marge) should tell her. This would be a blow but she needs it. I can't reach her. It will have to be you.

Counselor: You're saying that she might want to stay away just because she wouldn't want to hear what she might have to hear. You see this as Marge's job.

Marge: O.K. I'll bring it up to her but it may not do any good.

Counselor: Well, let's leave it at that. We're over our time. From my point of view, I would be quite willing to have her come with you or I could see her separately if she wished. And, if you wish to, you can convey that to her from me.

Since this couple disagrees on most things, it's not surprising that they disagree here, too. Yet we notice that some beginning of joint relationship has started to emerge. So, even if the mother does not come, at least some kind of beginning unity has been established between them. The issue of the wife's mother, rather than blocking them as it did before, has at least some unifying tones now.

FAMILY COUNSELING

If the mother chooses to come with them, then marriage counseling has fused into family counseling. This new relationship can be sustained as long as they find it helpful. They have the option to return to marriage counseling as a couple, and the mother may choose to come separately to see the counselor, particularly if she begins to face herself more directly. She may, for example, confusedly recognize that she's hurting their marriage, and also see that her own fears and conflicts are indirectly causing her to do this. This might then be the beginning of counseling for her about the special issues and anxieties of old age.

Children too, are most important as major factors of reconciliation and motivation to continue the marriage. Sometimes, especially with older children, they too can be included in the counseling sessions when the issues separating the married partners also concern them. Such "milieu" family counseling can fuse out of a relationship that initially began as individual or marriage counseling. In such milieu counseling, as in group counseling, the counselor tries to understand and relate each person's feelings and views—letting the group flow and relate through him. Often the children's awarenesses, accepted and understood in this way through the counselor, are a revelation to one or both parents since, without this setting, the children could never express themselves so openly and deeply. This kind of deep family interchange, more than any other factor, can often bring reconciliation and renewed attempts to "get along especially for the sake of the children." But this can mean more than that. Behind it can be a more profound awareness of what each married partner now really means to the other members of the family, and an enriching sense of the significance of the role of both married partner and parent.

DIAGRAM

While we have discussed individual, marriage, and family counseling as occurring separately, they can also, then, be related. The following diagrams show how this can come about.

In Diagram I, we see marriage counseling in the two main parallel lines representing husband (H) and wife (W). The H angle represents instances where the husband feels he wants to discuss personal material about, let us say, his work, in an individual counseling interview. Given the option by the counselor, he may choose to have his wife present to observe his interview or interviews so that she can understand his work situation better, even though she has no part in it. On the other hand, he may choose not to worry or involve her, and therefore may prefer individual counseling for this. This may go along in a separate relationship with the counselor, while the marriage counseling continues at another time.

The same process of individual counseling may occur with the

DIAGRAM I

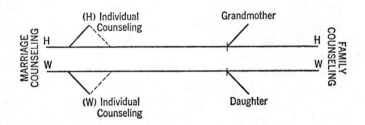

DIAGRAM II

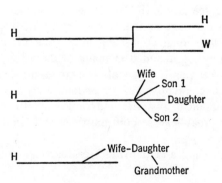

wife, indicated by angle W. The wife, for example, may have grave fears of childbirth, or some other personal anxiety for which she feels individual counseling would be necessary. Again, she can be given the option of her husband's presence as an observer, so that he may better understand the cause of her fears, or she or he may prefer that he not be present. This, too, can be concomitant with continuing marriage counseling.

Moving to the right (Diagram I), we see marriage counseling extending into family counseling. This develops in the process of marriage counseling or individual counseling, when the couple feels that issues which disturb them as husband and wife also significantly involve other family members. Let us assume, (as in Diagram I), that strong differences over the conduct of the teenage daughter also involve the wife's mother who is living with them. The grandmother and the granddaughter, let us say, "form a team" against the mother, or so she feels. The husband realizes he is caught in the middle, as now the grandmother, now the mother insists that he do this or that about the conduct of the teenage daughter. And the father, too, may have his own tensions with his daughter.

As this picture emerges from the husband and wife sessions, all four people could be given the option of coming together—with the counselor sensitively in the center, understanding the varying and conflicting viewpoints of all four. Marriage counseling may be resumed after a number of sessions of family counseling, or it may resolve itself into family counseling, as the broader issues prove to be the greater causes of tension between husband and wife.

In Diagram II we see an alternative, in which individual counseling could lead to marriage or family counseling. In this case a person coming for individual counseling may grow to recognize that his wife or family are included in many of the issues that he previously thought were purely personal. The counselor then offers him the option of concomitant marriage or family counseling. He in turn offers this option to his wife and/or family. In this way, individual counseling may lead to both marriage and family counseling.

Since family counseling and individual or marriage counseling are related, as well, to group counseling and group discussion, we will consider some aspects of these latter techniques in the next chapter.

NOTES

[1] John F. Cuber and Peggy B. Harroff, "The More Total View: Relationships Among Men and Women of the Upper Middle Class," *Marriage and Family Living,* 25 (2), May 1963, p. 144. (To arrive at these conclusions, a sampling of 437 persons between the ages of 35 and 55 were individually interviewed.)

12
Group Counseling

WE HAVE SAID that marriage, family, and group counseling are closely related. Learning experiences and group discussion can also include group counseling or pattern their relationships upon such counseling. Religious guidance and pastoral counseling, too, are often aided by group counseling skills. Consequently, this chapter will consist in a brief discussion of group counseling. Later chapters will develop this further, especially suggesting ways it relates to discussion and learning.

SKILLS FROM INDIVIDUAL COUNSELING

The basic awareness and skills of individual counseling are equally essential to group counseling. One might say that one aspect of group counseling consists in giving each person in the group the same sense of being really understood by the counselor that he receives in individual counseling. The importance of this is that it secures each person in feeling understood, even when others may reject or confront him.

NEW DIMENSION

As we saw in the consideration of limits, the presence of others gives a whole new dimension to group counseling and makes it a more central phase of living rather than the specially tailored personalized relationship of individual counseling. Here, particularly, is one of the main assets and stimulants of group counseling. The *whole group* is engaged together at a deeply personal level, not simply the counselor and one or two persons, as in individual or marriage counseling.

DISTINCTIONS

In any discussion of group counseling, it seems important now to distinguish between small, intimate family groups, or groups at least intimately related by the same personal issues, and larger groups that begin somewhat impersonally. We may call the first, *familial* or *intimate* groups, to suggest their close relationships at the beginning of the group counseling process.

If we regard the intimate group as receiving *particular* group counseling, we can then distinguish it from *general* group counseling. A further classification: the group formed clearly and exclusively for counseling, and the group that has originally formed itself for some work project or discussion topic. The group counseling process in this latter case would be ancillary to the work project or the more intellectualized discussion relationship. This distinction is necessary, as we will discuss in detail later, because there are obvious differences in the dynamics and motivations of a group that assembles exclusively for group counseling, in contrast to a group which assembles for another purpose.

In our present discussion then, we will consider, first, the intimate familiar group, such as the members of the same family; secondly, the group counseling process as such in a group consciously assembled for group counseling; finally, the use of group counseling and individual counseling in groups assembled for another purpose, e.g., students, or a discussion group, or those joined in a work project.

INTIMATE GROUP

We can begin then with counseling of intimate groups. Even here, however, one further distinction would seem necessary so that we can allot special treatment to the area we call marriage counseling. Usually, as we have seen, when we refer to marriage counseling, we mean the counseling of husband and wife, together or separately, centered on aspects related to their marriage. This would clearly be somewhat different from, although related to, family counseling in which husband, wife, and some or all of the children or intimate relatives might be included in the group counseling. While both groups would be concerned with marriage and the family, in marriage counseling husband and wife would tend to look at their relationship with one another much more directly, while regarding the children and relatives only indirectly. The reverse would be true, to some degree, in family counseling.

People related intimately in other ways, such as a small group working in an office together or on a research project or in a particular department, for example, while directly related to one another at a deep personal level in their common occupational concern, would not usually be so totally related as people in marriage or family counseling.

This would not always be true, however. Cuber's study, among others, reminds us that we may be romantically exaggerating the closeness and meaningfulness of marriage and family relationships, whereas, for many people, the deepest and most fulfilling relationships occur outside of marriage and the family.

We have grouped family counseling and small group counseling together because both have the characteristics of smallness, a common and somewhat intimate relationship together, and a focal point of tension and conflict around which personal reactions occur. In all this, such family or intimate groups differ from other groups that may be larger (fifteen or so, as against from three to six), and whose members begin as strangers to one another, with no shared experiences as a group, and no intimacy together. The same concepts as those of family counseling can, in general, apply to a group of people in conflict over a common project of any kind, provided the project engages them and is shared together in a serious way. This could also be true of common job responsibilities, faculty groups and similar situations.

FAMILY COUNSELING

Differing from marriage counseling, family counseling, as the name implies, would be concerned with issues that disturb people who live together as a family—and "family" here can be extended to include small groups with a common work relationship, etc. The focus is not only on husband and wife but on all the family members or all associates in a work or study relationship. The initiating factor can often be the difficulties of one or more students in the school, etc. Beginning with these concerns, the discussion slowly spreads to issues which affect and involve the whole family.

To return to the example given under the discussion of limits, disciplinary issues, at a high school level can be effectively dealt with not simply by censoring and punishing the high school student but also by directly involving one or both parents and, sometimes, other family members. Since many, if not most, school problems, especially in matters of discipline, are also the result of home situations, family rather than individual counseling can be an efficacious way of reaching the more basic causes of many school conflicts.

In the earlier example, the dean of studies, after a limited number of conduct violations, asked the student to bring one, or, if possible, both parents to the school with him. These appointments were scheduled in the evening if necessary. It was the boy's responsibility to explain to his parents why they were there. The dean, in this situation, acted as group counselor, clarifying and penetrating in his responses the exchange between the parents and the student and between the parents themselves. Only at the end did he present information that he felt was necessary, but even this, according to his report, rarely occurred. We saw from the statistical report that this proved an effective method for reducing the serious violations of school discipline.

In a similar way, family counseling can be inaugurated between one or more adolescents and their parents, between a person dating or engaged to someone "unacceptable" to his or her parents or, in fact, in any conflict involving various members of a family together.

SPECIAL DEMANDS ON COUNSELOR

Here, of course, even greater demands may be made on the counselor, since he must now reach out to and understand three or more people as they struggle to communicate together through him. While his function is fundamentally the same as in individual or marriage counseling, he has the added complexity of following each one closely and keeping the exchange related to him by his intervening, understanding responses.

This is a most important function since it keeps people from open quarrelling and painful confrontations without the advantage of hearing what it is they said, as filtered through the counselor. In all group counseling, it is very important that client expressions of any significance be directly responded to by the counselor before the other person answers. To achieve this, this counselor must often directly intervene and delay the other's reply until the first person has heard the counselor's sensitive awareness of how he feels.

As we discussed in treating marriage counseling, this sensitive counselor intervention accomplishes a number of things. First of all and perhaps most importantly, it gives the client who has just spoken, a genuine sense of feeling that he is always understood, even though others may then attack him or distort what he said, in their reply. Moreover, the other person or persons, geared for attack or distortion, have a chance to share empathetically in the sensitive way the client was understood by the counselor. This often lessens the intensity of their feelings and can even disperse them. What they might have said, therefore, without the counselor's response, they will not now say or they will say it with perhaps a lessening of hostility and distortion.

At first, this kind of counselor intervention may seem a little strange, and clients may attempt to run right over the counselor in the intensity of their feelings and reactions. Gradually, however, they grow used to his responses and they begin to wait for them before they themselves reply.

SIMILARITY

Other intimate groups assume many of the same characteristics of family counseling, inasmuch as the individuals already know one another somewhat, and they have at least one or more common concerns that deeply involve them. Their conflict about these common concerns is usually the explicit reason why they desired group counseling. Depending on the intensity of conflicts and feelings, and the extent of personal commitment, this process may center solely on common issues, or it may move into more personal concerns. As new material appears, especially of the sort that is uniquely applicable to only one person, the counselor (as we will discuss also under general group counseling since it applies there too) should hold up to this person the fact that he is beginning to reveal himself in intimate detail. The client now is given the option of individual personal counseling, or he and the group can discuss the degree to which they wish such personal data to be shared together. Usually the group will resolve the issues by more clearly defined limits which leave everyone more at ease and secure. Here unanimous agreement, at least by a show of hands, seems necessary so that the agreement on the defined limits is clear to all. If the counselor himself has reasons for asserting his own limits as to how far he can handle personal discussion in a group, he should say so openly. He will be more at ease himself, and as a result, more secure with the group and more likely to do a better job within the limits where he feels competent.

GENERAL GROUP COUNSELING

One of the main differences between general group counseling and the other types of group counseling we have discussed, is that as a rule the general group is larger and, in addition, the people are either complete strangers to one another, or only slightly acquainted. Some, of course, may be intimate friends. A common form of marriage group counseling is a group of married couples who already know one another or, at least, have common concerns, for example, small children, handicapped children, etc.

The group begins, therefore, with much less identity as a group, since the members have little or no relationship to one another. Some identity can be achieved by simply dividing the large group into smaller groups, each of which have some identity. Such identity can be simply a matter of being in the same ward in a particular hospital. In a military setting, division according to rank may seem helpful and even necessary because of the peculiar demands of military life. Groups can be divided also according to age or designated status such as adolescents or young married people.

While such divisions help in bringing about some homogeneity —and this, where possible, is certainly desirable—yet ordinarily, in general group counseling, we are faced with a group whose intent is to get individual personal help through the group exchange and not through any other sharing.

Consequently, the fact that the members are unknown to one another can constitute an advantage, since it gives a unique quality to the relationship, Often it allows a special freedom since these people do not see one another in other circumstances and need not and often do not choose to be friends outside the group counseling relationship. In this sense, the relationship of the members with one another has something of the same quality as the relationship with the counselor. Its aim and even exclusive purpose is counseling and no other relationships need impinge upon this purpose.

There seems to be no fixed agreement about the maximum size of a counseling group. Ten seems to be a commonly accepted number, although often fifteen or twenty seems a workable group, especially if they have a deep concern in common, like unwed mothers, mothers of small children, alcoholics, members of the same hospital wards, etc.

MISTRUST

The group counseling process generally begins in a way not unlike individual counseling. The mistrust of the counselor, however, is heightened by the mistrust with one another. Consequently, it may take an even longer time and greater patience and understanding on the part of the counselor than individual counseling, before the group begins to feel free to express themselves to the counselor and to one another.

The most common way this mistrust is expressed is by silence. Often no one wants to say anything. The counselor can become a prey to his own anxieties that the counseling will not even begin. Here he has to trust to the fact that each member of the group

came of his own accord for group counseling and there is, therefore, in the assembled group, a powerful dynamism to bring this
about. He must be willing to trust himself and the group and
neither be threatened, anxious nor in any way persuasive or cajol-
ing until these hidden forces begin to emerge. This usually will not
take long if the counselor in his anxiety does not say or do things
to impede rather than further the group process.

FROM NEGATIVE TO CONSTRUCTIVE VIEWS

In the following excerpt, members of the group are somewhat
familiar with one another and so are soon free to become negative.
We notice how this gradually produces expressions of positive and
constructive attitudes, as the negations are accepted.

In this illustration, the high school faculty member is also the
class discussion leader for a group of high school seniors. He was
at the assembly meeting and is aware of the tension that was
produced by the reading of new rules controlling autos and smoking, as well as those bearing on the manner of girls' costume, plus
a regulation forbidding girls to use the Coke machine in gym
clothes.

The leader is prepared for group counseling and so structures
his relationship to the group. In the beginning they are given an
option to continue their accustomed discussions or to react directly
to what has just occurred in the assembly.

Leader: Well, this is our third meeting, and as you know, we've used
this meeting for a kind of discussion together. This is a rather large
group for a discussion, I agree, but nonetheless, it seems to have
worked out. As you recall, I mentioned too, that sometimes these
discussions can get personal and may get into some things that have
you disturbed or upset in some form. And we can allow for that too,
even though in general, we usually intend to talk about political and
social situations and similar topics, such as we did the last time. You
recall we talked about DeGaulle and other world leaders and the issues
of peace.

We can do this again now, but we're also allowing for the possibility
that we may want to get into more personalized and more immediate

issues too. It's your option, and by option, we mean, of course, your choice, your freedom to decide as a group what things you want to discuss. So, as before, I'll leave it up to you to start the discussion . . . (pause)

Student 1, Boy: I dislike what the principal said. He doesn't understand the way things really are.

Leader: You're referring to the assembly meeting we just had.

Student 1: Yes, I worked last summer and I work evenings, and I just bought my car. I bought it with money I got because I worked all summer on a construction job. And, if you stop to think about it, I'm almost 18 years old, and pretty soon I'm going to be drafted, and it seems to me . . . I just don't quite understand . . . you ride the CTA, you don't want a car . . . I've seen you getting off the bus every morning . . . I don't know about you, but now I have this new Chevrolet convertible, and I worked two summers, and I work evenings.

PERMIT RELEASE

We are beginning to see an emotional involvement. The question is whether the leader should break in on this student. If he stops him too quickly, he is really saying to the whole group: "I said you could bring in personal material, but I'm not going to let you." So it seems better to let this first person talk himself out. Even if the group grows a little weary, they are reassured that the leader is going to listen. Later, he may perhaps break in with a response if another person starts to talk too long, when the group is assured of normal acceptance from the leader.

Student 1 continues: Well, I don't think you teachers understand because as I said, a parking lot is to protect the cars . . . I paid over $3000 for my car and they strip convertibles. You walk, you live close, you don't have to worry and Miss M——, she's got that old Ford, she don't need to worry but she's faculty and she can be in this parking lot and Joe, here, he sometimes brings his father's Oldsmobile—it's necessary, he lives a long ways.

Leader: Well, what I get here is that . . . you worked hard to get your car. It's yours. You may be going into the service. You may be doing anything that an adult man is asked to do soon. Then you figure that I and other faculty members don't have a good car or they don't have a car at all; you just feel that this is unfair and unjust to you, and perhaps to many others like you.

Student 2, Boy: Well, I wanted to come to this school, and I live almost 18 miles away, and I had to get permission to come to this school. Now, I can't come to this school if you're not going to let me drive my car. There's nobody I can take with me from where I live. Now, what am I supposed to do?

Leader: You feel that in your case your car is justified. The rule doesn't seem to allow for you because you have no students to bring.

Student 3, Boy: As far as these cars are concerned, I think we can all get around this because we can band together in a car pool.

Leader: You see a solution.

Student 4: I think that all this procedure was undemocratic. There should have been a polled vote instead of allowing the faculty and Student Council to make such a major decision.

Leader: Jack, your point is that this involves everybody, and it wasn't something that should have been just dropped down in a private decision . . . that everybody's reasons and contributions ought to have been made.

Student 3: Right. I agree with that too. But it hasn't been done that way . . . we should get back at the school by banding together and taking some action, maybe as I suggested, by setting up car pools, we could still bring our cars.

LEADER THREAT

The leader could be threatened here. If he is threatened, then he may trigger the group into threatening him more. So he handles this simply as a negative emotion.

Leader: Well, Joe, as you see it, this thing wasn't done democratically, and there might be a way to get revenge, in a sense, or get around it, if the group set up, say, group car pools and so expressed their own view of this.

Student 5, Boy: You're our teacher. I'm just wondering—I feel very personal about you as our own teacher—I'm just wondering where you stand on this issue. You with us or against us?

Leader: You wonder where I am, what view I take?

This kind of question is a common situation in group, as in individual, counseling. People may ask the leader what appears to be a direct or even attacking question, yet in reality, if he simply responds to their inquiry, the group counseling discussion goes right on. If it is a real negation or a genuine question, it will usually be brought up again by the same person or someone else. Then it should be directly accepted and, if need be, an explanation or opinion given. The leader, however, must be willing then to accept and respond to the group's expression of resistance and even hostility to him. The leader sees and responds to these as he would to other forms of group negation.

Student 6, Girl: Well, I feel sorry about the boys not being able to use their cars, but what really bothers me is that, well, that the women teachers are going to tell me how to dress. Now, some of these teachers look awful and I refuse to dress like that.

Leader: You're more disturbed, as I get it, by the question of the girls' dress . . . that issue is a greater one for you. You don't like to see yourself and the way you dress compared with some of the women faculty members.

Student 6: At least with the boys, it's a question of the whole faculty. But with the girls, it's going to be a question of one teacher and her, maybe way-out, views about how I should dress. Not only are you taking away a sense of democracy, but you're also taking away a sense of whether I know what is proper dress, too. So, you are taking away my choice of whether to be proper or not.

Leader: What seems unfair to you is one person making this decision. I gather that you feel it is a personal encroachment on your rights, that these are things you should decide for yourself.

Student 7, Girl: I think that as girls we should be allowed to smoke and I don't think a teacher has the right to tell the girls that they can't smoke just because she doesn't like smoking.

Leader: Again, the feeling is that smoking is your choice, and not the teacher's decision for you.

Student 8, Girl: I think if clothes are worn to prevent exciting the men, I think the men should judge what we are going to wear. And if the men are going to judge what we're going to wear, what about the boys walking around in their tight pants?

(This gets some hooting because the group knows that Jane usually makes statements like this.)

Student 9, Girl: Could I say to Jack about that democratic election . . . I'm a member of the Student Council, and we held a general election in September and all the students were supposed to vote. We represent the student body, and if he didn't vote in the general election, then he was obviously uninterested then. Personally, I don't care. I ride my bike to school.

LEADER'S FAIR BALANCE

This is a positive development. The student herself might be apt to overstate her position if she is encouraged. This may alienate her from the group. Because this seems to be the first statement of law and order, there is a danger of overselling it here. So it is simply presented back in the same way. The leader must hold his sense of fairness and honestly trust the group's ability to come to some balanced judgments themselves.

Leader: So, if Jack and the other students were really interested, they should have been at the meeting and had their say then. That's your view.

Student 10, Girl: I want to get back to the rules for the girls. Besides that, the regulation about the Coke machine. We're never away from class when we go down to get a coke. We're always at our next class on time, and that just seems so incidental, that there's nothing to it except to restrict us.

(This is complicated by the fact that the principal did not say what actually went on, and many of the students do not know all the difficulties that have occurred there.)

Leader: The coke-machine rule seems pointless to you.

Student 11, Boy: I talked to two student Council members on the way back to class, and they say all they do is sit in on the meetings, and they don't really have any say, and like Jack said, it's not a very democratic procedure.

Leader: You're questioning just how much real participation the Student Council actually has.

Student 12, Boy: Well, I think all these new rules are stupid. Ever since we've come here, every year there are rules made and something is taken away and nothing is given us. Now everybody knows the real reason about these cars, that old spinster down the street got mad because someone walked on her lawn. It isn't because of cars; she doesn't want kids around there, and the coke machine, that's because some teacher thought the kids were making noise in the hall—right away a rule is put down.

Leader: What you see is a series of rules. You don't see any logic to this, any point to it. As far as you can see, this whole business comes from the complaint of one or other people. These people's complaints —you feel this is what triggers this thing off, that they're really not balanced regulations at all.

Student 13, Boy: I would like to indicate to the representative of the Student Council that the comments made here today seem to have a very negative tone, and perhaps the Student Council and members that voted are not truly representing us. Maybe if they take note of that at this time they can change their behavior and really represent us in the future.

Leader: You're sort of supporting Jack's point that, as I get it, the Student Council ought to really represent the students in this, not just be a rubber stamp group . . . that the members of the Student Council here ought to pick up these comments and do something about them in terms of the faculty. In other words, you see the Student Council members as responsible for relaying this or in some way acting upon what is said here.

Student 14, Boy: Yes, I think we ought to have a class meeting, make motions, so all the seniors are behind this. First, though, I think we should have discussions like this and in smaller groups. I really think the faculty would go along with this. I mean, it's not really such a bad school. We all know that. (Some clapping)

Leader: Yes, you're proposing some meetings and some suggestions in advance, motions, etc. You're pretty sure the faculty would go along.

Student 15, Girl: I agree and I think a lot of others do too from the applause Bill got. But I think it's good to let everyone have their say. You know, we talk a lot about democracy, and I think we need to learn to practice it.

POSITIVE EMERGENCE

As with individual counseling, positive forces in the group start slowly to emerge as negations and hostilities are accepted by the leader and responded to in a sensitive, perceptive way. Gradually forces for unity and joint group reasoning and resolution begin to assert themselves. Without undue emphasis but in the same balanced way that he made negations cognitive, the leader catches and clarifies these group insights, positive commitments, and proposed plans. There is thus a slow but evident growth in group unity and group sharing. Even those who are hostile and resistant still are more likely to cooperate after the group has heard and understood their objections. They are less isolated. Even though their negation has been rejected, they are assured of some personal acceptance because they got a hearing. This often is all they really wanted.

Much more goes into group counseling process and skill than is illustrated here. From this we can see, however, its importance in aiding a group to express itself and share together in place of simply being isolated individuals in the same room. In later chapters we will extend this discussion of group dynamics further and add other illustrations of group counseling interaction.

COMMUNITY PROCESS

What we are seeing emerging in our discussion here and in the general areas of counseling therapy, is a concept of community inter-relationship and action. Applied to an educational setting, in what we are calling "community learning," for example, while the group experience engages each in a learning process, it also involves him personally in his own self-investment. This kind of group process can be conceived of as both community learning and operational group counseling therapy. It is community learning insofar as the group is learning together and acquiring facility over a new area of knowledge. But it could be called operational group counseling therapy inasmuch as the nature of the learning system engages them with one another and themselves at deep levels of their whole somatic, instinctive, emotional as well as intellectual awareness. This leads us to group discussion and counseling, and to a counseling type of learning experience, both of which we will now consider.

13

Group Counseling and Group Discussion

THE QUESTION might be raised whether one can distinguish clearly between group counseling and group discussion since, as we have seen, these are often combined and interrelated. But some distinctions can and, often, should be made. Since group counseling can be more personally involving, it is necessary for this to be understood and accepted by everyone whenever what seemed to be a discussion has, in fact, become counseling.

COMPARISON

Group discussion as distinct from group counseling has, as its main emphasis, the *understanding of meanings*. As such, it tends to be logical and intellectual. The discussion leader focuses on the meaning or idea content of what is said. *Group counseling,* on the other hand, is concerned with the identity of *value content* through understanding *emotional reactions,* including those we would call *instinctive* and *somatic*. The counselor's responses in a group would bypass, to some extent at least, the meaning content and concentrate on the emotion itself. As we have seen, the basic purpose of such responses is to uncover and symbolize emotion and value in the language of cognition.

We have also seen how a value-oriented educational relationship, because it extends to personal areas, can be especially complicated. In resistance and self-protection, I can reinforce my "not knowing that I do not know." I am not in a learning state because I do not open myself up. To reach a learning state—the next stage, where "I know that I do not know,"—is not an easy transition.

DISCUSSION SKILL

Consequently, deep emotions often occur in any learning experience. We will especially explore this in the next chapters. Here we note that, while the discussion leader must be aware of these emotions and may respond to them, his focus is still on the idea-content of what has been said. His response is mainly intended to further intellectual exchange and the group's pursuit and development of ideas. He touches on emotions then, to clear up a blocking in this intellectual idea process, not to pursue the emotions themselves to their value sources, unless the group itself really desires this. Some option should be given the group, or at least some notification, so that they know this is now what the leader is doing. Otherwise, the personal material unfolded can grow increasingly threatening for some of the group members, and they may be made hostile and resistant by such personalized discussion.

Since the main purpose of group discussion is the exchange of ideas, the clash of personalities and the emotional, instinctive, and somatic involvements and conflicts which ensue are, in general, seen as secondary, especially in the earlier stages of group discussion. Stated another way, while all the elements of group counseling are present, the group has in fact not assembled for group counseling and therefore, has not consciously agreed to anything but the sharing and contrasting of ideas together.

COUNSELING EMERGENCE

What can emerge, and usually does come up in any prolonged series of group discussions, is a somewhat intense series of personality conflicts which may take the discussion away from the main theme and leave it snarled in a tangle of somewhat unexpressed and unresolved emotions. When this occurs, group discussions have taken a bypath, while three or four control the group for their own basic personality needs, and leave the others hostile and rejected. At such times, some kind of group counseling seems called for if the group is to attempt to restore unity or even to prevent the total disbanding of the group discussion project.

Individual counseling may also be necessary when in the process of group counseling about the issues that impede discussion, areas that are highly personal for one or more of the group members begin to emerge.

DISCUSSION TO COUNSELING

To turn a group discussion into group counseling, it is, first of all, fundamentally necessary for the group leader to have sufficient counseling skills to handle the complexities that may occur in group counseling. In addition, he must be able to recognize the differences between the intellectually coordinating responses that are the main purpose of the group discussion leader and those more penetrating emotionally clarifying responses that can quickly involve the group in group counseling.

Because of the personal threat aspect, a discussion group should not be turned into counseling without at least some awareness on the part of the members that this is what is happening. They should know that there is freedom to express emotions and personal reactions and that, if they choose to do this, it will be understood and responded to by the counselor, and accepted and understood by the other group members. The leader must also reconceptualize his function as a counselor in order to change his attitudes, responses, and sensitivity accordingly. The group too, at least in a general way, needs to understand this changed relationship with the counselor. The reverse process can follow when the group clearly returns to intellectual discussion.

INTENSE EMOTIONAL INVOLVEMENT

There is a subtle kind of shame people may feel when, in the need of the moment, they say certain emotionalized and personal things. Given a day or so to think it over, they may be ashamed of what they did and hostile to either the group or the individual they think caused this. They may not come back to the group, if it is a free group; or if there is some type of required attendance, as for a seminar or class, they may remain uncooperative thereafter.

In other words, in an intellectual discussion the group is considering a theme or topic removed from themselves; the topic involves them only secondarily in their basic emotional and instinctive needs. While they may be in conflict with individual group members, these conflicts can be settled intellectually as differences of viewpoint, without necessarily arousing deep and somewhat uncontrollable emotions. As long as differences add to the group reasoning process of comparison and contrast, and conflicts are accepted with ordinary equanimity by group members, the group can remain focused on its original purpose, mainly, group discussion.

When, however, suppressed or uncontrolled emotions start to appear, faces can flush, palms perspire, heart action accelerates, and sharp and harassing personal remarks may emerge. As the group starts to divide into the angry, the resistant, the embarrassed and shocked, etc., the group discussion leader has a group counseling situation on his hands, whether he recognizes it or not. For such a contingency in a group to be utilized constructively, deepen the group's relationship to one another, and add significantly to the ultimate value of the group's experience and sharing, a sensitive group counseling skill on the part of the discussion leader is necessary.

PERSONAL THREAT

When the group discussion is focused on ideas, any emotional personalized expression can be disturbing to both the person and the group. If a group or a person is unprepared, what seems to be a simple exchange can be much more personal than it appears. It may not have seemed important to the observer or the group leader; yet, the individual involved may be hurt and upset. As we have seen, emotions tend to cause us to narrow our view and exaggerate reactions. A person may feel he was "made a fool of" by the group or the leader even when, to many in the group, this may have seemed just a spirited exchange of ideas.

The leader then must allow for the fact that a person in an emotional state tends to make "a mountain out of a mole hill," and what may seem to be minor in itself can be rejecting, and render him antagonistic. This is a main reason why it seems unwise, under the appearance of a discussion, to move people quickly into counseling.

GROUP OPTION

If the leader feels that group counseling is probably going to evolve out of a group discussion, people should be given some sort of option about entering into group counseling. If such anticipatory option is given, people are not nearly so threatened by what may then occur. So, when the leader anticipates that there is likely going to be a need of group counseling, this should be announced in advance with some kind of general statement, for example:

As you know, our purpose here is to have a discussion and exchange of ideas; however, some of these issues can get us personally involved. Strong positive or negative feelings in ourselves and others about some of these topics is clearly understandable. So, as leader, I'll recognize your feelings in this way, even though our main purpose is still discussion.

This opens up the possibility that some exploration of feelings may occur, but it has not shifted the focus from discussion. If any doubt exists, a show of hands may determine differences about instituting group counseling. These can be discussed before a final group decision. Such a procedure can prevent a possible backlash of anxiety and insecurity after a counseling group session. Group members who show some emotion or express personal reactions, know in a general way that this is what people sometimes do in this type of counseling, that the leader expected it and would understand and nobody would be surprised.

GROUP THERAPY

Relationships directly entered into for group therapy, of course, do not ordinarily demand this kind of structuring or clarification since their purpose is already clear. It is not our intent here to treat such therapy in detail, except to suggest that it resembles the group counseling process but generally implies a more personally disturbed and disorganized group membership. It usually takes place, therefore, in a hospital, clinic or similar therapeutic setting with the supervision and responsibilities that such settings provide.

LEADER INTERVENTION

The further question may arise: when is a group counseling release moving toward something too personal, and what may be done? This is the option of the leader, the group and the persons involved. One factor, for example, could be the degree of homogeneity of the group. Mixed groups of the same age would be more homogeneous than mixed groups of varying ages. Parents and children together would have less freedom than children alone or parents alone.

The leader may sometimes have to judge how intimately to let a person express himself before he intervenes. The person, already caught up in his emotional release, may not be capable of blocking himself at that moment. When the leader begins to have the feeling that a person may be moving too rapidly into personal revelations, the leader can intervene and offer the person an option.

While it may seem abrupt, such intervention allows the person to calm himself a little and gain a kind of breathing space where he can then decide to continue or not. What is said does not matter so much as the fact that it gives the person an opportunity to pause in his personal release. The wording, however, might be something like this:

You may feel that you know this group well and you are secure with them, and you may want to go on with this. I just thought I'd intervene momentarily because, you don't need to continue unless you wish. You can share this with the group or I would propose that maybe you would like to discuss this with me afterwards, if you feel you'd like to talk it out with someone. We could maybe get together after class for a few minutes and you could talk about it then.

This statement affords the person a chance to reflect and gives him the choice of the privacy of personal counseling. This is more important than what is said. In an emotional state, a person needs to pause and so collect himself, then, given this option, he can decide either way. People often come for individual counseling if they are given such an option. They welcome the relief given them. They recognize the leader's sincerity in blocking them and giving them a moment to think over what they wished to say. This adds to their trust.

When the private session begins, it often may start quite differently because the person may begin more directly with: "Well, what I really wanted to say was . . . but I didn't want to say it in front of the group." Before, he was in a kind of compromise-state which he now can resolve into the personal issues he really wants to talk about.

GROUP AS PERSON

A basic idea in considering the group process itself, is to view a counseling discussion group as, in some respects, similar to one person. Individual counseling, as we have seen, usually begins with the expression of negative emotion; this gradually becomes positive as insights and choices emerge. Some similar process seems to come about in group discussion counseling. But for this to occur the counselor-leader must be able to accept and clarify the group's negative feelings. Only slowly then, do more positive feelings and comments begin to emerge. But if the leader becomes threatened, he can impede or even prevent this process by making the whole group resistant. Having been promised freedom to express themselves, a group can become silently resistant, openly hostile or artificially participant, if they sense no genuine understanding and acceptance from the leader. This applies especially to those who express negation or even resistance to him. Since such negations often are communicated as soon as the group begins to trust the leader and one another, this can be a crucial phase. Accepting and understanding negative emotional releases in group as in individual counseling, seems basic to any developing process.

VARIATION IN SKILL

In the discussion as such, one of the main purposes of the leader is to understand each person's expression, to coordinate it with the contributions of the others, and to show by comparison and contrast how the group's ideas are interrelated. In this way, the individuals in the group can, in a sense, think together, formulating into a common intellectual awareness a wide mosaic of varying points of view and reaction. While all these contributions will be accompanied by some degree of tension and reaction, obvious or repressed, the leader filters out the emotional tones, since his main purpose is to coordinate the ideas expressed.

When, however, emotional tones commence to dominate to such a degree that they begin to disrupt and impede the group intellectual process, the leader, now consciously becoming group counselor, responds not only to the intellectual expression itself, but to the emotional tones surrounding these expressions. For example, a person in a group may say: "I disagree with that point because it seems that . . ." and express highly personal material that is still fundamentally intellectual in content. Another may say, however, "well, I strongly disagree and in fact, I think that remark was uncalled for. I think there are a number of people here who seem to always take the opposite side of what some of us say, and I think what some of us say is not as ridiculous as they are trying to make it." In an expression like this, we notice the same intellectual disagreement, but also somewhat deep feelings of hostility and resistance because the person feels that he and some others are being made to appear foolish. The person has not only stated his disagreement, he has also stated some deep feelings and one clear reason why he has these deep feelings.

TEMPORARY COUNSELING

Now if the leader, as counselor, chooses to respond to these feelings, he has initiated a temporary counseling relationship with that person. As the group takes up his response, counseling has begun with some or all of the group members. The counselor might say, for example: "You disagree but, if I understand what you have said correctly, you also feel that some of the group members are constantly taking the opposite side and this makes you resistant and even hostile because you do not feel what you present is foolish in any way."

Someone might then say, "Well, I don't see how we can have any kind of a discussion if every time we disagree someone's feelings are hurt. I don't think anyone is trying to make anyone else ridiculous. We just don't all agree—that's all!" The group is now clearly engaged in group counseling as they begin to unfold their feelings and reactions on the issue of some people being hurt when others disagree.

At this stage, the leader may find it helpful for himself and the group, to offer the group an option to discuss openly the various feelings that have been disguised to some degree up to this point. He may say, for example, after two or three more expressions of this sort, "Some people seem to feel rather deeply not only about this topic but about their relationship with one another. Perhaps we might want to discuss openly some of the feelings that may be impeding our discussion." In this way, he is clearly alerting the group to the change in focus that is occurring. Very often in the discussion about whether one should discuss feelings or not, the group can clear up some of the feelings that have been temporarily impeding their discussion. More relaxed, they can return to the intellectual disagreement, with resentments somewhat dispersed, at least temporarily.

CONTINUED COUNSELING

At other times feelings may be so strong and some or all of the group members may be so deeply involved, that the whole remaining time of that session will become group counseling. Normally, time should be called at the ordinary ending of the meeting. The leader, however, may offer the group an option to stay longer to discuss their deep involvement, and this can be shown by a raising of hands. It may be better here also to allow those who feel they must leave, the option to do so without feeling guilty. If not enough time remains for a stay of say, a half hour, the leader may propose the option of beginning the next meeting at the same feeling level with which it ends and so continuing group counseling.

At the beginning of the next meeting, he can then offer the group a further option to continue to unfold the divided reactions that impede them. Or, on the supposition that the intervening time may have solved the issues, the group may wish to continue their intellectual discussion.

By such methods one sees that the group leader interweaves group counseling whenever he feels it is necessary to facilitate a bogged-down process of group discussion. He does not establish consistent group counseling, however, unless the group, recognizing its deep involvement with one another as more basic and even more valuable than the group discussion topic, clearly decides to change the group discussion into group counseling.

When this occurs, we clearly have a new group of the same persons, who have now switched the focus from meeting to discuss together, to a conscious choice of meeting for group counseling. The role of the group leader has been eliminated and he, or another skilled person, should now function as group counselor.

INDIVIDUAL COUNSELING

Individual counseling may emerge out of group discussion when it becomes clear that the personal conflicts of one or two individuals are not really shared by the rest of the group, even though they are to some degree impeding the group discussion process. This can become evident when the group wants to continue the group discussion with only one or two people dissenting and interrupting on the basis of their feelings.

The group leader might then intervene with a counseling option such as: "I realize that you personally feel quite deeply about this, that you are negative and resistant to this discussion—if I understand your reaction—but (and here he may wish a show of hands from the group to make his point evident) the group seems to want to continue the discussion. I wonder if perhaps we should not continue our discussion on the topic we have prepared and if you would like, you and I might meet afterwards to talk out a little more your own reactions. Would you be free to stay ten or fifteen minutes afterwards?"

This kind of option statement made after two or three counseling responses, that is, giving the person the genuine feeling that the leader understands his feelings and resistances, would often be accepted by the person since he now feels warmly toward the leader and is somewhat aware—especially after he has seen the show of hands—that he is, in his own emotional involvement, impeding the desire of most of the group. A person can, in fact, often be grateful to the group leader for offering him a gracious way out of a somewhat embarrassing impasse that his feelings have gotten him into.

The group is also helped by this option because they are relieved of any guilt they might have had if they had just run over the feelings of one or the other of the group members.

LEADER LIMITATIONS

The limited interview after the group meeting could help the person probe, unfold and understand his feelings toward the group experience. Sometimes this can be adequately accomplished in the allotted ten or fifteen minutes. Otherwise a later personal interview series can be offered the person either with the group leader, if he is a skilled counselor, or with some other skilled counselor who has time available for such a personal counseling series. Here the leader must be careful not to assume responsibilities and obligations toward an individual group member which he cannot discharge, either because he lacks skill or sufficient time, or because he feels such a counseling relationship would impinge on his position as group leader.

Here, too, the group leader must recognize his limitations when serious psychological disturbances begin to appear. Here he should make considerate referral to competent, professional help whenever possible. As an alternative to this, he may consider the person's disturbed stage to be such that it is preferable as group leader to encourage the person not to continue in the group. When the group recognizes the person's absence, the leader's reasons for not wishing him to continue in the group should be briefly but sincerely stated to the group, so that it is not left with undefined guilt and insecurity about one member's continued absence.

COUNSELING IN LEARNING PROCESS

As we have pointed out earlier, we see counseling as a basic part of the learning process and not simply as an adjunct to it reserved, perhaps, for only the "failing" or "problem" student. Consequently, we see the school of the future offering ordinary occasions for counseling for every student to aid him in the final assimilation and personal application of what he is learning. In the meantime, however, teachers often encounter situations in the process of classroom teaching that call for group or individual counseling. Since teachers are being made increasingly aware of counseling skills, these can prove useful in many learning experiences.

Similar to the use of counseling in group discussions, the classroom, while tending to focus on the intellectual process, involves, in fact, the whole person of the student, often at a complex emotional, instinctive and somatic level. Going to school usually covers a long period of the day and such reactions can be even heightened by the special demands that school makes. There is, in addition, the threat of examinations, low grades and the high degree of competition that can exist in a particular class. The teacher, too, as a result, is usually far more involved and committed to his topic than a discussion leader would ordinarily be. These and other factors are special circumstances that may call for group or individual counseling to clear up a learning block.

The emergence of a counseling need can occur during a class session, in a wide variety of ways. In general, however, it will be in a situation similar to that described in group discussion: there will be the obvious expression of emotion and tension, usually coupled with some personal statements somewhat out of the context of the intellectual point or exchange. The classroom may compound all this, however, since it places a much greater premium on intellectual understanding. There is also much more personal involvement by the teacher and the threat of a low grade is always in the background.

COMPLICATED TASK

One of the most difficult phases of this contingency of counseling need in a classroom is the complication this creates for the teacher himself. To be deeply involved in an intellectual presentation and then to be suddenly faced with the demand to reverse oneself and become an understanding counselor can be, in itself, a very threatening about-face. Yet this is what seems necessary if the emotional impasse that can occur between the teacher and the student group or an individual student, is to be avoided.

Consequently, there is the complicated task of both intellectual presentation of a topic, at a more or less intense level of personal engagement, and, at the same time, the ability to invoke a counseling relationship in the midst of this presentation. To have the fluidity, in the process of involved teaching, to switch to an emotionally understanding and sensitive reflection of one or more students, places a great burden on the teacher-counselor's understanding and use of himself.

TEACHER INVOLVEMENT

Perhaps at no time is it more difficult to try to understand the feelings of someone else than when one is deeply and psychosomatically engaged in struggling intellectually with the presentation of one's own ideas. Here all the resources in one's personality are bent on *being understood by the student,* at least intellectually. One can sense how deeply rewarding this is to the teacher when one or a number of students so understand him. Geared as he is then for this kind of intellectual appreciation of what he is saying, the teacher is in the exact opposite mood from that which would characterize a counselor. To jump, within a space of a minute or so, from a teaching psychological mood where one is seeking to be understood, to that of a counselor who understands—with no intervening adaptive stages, is, therefore, a most exacting challenge.

TEACHING AIDS

One solution would be some kind of team teaching. This solution needs to be explored at much greater length. Here, two people, at least, would teach a given class. One might be primarily the class counselor and discussion leader, and the other the teacher, in the sense of having the responsibility for intellectual presentation, clarification, and the answering of knowledge-centered questions. Depending on the nature of the statement of an individual student or student group, either the teacher or the discussion leader-counselor would handle the response and continue to center the discussion, as long as it remained in his area.

A variation of this may be seen in those situations where through television or film, the intellectual presentation has already been made. The teacher, while he may be answering and clarifying the intellectual material, would be emotionally much freer to adapt himself to the position of discussion leader and group counselor. This, in fact, may be one of the natural outcomes of the increased use of teaching machine aids as an adjunct to the classroom. It could, in fact, free the teacher for these more personalized relationships in discussion and counseling.

SELF-DISENGAGEMENT

Difficult as it may seem, however, it is actually possible for the same person to train himself so that, even though he may be deeply engaged in the intellectual presentation of a topic, he can consciously come out of this intellectual depth. He is able sensitively to give himself over to understanding the emotional conflict and intellectual confusion of an individual student or group of students.

But, as we can see, this would require not only skill in group and individual counseling, but also practice in disengaging oneself quickly from the peculiar kind of personal self-involvement that intense intellectual presentation calls forth. If he can do this, however, the teacher will often find classroom experiences far more vital and communicative. No matter how clear an intellectual presentation is, it always runs the risk of being solipsistic in the way it centers everything around the thoughts and actions of the teacher himself. He is imprisoned, in a sense, by his own ideas. If he judges students largely on their ability to give him back almost exactly what he has said, he further tightens the bonds of his own involvement with himself. He is freed of this self-projection only when he can, in a sense, leap out of his stream of intellectual consciousness and engage himself in struggling to understand, penetrate and verbalize the complicated feelings of someone else.

This psychological leap may be all the more difficult because often, in a classroom setting, the student feels he has to protect himself by cloaking his emotional reaction, under the guise of an intellectual question. The teacher's first clue of the need for counseling responses may, in fact, come only after he has attempted once or twice without success, to give intellectual clarification to a questioner or group.

DISPROPORTION CLUE

The awareness of counseling-need seems often to hinge on the teacher's realization of a kind of disproportion between the student's resistance and obtuseness and the degree of difficulty of the intellectual material. Somewhere along the line of his recurrent explanations, the teacher sees or feels that somehow this material should not be as difficult to understand as some of the students are making it.

It is at this point in an exchange of question and answer that the teacher must listen carefully for possibly disguised emotional tones of conflict and confusion. He then has the option of switching to a counseling relationship until these barriers have been removed and clearer intellectual exchange is again possible. He has, of course, the alternative of not choosing a counseling relationship and ending the question and answer exchange in the hope that through discussion with other students or a night's sleep, the students involved will have worked their own way out of the impasse.

LEARNING COUNSELOR

Once one chooses to be a counselor, in such circumstances, one uses largely the same skills that we have already explained. What is peculiar about teaching is rather this special complexity, that one must suddenly, and sometimes unexpectedly, make the exacting operation of switching from a highly concentrated intellectual functioning to another involving emotional, instinctive and somatic sensitivity. To be able to do this, however, is to enrich the classroom experience both for the teacher and students. Such an ability would demonstrate on the part of the teacher a proficient and subtle use of himself, simultaneously as a teaching and counseling instrument. He would become a learning counselor. This would, at the same time, open up the learning experience to include much more personalized elements on the part of the students.

In a classroom setting, even more than in a group discussion, the intellectual presentation would still occupy the center stage. It would be unfair to students and teacher alike, were the classroom simply to become a place for group counseling. The purpose of counseling in this situation, then, would be short-termed. It would be aimed primarily only at discharging or removing immediate blocks to learning. But for an individual student who so wished, it might also clear the way for his entrance into a separate group or individual counseling relationship. In this sense, then, classroom experience could be a fruitful means for individual students to face the need for and make use of counseling interviews as a basic aid to their own learning process. In this way, too, an increasingly smooth relationship between teaching and counseling could be furthered.

Such a viewpoint, of course, furthers the aim of education for values as well as meanings. It sees the teacher as a learning counselor who supports each student in the learning process. The teacher function would no longer be simply focused on imparting information and explaining it. To achieve this more adequately, also implies a greater use of teaching aids and apparatus. These issues will be treated in greater detail in the next section.

PART THREE
Education for Self Investment

14

A Counseling Model in Learning

BASIC to the relationship of counseling, psychotherapy, and values is the nature of the educative process itself. In our earlier discussion of meaning and value, we proposed that the educational process extends along a continuum from the impersonal to the highly personal. In this process, one searches for and so seeks to find adequate life meanings. He then tries to make them operationally sound personal values. This present discussion will consider some learning experiences from this point of view of personal involvement. But most of the material reported here can be applied to therapeutic situations, or in fact to any life conditions, especially where adaptations to others and conformity to limits are necessary.

Any discussion of the educative process has really to start with the relation of conflict, hostility, anger and anxiety, to learning. This has been overlooked in many of our present educational methods because, as we have seen, we are apparently still victimized to a considerable degree by concepts that are both exaggeratedly intellectual and competitive. The "good" student is still presumed to be able to learn best in an intellectualized and individual way, with little or no consideration given to his emotional somatic involvement or his need for a community learning experience shared with other students.

LEARNING MODEL

Recently we have been doing research in the learning of foreign languages through a counseling-therapy type of relationship.[1] This research has made increasingly clear the interweaving of the whole personality process in learning. We wish her to draw on some of these learning experiences to illustrate and clarify this, and at the same time to show how any kind of teaching or guidance encounters many of the same personality subtleties.

The learning relationship—in this case, foreign language learning—can, in fact, be viewed as a model of the process by which many other groups and individuals learn. While this discussion is directly related to the learning of foreign languages in a counseling-psychotherapeutic way, it has implications beyond this in that it can readily be adapted to the learning of other subjects, especially those that become charged with fear and anxiety.

BROAD IMPLICATIONS

But the implications also extend to the areas of personality adjustment and personal value commitment, to legal and moral codes, to religious values, and to all those situations where a person must adapt himself to the demands of others, no matter what his internal preferences may be. In such situations, he cannot be guided simply by what is comfortable and secure for him. Rather he must undergo even pain and anxiety, if necessary, in order to fit himself to the boundaries and rights of others.

The struggle to learn to speak a foreign language aptly demonstrates many of the issues in this kind of conflict. To speak German, for example, one must give up one's security and comfort in English sounds and adapt to the demands not simply of the German person but of the whole grammar-pronunciation structure of what is considered proper German. This kind of language encounter contains in embryo most of the psychological experiences that any severe social adaptation entails. We can study this process psychologically and at the same time measure the effectiveness of the group process both by the psychological changes in the persons themselves and the degree to which they have learned to speak one or more foreign languages with foreign natives.

This project reveals, in a psychological research spotlight, some of the knottiest questions that arise in studying extremes like social rebels or isolated individuals who resist socialization. At the same time, we can observe more ordinary conflicts which act as barriers to personal communication, like those, for example, between husband and wife, or similar blockings in relating to others.

RESISTANCE TO LIMITS

We have, too, in the resistances to grammar and pronunciation, reactions that are similar to resistances to ethical, legal, and religious standards of conduct. Many times, deep personal reasons come forward—going back often to early childhood—which reveal the person's resistance is not limited to the language experience but extends to a wide area of what he sees as the outside imposition of any authority. Yet, paradoxically, he may see, too, that if he wishes to learn a foreign language, be a Christian, a law-abiding citizen, etc., he must take himself in hand and submit to these demands. They do not come, as he may at first *feel,* from another person's domination of him and superiority over him (the language native in the group to whom he may at first direct his resistance) but from the whole fabric of a social structure of which, by his very presence in the class, he desires to become a part, and according to whose norms, he wishes finally to change himself and learn to operate effectively.

MEANING BECOMING VALUE

Stated another way, one could say that the absorbing of meanings so that they become values, resembles and imitates the process by which I first approach and ultimately integrate and speak what was originally a foreign language. In this sense, the popular expression, "He speaks my language," or "I don't speak his language," catches something of the broader self-involving aspects of any value-learning. It comes down finally to learning to communicate comfortably and securely with oneself and others in this new value system.

As we will see, too, the learning process itself initiated here, has much in it that is similar to the psychological incarnate-redemptive process by which a person in counseling and psychotherapy acquired a renewed sense of the worth and value of his total self. As for the remote and almost God-like figure of the native language experts, as first viewed by the learners, we see them gradually come to share, in the learners' eyes, the common human condition. In the shared humanity of weakness and confusion, as they learn a common unknown foreign language together, there is renewed motivation for the student to identify with the expert in his own language. By such deep feelings of personal belonging, the learner is then positively urged to grow more and more in this new and different manner of self-reference and communication. He thus begins to grow a new self in the foreign language, a self that sometimes, in some ways, he may prefer to his native language self.

CONSTRUCTIVE-DESTRUCTIVE

The complicated and subtle part conflict, hostility, anger and anxiety play in learning recurred repeatedly in almost all aspects of this foreign language learning research. To a certain point, we can call these *positive* factors, for they engage one in the learning experience; they are forms of commitment and involvement. Beyond that point, however, they seem to become destructive forces; they block the student, make him want to escape the whole experience, or arouse him to a defensive kind of learning. Such a defensive learner often tends to disregard what he has learned as soon as it has served its defensive purpose, apparently because the whole experience has been so painful. Many students, for example, spoke of the deep hostility they had toward foreign languages as a result of previous classroom experiences. In their negative anxiety and conflict, most had defended themselves against this threatening situation by getting a passing grade—some even a high one. But afterwards it was difficult and painful for them even to try to speak this particular language in our research group.

LEARNING PROJECT

For our research project on the learning of foreign languages, at the college and graduate level, we chose four languages: French,

German, Spanish and Italian. We thought that accepting volunteers would produce graduate students and college students, and later, groups of high school students and any interested adults, with various levels of knowledge of some of the languages, but few with a knowledge of all four. This way each one could begin fresh in at least one language, with neither advantages over others nor previous negative experiences to impede them.

But we also used this approach with individual high school language classes—in Latin and Spanish. Our project also included very small children (two to three years), and elderly people in a home for the retired. Groups of "head-start" and slow learners were also taught English, as part of this research project.[2]

INITIAL ANXIETY CONFLICT

To illustrate the anxiety-hostility-conflict involvement in learning, let us reconstruct an experience which we conducted a number of times in different languages. This kind of experience was not the focus of our research, but it may help clarify some initial conflicts that seem to be present at the beginning of a foreign language learning encounter. The following was in French but could be paralleled in other languages.

To begin with, we chose four people from our group who, as we knew from their scholastic records, had only a year or so of high school or college French. We put them in a room and asked them to speak as much French as they could, using English for words they did not know in French. No one of the four people knew how much French the other three knew.

The first reaction of the four was far from being simply an intellectual one. The four people confronting each other anxiously wondered how much the others knew. They experienced needs for both reassurance and group equilibrium. Each hoped that the others knew no more French than he, and so would be on his same level. In primitive and probably regressive defense of himself, each person was already prepared to resist anyone who had learned more than he. It was, therefore, necessary for him to begin to explore the situation causing his anxiety with something like: "je

... uh ... uh ... never really had much français." He was admitting his ignorance, defending his ego, and to some degree pleading with the others not to be any better in French than he. Another student, obviously relieved to find that there was at least one other person identified with him, would say something like: "Oh, I'm glad there is somebody here who doesn't know any French either." Two of the people were already pleased with their ignorance, and finding a degree of comfort in it, were now fearful of the other two, lest they knew more. Soon the third person came forward and joined the group of the ignorant. Finally, when it became evident that the last person also knew no more than the others, the group settled to a security equilibrium—no one's knowledge threatening anyone.

If, however, we chose one person who knew more, he seldom felt really secure in his superior knowledge. Rather he usually tried to minimize his knowledge, and even apologize for it, since he recognized his threat to the group's security and his own isolated position in regard to the other three.

URGE TO TEACH

To add to the experience, in a few instances we had a native person, in one case a French girl who had been in this country only six months, sit outside the door and listen to these four people struggling painfully with her language. It is not hard to envisage her feelings as she sits there. During her six-month stay in America, she had already been daily humiliated and submissive while people corrected her English. Her position in English was, in other words, much like that of a child. Now by contrast, her adult self was strongly involved. Afterwards she said she was intensely identified with the four students and their obvious need of French. She wanted very much to help these Americans in return for the help she had received in English. She also wanted to be related in her French self with Americans. It would make her feel like the adult she really was, instead of the child she had been feeling. She wanted to help these people who, as she logically saw, needed her. She had, in other words, many of the qualifications and urges of an expert teacher.

THREAT OF KNOWING

We then asked her to go into the room and sit at a slight distance from the group. The four people in the room had by this time become comfortable and at ease in their shared ignorance, and were having rather a good time exchanging whatever words they knew and using English for what they did not know. They knew this girl by sight, knew that she was French.

In a few minutes they became silent. Like a sudden draft of cold air, her entrance had frozen them. The French student was thus completely frustrated in the greatest potential fulfillment she had had so far in America. She, in turn, soon found herself both disturbed, hostile and embarrassed. In place of needing her, she realized that the people were not accepting her, had asked her no questions, did not seem to want her help. Soon after they stopped talking, she felt they were throwing angry glances in her direction. Perhaps in reality, the glances were more anxious than angry, but anxious glances were often interpreted as angry ones by the person to whom they were directed. Sometimes they were anxious and aggressive at the same time.

If one continued this process, rather than ending it here, one solution the group commonly arrived at was to become exaggeratedly dependent on the French expert, asking her reassurance and help with every word and phrase, even those they knew and may have used before. This apparently was, as we shall discuss later, a passively aggressive way of handling their resistance and resentment. In such a resolution, the expert gains no real relationship to the group except that of an adult to helpless children.

This reconstructed experience, while simple, serves to show some of the negative dynamics created against an expert by people who, having become secure in their comfort state, seem defensively to band together against the "enemy" who knows too much. They are resentful toward the person who tilts their security equilibrium.

COMMON LEARNING CONFLICT

We see here an example of the psychological conflict that is often if not always initially involved between the person who is informed, who can and is eager to give his knowledge, and the people who are blocked from accepting that help by the hostility arising from their anxiety and ignorance. This is clearly a counseling therapeutic situation as well as a learning one. Yet this kind of conflict seems intrinsic to at least the first stages of learning. What often goes on in a classroom, for example, is the end effect of the attempts of both groups—the teacher and those who are to be taught—to resolve this kind of complicated psychological involvement with one another. They seldom resolve it in a counseling way, but rather almost by chance, depending on the immediate circumstances. For some students this may have serious negative after-effects.

INVERSE RATIO PARADOX

By way of contrast, we found it interesting to see what happened when we chose a different group of four, all of whom knew a good deal of French, although, when the group first came together, no group member knew how much the others knew. Again, anxiety was evident at the beginning. The first speaker usually said something like: "Well, I have had some French, but . . ." Each one tended to play down his ability until it became clear that they all spoke fairly fluently. If we brought the native French person into the room after the four students had assured themselves of their security, the threat was minimal. They were usually able to make use of the French expert's help when needed, with anxiety but without serious conflict. There is, then, apparently an inverse ratio here: the greater the need, the greater the resistance to expert help; the less the need, the more willingness to accept such help. Apparently, this is, in another guise, the age-old truism—"to him who has, will be given," and the issue of "saving the saved."

AFFECT-COGNITION MODEL

This brings us then to a consideration of some more complicated arrangements and procedures. As we have said, the main aim of our research was to establish a learning experience through a relationship which imitated counseling therapy and which was as deeply involving of the whole person of each student. We wanted some kind of *total experience,* not simply an "intellectual" one.

In our attempt to accomplish this, we took as our model *the affect-cognitive inter-communication* that seems to constitute a basic aspect of the counseling relationship. One of the functions of the counseling response, as we have seen, is to relate affect, emotional, instinctive, or somatic, to cognition. Understanding the language of affect, or "feelings," the counselor responds in the language of cognition. From our point of view, this is one of the chief dynamics occurring in the counseling therapy process. The person has affects for which he cannot supply adequate cognition, but which he tries to communicate in words to the counselor. He gets back from the counselor, in a sensitive and understanding relationship, a cognition of his affect that he can hear, absorb, and then compare with his affect. He often expresses successful cognition with such phrases as, "I am beginning to see." Before, he had only confusion and conflict as he tried to recognize his own feelings. It was apparently his attempt to put these confused and conflicting feelings into words, and the counselor's understanding and return communication, that slowly gave him this increase in cognition about himself.

We can say then that the counselor tries to speak the language of cognition, but also understands the language of affect, and that the client tends to speak the language of affect, but hears back, and therefore is able to absorb, compare, and understand the counselor's language of cognition. In this way, he slowly learns to speak a more cognitive language to himself. As a result, in place of confused feelings, he begins to "understand himself better," as he will often say. Seen in this way, we have a sort of two-language communication taking place.

LANGUAGE-COUNSELOR
GROUP COMMUNICATION

This awareness of a two-language model in the counseling-therapeutic process led us to choose the learning of foreign languages as the area for our attempt to interrelate counseling and learning in a unified experience. We adapted this conception to foreign language learning in the following manner. As has been said, we chose four languages: French, German, Spanish, and Italian. In this way, if a person was well-trained in one language—French, for example— he could, when he desired, attempt to speak German, Spanish or Italian. It rarely happened that a person was secure in all four languages; hence, people could switch around and so experience various levels of linguistic difficulty, anxiety, and conflict in communication, in proportion to their competence.

To help him communicate in the foreign language, each person had a language counselor who was usually a native speaker of that language. This person came to be considered as a kind of "linguistic parent-substitute," or a language "other-self." Sometimes he was thought of as a sort of linguistic "iron lung."

The four, five or six people sitting in a circle did not communicate with one another directly at first, but through these "other language selves." If, for example, the first person to speak wanted to say to the group in French: "It is a beautiful day today," and he knew little or no French, he turned to the French person slightly behind him, and said this in English. The others in the group overheard the English and therefore knew what the person wanted to say in French. This was called the English "over-hear." We notice this was not a direct communication but more as though one might eavesdrop or monitor an exchange between counselor and client.

The French person then gave back, in the manner of a counselor's response, the French words: "C'est un beau jour aujourd'-hui." The student turned to the group and repeated the French words as they were given to him. This was his first real communication to the group. He was helped by his French counselor to speak each word correctly. This same procedure was followed in the other three languages.

SPEAKING FOREIGN LANGUAGE

This process resembled the way a swimmer turns his head to breathe in air, then turns back to the water to breathe out. It enabled the person, from the very beginning, to speak to the group in a foreign language, with the expert's help. The language counselor expert—like a psychological counselor—was warm, secure and reassuring. The language counselor's tone and manner strived to convey the same deep understanding of the client's anxious, insecure state as he might experience in a good counseling relationship.

HANDICAPPED REGRESSION

This language counseling arrangement allowed us to see a number of psychological processes begin to operate. Since the foreign language counselor was a kind of parent-figure, an infantile emotional regression relationship soon emerged between him or her and the client. The group in turn became both children and handicapped people. All had parent-figures and, like handicapped adults, all were breathing through linguistic iron lungs as they communicated and related to one another.

In a comparatively short time the group became adapted to this handicapped way of speaking in four languages. Much like paraplegics learning to play basketball, they gradually became more natural and efficient. They soon could carry on what became increasingly an ordinary conversation, except for the much more intensive psychosomatic engagement that such a "handicapped" conversation involved.

Each one could advance independently in speaking a language according to his ability, getting help only when he needed it or made mistakes. Later, as he advanced, more minute corrections were made and special idiomatic expressions were supplied by the expert language counselors. This progress was divided into five stages, each marking a difference in his relationship to the counselor and the group as he grew more secure and independent in one or more languages.

COUNSELING-FOREIGN LANGUAGE RESEARCH:
DESIGN OF THE DIFFERENT POSITIONS IN LANGUAGE-COUNSELING DISCUSSIONS

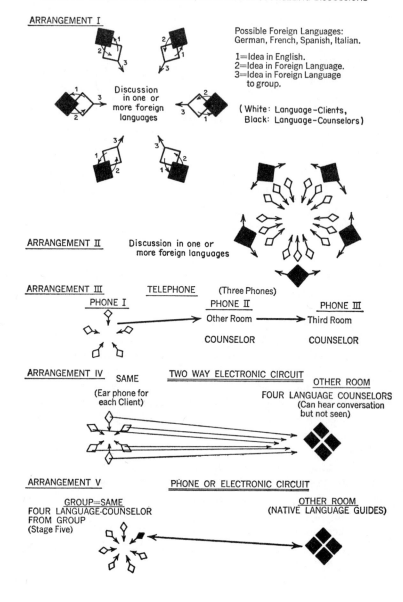

ARRANGEMENT I

Possible Foreign Languages:
German, French, Spanish, Italian.

1=Idea in English.
2=Idea in Foreign Language.
3=Idea in Foreign Language
to group.

(White: Language–Clients,
Black: Language–Counselors)

Discussion
in one or
more foreign
languages

ARRANGEMENT II   Discussion in one or
more foreign languages

ARRANGEMENT III   TELEPHONE   (Three Phones)

PHONE I   PHONE II   PHONE III
Other Room ——————→ Third Room
COUNSELOR   COUNSELOR

ARRANGEMENT IV   SAME   TWO WAY ELECTRONIC CIRCUIT
OTHER ROOM
(Ear phone for
each Client)   FOUR LANGUAGE COUNSELORS
(Can hear conversation
but not seen)

ARRANGEMENT V   PHONE OR ELECTRONIC CIRCUIT

GROUP=SAME   OTHER ROOM
FOUR LANGUAGE-COUNSELOR   (NATIVE LANGUAGE GUIDES)
FROM GROUP
(Stage Five)

STAGES OF GROWTH

The following outlined plan was given to each one:

Stage I

The client is completely dependent on the language counselor.
1. First, he expresses *only* to the counselor and *in English,* what he wishes to say to the group. Each group member overhears this English exchange, but is not involved in it.
2. The counselor then reflects these ideas back to the client *in the foreign language* in a warm, accepting tone, in simple language especially of cognates, in phrases of five or six words.
3. The client turns to the group and presents his ideas *in the foreign language.* He has the counselor's aid if he mispronounces or hesitates on a word or phrase.

This is the client's *maximum security stage.*

Stage II

1. Same as above.
2. The client turns and begins to speak the *foreign language* directly to the group.
3. The counselor aids only as the client hesitates or turns for help. These small independent steps are signs of positive confidence and hope.

Stage III

1. The client speaks directly to the group *in the foreign language.* This presumes that the group has now acquired the ability to understand his simple phrases.
2. Same as (3) above.
   This presumes the client's greater confidence, independence and proportionate insight into the relationship of phrases, grammar and ideas. Translation given only when a group member desires it.

Stage IV

1. The client is now speaking freely and complexly *in the foreign language.* Presumes group's understanding.

2. The counselor directly intervenes in grammatical error, mispronunciation or where aid in complex expression is needed.
   The client is sufficiently secure to take correction.

Stage V

1. Same as IV.
2. Counselor intervenes not only to offer correction but to add idioms and more elegant constructions.
3. At this stage, the client can become counselor to group in Stages I, II, and III.

As ease in conversation developed through this language-counseling arrangement, psychological complexities began to appear. Some were repeated in each successive group so that they seemed predictable. Intense relationships with the counselors emerged as well as jealousies and rivalries with other group members. Hostility to oneself and others was very strong in some. Gradually open anger was able to be expressed, especially as the members of the group grew to trust one another. There was evident regression in the group in proportion as one knew little or nothing about the language he was attempting to speak. Many expressed feelings, emotions and fixed reactions similar to those they remembered from early childhood. "We are all children around a sand-pile," was a commonly accepted concept for those in stages one and two.

At the other end of the scale, as people began to speak freely and independently in stages four and five, intense resistances to the counselors sometimes emerged in a manner that appeared to be similar to that of an adolescent struggling to become an independent and self-responsible adult.

DOMINANT-SUBMISSIVE ATTITUDES

In other ways, too, the relationship between the group and the counselors proved revealing. There were, among other things, implications about the hidden attitudes and needs of a person in an expert or teacher role and how this affects the group relationship.

One aspect of this was the degree to which people who stayed only in their most capable languages and so protected themselves by being superior, at the same time often felt alienated from many group members. This was especially true of the native experts.

Since people who were native expert langue counselors in one language, were much less expert in at least one other language, an interesting relationship usually developed between these people and the other group members. When they were expert language counselors, for a comparatively long time they were never considered part of the group by the other group members nor did they themselves really feel part of the group. This was true even though members could be deeply attached to them in their language-counselor identification.

Urges in both the group and the language expert seemed to combine to bring this about. The group, as we have seen, tended to be hostile to anyone who knew too much. This produced various reactions. One common reaction, as in controlled hostility, was to alienate the expert. One of the ways to accomplish this seemed to be to make him appear a kind of god, and so remove him from any human conditions, to put him in what we have called a "non-incarnate" state. Creatures can be seen as totally dependent on this "non-incarnate God." There is almost no communication except that of helpless, dependent people toward a god-figure, who determines what is right, how things are to be done. Here we can go a step beyond the infant-parent-figure dependency to a mode of creature-creator dependency.

ALIENATION OF KNOWER

This god-like position, however, while giving the native counselor great prestige, had the painful adverse effect of removing him from any sense of sharing or belonging to the group. He was simply the one who knew every word and every construction, and so seemed to have a kind of absolute, unquestioned power and supremacy.

One example will illustrate this reaction between such an individual and the group. A student in the group was an Italian who came to the United States at the age of fifteen and was now a graduate student. At the time he joined the group we were not insisting that people try any of the other languages besides the one they knew well. He was, therefore, in the god-role in Italian and spoke fluent, correct English as well. He was also fairly competent in French. He was, however, hopelessly incompetent in German. It slowly came to him that he was almost completely alienated from the group. In other words, he was too perfect to be considered as having any share in their blundering anxiety and confusion. He felt excluded as if, he said, he did not "belong to the human race."

This is similar to the non-incarnate hostility and removal from themselves that people often express at the beginning of counseling. He was, of course, at the same time, very aware of his feeling of powerful superiority. He also felt a vengeful satisfaction at their inadequacy, which he enjoyed because of his earlier humiliations in high school when he had painfully to learn English.

In a counseling interview about this, he decided that at the next meeting of the group he would struggle to speak German for the first time. He saw that this decision meant giving up his superior position and showing himself to the group in a helpless human state. He carried out his resolution and for the first time he no longer felt alienated. He described experiencing a deep sense of his own weakness and of having his weakness understood. The group now accepted him, too. In place of his dominating power, he had gained a sense of worth through a sort of Sullivanian "consensual validation," apparently. One might describe this also as a kind of human redemption following upon the acceptance of incarnation. He felt he belonged at last, because he was now in reality an ignoramus like everyone else. He had become "engagé" in the human condition by submitting to the humiliation of his ignorance in German. In giving up his pseudo-divine power position, he had gained human community and belonging.

WILL TO AID COMMUNICATION

Another significant aspect was the manner in which the experts as language counselors had slowly to give up their "will to power" over their clients, and see them grow to be increasingly independent of them. One is reminded here of how the expert had to accept the Scriptural proposition: "he must increase, I must decrease," in regard to his client. One might suggest, too, that this resembles some of the issues between adolescents and parents, as the adolescent struggles to find his own unique and independent meaning as an adult.

This began to be evident when the learner reached stage three in a particular language. Here he started to use words and phrases he had learned. With this came a surge of independence, a desire to be free of the counselor, in marked contrast to the warm, almost womb-like dependency of stages one and two. Now the learners began to struggle painfully and sometimes angrily with themselves to "say it themselves." The counselor had to be very sensitive here to discern when he was really needed or when, on the contrary, persons wanted time to find, on their own, the required word or phrase.

In the third stage, as we said, the client, having gained greater confidence, independence and proportionate insights into the relationship of phrases, grammar and ideas, spoke immediately to the group in the foreign language, without any English communication of his ideas to the counselor. Only when he clearly needed help did he turn to the counselor with the English expression of what he wanted to say in the foreign language. Here the counselor with a surprising intuition sometimes already knew the word or phrase the client was struggling to use and could often supply it to him, without any English communication between them. The very intensity of the concentration of their communication together, and the deep relationship and security which both had, seemed to produce this joint understanding.

The following excerpt from one of the language counselors—a student from Germany—describes a subjective reaction to the client-relationship at this stage:

I had to relax completely and to exclude my own will to produce something myself. I had to exclude any function of forming or formulating something within me, not try to *do* something but instead letting enter into me without any restriction, what the person says, and being completely open to everything he might say, foreseeing with calm, not hoping or wishing that or this word might come forward; not concentrated on what the person might say, i.e., on the contents of the speech, but on the person himself, completely accepting him and at the same time trying to understand what *he* wants to say, not *what* he wants to say.

Together with the other person (client), I concentrate on his process of trying to find this word or that expression joining into this process with sympathy and understanding. I do not allow myself to feel embarrassed about his hesitation, momentary silence or stuttering, in order not to bring up any tension, which would make him self-conscious, but I sort of try to find the word myself, and as I do not know what word is wanted—I am just joining in the process of thinking with the other person. Thus, so to say, both of us are thinking in combined effort. It is important that there be in me no willing or wishing, but a relaxed state of almost passiveness, which is, however, creative as it provides additional creative force to the other person. I try to be relaxed, without any personal anxiety that he do well. I would not be disturbed in the least, if there would come forward a completely wrong sentence or word or bad pronunciation, since I do not wish to hear something particular that I have in mind myself. Thus, this situation differs widely from teaching. I am almost indifferent to what is said, or better, to how the other person puts it, as there is a deeper level of communication, which need not cling so much to words, which are but the outward appearance of what is communicated. I feel like I am walking along a path with the other person towards a common goal.

What we see here is a delicate sense of "will to community" taking the place of "will to power." The focus on teaching gave way to the joy of sharing in a person's independent learning growth.

From another language counselor:

Being a counselor to two people who want to have a conversation in my native language: Their conversation is flowing through me. I am participating in one continuous flow of thoughts, that goes through me in two directions. I have a humble role: people refer to me only when they need help. The rest of the time they are having a conversation among themselves. Nevertheless I am not excluded from the conversation. I am participating in a passive role, giving myself to what they want to say, not producing something myself. Giving myself to the others, helping them so smoothly that they forget to realize that there is somebody without whom they would not be able to perform all this, somebody who gives them their security.

The reward here for the expert seems to be the sense of consensual validation that his presence—even in its silence—brought to the learners. To be accepted, to belong in the language of the native, to feel the warm secure approval of silence or limited correction, was a powerful motivation for the learner to speak with even greater clarity and accuracy. Almost as for a little child learning to walk or talk, the secure acceptance and approval of one's independent achievement was always there, and never more so than in silent reassurance.

SENSE OF GROWTH

The following learner comment gives both the surprise at this growing language security and the awareness of how the counselor played a part in this:

I was very much surprised at the fact that I would get anything out of the language research in German. I was more surprised by my ability to understand German, as the different speakers spoke it in our conversations. I found it much simpler than I had expected because I began to see its relationship to English and to understand it in terms of its relationship to the English words. I noticed that I did not so much discover a facility of detecting words as I discovered a facility in detecting general ideas. I found an ability to understand the general ideas and consequently to laugh at jokes in German, rather than listening for the English words. I also was very much surprised at the fluency with which the words were pronounced. I could discover that the words were flowing through me and that there wasn't a hard stereotyped pronunciation but rather the words were an extension of my English vocabulary.

Part of this I attributed to the facility of the counselor, who enabled me to feel very much at ease in the language; and consequently allowed the words to flow from herself through me into the group.

The following comment is from a person who had previously studied French but was blocked in speaking:

With regard to French, I noticed several things, one of which was definitely more of a facility in speaking French; I made more attempts to speak French. Before I would be blocked in speaking with anyone from France. I found myself now wishing to converse in French and not being so much impeded by my lack of knowledge. I found too, in French, the language flowing through me from the counselor, rather than a previous setting up of the sentences in English and translating into French in my mind and then trying to speak in French. I noticed no difficulty with pronunciation whatsoever, and this was, I believe, due to the encouragement of the counselors. I found that the French was far simpler for me too, because I could again see its relationship to English and I noticed that from speaking French through the Counselor I tended to listen for the more Norman-sounding words and I tended to choose those words which were more Norman when I was speaking French.

I was also very much amazed that, when I addressed the group in conversation, that there was in me no notice of the fact that I was speaking French, but rather, simply an extension of myself into the group; I was not so much concerned with how I pronounced the words, and to my amazement, I was pronouncing them with relative accuracy. I was not conscious of what word I was using or choosing, but in one span of time I found myself becoming more aware of the words which occurred more frequently and also found myself more anxious to speak on my own, without the counselor's aid.

TURNING POINT

Some years ago Brachfeld pointed out the turning point evident in language learning: :

Many years of experience in learning languages has given me the conviction that there is a "Turning Point" in language study. This "Turning Point" has very little to do with intelligence, talent and so forth. Psychologically, it is rather akin to courage. In three foreign languages, I can clearly remember my "Turning Point." In a fourth one, I believe that I have not yet arrived at, but I am already very close to, the "Turning Point."[3]

This "turning point" or what we call the "language threshold," was very evident in our research. Some students even recalled the precise day when this sense of belonging, this passing over the threshold, occurred in one or the other of the foreign languages. It was closely related to a deep sense of psychological belonging and sharing with the language counselor.

In fact, one of the main results of this counseling-learning relationship was that it seemed to enable students rather rapidly to pass over this threshold of confidence and away from fear, uncertainty and strangeness. In one semester, even, many seemed to acquire a positive identification with the four foreign languages and a confidence and security that they could learn to speak and understand them. In other words, they felt strongly that they belonged to these languages. These languages were no longer strange and threatening for them.

A second result, interrelated with the first, was the overcoming of strong personal blocks against a particular language itself or the people it represented. These blocks existed in at least one language for over half the students. These resistances were caused either by unfortunate earlier experiences in trying to learn the blocked language or by national or cultural hostilities to a particular people.

This "turning point" process we might also consider the movement from meaning to value. At these stages, the language had become a value—the person had begun to invest himself in it, aided by the warm and secure personal acceptance and understanding of the expert counselor.

DEEPENING COMMITMENT

Similar types of group engagement and individual change emerged in the process of these linguistic experiences. People who were just curious about the research or only vaguely interested in learning a foreign language, became increasingly more deeply committed to the language experts and counselors and to one another. At first, for example, conversations would begin with the usual banal topics like "the weather" and "what did you do over the week-end?" These topics were similar to those in any group whose members do not know, or feel secure with one another.

Gradually, however, relationships deepened. At this stage, one member would usually introduce the first "breakthrough" by beginning to speak of his or her feelings, especially of anxiety. Sometimes deeper communication began with freedom to express hostility toward one or more other group members or to the counselors. Thus, negative emotions emerged and the group grew able to express them with increasing security. Slowly, positive attitudes came forward, too, with the whole group sharing in the excitement of each one's language progress or new personal insights or achievements.

COMMUNITY LEARNING

We came to call this mutual support and strengthening process "community learning", in contrast to the "laissez-faire rugged individual" learning that most classroom experiences seem to have afforded these people. There was often an atmosphere of enthusiasm and shared achievements similar to that of amputees beginning to walk on artificial limbs. Negations were still freely expressed but with little or none of the self-consciousness about, say, anger, that had marked earlier releases.

Obviously, not all students remained in the research groups long enough to attain to stage four or five in all four languages. But a significant number did, so that easy conversation in all four languages could occur and they could then become "counselors" to new groups. More common was significant speaking proficiency in one or two languages, and less adequate comprehension of the other two or three. Some remained only two semesters. Even here, however, they often then entered regular classes in a particular language, more motivated to learn and more positive toward the language as a result of the language-counseling experience. A number of the more advanced arranged to go to Europe, some for a year, some for a summer. As a result of the security and enthusiasm they had acquired, they now desired an even more complete linguistic and cultural experience.

As the more advanced group members became "counselors" to new groups, the native speakers of the languages became "experts" who backed up the counselors, checked recordings for mistakes, etc. Experts guided the counselors who in turn had full responsibility for the clients. At this stage the clients, we found, could often relate more easily to these intermediate people. The counselors did not seem so distant, since they were sometimes being corrected, too.

GROUP SHARING AND MOTIVATION

In one study an American university group, in French-Canada to learn French, met together for six weeks, using this counseling-learning relationship. In their evaluation, all but one reported positive reactions and achievement, especially in motivation, to continue to study on their own:

I think eventually I will study much more on my own. If I had been forced to study, I would have learned more, but I would have never got to that point. We had to pass through that period, whether we liked it or not.[4]

Some typical evaluative comments were:

I don't think we experienced freedom until a week and a half ago. We really expected and we still expect the person running the course to tell us what to do and what not to do . . . At the beginning of the course, we were still thinking in the traditional methods. We are so engrained in having somebody running the course. That hindered us more than anything else.

We are just beginning to realize that it is up to us . . . up to the group to decide how you want to learn . . . It comes from the group, and the group decides to do it: this to me was the biggest thing![5]

A strong sense of group belonging was reported by everyone but one (Edward), who insisted:

The group as such is really nonexistent. It is individuals within a group that act, and then you get accord or discord.[6]

His general behavior outside the language experience corresponded to this "loner" alienation.

The report commented:

Edward's behavior during the summer was perfectly consistent with those words: groups don't exist.[7]

This suggests that strongly isolated value patterns will persist in such a learning group, and so resist the group's efforts at acceptance and affiliation.

By contrast, the others all felt a strong group tie and its aid in motivating them:

I noticed that, when the expert started to divide the groups, no one ever said: I don't want to be in that group. I don't want to go with that bunch, because of the group feeling that was there from the start. We all wanted to help one another to learn French.[8]

Another comment pointed out how the student had "to learn you people" before he began to really learn French:

I think this is one of the most painless ways to learn that I have ever got into. It was left to my own motivation to study. Not only did I learn French, but I've got to know a lot of tremendous people in the meantime. This experience of living with you, guys, ya, it has been great. First of all, I had to learn you people, before we could get down to business. During the first two weeks, we were like people going to Mass without knowing each other. But after that, we could relate with everyone, even with people whom you might think you could never possibly work with.[9]

POSITIVE SELF-CONCEPT

We are now gathering data to see if we can further determine the relationship between personality change and the learning process. Some evidence seems to indicate the possibility that significant change in positive self-regard may be related to gain in foreign language speaking competence. This seems to have been so for particular individuals. Some have commented on the notable positive changes they have seen in themselves, which also have been reported by others who know them well. These have usually corresponded to their gain in speaking ability in one or more of the four languages. Through the use of attitude scales, Q-Sort methods, personality evaluation and similar material, we hope to gain greater understanding of the factors which bring about these positive changes as well as greater foreign language communication competence.

One study made of this research group, contrasted the learners' changing views of themselves from negative to positive self-attitude towards the four foreign languages, as the group experience proceeded. As they became more realistic in their self-concept about what they could learn, they began, at the same time, to gain in their ability to speak and understand.

As discrepancy between self-perception and ambition is reduced, proficiency in language tends to increase.[10]

There also seemed to be a more realistic self-attitude toward how much they could achieve linguistically instead of exaggerated learning goals far beyond them, or negative defeatist attitudes.

The experimental members, as a group, not only grew in self-acceptance but also in greater consistency between their self-perceptions and their aspirations.[11]

Some preliminary findings seem also to suggest the rather surprising possibility that some people in this type of community counseling learning may be able to learn comparably in four languages what classes in one language learn in approximately the same time. This has been apparent with particular individuals who made high gains in individual languages as tested by standard language achievement tests and by an aural test especially standardized for our research. Whether this can be found to be generally evident, is not yet clear. It may be that some persons are more strongly motivated by this kind of learning experience and that this accounts for their gains in foreign language competence. Differences in the experts and the counselors might also help explain some of these variations in what individuals learned. No outside assignment or study was suggested or encouraged but this could also have made some differences.

CONFIDENCE IN LEARNING POTENTIAL

In general, however, the main result for many seemed to be the awareness of being much less anxious in their approach to the learning of foreign languages and of having acquired confidence that they themselves could really learn to speak, as well as read and write, these languages. Such an experience might, therefore, better prepare them for further ordinary classroom learning in these languages. In the light of the fears that many had in the beginning, this in itself seemed a significant advance for them.

One implication here seems to be the necessity of methods that incorporate counseling more immediately into the complications of any learning experience. For this, we have to rethink the whole educative process in a non-Cartesian way, seeing it not simply as an intellectual but as a unified personality encounter. An intellectualized model gives us only a partial view, and so forces us to leave out of consideration many other significant factors. New ways of relating are necessary if we are to bring into full play, the complete and genuine involvement of teachers and learners together, and with one another.

LEARNING IS PERSONS

In this kind of community learning where the conflict, hostility, anger and anxiety intrinsic to learning are shared, intellectual development would be an important and central but not an exclusive aim. Counseling and procedures patterned from it, would then have a basic and effective function. This would especially open the way for making values as well as meaning, a main aim of the educative process.

One can see here a model for learning that could at the same time be personally therapeutic. The student's growth in self-worth as well as his total person, are engaged. In the focus simply on intellectual knowledge, education gives, at best, meanings, not values. People often are not moved to make any real self-invest-ment. If this is to come about, we might see the deep sense of commitment expressed by the language expert and the reciprocal sense of identity, belonging and engagement expressed by the learners, as a model of the kind of learning experience that could be both therapeutic and constructive, as it furthered genuine and independent maturity.

What is involved here then, is that "learning is persons." That is, real learning demands investment in self and others, and au-thentic relationship and engagement together. Knowledge of mean-ings can be acquired from books, lectures and various teaching devices. But to make what one has learned a value demands "the courage to be as a part and the courage to be oneself."[12] It involves, in other words, the process of maturity itself, and so engages each learner in a constructive and creative growth in greater possession of self and commitment to others, as well as in a therapeutic process.

NOTES

[1] Charles A. Curran, "Counseling Skills Adapted to the Learning of Foreign Languages," a report on the plan of this research and on some earlier findings, in the *Menninger Bulletin,* March 1961. A later report was published at Loyola University, Chicago, February 1965, "A Counseling-Psychotherapeutic Methodology and Associated Learning Apparatus."

Demonstrations and theoretical discussions have been presented at a variety of meetings, among them: The Kansas State Language Teachers' Assn., April 1960; The Spanish Language Teachers' Assn., February 1963; Chicago Teachers College; The Midwest Psychological Assn., May 1963; and two National Defense Education Act Teacher Training Institutes at Rosary College, June 1962 and Mundelein College, July 1963.

Some presentations of color films of high school classes learning Latin and Spanish were made in a week workshop devoted to study and discus-sion of this research and viewpoint. It was held at Barry College, Miami, Florida, February 1968.

[2] The following people were involved as leaders or learning counselors: Latin in High School, Daniel D. Tranel; Spanish in High School, Rosina Mena Gallagher; English with Slow Learners, Jenny Rardin; French (In Quebec) with American College Students, Yves Begin; French with the aged, Roland Janisse; English, Spanish and French with Small Children, Rosina Mena Gallagher and Jenny Rardin.

[3] Oliver Brachfeld, "Individual Psychology in The Learning of Languages," *International Journal of Individual Psychology*, 2 (1), First Quarter, 1936, pp. 77–83.

[4] Yves Begin, "Evaluative and Emotional Factors in Learning a Foreign Language," Doctoral Dissertation, Loyola University, Chicago, June 1968, p. 108.

[5] *Ibid.*, p. 105.

[6] *Ibid.*, p. 106.

[7] *Ibid.*, p. 107.

[8] *Ibid.*

[9] *Ibid.*, p. 108–109.

[10] Juan B. La Farga, "Learning Foreign Languages in Group Counseling Conditions," Doctoral Dissertation, Loyola University, Chicago, November 1966, p. 105.

[11] *Ibid.*

[12] Tillich, *op. cit.*, p. 187.

15

Counseling, Teaching Apparatus, and Learning

WITH ALL the confusion of our technological age, there are yet many obvious and significant advantages. One of these, fortunately, is occurring in education itself. Technical developments in learning equipment and information-giving apparatus seem now to make it increasingly possible for teachers and others to be freed for more attention to the personalized tasks of the educative process. Years ago Eric Gill remarked that what a machine can do as well or better than a man is unworthy of a man's labor.

So too with teaching. The understanding and adequate design and use of machines and apparatus now appear to make possible the freeing of the person of the teacher to do for another what only a *human person* can do. He can become a learning counselor, as the various types of apparatus take over more onerous and less personal phases. The many information-giving tasks and the rote-drill and practice aspects necessary to learning can often be done as well or better with the aid of learning apparatus. This leaves open—as a new and exciting educative area—the special promise of penetrating understanding and sharing in a learning experience that only genuine and authentic human communication can really make possible—the truly creative relationship.

In our consideration of the pursuit of values and of counseling as a normal part of this process, we are also, in a way, redefining one of the main aspects of counseling. That is, we are not viewing it as a special aid for troubled persons alone. We are rather seeing counseling as a personal relationship and skill for the use of everyone in the more efficient evaluation and resolution of each one's

323

empirical life situation. This is, moreover, especially applicable to the educative process if counseling is conceived as the final state in the personal integration of what is significant and meaningful. So, from this view, as we have said, counseling with oneself or through another would be a normal and necessary part of any learning experience.

THE LEARNING COUNSELOR

Any discussion of counseling as a normal part of the educative process, however, immediately introduces a two-fold concern. First, how do the information-giving tasks and routine rote-drill memorization—as for example, the study of vocabulary and the study and practice of grammatical rules in language—enter into this process by which counseling would be a central function of the teacher? Second, how, in the ordinary course of present school-room arrangements with thirty to forty students in each class, would the teacher, granting his ability as a counselor, have time for any counseling relationship with groups or individual students? The legitimacy of both of these difficulties has caused us, in our research over the last ten years, to concern ourselves with ways of meeting and resolving these issues. We have not, of course, arrived at any final solution.

One project has been the designing, testing, and, finally, use in the classroom of a variety of teaching machines and other learning apparatus. In various forms, these machines and apparatus were not designed to be simply teaching machines, as, for instance, Skinner proposed.[1] We did not disregard such Skinnerian-type apparatus, but placed emphasis on the special purpose we had in mind in our designs: to facilitate an educative process modelled after the counseling relationship, and thus free the teacher to function increasingly as a learning counselor. Rather than an information-giver or the central object of a drill, with its right-and-wrong-answer kind of learning, the person of the teacher can emerge in a new learning-counselor dimension.

COMMUNITY AND
TOTAL PERSON LEARNING

Moreover, a further and central concern for which the different kinds of apparatus have been designed is to *personalize* their use as well as to facilitate community learning. In addition, they are intended to enable every student to have an active and concentrated psychosomatic involvement in the learning process at all times.

Like an athletic team, the students in community learning motivate and stimulate one another as they, individually and as a group, struggle to succeed in the learning task. In this sense, they are not concentrated directly on the teacher. Their learning difficulties and negations are not projected on him or her but rather they are concentrated on the task-oriented apparatus which they themselves control and direct, and which is the object of their learning concern and engagement. In this they succeed or fail with themselves and with the group. Such a learning process can engage all the students together. Their learning difficulties are in no way related to the teacher-figure. In place of being up in front and the center of their focus, the teacher, as learning counselor, stands toward the back or in the center of the class as a part of them. He is there ready to aid them individually and support them in their learning task.

THE LEARNING APPARATUS SYSTEM

In its variety of forms, this apparatus has been named the Chromacord ® Teaching System.* Corresponding to its name, as we shall explain, the system involves the use of a moving perceptual field of a learning visual tape in combination with a codal system of eight color signal lights and keys to activate them. The apparatus can be used by individual students or it can be shared together by two, three or a large group of students.

* Chromacord Company, P. O. Box 3856, Merchandise Mart, Chicago, Illinois 60654.

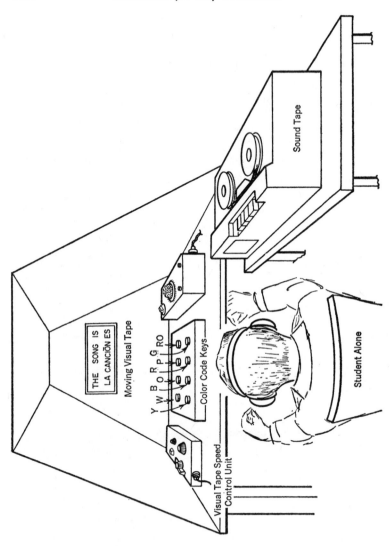

THE SONG IS
LA CANCIÓN ES

Moving Visual Tape

Sound Tape

Y W B O R P G RO

Color Code Keys

Visual Tape Speed
Control Unit

Student Alone

GROUP PARTICIPATION

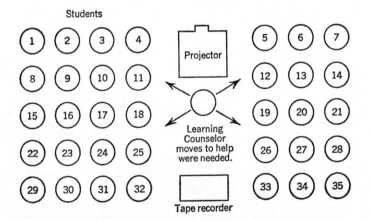

Wall of Learning Lanterns

Students

Projector

Learning
Counselor
moves to help
were needed.

Tape recorder

Each student has color keyboard (eight keys, one for each color: yellow (Y), blue (B), red (R), green (G), white (W), orange (O), purple (P) and rose (RO) corresponding to the Learning Lantern with his number. Students volunteer to control projector and tape recorder.

Chromacord ® U.S. Patent #3396308

THREE STUDENTS

At set time intervals students rotate seating positions.

Third Sound Monitor	*Second* Learner	*First* Visual Monitor
1. Programmed sound tape matching visual tape gives him exact pronunciation.	1. Controls speed of moving visual tape.	1. Programmed visual frame contains correct color analysis.
2. Monitors learner's pronunciation with bell (correct) and buzzer (mispronunciation).	2. Maximum learning: Color analysis and pronunciation are closely monitored by students 1 and 3.	2. Monitors learner's color analysis with bell (correct) and buzzer (error) unit.
3. Practices color analysis.		3. Practices color analysis.

Color symbols used in illustration:
yellow (Y), blue (B), red (R), green (G), white (W), orange (O), purple (P) and rose (RO).

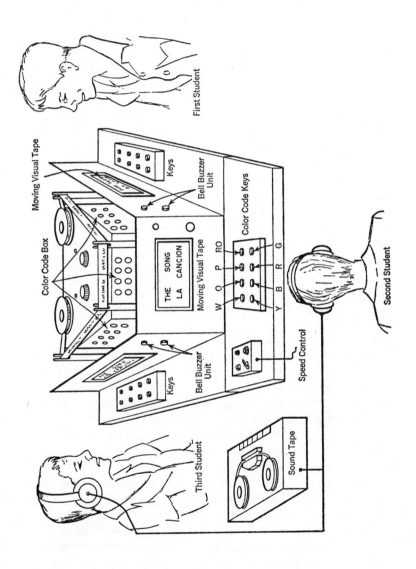

In its various forms, the apparatus may be used, for example, by one student working alone. In what might be described as a learning reinforcement color-discriminating system, he responds with color code analysis to the visual tape as it goes by, and then sees whether he is correct or has failed, according to the reinforcement program as the tape moves. At the same time, he is hearing a sound tape which corresponds in pronunciation to what he is seeing. But he can control this separately so that he himself has the learning task of directing the synchronization between the sound and the words he sees. By the use of color code keys he then can also discriminate and analyze the grammatical and linguistic content of what he sees and hears. In this sense he is *playing color* as he hears and sees—hence the name "Chromacord ®."

For such individual use, the visual and sound programming—modelled after the counseling learning relationship described in the previous chapter—can seek to provide the same type of freedom from anxiety and threat. The apparatus is *for* the learner, not against him. It is to aid him. It is completely under his control. As one student said, "No matter how many times you repeat it and make mistakes, it never embarrasses you, makes you feel a fool or changes the tone of its voice." It never tires repeating, no matter how long it takes the student to learn.

Moreover, as, for example, in the use of popular foreign songs, the sound tape can be warm, pleasant and sentimental, if this suits the learning mood of the student. Sometimes grammar and pronunciation can be better learned this way and the songs retained as models, as the student continues to sing them afterwards.

Similarly it can be used for the improvement of English in "Headstart" or "Upward bound" programs, as well as in ordinary English classes.

This same apparatus in a slightly more complex form has a three-way aperture. Here one student is the visual monitor who sees the correct answer in the programming while, at the same moment, a second student, in the central position, is the learner. He pushes the various colors to correspond to what he feels or thinks is the correct response. The student in position One, the monitor, immediately signals and in some instances, scores whether he is correct according to the programming on his visual scope. The student in the third position, is the pronunciation monitor. In his turn he hears the sound tape's correct pronunciation. Then as the learning student pronounces, he rewards the pronouncing student if he feels his pronunciation corresponds to the one he has just heard. Together then they listen a second time to the pronunciation. So the student in number Three position rewards the student who has pronounced correctly according to the sound tape pronunciation that he has heard.

If each student changes places every ten minutes, for example, then in a given half-hour all three students have had learning experiences as learners and as monitor-correctors. To monitor vision or sound can often be as good a learning experience as to be in the number Two learning position.

This also can be used by a class of students. But to explain this, let us first consider some more general aspects of the classroom use of this system. The main purpose of the learning apparatus is not simply to be a teaching machine but rather to be personalized and to facilitate the ease and freedom with which the students can learn together and communicate in learning with one another. In addition, its intent is to put the teacher—now seen as learning counselor—in a position of aid and support, warmth, acceptance and understanding, in place of the usual position that the teacher occupies.

This teaching apparatus system and its corresponding counseling-learning relationships have been used over a five-year period in high school, college and graduate school classes in America, Italy and Canada. These projects have involved the learning of French, Spanish or Latin, or in learning a four-language combination of French, German, Spanish and Italian similar to that described in the previous chapter. This system and its learning-counselor functions have also been used with small children and underprivileged older children in improving English, spelling, grammar and pronunciation.

CHROMACORD LEARNING
RESEARCH REPORT

The following is a description of a Latin sophomore high school class taught by the Chromacord method (this group is called experimental) was contrasted with an ordinary class taught by the same Latin teacher in his accustomed manner.

We will quote in detail from this report for the purpose of consistency.[2] The experiences reported here, however, are typical and were similar if not identical to the experiences in group belonging, sharing, positive motivation and personal change, in all the other groups. Tranel explains the contrast in the two High School Latin classes:

In this experiment two groups of sophomore students were actually involved, the experimental group and a control group. The control was taught according to the traditional method (excluding such methods as those of Sweet, Most, *et al.*), while the experimental group was taught with the Chromacord®.

Here is a description of how this system was used in a normal high school classroom:

What is the Chromacord® Teaching Machine and how was it employed? The machine itself may consist of any number of units, depending upon the class enrollment. Each unit, or learning lantern, consists of a wooden box one foot square and six inches deep, with a Plexiglas facing. Eight light bulbs of different colors are mounted inside, each color having a definite significance. For example, red represents either masculine gender or perfect tense; blue represents either feminine gender or future tense, etc. From each lantern there extends to the student an electrical cord, with a set of switches at the end by which he can control the lights. Ideally each student has his individual learning lantern and switches, so that if there are twenty students in the class, there will be twenty learning lanterns placed one on top of another, forming a panel at the front of the room. It is not, however, necessary that each student have an individual lantern, since any number of switches can be connected to the same lantern.

In the experiment, students were seated in the normal classroom arrangement. A panel of twenty learning lanterns for the twenty students in the class was displayed at the front of the classroom, and each student controlled a set of switches. An overhead projector was set up, from which a Latin word or phrase or sentence was projected onto a screen at the left of the lanterns. An English translation was directly above the Latin. As one of the students read aloud a Latin word from the screen, all the students flashed on their lanterns the colors necessary to parse the word in detail. For example, if *aquam* appeared on the screen, blue, indicating feminine, and amber, indicating accusative, should appear on each lantern. At the same time, another student would call out the translation, and another would give a cognate, or "security" word, as an aid to memory. If all students flashed correct lights, a bell sounded, indicating that the group was ready to move to the next word. If one or more students flashed the wrong colors, a buzzer sounded, and progress was delayed until an explanation, sometimes by the teacher, was made and all lights were correct.

Let us look at this in more detail. Suppose that the following Latin sentence from Caesar's *Gallic War* appeared on the screen from the overhead projector: *Hi omnes lingua, institutis, legibus inter se differunt.* The following series of colors appear on the lanterns in succession as one student reads aloud each word of the sentence, a second reading the corresponding English translation above it, and a third giving the cognate: red and white for *hi,* indicating masculine nominative; red, white, and yellow for *omnes,* indicating a masculine nominative adjective, modifying *hi;* blue and purple for *lingua,* indicating feminine ablative. After each word is parsed in this way, the entire sentence is read aloud in Latin by a student and the entire translation given by another. The same sentence now appears on the screen a second time, but without the translation written above, and the process with the lights is repeated. In this way an average of from twenty to twenty-five lines can be completed during a class period of forty-five minutes.[3]

Vocabulary can be presented in the same manner, and any other material from a text or reading, such as *Virgil* in Latin. When necessary and helpful, the students can make the visual tape themselves and color it properly so that it can be projected. Overhead projector tape and ordinary paper tape, run through an opaque projector, were both used. The codal numbers 1, corresponding to yellow; 2, corresponding to blue; 3, corresponding to red, etc. up to 8, corresponding to rose, was used on the overhead projector tape, since it does not reproduce color. Students quickly adapted to this relationship of say, 4, to green. While it is not as colorful and attractive as the colored underlining of a word, for learning purposes it functions as well, and provides an added discriminatory reinforcement.

LEARNING ROUND TABLE

Another system was used for vocabulary sentence learning, and the review of student conversation was also used for smaller groups of six to eight students. This is called the "Learning Round Table." The following is a description of its use for the purpose of learning Latin vocabulary.

The same system of colors was employed in the learning of vocabulary, but instead of an overhead projector, a rotating circular table was used. Five or six small reading stands were placed around the edge of the table, and, as it rotated, one of the students would place an 8″ by 11″ sheet of paper on a stand. On each sheet was a Latin word, with genitive, gender, and English meaning written toward the bottom. One student read the word aloud as it circled past him, another read the genitive case, a third the gender, and a fourth gave a cognate. For example, if the word *equus* were to appear on the rotating table, then red signifying masculine, white signifying nominative, and amber signifying genitive would appear on the lanterns, as nominative, genitive, gender, and cognate were called out by various students.[4]

STUDENT LEARNING RESPONSIBILITY

Responsibility, group cohesion and support, a different regard for the teacher now seen as learning counselor, all emerged in this and other similar classroom experiences. The following comment by the teacher—now become Latin counselor—indicates this:

One of the most striking phenomena was the amount of responsibility the students assumed for their own learning. A minimum of pressure was required to keep the students alert and attentive. The group seemed to realize instinctively that if any individual member were remiss in his part of the total performance, the entire group was adversely affected. Thus the group itself served as a motivating force to each of its members. The authoritarian image of the teacher was minimized, thus reducing anxiety and creating greater learning readiness. The group itself became the authority. If any individual failed, he reflected the failure of the whole group. This became evident when, for example, a particularly difficult passage or construction was under study and the majority got it wrong; the reaction might have been summed up in a statement such as "We did badly on that one," a remark most probably made by someone who actually had got it correct. Apparently such a student had become so identified with the group that he regarded their failure as his own.

It was readily observable that students of the experimental group were highly motivated to learn in order to avoid isolation from the group. In order to achieve a sense of belonging, a student needed to become totally involved in what was taking place and to become identified with the other members of the group. After a time he seemed to realize that he was learning not in alienated isolation, but as a part of a community endeavor in which he was expected to contribute something to the community and would receive something from it in return.

In the context of the preceding situation, the nature of homework took on an entirely new connotation. Each student was able to see clearly the areas in which he was deficient. Since he saw himself as part of a community effort to which he had to contribute if he were not to hinder the progress of the community, he was motivated to study his areas of deficiency on his own. For example, if a student was consistently unable to recognize a subjunctive, he would concentrate on that area on his own until he was able to get it correct and thus make himself an integral part of the group. He could be proud of returning to class on the next day and making this contribution to the group.

In the kind of learning atmosphere which prevailed, it seemed almost impossible not to be personally and intensely involved, since the student was simultaneously occupied with sight, sound, touch and motion. One student commented that although this was probably the most difficult work he did all day, it did not seem so because he had no time to think about it as such; only after the class period did he realize how tired he was. Much of the drudgery frequently associated with learning seemed to have been eliminated, replaced by excitement and challenge.[5]

POSITIVE TEACHING ENGAGEMENT

It becomes apparent that this kind of learning arrangement and process would have significant effects on the teacher's self-concept. Rather than seeing himself in the usual isolated and father-figure or God-figure role, he found himself openly engaged, too. And so he could admit, without defense, his own need to belong and to give and receive. He became incarnate in the learning situation with his students. He was then in a position to be more of a learning counselor and consultant than a removed "teacher."

My own reactions to the two groups were quite different. In the contrast of interaction and personal involvement between the two groups, I came to a realization of the student's gift to the teacher. The teacher naturally looks for response to the ideas, the facts, and the subject matter which have been his gift to students. The more spontaneous the response, the greater the reward. In the control group, the response, though often given, was frequently given far from spontaneously and freely. Since it was difficult for the teacher to accept the response, defensiveness and tension arose between teacher and student. In this same group, where there was little emphasis on personal interaction, the teacher's primary aim was to present facts. The student, however, did not always regard this as a gift. He often felt that he was being forced to accept something that had little meaning for him, and consequently he resisted it. In the experimental group this difficulty was obviated by the fact that the student was largely giving to himself what he had attained.

In the control group, much of the learning was defensive and was forgotten as soon as the need for protection was no longer there. Perhaps this will explain why the experimental group did better in the retesting. Since they felt no need to be defensive in the original learning situation, they were freer to enter fully into the learning situation.

In the experimental group, my role as teacher assumed a different meaning. It became more like that of an expert consulted in unusual situations but otherwise remaining in the background. As a result, I felt freed from the burden of teaching, which was carried by the Chromacord®, and I could truly interact with the students.[6]

CONSTRUCTIVE VERSUS
DEFENSIVE LEARNING

One teacher notes here, too, the degree to which what we have called "defensive" learning and greater passivity were evident in the ordinary class situation. By contrast, with the aid of the learning apparatus to facilitate psychosomatic involvement and group cooperation, the teacher became a supporter and the students could actively and positively engage themselves and one another in the learning progress:

A further observation on my part as teacher was that of the lessening of the distance between knower and learner. The threat that this distance can create was sharply brought out in the control group as contrasted to the experimental group. Since in the experimental group the students were actually teaching themselves, thus assuming an active role, they were not forced into a position of humiliation by their ignorance. On the contrary, in the control group it seemed that the students' own ignorance was constantly on display before their eyes because of the relative passivity of their role. Even though the students in the experimental group were teaching themselves, they nevertheless had the security of knowing that they were not learning incorrectly because of the presence of the teacher in the background. If learning involves a process of personal change, then perhaps the reason why the students in the control group seemed more resistant to learning, was that they resented having something done to them, rather than doing it themselves. In the experimental group, although the students felt some pressure to change, to learn, it was for an entirely different reason, namely, so that they would have something to give to the rest of the group.[7]*

Many other phases of this counseling learning process might be discussed in detail here. But this is beyond our present scope. What seems more apropos for the present treatment is to understand the quoted comments to be somewhat typical of the general results of our experience with a variety of learning groups.

This suggests the possibility that teaching machines and similar

---

* Two color films and accompanying sound tapes are available. These were made during the actual classroom use of this system, in classes of Latin and Spanish for high school students.

aids, thought out and designed from the point of view of the unified person, may noticeably aid the personalization of learning. This is the opposite of what is often thought—that mechanization is depersonalizing and degrading, turning the learner into a kind of robot. But as Whatmough said: "What the human mind has done, the human mind *ex hypothesi,* can cope with."[8]

That is, we can see a teaching device such as the one we used in its various forms, as designed to free the expert for more personalized functions. So, while the machine aids in the rote and informational learning, the teacher is freed to spend time in those guidance and counseling relationships which only a human being can perform.

NOTES

[1] See B. F. Skinner, *Verbal Behavior,* New York: Appleton-Century-Crofts, 1957.

——, "Teaching Machines," *Science,* 128, 1958, pp. 969–977.

——, *The Technology of Teaching,* New York: Appleton-Century-Crofts, 1967.

See also A. Waldman, "Programmed Instruction and Foreign Language Teaching," *Trends in Language Teaching,* ed. A. Waldman, New York: McGraw-Hill, 1966.

[2] D. D. Tranel, "Teaching Latin with the Chromacord®," *The Classical Journal,* January 1968, 63 (4), pp. 157–160. This research was also presented in a detailed discussion and the showing of color films at the National Meeting of The Classical Language Association, St. Louis, Mo., February 11, 1968, by D. D. Tranel.

[3] *Ibid.,* p. 158.

[4] *Ibid.*

[5] *Ibid.,* pp. 158–159.

[6] *Ibid.,* pp. 159–160.

[7] *Ibid.,* p. 160. (orig.)

[8] Whatmough, *op. cit.,* p. 68.

16
A Value Learning Theory

WE CAN NOW consider some further aspects of this kind of counseling therapy model of a value learning process. Here our aim will be to see if we can arrive at some concepts which might be basic to a value-type of learning theory. Or, understanding this in our special meaning of value, we might call this a self-investment learning theory. By this we would be distinguishing it from mere reinforcement conditioning, on the one side, and a purely abstractive kind of intellectual learning, on the other.

This treatment is, of course, too brief for any final or complete presentation. It will, however, indicate the direction such a theory would take. It will also give some basis for it in neurological and psychological viewpoints. Such a theory would be built on a concept of the involvement of the total human person in learning. It would not consider a separate animal learning process. Nor would it see some parallel intellectualized process separate from man's incarnate unity with himself. It would, in other words, try to avoid the Cartesian-Kantian structures and dichotomies with which our present culture is still so heavily laden. It would see man as learning in unity with himself and in community with others. He would not then be thought to learn best in isolation or in competition with others.

While this concept of learning counseling and its associated apparatus was developed after the model of counseling therapy, it is interesting to note the degree to which it is similar to the conclusions of some recent neurological studies and of organismic or holistic concepts. To illustrate this, we will quote, in some detail, first Eccles and then Goldstein, and compare them briefly with the counseling learning experience and its associated apparatus.

339

In any consideration of a human learning theory, we must begin, as we have said, with negative anxiety and the negative emotions of defense, hostility and similar reactions. These prevent the human person from a total kind of self-investment. It is only with this kind of inner directive self-investment that human learning in its most adequate form, can occur.

In the counseling-learning relationship and its associated apparatus, total self-investment is furthered, first by the security gained through the language counselor. This enables the person to abandon himself to the learning experience in the totality of his whole person. This, as we can see, is quite different from simple conditioning which would involve only a part of himself. From the regressive dependency of stage one, the person moves through the gradual independence of stages two, three and four, to the total independence of stage five. At his own speed and according to his own degree of security and desire, the learning client can increasingly move himself into the self-assertion and growing responsibility of speaking a foreign language himself, with less and less dependency upon, and need of the language counselor.

This is the same kind of delicate process of self-investment which encourages the person, in counseling and psychotherapy, slowly to take hold of himself and gradually to become inner-directed. In a similar way, the learner becomes invested in an ever-increasing degree in the learning experience itself. By the time he has arrived at stage four, for example, he needs the learning counselor only for precise idioms and the minute details of grammar or pronunciation. This frees him from the anxiety of being forced to learn too much all at once. Only in stage four are the maximum demands of the learning experience put on him. By this time, through the slow evolution of self-investment in the previous three stages, he is ready for the final complexities of the learning experience. He does not therefore become quickly panicked and he is not made defensive, when corrections are offered him. On the contrary, he is open and ready for them.

We have already seen how the color coding and associated discrimination devices are designed to add to the ease of involvement and commitment to the learning experience and to the group.

But even in the programming itself, in the way the visual tape is prepared, for example, more than simple conditioning is invoked. Rather, the transition from the security of the known, to the anxiety of the unknown, is carefully guided to minimize threat and insecurity. All visual and sound tapes are guided by this goal. The word-programming, for example, follows "security" clues to relieve this anxiety and threat. The following explanation may help clarify this.

In the transition from the English word to the foreign language word or vice versa, a series of steps was devised to prevent the blocking kind of anxiety which usually is produced by the complete newness and strangeness of a foreign word or expression. This is done by taking advantage of the well-known fact that English is a combination of Saxon and Norman words. The Saxon words are, therefore, similar in origin to the Nordic languages, particularly German and the Norman words are similar to French, Spanish, Italian and Latin. Since Russian has a large number of French and Latin words, this method is also adaptable to Russian, once the peculiar strangeness of the new alphabet is overcome. By these transitional adaptations, in the visual and sound programming, anxiety and memory blocking through panic was reduced by moving the student securely from a known English word with a similar meaning, to the strange unfamiliar foreign language word, whether German, French, Spanish, Italian, Latin or Russian.

With the English word "black," to give one example, the student was encouraged to "feel" blackness and not simply see or hear the English word. The tape then gives him, in sequence, "swarthy," "negro," "negro," "negro," "negro" and "charred." These would be security words for German, French, Spanish, Italian, Latin and Russian, respectively. In the color code, "swarthy" and "charred" would be *amber* (like the middle color of the traffic light) indicating some hesitancy and caution in the passage to the foreign word. "Negro" by contrast, would be *green,* that is, a direct passage over to the foreign language word. *Red,* not necessary here, would indicate a word demanding special adaptation. There would then be a

gradual movement from *black, swarthy* s $\overset{ch}{}$ war $\overset{z}{}$ to "schwarz." The $\underset{(v)}{}$

"v" underneath suggests the change in pronunciation. The "ch" and "z" would be in yellow, the color for German. "Charred" would, in the same way, gradually become "chörnii", in Russian.

A *"red"* word or phrase requires a "nonsense", or more personal security relationship. That is, since the words have no evident relationship in English and the foreign language, each student is free to make up his own connection. This is sometimes taken from an incident in his own personal life, or from some other relationship that he has devised. He explains his chosen word to the other students, and they may accept this explanation or offer their own versions of a security clue for a particular word or phrase.

The insecurity of not knowing a strange word is not nearly so great, when one moves in this fashion. By slow stages the new strange word becomes quite familiar, so that the final stage, the foreign word, is then comparatively obvious and not threatening at all. For example, in moving from "black" to "swarthy," on the visual tape, one sees "swarthy" crossed out and the German put above it. One then sees the yellow letters of German fuse into the remaining black letters of English. The final word, "schwarz," is obvious and familiar, when the student arrives at it on the tape programming. This is one example of how the anxiety-security self-investment system followed even in the programming, would be clearly different from a simple conditioning-response conceptualization.

NEURAL MEMORY

In a more general consideration of this learning theory, we have already sufficiently stressed the psychosomatic unity of the person in contrast to our present cultural dichotomized attitude, and how the latter affects, among many other things, our manner of teaching. Most pedagogy is still exaggeratedly intellectual, taking little or no cognizance of the complicated total-person aspects, beginning with the neural foundations of memory.

The literature of what might be called the learning process, including the phenomena of conditioned reflexes, is so great it is impossible to review it here. Morrell has made a recent survey especially of the neural basis of learning. The following is a brief explanation of this process:

It is generally recognized that there are two varieties of psychic memory. *First* of all *there are brief memories,* for seconds or at most minutes, many examples of which have recently been considered by Brown (1964). One example is the ability to repeat sequences of numbers that have been read out. After a few seconds or minutes this memory is lost beyond all recall. Following Hebb (1949), Gerard (1949), and Burns (1958), one can postulate that such a memory is subserved by a spatio-temporal pattern of propagated impulses. So long as *this specific pattern is preserved* in a dynamic operation, *retrieval is possible.* The spatiotemporal pattern forms a dynamic engram such as Lashley would have envisaged. The *second* kind of memory is distinguished by *its enduring character,* even for a lifetime, and has been shown in many experiments to survive, even when the central nervous system is reduced to a quiescent state, as by deep anesthesia, coma, or extreme cooling. Such memories must therefore have as a basis some enduring change that is built into the fine structure of the nervous system, and that is often referred to as a "memory trace," so that we have what is called the "trace theory of memory" (Gomulicki, 1953).[1]

Let us look now more carefully at some comments by Eccles. In the following excerpt he makes clear how a codification process, such as the learning apparatus uses in terms of color analysis, would correspond to the basic encoding that seems characteristic to the synaptic connections of the nerve cells:

The specificities are encoded in the structure and in the synaptic connections of the nerve cells, which are arranged in the unimaginably complex patterns that have already been formed in development. From then on, all that seems to be required for the functional development that we call learning, is merely the microgrowth of synaptic connections already in existence.[2]

CORTICAL REPLAY

However, it is not enough simply to have "memory traces." There must be a living experience that is not only hypothalamic but cortical. In the learning apparatus previously described, this is brought about by the playing of the color code as the sound and the visual tape moves, so that there is a direct engagement in playing analysis, much as one might play music. In this case, however, the playing is in colors and the colors are cortically significant. They are "replayed in the cortex." We notice that this corresponds to Eccles' description:

The flow of specific information from receptor organs into the nervous system will result in the activation of specific spatiotemporal patterns of impulse discharges. The synapses so activated will grow to an increased effectiveness; hence *the more a particular spatiotemporal pattern of impulses is replayed in the cortex,* the more effective become its synapses relative to others. And, by virtue of this synaptic efficacy, *later similar sensory inputs* will tend to traverse these same neuronal pathways and so *evoke the same responses,* both overt and psychic, as the original input.[3]

The same responses,—for example, the equivalent meanings of French and English words—either from counseling conversations or vocabulary list—are repeatedly re-presented to the person. As a result, when one sees French, for example, English immediately occurs; or as one sees English, French sound and vision and meaning are evoked. In this way the same responses, both overt and psychic, are evoked as a result of the original input.

It is obvious therefore that if such neural retrieval memory and cortical replay is a fundamental basis of learning—as of a foreign language—more precise sensory psychosomatic involvement must be provided the student than simply sitting in his seat and passively listening. He must be somatically or physiologically, as well as intellectually engaged.

ACTUALIZED-PERSON LEARNING

But in man, the subtlety of his unitary being makes necessary more than simply repeated and re-enforced neural experience. So Goldstein, in his distinction between "practice" and "drill," points out the importance of combining with this, the inner experience of an insightful and actualized personality, if fruitful knowledge is to be acquired:

Practice and Drill. Regarding the performance of the organism, there is a fundamental difference between practice and drill, a difference only too often overlooked.* Both aim at the best performances possible, but practice aims more to attain the optimal performances attuned to the nature of the organism, whose development, to the highest perfection possible in a given environment, is the objective. For this purpose, a knowledge of the organism's essential nature is necessary, and the task consists in bringing forth the greatest adequacy between organism and environment. Thus all practice implies those *inner experiences,* which we have described as characteristic of preferred behavior, no matter which performances are involved. With that goes the experience of an *actualized personality*. From this alone springs *true* insight and the acquisition of *fruitful knowledge*—all of which is fundamentally different from drill and rote learning.[4]

The deep engagement of the whole person in the counseling learning experience and its increasing kind of self commitment, would seem to provide this sort of inner directed and "fruitful knowledge" experience. Students completely control not only what is said but how it is said and, under certain conditions, they determine the nature of what is being studied. Such a learning process, engaging each person as well in a counseling search for self-insight, would also be an effective way of "actualizing the personality." This can produce insight into the experience which the person is undergoing both as counseling and as learning.

In the model of conditioning, by contrast, the animal is made to focus on one part of its organism, for example, the flowing of saliva, associated first with the food and the ringing of the bell, and later, with the ringing of the bell alone. The animal is purely passive in this process and is usually restrained in some way.

We observe the exact opposite of this in the counseling-learning experience involving the apparatus. Here everyone is free to cooperate, free to speak or not to speak, to choose whatever topics he wishes to talk about in terms of his personal emotions, free to invest in greater or lesser degree of psychological openness as he reveals himself to the group and at the same time, free to choose from a variety of codal colors, the various forms of color analysis

* By *drill,* we mean every sort of so-called training, without primary insight.

Education for Self Investment

which seems to him to correspond to the right discrimination. This is very different from a simple conditioning process, for it involves the whole unitary psychosomatic human person, engaged with himself and others, in a free and self-invested kind of learning.

Even the tape makes a difference here. It is not a film strip. The tape is paper or paper cards put together. One advantage of this methodology is that the tape can be quickly made up by the teacher or by the students themselves and immediately put to use. If a filmstrip effect is desired, a colored strip can be run through an opaque projector and shown to a large class on a screen. Tapes can, of course, be shown over and over again. But they are the spontaneous and living product of the group experience together— not a "canned" or pre-determined script.

The fundamental difference between human learning and animal conditioning is clarified by Goldstein, as he explains how an animal is trained and so learns by drill:

In drill, the acquisition of a certain performance is at first quite unrelated to the nature of the performing being. It is achieved by bringing a somehow isolated part of the organism into establishing such a firm tie between the two, that the external event (stimulus) is followed by the performance (response) with the greatest promptness. The prototype of the drill is the conditioned reflex. Such a reaction-bond depends, in principle, upon a safeguarding from all possible interferences. This safeguard is furnished by the prevailing isolation while the performance in question is in demand.[5]

Drill, then, is this kind of conditioning isolation. The animal is made passive and deprived of his individuality:

In the animal, this safeguard is accomplished by preventing, through force, all performances which are essential to the animal, except the one reaction in question. Gradually, on account of the special arrangement, the animal comes into a condition in which this isolation of certain events takes place *almost passively* without any resistance on its part. *The animal has been gradually deprived of its individuality.* Usually, drill remains a continual discomfort for the animal, and is tolerated because of anxiety (punishment) or its counterpart (reward).[6]

All the responsibility is with the trainer. Applied to persons, this would be a teacher-centered or operant-centered apparatus:

Drill is the more successful, the more the trainer manages to press the *adequate* performances into the service of the drilled actions; in other words, the more he can bring drill into relationship with the natural potentialities of the respective organism. Then it becomes best fixed and rooted, and may even become somewhat agreeable to the animal. In this respect, bad and good drill differ, inasmuch as the latter always contains a great deal of practice.[7]

To say that "drill is the more successful, the more the trainer manages to press the adequate performances . . ." suggests a directive kind of learning. It implies manipulation on the part of the one doing the training rather than any free investment on the part of the learner. Consequently in this type of learning, if the human person does grow to find it pleasant, it is apparently only after the experience has evoked some kind of self-investment and commitment on his part.

In contrast to this, we see that the counseling-learning process and apparatus, engages the unique individual in the learning process in a "special method of learning." He is free to select the material in the counseling discussion process. He has freedom in how he uses the counselor to help him learn, and he chooses the topics he wishes to discuss as well as whether he wishes to speak or remain silent. In using the apparatus in a group, he does not have to operate the lights. But his lantern remains dead if he does not do so, and in that sense he is not participating in the community learning experience. He has the help and support of the group without feeling forced. This corresponds to Goldstein's explanation:

In human learning, drill also plays a particular part. But that it is not the adequate method of learning can be appreciated immediately from the fact that the learning of any inadequate performance is extremely laborious and tedious. In any event, the "acquisition" of adequate performances succeeds much better. From this follows the expediency of *a special method of learning*. The learning must be inspired by the *aspect of adequacy for the respective individual* with regard to the selection of the material as well as to the method of learning. But this procedure, oriented on adequacy, is usually not sufficient. Corresponding to the imperfect adequacy of the environment to his nature, man has more or less to take recourse to drill. However, *drill*—if it is not to be doomed to failure—*must become substantially* related to the personality of the learner.[8]

Practice or drill then to be effective in human learning, must engage the total person and effect self-investment of the learner. Drill or any kind of adequate practice is

. . . *only effective through insight into, and realization of, its necessity,* on the part of the learner. It is only fruitful, as *voluntary, deliberate "self drill."* In this respect, human learning by drill does not involve a complete aberration from the basic trait of "biological acting," which ultimately arises only when it is necessary to help a being to actualize itself.[9]

In contrast to ruling out individuality, isolating and particularizing and passively conditioning the animal, human learning, while using drill and its corresponding conditioning neural process, must do much more. It must further personal individuality and the total engaging of the insight and commitment of the person. Only in this way is "adequate" human learning acquired:

Man is probably the only creature which possesses the potentiality of partitive isolation within his organism and, by his own will, of exposing parts to stimuli. In this way, *these parts* become attuned to stimulus settings in such a way that, under the same environmental conditions and under the volitionally produced identical isolation, *the same performance* sets in. To a certain extent, we need such "inadequate" performances in order to cope with the world. Yet they are not so completely inadequate, as long as they are *acquired with insight* into the inescapable demands of the world, and as long as one is determined to deal with these necessities even in an "inadequate" way. From this it follows that human learning does not always represent adequate practice, insofar as it consists in drill.[10]

In his insistence on "insight," Goldstein could be said to be describing a personality process as well as a learning experience. Consequently, the model of a counseling relationship and the patterning of apparatus from this model, would seem to be an effective way of achieving this kind of free, self-invested commitment to learning. In this commitment, actions of a unitary person and self-insight could go together.

ADEQUATE AND INADEQUATE LEARNING

The fact that inadequate human learning seems always "extremely laborious and tedious" no doubt often contributes to the state of defensive learning we previously described. That is, the student, bored or even hostile, learns simply to defend himself against a poor grade or the public humiliation of failing in a recitation before others. But he resists this learning and feels no part of his person is engaged. He therefore makes no self-investment in what he learns, and so quickly discards it when the class and the threat of a poor grade is passed. For self-investment to occur, or what Goldstein calls "adequate" learning, such a student may still need a counseling opportunity to detraumatize himself from this defensive state, even when it may have gained him a good grade.

A maturity, or therapy of limits, is also suggested here, in Goldstein's insistence on acceptance of the "inescapable demands of the world." Such a "conforming to limits" process aids, as we have said, the growth in personality maturity. A basic aspect of value oriented learning would be that it provides occasions for such maturity growth.

These concepts of Eccles and Goldstein and the insistence on the human necessity of some kind of "insight" would heighten the importance not only of counseling-learning kinds of experiences, but also of apparatus patterned after such experiences. Such a model and the self-investment learning theory behind the model would be different from the present commonly used teaching apparatus. The intent would not simply be neural conditioning. Such apparatus would rather be integral to the kind of unitary person, self-invested learning we have been describing.

One might say then, that while animal learning is passive and particularized, human learning, at its best, is self-invested and total. "Drill," as Goldstein maintains, "must become substantially related to the personality of the learner." This applies as well to all aspects of learning. This is the special mark of man, that he is value-oriented and purposive. These values are unique and personal. Unless such self-investment is engaged, he may learn but only extrinsically and in a conditioned way. Such learning forms no part of his insight and inner experience. His negative anxiety, threat and insecurity must be resolved positively and insightfully if they are to become motivating and constructive challenges to learning achievement.

PERSONALIZED LEARNING

The learning counselor relationship, even more than the learning apparatus, would be a fundamental part of such an educative process, following from and related to this value learning theory. It would especially provide the inner experience, direction and insight previously discussed, and would aim at engaging and involving teacher with student, and students with one another in a committed total-self relationship to learning. It would consist not only in acquiring new meanings but also in the self-investment of teacher and learners in these meanings and in one another.

Learning apparatus systems, then, in this theory, would be seen not simply as re-enforcement aids but as indispensable elements. They would be necessary to free the learning counselor from many learning tasks, and so enable him to concentrate his most personal and effective forces on the final assimilation stages of learning. In this way, learning would increasingly become an experience with *persons*—each deeply committed in his total self.

Moreover, this counseling-learning process and associated apparatus need not be restricted to foreign language learning. The same concepts could be used—as one member of the group has used them—in the teaching of mathematics. Other subjects, such as anatomy and history, have been experimentally adapted to this method. In fact, it seems likely that it is adaptable to most subjects that are now taught in schools or universities.

But, whether this proves so or not, our main concern has been to show the direction a value kind of learning theory would take. We also wished to show some initial steps at least, in both the learning relationship and associated apparatus, that might implement greater total self-investment in each learning experience. This would aim at providing learning experiences that engage the unitary human person, thus avoiding the animal-intellectual dichotomy.

We have explored some aspects of such a unified learning theory. It is especially centered in the relationship of counseling to the educative process and to the search for meaning and pursuit of values. The question of learning theory is, however, part of a still larger question involving not only values but the nature of reality itself and the quality of authenticity that any creative affiliation would require. We will especially consider some of these broader issues in the concluding chapter.

NOTES

[1] J. C. Eccles, "Conscious Experience and Memory," *Brain and Conscious Experience,* ed. J. C. Eccles, New York: Springer-Verlag New York, Inc., 1966, p. 328. (Italics mine)

See also:

F. Morrell, "Electrophysiological Contributions to the Neural Basis of Learning," *Physiol. Rev.* 41, (1961 b), pp. 443–494.

J. Brown, "Short-term Memory," *Brit. Med. Bull.,* 20 (1964), pp. 8–11.

B. D. Burns, "Some Properties of the Isolated Cerebral Cortex of the Unanaesthetized Cat," *J. Physiol.,* 112 (1951), pp. 156–175.

R. W. Gerard, "Physiology and Psychiatry," *Amer. J. Psychiat.,* 106 (1949), pp. 161–173.

D. O. Hebb, *The Organization of Behaviour,* New York: Wiley, 1949.

B. R. Gomulicki, *The Development and Present States of the Trace Theory of Memory,* Cambridge, Eng.: Cambridge University Press, 1953.

Any of a wide variety of learning texts will give other, more general surveys of learning theory.

[2] Eccles, *op. cit.,* p. 337.

[3] *Ibid.* (Italics mine)

[4] Kurt Goldstein, M.D., *The Organism,* Boston: Beacon Press, 1963, pp. 501–502. (Italics mine) Reprinted by permission of the Beacon Press, copyright © 1939 by the American Book Company, © 1963 by Kurt Goldstein.

[5] *Ibid.,* pp. 501–502.

352   *Education for Self Investment*

[6] *Ibid.*, pp. 502–503. (Italics mine)
[7] *Ibid.*, pp. 502–503.
[8] *Ibid.*, p. 503. (Italics mine)
[9] *Ibid.*, p. 504. (Italics mine)
[10] *Ibid.*, pp. 503–504. (Italics mine)

CONCLUSION

Values, Reality and Creative Affiliation

THE GREAT ADVANCES in counseling and psychotherapy which have characterized our age have not only changed our outlook with regard to ourselves but they have also influenced and shaped our relationships with one another. Despite this, study and research in these fields must be cautious in drawing exaggerated or extreme conclusions about the effectiveness or the ultimate adequacy of many theories or methods.

One might say that, in some measure, earlier psychoanalysis and some forms of counseling and psychotherapy finds an historical parallel in medical therapy, namely, an exaggerated enthusiasm for what could be achieved. In drug therapy, for example, there is a long-standing quip about doctors who "rush to use a drug while it can still cure." Sensational new curing phenomena somehow become much less spectacular with time.

In *Research in Psychotherapy*, Whitehorn makes the following comment:

During the hey-day of psychoanalytic pretensions, its proponents viewed that method of therapy as the one and only instrument for getting at, and really curing, the cause of mental ills; but experience and comparisons have led to a more general recognition of the imperfections and limitations of psychoanalysis. During this reevaluation melioristic aims in psychotherapy have regained respectability. The melioristic approach may be characterized as that in which one views the patient as a person functioning not very well or very happily and seeks to help him to a better mode of functioning, as contrasted with the perfectionistic view of seeking to achieve the complete elimination of his disease, through the radical cure of its cause.[1]

355

In our consideration of some broader implications then, we are rather concerned with the trends and directions which some of our present awareness in counseling and psychotherapy seems to reveal. In this area, it is quite apparent how much we have yet to learn and, at the same time, it is clear that we have much to gain from other areas in psychology, science, and general learning. Here, we attempt to bring together the implications of some of these areas, without presuming to settle the issues raised. Rather our purpose is to explore briefly what the findings may contribute to our present understanding, and what they may suggest in the direction of further knowledge, research, and development.

It is evident too, as we discussed earlier, that the analogy or model of "health" and "sickness" implied in the word "therapy," is not totally adequate. For, in addition, we are also dealing with a process that has something to do with growth. Defined this way, we are talking not about "illness" but about "immaturity." So the same report comments that:

. . . Some systematic conception of immaturity appears necessary in dealing with the problems aptly called "unfinished business," which we so often encounter in psychotherapy. By this phrase, I refer to those vague yet resentful ruminations, and those repetitious reenactments of issues involved originally in some long-ago conflict not adequately resolved at the time and therefore remaining to pester the patient in poorly recognized ways until the basic issue can be faced, cleared up and properly settled to the patient's satisfaction. In suitable cases one can also envisage progress from low levels of immaturity toward higher levels as a reasonable goal of therapy, and even evaluate such progress on a scale.[2]

RESTORATION OF VALUES

We have stressed throughout this book the degree to which the process of counseling therapy seems to imply a basic commitment or investment of the whole self to certain goals, purposes, situations and other persons. This can be either a conscious or unconscious investment. We have concluded that any consideration of counseling and psychotherapy seems to bring us face-to-face with the question of values.

Consequently, a significant contribution of counseling and psychotherapy to the whole field of psychological investigation, research and knowledge is the degree to which it reveals this fundamental importance of values. In this it is restoring to psychology and to all the behavioral and "healing" sciences, an aspect of the human condition that was for a time somewhat neglected and overlooked.

Kohler has remarked:

Human living would simply collapse if all value experiences and corresponding activities were suddenly to disappear. Is the psychologist permitted to ignore the most important parts of his subject matter? And is not his decision to deal only with neutral facts strangely at odds with his own contempt of value? Clearly, his own love of neutral facts and his contempt of value are clear instances of powerful valuation.[3]

Wolberg highlights the issue for counseling and psychotherapy:

Ultimately, successful psychotherapy must accomplish an alteration in the patient's sense of values. These, accretions of many units, fashion drives and action tendencies that operate in the service of adaptation. Many of the value systems are products of the individual's cultural heritage, subtly passed along through educational promptings. These embody moral codes whose origins date back to the earliest phases of man's history, the lineage of social tradition, redesigned to conform with the sanctions of the modern world. Many are the protocols of parental prescripts, incorporating neurotic ideologies; or the product of pleasureable biological drives or their sublimated derivatives; or the reverberations of self-needs; or responses to anxiety; or credendas of the conscience that deal with issues of duty, responsibility, obligation to others and to the world. The sum total of these values, alternating, fluctuating, fusing, receding, makes for the uniqueness of the individual, more or less determining the quality of his adaptations. A consideration of values is, for the psychotherapist, of fundamental importance, not only in terms of detecting sources of conflict, but also of working toward goals in therapy, in service of the end results he ideally seeks to achieve.[4]

In *Research in Psychotherapy,* Whitehorn makes this point, too, when he says:

Beyond the goal of health, as it may be defined strictly, lies a region of value judgments, regarding preferences as to what life and health are for. High value placed upon freedom, or upon conformity, may implicitly determine the strategic aim of the therapist. Behavioral manifestations of these value-orientations are important factors in the processes of psychotherapy.[5]

Whatever else our present awareness of counseling and psychotherapy implies, it seems evident that we must include values. We have therefore tried to show that a great part of the counseling therapy process and its skill is taken up with unfolding, clarifying and re-sorting these values. It involves, in a word, *evaluation.*

We might then speak of a value "package," in the sense that the operational motives contained here are often implicit, folded or "wrapped-up." Even though a person is acting on the motives, attitudes and goals they contain, he may not in reality see these aspects at all, or only confusedly, as through thin wrapping paper. A basic aspect of the counseling therapy process consists in unwrapping and identifying clearly the contents of these value "packages."

In maintaining that values are "charged" with emotions, we mean that since they involve goals and motives to which a person has already committed himself—at least implicitly—they are also the basis and the source of his feeling state. At the beginning of a counseling process, however, all he may really be aware of, are "feelings", and even these may need to be recognized consciously. This is the initial help the counselor or therapist gives him. In this way begins the search and pursuit of the person's value system.

We can also see that this concept of values involves going out of the self to the operational situation and the investment in goals and purposes related to other persons. This adds the dimension of the *other* to the ideas of *self-concept* and *self-actualization.* These points of view in personality dynamics, attributed to Raimy and Rogers[6] and Maslow[7] respectively, have added much to our comprehension of the person. One can see, of course, that to make any investment in the other, one must first, in some form, have invested in one's own self-concept and self-ideal. It is also evident that for this investment to have any real significance, it must first be actualized in the self and in some measure at least, fulfilled. Nonetheless, the actual self investment of going out to the other in a genuine commitment and the concepts of engagement and involvement that this implies, are more sharply and cleanly suggested by the word "values." In this sense, then, we can say that man is his values and so, by his values, one can know in a measure what he is. And a relationship will contain as much or as little as each one chooses to invest in it.

Because the perceptual field of interlacing values—conscious and unconscious, implicit and explicit—is capable of being reorganized and re-sorted, different options are possible. Optional freedom or choice, then, seems related to this capacity of the person in counseling therapy to restructure his own perceptual field. Rogers earlier pointed out:

We discover within the person, under certain conditions, a capacity for the restructuring and the reorganization of self and consequently the reorganization of behavior, which has profound social implications.[8]

This, of course, is limited and mitigated by not only the value system that he has invested in, but also by the constrictions of his own unique self and the empirical situation. Nonetheless, counseling therapy seems also to provide the possibility of and the occasion for the reorganization and resorting of conflicting value systems, and so provides for a different kind of option and operational pattern. Put into practice, it seems often, to the client, more consistent with reality, more appealing, fulfilling and rewarding, and, consequently, he is encouraged to continue in this new operational pattern option.

THE NATURE OF REALITY

But the experience and data of counseling and psychotherapy do more than introduce the issue of values, important and significant as this is in itself. They entail a number of other related issues.

One further implication seems related to the nature of reality itself. As we stated earlier, one of the results of the counseling therapy process is

. . . the unfolding of and growth in the realization of an inner value system. But it is not simply solipsistic. Rather it enables a person to relate better with others and with the life situations in which, here and now, he finds himself.

We see in the counseling therapy process, then, a similar unfolding of an inner value system that is yet objectively effective in producing a better operational fulfillment and achievement. Operational reality, by implication, has apparently some kind of reasonable substructure (granting all its apparent disorder) into which the client's own reasonable process penetrates. The counseling therapy process ultimately facilitates not only a more reasonable integration and control of the personality, but also somehow a better, more adequate way of living.[9]

UNITARY EXPERIENCE

In counseling therapy this unfolding process is partially achieved through what Polanyi calls "the insight that relieves our puzzlement."[10] This comes about through verbal communication between client and counselor or therapist. But, as Maritain says, "it is not language that makes concepts but concepts that make language."[11] So, using a linguistic model, when we say "I am," it is not only a statement about the self but it is also the result of an intuition of being or *is-ness*. "You are," "he is," and "it is," "we are," and "they are," all partake of this same intuition. One thus experiences *is-ness* and formulates or expresses it linguistically. What one is then, or sees himself as—in the sense of a statement of self-concept, "I am disgusted with myself" or "I am pleased with myself" etc.—is basically an extension of this *is-ness,* that is, awareness of reality-contact.

This is, of course, the common sense assumption we all live by and that "science" at some point must imply and fall back on. This existential experience is not simply the object-subject relationship of uninvolved knower but it is the involvement of the whole person in reality or world engagement. Thus Goldstein comments:

For the individual is here involved in his totality, while in the subject-object world he is considered from an isolated and isolating point of view which we may prefer for some special purpose. In order to enter this sphere of immediacy we have to try to neglect somewhat the "natural science" attitude which appears unnatural in this sphere since it does not comprise total human nature. The experience of immediacy cannot be reached by the discursive procedure or by any kind of synthesis. It may be achieved only by surrendering ourselves to the world with which we come in contact without fearing to lose our relation to the ordered world.

Experience teaches us that we are able to live in both spheres, that the two spheres are not opposed to each other, that the sphere of immediacy also belongs to our nature. It shows that our existence is based not on objectively correct order alone but at the same time on comfort, well-being, beauty and joy, on belonging together . . . [12]

This is, as we have seen, a modern development which, in involving the person-in-reality awareness, breaks with the earlier Cartesian-Kantian view. Even physics itself, whose model of Newtonian mechanics so affected our present cultural attitudes towards ourselves and reality, no longer maintains this position. Rather, quantum mechanics suggests quite a different view. Heisenberg explains:

But at this point the situation changed to some extent through quantum theory and therefore we may now come to a comparison of Descartes's philosophical system with out present situation in modern physics. It has been pointed out before that in the Copenhagen interpretation of quantum theory we can indeed proceed without mentioning ourselves as individuals, but we cannot disregard the fact that natural science is formed by men. Natural science does not simply describe and explain nature; it is a part of the interplay between nature and ourselves; it describes nature as exposed to our method of questioning. This was a possibility of which Descartes could not have thought, but it makes the sharp separation between the world and the I impossible.[13]

One might call this the restoration of the self and the return to an awareness of an inner dynamic process in reality, of which man himself is a basic and essential part. There is therefore, no depersonalized observation and no totally uninvolved observer. Rather, reality and man constitute a common engagement together, an engagement that seeks to understand, but not necessarily always in the "clear and distinct" mathematical mode of Descartes.

Ideation and reflective awareness is not removed from unitary experience as "subjective" nor is there some special "objective" world that is above the perceptual equipment of each person. The unitary *is-ness* intuition of being is suggested by Schrodinger[14] and Eccles:[15]

. . . this objective-subjective distinction is illusory, being derived from a misinterpretation and a misunderstanding, as has been convincingly argued by Schrodinger. For example, he says: "Without being aware of it and without being rigorously systematic about it, we exclude the Subject of Cognizance from the domain of nature that we endeavour to understand. We step with our own person back into the part of an onlooker who does not belong to the world, which by this very procedure becomes an objective world. This situation is the same for every mind and its world, in spite of the unfathomable abundance of "cross-references" between them. *The world is given to me only once,* not one existing and one perceived. Subject and object are only one. The barrier between them cannot be said to have broken down as a result of recent experience in the physical sciences, for this barrier does not exist."

Observation can therefore be as genuinely applied to private, inner or "subjective" experiences as to "objective" experience, since, in fact, both achieve public status by symbolic and linguistic communication between observers. So Eccles concludes:

. . . that every observation of the so-called objective world depends in the first instance on an experience which is just as private as the so-called subjective experiences. The public status of an observation is given by symbolic communication between observers, in particular through the medium of language. By means of this same method of communication, our inner or subjective experiences can likewise achieve a public status. We report such experiences to others and discover that they have like experiences to report to us. A large proportion of our literature is concerned with such verbal communication of inner experiences, either of the author himself or of the characters that he so creates.[16]

What we have referred to as a mosaic, Eccles considers as a map:

This map or symbolic picture is essential so that I can act appropriately within this "objective world;" and, as we have seen, it is synthesized from sensory data so as to be effective for this very purpose. It is built upon spatial relations, but is also given symbolic information in terms of secondary qualities. For example, colors, sounds, smells, heat, and cold, as such, belong only to the perceptual world. Furthermore, it is part of my interpretation of my perceptual experience that my "self" is associated with a body that is in the "objective world;" and I find innumerable other bodies that appear to be of like nature. I can exchange communications with them by bodily movements that give rise to perceptual changes in the observer, for example, by gestures or at the more sophisticated level of language, and thus discover by reciprocal communication that they too have conscious experiences resembling mine. Solipsism becomes for me no longer a tenable belief. There is a world of selves, each with the experience of being associated with a body that is in an "objective world" comprising innumerable bodies of like nature and a tremendous variety of other living forms and an immensity of apparently nonliving matter.[17]

SCIENTIFIC SELF-QUEST

Seen this way then, the counseling therapy process of self observation, exploration and evaluation would not be dissimilar to the scientific quest generally considered.

Polanyi describes how he conceives the process of scientific quest in the following way:

It is a mistake to think of heuristic surmises as well-defined hypothetical statements which the scientist proceeds to test in a neutral and indeed critical spirit. Hunches often consist essentially in narrowing down the originally wider program of the enquiry. They may be most exciting, and may indeed turn out later to have been crucial, yet they are mostly far more indeterminate than the final discovery will be. The range of their indeterminacy lies at some point between that of the original problem and of its eventual solution.[18]

Far from being value-free, he proposes that personal values inspire the scientist:

Besides, the relation of the scientist to his surmises is one of passionate personal commitment. The effort that led to a surmise committed every fiber of his being to the quest; his surmises embody all his hopes.[19]

The final process might be said to resemble the process of insight and self-integration that occurs in counseling therapy:

You might expect me to conclude by showing how a problem is eventually resolved by the discovery of a coherence in nature, the hidden existence of which had first been sighted in a problem and which had become increasingly manifest by its pursuit. I must, however, first introduce another factor, the identification of which we owe to Henri Poincaré. In a classic essay included in *Science et Methode* (1908) he described two stages in the way we hit upon an idea that promises to solve a scientific problem. The first stage consists in racking one's brains by successive sallies of the imagination, while the second, which may be delayed for hours after one has ceased one's efforts, is the spontaneous appearance of the idea one has struggled for. Poincaré says that this spontaneous process consists in the integration of some of the material mobilized by thrusts of the imagination; he also tells us that these thrusts would be useless but for the fact that they are guided by special anticipatory gifts of the scientist.

It seems plausible to assume, then, that two faculties of the mind are at work jointly from the beginning to the end of an enquiry. One is the deliberately active powers of the imagination, and the other a spontaneous process of integration, which we may call *intuition*. It is intuition that senses the presence of hidden resources for solving a problem and which launches the imagination in its pursuit. And it is intuition that forms there our surmises and which eventually selects from the material mobilized by the imagination the relevant pieces of evidence and integrates them into the solution of the problem.[20]

By contrast with this description, the kind of experiment that is sometimes held up as a scientific empirical model may not be really this at all. Bakan comments that:

Most experimentation in the field of psychology falls considerably short of being able to be considered really empirical. Consider the ideal of the "well-designed experiment." The usual meaning of "well-designed" is that the outcomes of the experiment have been completely anticipated, and that one will not allow the experience of conducting the experiment to lead one to consider alternatives outside of the ones already thought of beforehand.[21]

EMPIRICAL OBSERVATION AND COMMITMENT

This is not, as we have repeatedly stressed, to gainsay scientific objectivity or information yielded by precise and detailed empirical observation and measurement. These are of primary importance. But we need to distinguish between psychology as genuinely empirical observation, that is, drawn from experience, and the much greater limits of mathematical calculation and rigorously controlled experimentation. Both can be scientific but they are by no means always synonymous. Nor are they opposed. But they need to be carefully distinguished if they are to be helpful and clarifying in advancing knowledge. Bakan explains that

Brentano (1874), at the time of the founding of modern experimental psychology, argued that psychology should be empirical rather than experimental; that the experiment was too far removed from experience to be able to tell us much that was significant. The very distinction—let alone the comparison—between the empirical and the experimental is one which many psychologists today might find hard to understand. In the culture of contemporary psychology the words are used synonymously. It is perhaps worthwhile to allow the possibility that the experimental may *sometimes* stand in the way of the empirical. The essential feature of any empirical epistemology is that it relies heavily on the contributions from experience. If the experimental method as it has developed in the field of psychology interferes with the processes whereby we may acquire knowledge from experience, then indeed do we have to review seriously the relationships between the experimental and the empirical.[22]

Moreover, in the context of deep personal commitment and authentic relationship that counseling and psychotherapy especially demand, "valueless" neutrality would seem to run the risk of appearing not only as a contradiction but worse, as a fraud or a pose. It might, too, under a "scientific" guise, turn out in fact to be a masque for manipulation, control and mastery over others rather than an authentic relationship. It might thus cast into doubt what one might choose to stand for as a human person. For such a mastery-complex would be quite different from a genuine investment in the other person, in his freedom and his right and need to pursue and form in himself his own personal value structure, helped by but unencumbered by the interfering values of the counselor or therapist.

Values uniquely fulfilling for each person, however, need not contradict values equally unique and fulfilling for others. Rather, a common atmosphere and climate emerges so that aspects of what is unique in each can also in some measure be common to all. In their common and symbolic quality, they can then be educative without being compulsive or abusive of unique self-fulfillment.

In fact, it is precisely here that counseling in particular can be seen not simply as therapeutic or related to illness but as an integral and necessary part of the educative process. For, through counseling, the meanings of education, their broad and deep extension through all the knowledge areas of mankind—past and present—become personal by being at the same time the unique investment and value of each learner. Such meanings thus engage themselves in and become the life-stuff of his own person through the digestion process of his own *euboulia,* with or without the assistance of skilled counseling. But, as with any skill, the learner can most effectively and efficiently achieve these results through such counseling.

RETURN TO COGNITIVE PROCESS

Meaning, then, adds to experience the *signification* which the immediate reflection upon experience produces. Experience, here, is that kind which consciousness brings. This immediate signification may be retained or changed by later and more prolonged reflection, as in a counseling therapy process. Man calls experience by a name, he signifies its meaning to himself, he gives it a symbolic sign. So, in this sense we might say that man is an experiencing—reflective—symbolic animal. He signs experience with meaning. As the word itself indicates, "conceptualization" is feminine, and it depends upon basic experience for the initiating of its signification process. Its meaning is then founded on such basic experience.

Here signification and value are not totally separate. Signification, however, tending as it does towards the universal, is less directly value-laden. It becomes so, as its symbolization is invested with personalized individuation or, what might be called, the "empirical situation." Lonergan sums up the intellectual insight process this way:

. . . insight is the source not only of theoretical knowledge but also of all its practical applications and, indeed, of all intelligent activity. Insight into insight, then, will reveal what activity is intelligent, and insight into oversights will reveal what activity is unintelligent. But to be practical is to do the intelligent thing and to be unpractical is to keep blundering about. It follows that insight into both insight and oversight is the very key to practicality.

Thus, insight into insight brings to light the cumulative process of progress. For concrete situations give rise to insights which issue into policies and courses of action. Action transforms the existing situation to give rise to further insights, better policies, more effective courses of action. It follows that if insight occurs, it keeps recurring; and at each recurrence knowledge develops, action increases its scope, and situations improve.

Similarly, insight into oversight reveals the cumulative process of decline. For the flight from understanding blocks the insights that concrete situations demand. There follow unintelligent policies and inept courses of action. The situation deteriorates to demand still further insights and, as they are blocked, policies become more unintelligent and action more inept. What is worse, the deteriorating situation seems to provide the uncritical, biased mind with factual evidence in which the bias is claimed to be verified. So in ever increasing measure intelligence comes to be regarded as irrelevant to practical living. Human activity settles down to a decadent routine, and initiative becomes the privilege of violence.[23]

But insight as we mean it and as we see it operating in counseling therapy, would be more than this intellectual awareness, more than perceptual *gestalten*. It would be *evaluative* in the most exact sense of that term, in that such insight would consist of tracing emotional reactions to their sources in the self-invested values of the person himself. The unfolding and clarification of this value system and the ability to resort and reinvest the self as a result of this clarification would constitute genuine psychological insight.

This leads us to some further implications of the linguistic model we used earlier. We might propose that the linguistic paradigm, especially in the forms of the verb "to be"—the verb signifying both being and existence—is basic to all self-other awareness and all communication within the self and with others. One might say that here we are at the heart of the whole counseling therapeutic communication because it depends finally on words and on a language paradigm—granting the presence of other significant factors. It is, as we have said, a language-of-affect–language-of-cognition communication.

Bruner and others point out how developments in therapeutic and personality theory have revived concern for the cognitive process:

The past few years have witnessed a notable increase in interest in and investigation of the cognitive processes—the means whereby organisms achieve, retain, and transform information. This increase in interest and effort should, we suppose, be counted as a "revival," since there was an earlier time (the years before the first World War), when the Higher Mental Processes constituted a core topic within psychology . . .

Finally, the revival has been stimulated by deep and long-term changes in personality theory. Freud's brilliant insights at the turn of the century focussed attention on what might appropriately be called the motivational economy of man's adjustment: the expression of inner drives and the resolution of such drives when they conflict. His formulations and their later extension were, in considerable measure, a revolt against the excessive rationalism of the 19th century. Cognitive activity was at first of interest to the personality theorist only to the degree that it illustrated the manner in which "rational" processes could be made captive of imperious drives and defenses. Here too there has been a significant change. Psychoanalysis and personality theory generally have become increasingly interested in what has come to be called "ego psychology," and the so-called synthetic functions of the ego grow more and more central. Perhaps the change can even be dated to the publication of two books in the late 1930's, one psychoanalytic, the other not: Anna Freud's *The Ego and the Mechanisms of Defense,* and Gordon W. Allport's *Personality*. In any case, as the ego came out of hiding, the interest in cognitive functioning came with it. If the work that came to be called the "New Look" in perception started off searching for manifestations of autism in perceiving, it soon became transformed into a search for links between general laws of perception and cognition on one side and general laws of personality functioning on the other.[24]

Later Bruner insists that the learning and utilization of categories is central to the cognitive process:

Two broad types of categorizing responses are obviously of interest. One of them is the identity response, the other the equivalence response, and each points to a different kind of category.

Without belaboring the obvious, identity categorization may be defined as classing a variety of stimuli as *forms of the same thing.* What lies behind the identity response is not clear, save that it is obviously a response that is affected by learning. It does not do to say simply that an object is seen as the identical object on a later encounter if it has not "changed its characteristics too much." The moon in its phases varies from a sliver to a circle, in color from luminous white to the bronzed hunter's moon. Sheldon (1950) collected a series of photographs of the same individual over a period of 15 years, the person standing in the same position against a uniform background. The photographs span the period from early boyhood to full manhood. As one riffles through the stack, there is a strong and dramatic impression of the identical person in the process of growth. Yet the pictures go through a drastic metamorphosis. Because such identity responses are ubiquitous and because they are learned very early in life, we tend to regard them somehow as a different process from other forms of categorizing—the recognition of two different people as both being people. Yet both depend upon what Michotte (1950) speaks of as the presence of a *cachet spécifique* or essential quality. They are both forms of categorizing. What differs is the nature of the inference: in the one case we infer "identity" from the presence of the *cachet*, in the other case "equivalence."[25]

A child in early growth stages has difficulty holding identity— living apparently in a kind of moment-to-moment "now." He grows in his identity ability:

How one comes to learn to categorize in terms of identity categories is, as we have said, little understood. Too often we have succumbed to the Kantian heritage and taken identity categories as given. Piaget's recent work (1953) and the work of Michotte (1946) leave the question open. Piaget speaks of the learning of identity as corresponding to the mastery of a principle of conservation of energy in physics. At certain stages of development, an object passed behind a screen is not judged by the child to be the same object when it emerges on the other side. Hebb (1949) proposes that certain forms of neural growth must precede the capacity for the maintenance of identity. Whether the capacity is "innate" and then developed by being extended to new ranges of events or whether the capacity to recognize identity is itself learned is not our concern here. It suffices to note that its development depends notably upon learning.[26]

That the counseling therapy process centers around this *is-ness* self-definition or self-concept is suggested by the existential awareness of both sameness and change:

That there is confusion remaining in the adult world about what constitutes an identity class is testified to by such diverse proverbs as *plus ça change, plus la même chose* and the Heraclidan dictum that we never enter the same river twice. Indeed, in severe psychotic turmoil one sometimes notes an uncertainty about the identity category that is the "self" in states of depersonalization, and a rather poignant reminder that the identity of self is even equivocal in normal states is provided by the sign behind a bar in the Southwest:

> I ain't what I've been.
> I ain't what I'm going to be.
> I am what I am.[27]

This helps explain why the cognitive process of the proper labelling and resorting of experience-categories, would constitute a central purpose and achievement of counseling therapy. What Polanyi called the "puzzling aspects"[28] of human experience are transformed into a solvable realization by means of a language-of-affect–language-of-cognition communication.

Rimoldi makes this interesting point:

The interplay between logical structure and language seems to be at the basis of our advancement in knowledge. The invention of new symbols may facilitate the performance of certain logical operations, and more complex logical operations are possible provided there is an appropriate language to express them.[29]

Adapting this to counseling and psychotherapy, we might say that many people, when they experience affects, are confusedly able to communicate these in the language of affect. But they are unable to understand or communicate them in cognitive language. In this sense, then, through the counseling therapy process, they would be learning a "new" language—in Rimoldi's terms—that is to say, they would be learning, for the first time, to speak cognitively of and to themselves. It is this type of language, with its more communicable symbols, that seems to facilitate genuine communication with the self as well as with others, and so results in a gain in genuine self-understanding as well as a better operational relationship. So, what a person previously described as "I feel", he can now describe as "I see" or "I understand". By these differences, he designates a gain in self-awareness through a "new" cognitive language which enlarges and extends his inner-self as well as his extra-self communication ability.

This does not mean any "clear and distinct" Cartesian resolution of the "puzzling aspects" of one's individual empirical situation, but it simply means the kind of clarity and release from conflict that makes some self-symbolization possible. This results in understanding adequate at least for a more fulfilling operational achievement—Whitehorne's "melioristic" goal. And this is achieved, as we have repeatedly stated, not in an atmosphere of cold, neutral, impartial observation but in the rich, warm and intense regard and convalidation of genuine personal communion.

CREATIVE AFFILIATION

We earlier discussed in detail those aspects still implicit in our culture which impede such authentic relationship and genuine engagement between persons. Such implicit "scientific" values can make us tend to be observers of life rather than being genuinely related and engaged. They therefore can really pull us away from the reality of ourselves and from other persons and things. So Kerr was quoted as saying:

We have neglected knowledge by contact in our abstraction-centered lives, have in fact almost persuaded ourselves that it does not exist.[30]

We have proposed that counseling therapy can aid us in this impasse by offering a model from which to develop and extend the means of authentic relationship.

In searching for a word to delineate this authentic relationship, we find difficulty with the term "friendship." As we have said, "friendship" tends to imply a relationship perhaps too remote and too undefined. In American society especially, it is common to assume such a relationship of friendship on even a first meeting. It is simply a form of open acceptance and in this it can also be artificial and false. This type of friendship is contrived and basically the opposite of the genuinely authentic relationship we are discussing. Consequently, because of the difficulties accruing from its present usage and connotation, the term "friendship," would not convey the authenticity that we mean here, except in the sense of the Latin "amicitia," a "benevolent love," actively communicating to another a sense of his unique personal dignity.

On the other hand, the word "love" is highly ambiguous too. Its present sentimental as well as sexual tones can somewhat distort its implications for genuinity in a relationship. "Love" rather conveys an area of relationship too broad and too all-inclusive. Its very extension and magnitude and all the things that can be understood by it, often tend to confuse rather than help delineate the nature of a relationship.

Consequently, we propose using the word "affiliation." By "affiliation" we mean a relationship which engages us in a real concern for the other and a conscious effort to convalidate his worth and dignity. Such a relationship, by definition, involves adequate communication. It is not enough, therefore, *simply* to wish another well (benevolence), to be concerned and "care" about him. This caring must be repeatedly conveyed in communication, so that he is and feels himself understood and accepted at the unique level of himself. His person and communication are not manipulated and controlled by another person. They are not subtly made the object of the other person's will to power over him. They are given their own unique meaning and value. By this kind of understanding relationship and response, one person constitutes for the other a genuine affiliation.

After indicating how few studies have been made on the conditions necessary to adequate relations between people, Schachter comments that

... people, in and of themselves, represent goals for one another; that is, people do have needs which can be satisfied *only* in interpersonal relations. Approval, support, friendship, prestige and the like have been offered as examples of such needs. There is no doubt that such needs are particularly powerful ones and that association with other people is a necessity for most of us.[31]

This does not mean that such affiliation would be always accepting of what the other person *does*. On the contrary, it can be a most confronting experience to hear oneself genuinely understood by another and in such mirroring, be forced to see oneself as one really is. Consequently, by "understanding," we do not always mean *approval* or permissiveness in regard to another's behavior. We mean a genuine caring about the other which strives to penetrate his emotional, instinctive and somatic being, as well as to intellectualize with him. Such a caring can result in helping him see the particular set of values which are actually motivating him. This can be very different from what a removed intellectual judgment of him might appear to reveal.

As to being permissive, genuine affiliation may, at times, be quite the contrary. Again, we quote Shakespeare (as in Chapter X, "The Maturity and Therapy of Limits,"): "Love is not love/ Which alters when it alteration finds." Convalidation of the worth of another can be shown sometimes by an honest standing against him. The difference here would be that in true affiliation, such standing against another would show "caring." The confrontation honestly emerges from this caring. It would then turn to understanding and helping a person pursue the confused value system that lies behind his present conduct. Such confrontation, seeking to be constructive, would, in its concern, convey both its authenticity and its positive regard.

The issue in affiliation, therefore, is not permissiveness or confrontation. The question is rather whether permissiveness or confrontation are used as disguises of will to power manipulation of another person, or are the result of a genuine will to communication with him. Only such communication can convalidate a worth and dignity that are uniquely in himself. This would constitute the state of affiliation between two or more persons.

CREATIVE CONVALIDATION

To add the concept "creative" to the state of affiliation, would be the final unfolding of an authentic relationship. "Creative" would suggest that such affiliations should be mutually encouraging, stimulating and achieving. They should bring out from each, in home, family, school, work and play, what is in the direction of one's better and more fulfilling self. They should, in a word, invoke and encourage the pursuit of each one's own excellence. Just such a pursuit of one's own excellence was an ancient definition of "humility," a word that now rather suggests the servility and artifice of Uriah Heep. But in its ancient sense, such a desire, firm in courage, constitutes a major motivating source of all other value pursuits.

Thus, a creative relationship would be free, so that each might search for and pursue his unique self, and encourage his own best unfolding and actualization. By striving to be genuinely understanding and reflective of another, such affiliation would convalidate the continual discovery and realization of self-potential.

But the values of freedom and the pursuit of one's own special excellence also include and require a self-conformity to limits sufficient to permit equal freedom and self-pursuit to others. These values will not be learned in isolation or in competition with others exclusively. They are apparently much more effectively learned by cooperative and joint effort at belonging and sharing. This does not preclude reflection and necessary removal for one's own unique self-exploration and unfolding. "The world" and people can be "too much with us." But such reflection will be accompanied by a respect and regard for others as well as for oneself. Hence, it will further one's growth toward mature other-centeredness, as well as a tranquility in one's own respectful self-regard. This is the kind of relationship we signify by the term "authentic." Such a relationship, too, would constitute "creative affiliation", because it would seek to provide the most appropriate conditions for the search and pursuit of values.

NOTES

[1] John C. Whitehorn, M.D., "Goals of Psychotherapy," *Research in Psychotherapy*, ed. E. A. Rubinstein and M. B. Parloff, Washington: American Psychological Association, Inc., 1959, p. 8.

[2] *Ibid.*, p. 8.

[3] Wolfgang Kohler, *The Place of Value in a World of Facts*, New York: A Mentor Book, New American Library, 1966, Introduction, p. vii.

[4] Lewis R. Wolberg, M.D., *Psychotherapy and the Behavioral Sciences*, New York: Grune & Stratton, 1966, p. 130.

[5] Whitehorn, *op. cit.*, p. 9. See especially the detailed treatment of

Charlotte Buhler, *Values in Psychotherapy,* New York: Free Press-Macmillan, 1962.

[6] C. R. Rogers, *On Becoming a Person,* Boston: Houghton Mifflin, 1961, pp. 163–181.
    See also:
    Raimy, Victor Charles, "The Self-Concept as a factor in Counseling and Personality Organization," Ph.D. Thesis, Ohio State University, Columbus, Ohio, 1943.
    ———, "Self-reference in counseling interviews," *G. Consult Psych,* 1948, 12,153–163.
    Wylie, Ruth C., *The Self Concept: A Critical Survey of Pertinent Research Literature,* Univ. of Nebraska Press, Lincoln, 1961.

[7] A. H. Maslow, *Motivation and Personality,* New York: Harper and Brothers, 1954, p. 214.

[8] Carl R. Rogers, "APA Presidential Address," *The American Psychologist,* 2 (9), September 1947.

[9] See p. 81.

[10] Michael Polanyi, "Logic and Psychology," *The American Psychologist,* 23 (1), p. 36.

[11] Jacques Maritain, *The Peasant of the Garonne,* New York: Holt, Rinehart and Winston, 1968, p. 14. Trans. by Michael Cuddihy and Elizabeth Hughes.

[12] Goldstein, *op. cit.,* Preface, p. ix. ·

[13] Werner Heisenberg, *Physics and Philosophy: The Revolution in Modern Science,* New York: Harper & Brothers, Inc., 1958, p. 81.

[14] E. Schrodinger, *Mind and Matter,* London: Cambridge University Press, 1958.

[15] Eccles, *op. cit.,* p. 324. (Italics mine)

[16] *Ibid.,* p. 325.

[17] *Ibid.,* p. 326.

[18] Polanyi, *op. cit.,* p. 41.

[19] *Ibid.*

[20] *Ibid.,* pp. 41–42.

[21] David Bakan, *On Method: Toward a Reconstruction of Psychological Investigation,* San Francisco: Jossey-Bass, Inc., 1967, Preface, pp. xii–xiii.

[22] *Ibid.,* p. xiii.

[23] Bernard J. F. Lonergan, *Insight: A Study of Human Understanding,* New York: Philosophical Library, 1957, Preface, pp. xiii–xiv.

[24] Jerome S. Bruner, Jacqueline J. Goodnow, George A. Austin, *A Study of Thinking,* New York: John Wiley & Sons, Inc., 1956, Preface, pp. vii and viii.

[25] *Ibid.,* p. 3.
    See also:
    W. H. Sheldon, a personal communication in 1950.

A. Michotte, "A propos de la permanence phénoménale: Faits et théories," *Acta Psychol.*, 7, 1950, pp. 298–322.

——, *La perception de la causalité* (1st Ed.), Louvain et Paris: Vrin., 1946.

J. Piaget, "Experimental epistemology," unpublished lecture at Harvard University, 1953.

[26] Bruner, *op. cit.*, p. 3.

See also:

D. O. Hebb, *The Organization of Behavior*, New York: Wiley, 1949.

Heinz Werner and Bernard Kaplan, *Symbol Formation*, New York: John Wiley and Sons, Inc., 1967, p. 418.

One may recall, in this connection, the indiscriminate use of early "time words," e.g., *yesterday, tomorrow,* used now for past, now for future (i.e., not-now). "In the mind of the child that which is not present—and this may refer to the past or the future—possesses a uniform character, viz., that of non-existing at the moment." (A Gregoire, *L'apprentissage du language,* 2 vols., Paris: Droz., 1937–1947, p. 129.)

[27] Bruner, *op. cit.*, pp. 3–4.

[28] Polanyi, *op. cit.*, p. 36.

[29] H. J. A. Rimoldi, M.D., "Thinking and Language," *Arch. Gen. Psychiat,* 17, November 1967, p. 575.

[30] Kerr, *op. cit.*, p. 214.

[31] Stanley Schachter, *The Psychology of Affiliation*, Stanford, Calif.: Stanford University Press, 1959, pp. 1–2.

Bibliography

Adams, James F. *Problems in Counseling: A case Study Approach.* New York: Macmillan Co., 1964.

Allport, Gordon W. *Becoming: Basic Considerations for a Psychology of Personality.* New Haven: Yale University Press, 1955.

——. "Mental Health: A Generic Attitude," *Journal of Religion and Health*, 4(1), October 1964.

——. *Personality: A Psychological Interpretation.* New York: Henry Holt, 1937.

——. "The Psychology of Participation," *Psychological Review*, 53, May 1945.

Ansbacher, H. L., and Rowena R. Ansbacher, eds. *The Individual Psychology of Alfred Adler: A Systematic Presentation in Selections from His Writings.* New York: Harper & Row, Harper Torchbooks, The Academy Library, 1964.

Aquinas, Thomas. *Summa Theologica.* Trans. by Fathers of the English Dominican Province. New York: Benziger, 1947.

Arbuckle, Dugald S., ed. *Counseling and Psychotherapy: An Overview.* New York: McGraw-Hill, 1967.

——. "Kinds of Counseling: Meaningful and Meaningless," *Journal of Counseling Psychology*, 14(3), 1967.

Ariés, Philippe. *Centuries of Childhood: A Social History of Family Life.* Trans. by Robert Baldick. New York: Alfred A. Knopf, 1962.

Aristotle. *Aristote: Ethique de Nicomaque.* Trans. by Jean Voilquin. Paris: Librairie Garnier Freres, 1950.

——. *The Ethics of Aristotle.* Trans. by J. A. K. Thomson. Maryland: Penguin Classics, Penguin Books, 1953.

——. *Introduction to Aristotle.* Ed. by Richard McKeon. New York: Random House, Modern Library, 1947.

379

Arnold, Magda B. *Emotion and Personality, Neurological and Physiological Aspects.* 2 Vols. New York: Columbia University Press, 1960.

――――. *Story Sequence Analysis: A New Method of Measuring Motivation and Predicting Achievement.* New York: Columbia University Press, 1962.

――――, and John A. Gasson. *The Human Person: An Approach to an Integral Theory of Personality.* New York: Ronald Press, 1954.

Augustine, Saint. *The Building of the Human City.* Ed. by Thomas P. Neill. Garden City, N. Y.: A Doubleday Dolphin Book, 1960.

――――. "On the Trinity," *Basic Writings of Saint Augustine.* Ed. by W. J. Oates. New York: Random House, 1948.

Axline, Virginia M. *Dibs: In Search of Self Personality Development in Play Therapy.* Boston: Houghton Mifflin, 1964.

Bakan, David. *Disease, Pain and Sacrifice: Toward a Psychology of Suffering.* Chicago: University of Chicago Press, 1968.

――――. *The Duality of Human Existence.* Chicago: Rand McNally, 1966.

――――. *On Method: Toward a Reconstruction of Psychological Investigation.* San Francisco: Jossey-Bass, Inc., 1967.

――――. "The Mystery-Mastery Complex in Contemporary Psychology," *The American Psychologist,* 20(3), March 1965.

――――. "The Test of Significance in Psychological Research," *Psychological Bulletin,* 66(6), 1966.

Barron, Frank. *Creativity and Psychological Health: Origins of Personal Vitality and Creative Freedom.* New York: Van Nostrand, 1963.

Bartley, S. Howard. *Principles of Perception.* New York: Harper and Brothers, 1958.

Beck, Carlton E. *Guidelines for Guidance: Readings in the Philosophy of Guidance.* Dubuque, Iowa: Wm. C. Brown Co., 1966.

Beck, Samuel J., and Herman B. Molish, eds. *Reflexes to Intelligence: A Reader in Clinical Psychology.* Glencoe, Ill.: The Free Press of Glencoe, 1959.

Becker, Ernest. *The Birth and Death of Meaning: A Perspective in Psychiatry and Anthropology.* New York: The Free Press, A Division of The Macmillan Co., 1962.

――――. *The Revolution in Psychiatry: The New Understanding of Man.* New York: The Free Press, A Division of The Macmillan Co., 1964.

Begin, Yves. *Evaluative and Emotional Factors in Learning a Foreign Language.* Doctoral Dissertation. Loyola University, Chicago, June 1968.

Benda, Clemens E. "Language, Intelligence and Creativity," *Journal of Existential Psychiatry,* 3(9), Summer-Fall,, 1962.

Berelson, Bernard, and Gary A. Steiner. *Human Behavior: An Inventory of Scientific Findings.* New York: Harcourt, Brace and World, Inc., 1964.

Berkson, J. "Tests of Significance Considered as Evidence," *Journal of American Statistical Association,* 37, 1942.

Boring, Edwin G. *History, Psychology and Science, Selected Papers.* Ed. by Robert I. Watson and Donald T. Campbell. New York: John Wiley and Sons, 1963.

Boy, Angelo U., and Gerald J. Pirie. *Client-Centered Counseling in the Secondary School.* Boston: Houghton Mifflin, 1963.

Brachfeld, Oliver. "Individual Psychology in the Learning of Languages," *International Journal of Individual Psychology,* 2(1), First Quarter, 1936.

Bradford, Leland P., Jack R. Gibb and Kenneth D. Benne, eds. *T Group Therapy and Laboratory Method.* New York: John Wiley and Sons, 1964.

Brammer, Lawrence M., and Everett L. Shostrom. *Therapeutic Psychology, Fundamentals of Counseling and Psychotherapy.* Englewood Cliffs, N. J.: Prentice-Hall, 1960.

Branan, J. M. "Client Reaction to Counselor's Use of Self-Experience," *The Personnel and Guidance Journal,* 45(6), February 1967.

Brennan, Robert E. *General Psychology: A Study of Man Based on St. Thomas Aquinas.* Rev. ed. New York: Macmillan Co., 1952.

Brenner, Charles. *An Elementary Textbook of Psychoanalysis.* New York: Doubleday and Co., 1955.

Bruner, Jerome. *The Process of Education.* Cambridge: Harvard University Press, 1961.

————, J. Goodnow and G. Austin. *A Study of Thinking.* New York: John Wiley and Sons, 1956.

Buber, Martin. *I and Thou.* Trans. by R. G. Smith. Edinburg: T. and T. Clark, 1937.

Bugelski, B. R. *The Psychology of Learning Applied to Teaching.* Indianapolis: Bobb Merrill, 1964.

Bugental, J. *The Search for Authenticity.* New York: Holt, Rinehart and Winston, 1965.

Bühler, Charlotte. *Values in Psychotherapy.* New York: The Free

Press of Glencoe, A Division of The Macmillan Co., 1962.

Buss, Arnold. *The Psychology of Aggression.* New York: John Wiley and Sons, 1961.

Campbell, David P. *The Results of Counseling: Twenty-Five Years Later.* Philadelphia: W. B. Saunders, 1965.

Carkhuff, Robert R., and Mae Alexik. "Effect of Client Depth of Self-Exploration Upon High- and Low-Functioning Counselors," *Journal of Counseling Psychology,* 14(4), July 1967, pp. 350-355.

Carmichael, Leonard. "Science and Social Conservatism," *Scientific Monthly,* 78, June 1954.

Carstairs, G. M. Review of "Normality, Theoretical and Clinical Concepts of Mental Health," by Daniel Offer and Melvin Sabskin, *Science,* 153, September 23, 1966.

Cartwright, Dorwin, and Alvin Zander, eds., *Group Dynamics: Research and Theory.* Evanston, Ill.: Row Peterson, 1956.

Cassirer, Ernst. *An Essay on Man: An Introduction to Philosophy of Human Culture.* New Haven: Yale University Press, 1962.

Cather, Willa. *On Writing.* New York: Alfred A. Knopf, 1949.

Cattell, Raymond B. *Factor Analysis: An Introduction and Manual for the Psychologist and Social Scientist.* New York: Harper and Brothers, 1952.

Cavanagh, J. R. *Fundamental Marriage Counseling: A Catholic Viewpoint.* Milwaukee: Bruce, 1957.

Clemens, Alphonse H. *Design for Successful Marriage.* 2nd ed. Englewood Cliffs, N. J.: Prentice-Hall, 1964.

Cole, Charles W., and Dean C. Miller. "Relevance of Expressed Values to Academic Performance," *Counseling Psychology,* 14(3), May 1967.

Contemporary Approaches to Creative Thinking: A Symposium Held at the University of Colorado. Ed. by H. E. Gruber, G. Terrell and M. Wertheimer. New York: Atherton Press, 1962.

Cottle, William C., and N. M. Downie. *Procedures and Preparation for Counseling.* Englewood Cliffs, N. J.: Prentice-Hall, 1960.

"Creativity," *Carnegie Corporation of New York,* Quarterly, 9, 1961.

Cuber, John F., and Peggy B. Harroff. "The More Total View: Relationships Among Men and Women of the Upper Middle Class," *Marriage and Family Living,* 25(2), May 1963.

Cullmann, Oscar. *Christ et le temps: temps et histoire dans le christianisme primitif.* Neuchatel et Paris: Delachaux et Nestle, 1947. English trans. by Floyd V. Filson, *Christ and Time: The Primitive*

Christian Conception of Time and History, Philadelphia: The Westminster Press, 1950.

Curran, Charles A. "A Counseling Psychotherapeutic Methodology and Associated Learning Apparatus," Loyola University, Chicago, February 1965.

————. "Counseling, Psychotherapy and the Unified Person," *Journal of Religion and Health,* 2(2), January 1963.

————. "Counseling Skills Adapted to the Learning of Foreign Languages," *The Menninger Bulletin,* March 1961.

————. "Counseling as Therapy and Self-Integration," *The Human Person.* Ed. by M. B. Arnold and J. A. Gasson. New York: Ronald Press, 1954.

————. "Nondirective Counseling in Allergic Complaints," *Journal of Abnormal and Social Psychology,* 43(4), October 1948.

————. "Personality Factors in Allergic Disorders," *Journal of Allergy,* 18, 1947.

————. *Personality Factors in Counseling.* New York: Grune & Stratton, 1945.

————. "The Physician's Understanding Heart," *Journal of the American Medical Association,* 188, April 13, 1964.

————. "Toward a Theology of Human Belonging," *Journal of Religion and Health,* 4(3), April 1965.

Dalbiez, Roland. *Psychoanalytical Method and the Doctrine of Freud.* London: Longmans, Green and Co., 1941.

Dawson, Joseph, K. Herbert Stone and N. P. Dellis. *Psychotherapy with Schizophrenics: A Reappraisal.* Baton Rouge, La.: Louisiana State University Press, 1961.

Dellis, Nicholas P., and Herbert K. Stone, eds. *The Training of Psychotherapists: A Multidisciplinary Approach.* Baton Rouge, La.: Louisiana State University Press, 1960.

Descartes, René. *Discourse de la Méthode.* Ed. by E. Gilson. Paris: Librairie Philosophique J. Vrin, 1935.

Devlin, William, S. J. *Psychodynamics of Personality Development.* Staten Island, N. Y.: Alba House, 1966.

Diamond, Solomon. *Personality and Temperament.* New York: Harper and Brothers, 1957.

Dinkmeyer, Don, and Rudolf Dreikurs. *Encouraging Children to Learn: The Encouragement Process.* Englewood Cliffs, N. J.: Prentice-Hall, 1963.

Eccles, John C. *Brain and Conscious Experience.* Study Week, September 24 to October 4, 1964, of the *Pontificia Academia Scientiarum.* New York: Springer-Verlag New York, Inc., 1966.

Edwards, W., H. Lindman and L. J. Savage. "Bayesian Statistical Inference for Psychological Research," *Psychological Research,* 70, 1963.

Eliade, Mercea. *Mephistopheles and the Androgyne: Studies in Religious Myth and Symbol.* Trans. by M. Cohen. New York: Sheed and Ward, 1965.

———. *The Sacred and the Profane.* Harper & Row, 1961.

Eliot, T. S., in the Preface to *The Need for Roots,* by Simone Weil. Boston: The Beacon Press, 1952.

Emig, Janet A., James T. Fleming and Helen M. Popp, eds. *Language and Learning.* New York: Harcourt, Brace and World, 1966.

Entralgo, Pedro L. *Mind and Body: Psychosomatic Pathology: A Short History of the Evolution of Medical Thought.* Trans. by Aurelio M. Espinosa. New York: P. J. Kenedy and Sons.

Erikson, E. H. *Childhood and Society.* New York: Norton, 1950.

Esper, Erwin. *A History of Psychology.* Philadelphia:: W. B. Saunders, 1964.

Evans, Joan, ed. *The Flowering of the Middle Ages.* London: Thames and Hudson, 1966

Fairchild, Johnson E., ed. *Women, Society and Sex.* New York: Sheridan House, 1952.

Feifel, Herman. *The Meaning of Death.* New York: McGraw-Hill, 1959.

Fenichel, Otto. *The Psychoanalytic Theory of Neurosis.* New York: W. W. Norton and Co., 1945.

Fincher, Cameron. *A Preface to Psychology.* New York: Harper & Row, 1964.

Frank, Jerome D. *Persuasion and Healing: A Comparative Study of Psychotherapy.* Baltimore: Johns Hopkins Press, 1961.

Frankl, Viktor E. *From Death-Camp to Existentialism.* Boston: Beacon Press, 1959.

———. "Self-transcendence as a human phenomenon," *Journal of Humanistic Psychology,* 6, 1966.

French, T. M. *The Integration of Behavior.* Chicago: University of Chicago Press, 1952.

Freud, Sigmund. *An Autobiographical Study: The Standard Edition of* the Complete Psychological Works of Sigmund Freud. Trans. by James Strachey. London: The Hogarth Press, 20, 1959.

——. *Basic Writings*. Trans. and ed. by A. A. Brill. New York: Random House, 1938.

——. *Collected Papers, II, Clinical Papers on Techniques*. New York: Basic Books, 1959.

——. *Freud and the Twentieth Century*. Ed. by B. Nelson. New York: Meridian Books, 1957.

——. "The Interpretation of Dreams," *Standard Edition of the Complete Psychological Works of Sigmund Freud*. Vols. 4 and 5. New York: Modern Library, 1950.

——. *New Introductory Lectures on Psychoanalysis*. Trans. by W. J. H. Sprott. New York: W. W. Norton, 1933.

——. *The Origin and Development of Psychoanalysis*. New York: Henry Regnery, 1955.

——. *An Outline of Psychoanalysis*. New York: Norton, 1949.

——. *The Problem of Anxiety*. Trans. by Henry Alden Bonker. New York: The Psychoanalytic Quarterly Press and W. W. Norton, 1936.

Fry, Edward B. *Teaching Machines and Programmed Instruction: An Introduction*. New York: McGraw-Hill, 1963.

Funkenstein, Daniel H., Stanley H. King and Maragret E. Drolette. *Mastery of Stress*. Cambridge: Harvard University Press, 1957.

Gardner, John W. *Excellence: Can We Be Equal and Excellent Too:* New York: Harper and Row, 1962.

——. *Self Renewal: The Individual and the Innovative Society*. New York: Harper & Row, 1963.

Gendlin, Eugene T. *Experiencing and the Creation of Meaning: A Philosophical and Psychological Approach to the Subjective*. New York: The Free Press, A Division of The Macmillan Co., 1962.

——. "A Theory of Personality Change," *Personality Change*. Ed. by P. Worche and D. Byrne. New York: John Wiley and Sons, 1964.

——. "Value and Process of Experiencing," *The Goals of Psychotherapy*. Ed. by A. H. Mahrer. New York: Appleton-Century-Crofts, 1967.

Getzels, Jacob W., and Phillip W. Jackson. *Creativity and Intelligence:*

Explorations with Gifted Students. New York: John Wiley and Sons, 1962.

Glaser, Robert, ed. *Training, Research and Education.* Pittsburg: University of Pittsburg Press, 1962.

Glasser, William. *Reality Therapy: A New Approach to Psychiatry.* New York: Harper & Row, 1965.

Glettman, Henry, and Joseph Greenbaum. *Preliminary Results of Depth Interviews and Attitude Scales of Inquiry into Political and Social Attitudes in Hungary of the Europe Press.* New York: Free Europe Press, 1957.

Gould, Thomas. *Platonic Love.* New York: The Free Press, A Division of The Macmillan Co., 1963.

Guardini, Romano. *The World and the Person.* Chicago: Henry Regnery Co., 1965. First published as *Welt und Person,* Wurzburg: Werbudd-Verlag, 1939.

Gurwitsch, Aron. *The Field of Consciousness.* Pittsburg: Duquesne University Press, 1964.

Hameline, Daniel, and Marie J. Dardelin. *La Liberté D'Apprendre: Justifications pour un enseignement non-directif.* Paris: Les Editions Ouvrieres, 1967.

Hamilton, Max. *Psychosomatics.* New York: John Wiley, 1955.

Handel, Gerald, ed. *The Psychosocial Interior of the Family: A Source Book for the Study of Whole Families.* Chicago: Aldine Publishing Co., 1967.

Harper, Robert J. C., Charles C. Anderson, Clifford M. Christensen and Steven M. Hunka. *The Cognitive Processes: Readings.* Englewood Cliffs, N. J.: Prentice-Hall, 1964.

Harris, Irving D. *Emotional Blocks to Learning: A Study of the Reasons for Failure in School.* Glencoe, Ill.: The Free Press of Glencoe, 1961.

Hartman, Heinz. *Ego Psychology and Problem of Adaptation.* Trans. by David Rapaport. New York: International Universities Press, 1958.

———. *Essays on Ego Psychology: Selected Problems in Psychoanalytic theory.* New York: International Universities Press, 1964.

———. *Psychoanalysis and Moral Values.* New York: International Universities Press, 1960.

Harvey, O. J., David E. Hunt and Harold M. Schroeder. *Conceptual Systems and Personality Organization.* New York: John Wiley & Sons, 1961.

Hayakawa, S. I. *Language in Action: A Guide to Accurate Thinking.* New York: Harcourt, Brace & Co., 1941.

Heath, Douglas H. *Explorations of Maturity: Studies of Mature and Immature College Men.* New York: Appleton-Century-Crofts, 1965.

Heisenberg, Werner. *Physics and Philosophy: The Revolution in Modern Science.* Planned and ed. by Ruth Nanda Anshen, World Perspectives, Vol. 19. New York: Harper and Brothers, 1958.

Henry, Paul, S.J. *Saint Augustine on Personality: The Saint Augustine Lecture—1959.* New York: Macmillan Co., 1960

Herr, Vincent V., S.J. *Religious Psychology.* Staten Island, N.Y.: Alba House, 1965.

Herrick, C. Judson. *The Evolution of Human Nature.* Austin: University of Texas Press, 1956.

Hilgard, Ernest, and Donald Marquis. *Conditioning and Learning.* New York: Appleton-Century-Crofts, 1940.

———. *Introduction to Psychology.* 3rd edition. New York: Harcourt, Brace and World, 1962.

Hiltner, Seward, and Karl Menninger. *Constructive Aspects of Anxiety.* New York: Abingdon Press, 1963.

Hitler, Adolf. *Mein Kampf.* Trans. by R. Manheim. Boston: Houghton Mifflin, 1943.

Hobbes, Nicholas. "Sources of Gain in Psychotherapy," *The American Psychologist,* 17(11), November 1962.

Honey, Karen. *Feminine Psychology.* Ed. with introduction by Harold Kelman. New York: W. W. Norton and Co., 1967.

Hovland, Carl I., Irving L. Janis and Harold H. Kelley. *Communication and Persuasion.* New Haven and London: Yale University Press, 1953.

Hunt, J. M. *Intelligence and Experience.* New York: Ronald Press, 1961.

Kant, Immanuel. "Fundamental Principles of the Metaphysic of Morals," *Kant's Critique of Practical Reason and Other Works on the Theory of Ethics,* 1898. Reprinted as "The Categorical Imperative," by Immanuel Kant in *A Modern Introduction to*

Ethics: Readings from Classical and Contemporary Sources, ed. by M. K. Munitz, trans. by Thomas K. Abbot, Glencoe, Ill.: The Free Press of Glencoe, 1958.

Kerr, Walter. *The Decline of Pleasure.* New York: Simon and Schuster, 1962.

Kiell, Norman. *The Universal Experience of Adolescence.* New York: International Universities Press, 1964.

Klausmeier, Herbert H. *Learning and Human Abilities: Educational Psychology.* New York: Harper and Brothers, 1961.

Knapp, Peter H., ed. *Expressions of the Emotions in Man.* New York: International Universities Press, 1963.

Kobler, Frank. *Casebook in Psychopathology.* Staten Island, N.Y.: Alba House, 1966.

Kohler, Wolfgang. *The Place of Value in the World of Facts.* New York: New American Library, A Mentor Book, 1966.

Lado, Robert. *Language Teaching: A Scientific Approach,* New York: McGraw-Hill, 1964.

————. *Linguistics Across Cultures: Applied Linguistics for Language Teachers.* Ann Arbor: University of Michigan Press, 1964.

La Farga, Juan B. "Learning Foreign Languages in Group Counsel- *and Counseling.* New York: Sheed and Ward, 1966.
of Psychology, Loyola University, Chicago, November 1966.

Laffal, Julius. *Pathological and Normal Language.* New York: Atherton Press, 1965.

Langer, Susanne K. *Philosophy in a New Key: A Study in the Symbolism of Reason, Rite and Art.* New York: Mentor Books, 1951.

Langmuir, Irving. "Langmuir's Address" (Presidential Address to the American Association for the Advancement of Science, 1943), *Science Newsletter,* 43, January 2, 1943.

Lantz, D., and Volney Steffle. "Language and Cognition Revisited," *Journal of Abnormal and Social Psychology,* 69(5), November 1964.

Lee, James M., and Nathaniel J. Pallone, eds. *Readings in Guidance and Counseling.* New York: Sheed and Ward, 1966.

Lemaire, Jean G., with Evelyne Lemaire-Arnaud. *Les Conflits Conjugaux.* Paris: Les Editions Sociales Francaises, 1966.

Lessing, Arthur. "Eros, Dionysus and Ontology," *Existential Psychiatry,* 1(3), Fall, 1966.

Lillie, Ralph S. *General Biology and Philosophy Organism.* Chicago. University of Chicago Press, 1945.

Lonergan, Bernard. *Insight: A Study of Human Understanding*. New York: Philosophical Library, 1957.

Lund, Helen M. *On Shame and The Search for Identity*. New York: Science Editions, Inc., 1961.

Lyons, Joseph. *Psychology and the Measure of Man: A Phenomenological Approach*. New York: The Free Press of Glencoe, A Division of The Macmillan Co., 1963.

MacMurray, John. *Reason and Emotion*. New York: Barnes and Noble, 1935.

Malamud, Daniel I., and Solomon Machover. *Toward Self-Understanding: Group Techniques in Self-Confrontation*. Springfield: Charles C. Thomas, 1965.

Malis, G. *Research on Etiology of Schizophrenia*. Trans. by B. Haigh. Preface by Hudson Hoagland. New York: Consultants Bureau, 1961.

Mann, Thomas. *Dr. Faustus: The Life of the German Composer Adrain Leverkuhn as Told by a Friend*. Trans. by H. T. Lowe-Porter. New York: Alfred A. Knopf, 1948.

Marcel, Gabriel. *Homo Viator: Introduction to a Metaphysics of Hope*. Chicago: Henry Regnery Co., 1951.

Maritain, Jacques. *On the Use of Philosophy: Three Essays*. New York: Atheneum, 1965.

———. *Philosophy of Nature*. Trans. by Imelda Byrne, to which has been added "Maritain's Philosophy of the Sciences," first published by Sheed and Ward in the Maritain volume of *The Thomist*, 1943. New York: Philosophical Library, 1951.

Marx, Melvin., ed. *Psychological Theory: Contemporary Readings*. New York: Macmillan Co., 1951.

Maslow, A. H. "Beyond Self-Actualization," *The Challenge of Humanistic Psychology*. Ed. by J. Bugental. (In Press.)

———. "Fusions of Facts and Values," *American Journal of Psychoanalysis*, 23, 1963.

———. "Lessons from the Peak-Experiences," *Journal of Humanistic Psychology*, 2, 1962.

———. *Motivation and Personality*. New York: Harper and Row, 1954.

———. "The Need to Know and the Fear of Knowing," *Journal of General Psychology*, 68, 1963.

———. *The Psychology of Science: A Reconnaissance*. New York: Harper and Row, 1966.

————. *Religious Values and Peak Experiences.* Columbus: Ohio State University Press, 1964.

————. "Some Frontier Problems in Mental Health," *Personality Theory and Counseling Practice.* Ed. by A. Combs. Miami: University of Florida Press, 1961.

————. *Toward a Psychology of Being.* Princeton: Van Nostrand, 1962.

Maslow, A. H., and B. Mittleman. *Principles of Abnormal Psychology: The Dynamics of Psychic Illness.* New York: Harper and Brothers, 1941.

May, Rollo, ed. *Existential Psychology.* New York: Random House, 1961.

————. *The Meaning of Anxiety.* New York: Ronald Press, 1950.

————. *Psychology and the Human Dilemma.* Princeton: Van Nostrand, 1967.

Mayman, Martin. "Toward a Positive Definition of Mental Health." American Psychological Association symposium, September 1955.

McCall, Raymond. *A Preface to Scientific Psychology.* Milwaukee: The Bruce Publishing Co., 1959.

McCary, J. L., and D. E. Sheer. *Six Approaches to Psychotherapy.* New York: Dryden, 1955.

McDaniel, H. B., John E. Lallas, James A. Saum and James L. Gilmore. *Readings in Guidance.* New York: Henry Holt and Company, 1959.

McGavan, John F., and Lyle D. Schmidt. *Counseling: Readings in Theory and Practice.* New York: Holt, Rinehart and Winston, 1962.

McKeon, Richard, ed. *Introduction to Aristotle.* New York: Random House, Modern Library, 1947.

McKinney, Fred. *Counseling for Personnal Adjustment in Schools and Colleges.* Boston: Houghton Mifflin, 1958.

McLaughlin, Barry, S. J. "Values in Behavioral Science," *Journal of Religion and Health,* 4(3), April 1965.

McLuhan, Marshall. *Understanding Media: The Extensions of Man.* New York: McGraw-Hill, 1964.

Mednick, M., S. Mednick and C. Jung. "Continual Association as a Function of Level of Creativity and Type of Verbal Stimulus," *Journal of Abnormal and Social Psychology,* 69(5), November 1964.

Menninger, Karl A. *A Manual for Psychiatric Case Study.* 2nd ed. New York: Grune and Stratton, 1962.

————. *A Theory of Psychoanaliytic Technique.* New York: Basic Books, 1958.

————, Martin Maymen and Paul Pruyser. *The Vital Balance.* New York: The Viking Press, 1963.

Meyer, Leonard B. *Emotion and Meaning in Music.* Chicago: University of Chicago Press, 1956.

Missildine, W. Hugh. *Your Inner Child of the Past.* New York: Simon and Schuster, 1963.

Mittlemann, Wolff, and M. P. Scharf. "Experimental Studies on Patients with Gastritis, Duodenitis and Peptic Ulcer," *Psychosomatic Medicine,* 4, May 1961.

Montaigne, Michel de. *The Autobiography of Michel de Montaigne.* Ed. by Marvin Lowenthal. New York: Vintage Books, 1956.

Morgan, John. *The Psychology of Abnormal People.* 2nd ed. New York: Longmans, Green and Co., 1940.

Mowrer, O. H. *The New Group Therapy.* Princeton: Van Nostrand, 1964.

Murphy, Gardner. "Pythagorean Number Theory and Its Implications for Psychology," *The American Psychologist,* 22(6), June 1967.

Mussen, Paul H., and John Conger. *Child Development and Personality.* New York: Harper and Brothers, 1956.

Mustakas, C. E. *The Self.* New York: Harper, 1956.

Nunokawa, Walter D. *Human Values and Abnormal Behavior.* Chicago: Scott Foresman and Co., 1965.

Nurnberger, John I., C. B. Ferster and John Paul Brady. *An Introduction to the Science of Human Behavior.* New York: Appleton-Century-Crofts, 1963.

Odegard, Peter H. "The Social Sciences and Society." An editorial in *Science,* 145(3637), September 11, 1964, from *The Educational Record,* 45(190), 1964.

Ogden, C. K. *Opposition, A Linguistic and Psychological Analysis.* With a new introduction by I. A. Richards. Bloomington: Indiana University Press, 1967.

Opler, Marvin K. *Culture and Social Psychiatry.* New York: Atherton Press, 1967.

Patterson, C. H. *Theories of Counseling and Psychotherapy.* New York: Harper and Row, 1966.

Pearson, Karl S. "Statistical Concepts in Their Relation to Reality,"

Journal of the Royal Statistical Society, 17, 1955.

Peck, Robert F., Robert J. Havighurst, Ruth Cooper, Jesse Lilienthal and Douglas More. *The Psychology of Character Development.* New York: John Wiley and Sons, 1960.

Pei, Mario. *The Story of Language.* Philadelphia: J. B. Lippincott Co., 1949.

Pepinsky, H. B., and Pauline Pepinsky. *Counseling Theory and Practice.* New York: Ronald, 1954.

Perls, Frederick S., Ralph F. Hefferline and Paul Goodman. *Gestalt Therapy, Excitement and Growth in Human Personality.* New York: The Julian Press, 1951.

Peters, Herman J., and James C. Hanson, eds. *Vocational Guidance and Career Development, Selected Readings.* New York: Macmillan Co., 1966.

Petrie, Asenath. *Individuality in Pain and Suffering.* Chicago: University of Chicago Press, 1967.

Piaget, Jean. *The Construction of Reality in the Child.* Trans. by Margaret Cook. New York: Basic Books, 1954.

———. *The Language and Thought of the Child.* Trans. by Majorie Gabian. Preface by Professor E. Claparede. New York: Meridian Books, 1955.

———. *The Origins of Intelligence in Children.* Trans. by Margaret Cook. New York: International University Press, 1952.

———. *La Psychologie de l'Intelligence.* Paris: Librairie Armand Colin, 1956. Eng. trans.: *Psychology of Intelligence,* Humanities Press.

Plato. *The Republic.* Trans., introduction and notes by Frances Macdonald. Cornford: Oxford University Press, 1945.

Polanyi, M. *Personal Knowledge.* Chicago: University of Chicago Press, 1958.

Porter, E. H. *An Introduction to Therapeutic Counseling.* Boston: Houghton Mifflin, 1950.

Pressey, Sidney L. *Psychological Development Through the Life Span.* New York: Harper and Brothers, 1957.

Priestley, J. B. "Eroticism, Sex and Love," *Saturday Evening Post,* April 29, 1963.

Prothro, E. Terry, and P. T. Teska. *Psychology: A Biosocial Study of Behavior.* Boston: Ginn and Co., 1950.

Pruyser, Paul. "Is Mental Health Possible?" *Bulletin Menninger Clinic,* 22, 1958.

Rank, Otto. *The Trauma of Birth*. New York: Harcourt, Brace and Co., 1929.

Rapaport, D. *Organization and Pathology of Thought*. New York: Columbia University Press, 1951.

Reeves, Robert B. "The Total Response," *Journal of Religion and Health*, 4, April, 1965.

Reisman, David, *et al. The Lonely Crowd*. New Haven: Yale University Press, 1961.

Restle, Frank. *Psychology of Judgment and Choice: A Theoretical Essay*. New York: John Wiley and Sons, 1961.

Richter, C. F. "Sudden Death Phenomenon in Animals and Humans," *The Meaning of Death*. Ed. by Herman Feifel. New York: McGraw-Hill, 1959.

Ricoeur, Paul. *The Symbolism of Evil*. Trans. by Emerson Buchanan. New York: Harper and Row, 1967.

Rimoldi, H. J. A., Hermelinda M. Fogliatoo, James B. Erdmann and Michael B. Donnelly. "Problem Solving in High School and College Students." Cooperative Research Project No. 2199, Loyola Psychometric Laboratory, Loyola University, Chicago, Ill., 1964. (Unpublished.)

Roebuck, Julian, and S. Lee Spray. "The Cocktail Lounge: A Study of Heterosexual Relations in a Public Organization," *Reflections*. Merck Sharp and Dohme, 2(5), 1967.

Rogers, Carl. "APA Presidential Address," *The American Psychologist*, 2(9), September 1947.

———. *Client-Centered Therapy*. Boston: Houghton Mifflin, 1951.

———. *Counseling and Psychotherapy*, Boston: Houghton Mifflin, 1942.

———. A Note on "The Nature of Man," *Journal of Counseling Psychology*, 4(3), 1957.

———. *On Becoming a Person*. Boston: Houghton Mifflin, 1961.

———, ed. *The Therapeutic Relationship and Its Impact: A Study of Psychotherapy with Schizophrenics*. Madison: University of Wisconsin Press, 1967.

———, and Barry Stevens. *Person to Person: The Problem of Being Human: A New Trend in Psychology*. Walnut Creek, Calif.: Real People Press, 1967.

Royce, James E. *Man and His Nature: A Philosophical Psychology*. New York: McGraw-Hill, 1961.

Royce, Milford O. "Caring for the Whole Patient." Palmer House

Banquet, Anderson Foundation, November 10, 1966.

Rubenstein, Eli A., and Morris B. Parloff., eds. *Research in Psychotherapy*. Washington, D. C.: National Publishing Co., 1959.

Ruesch, J., and G. Bateson. *Communication: The Social Matrix of Psychiatry*. New York: Norton, 1951.

Ruitenbeek, Henrik M., ed. *Psychoanalysis and Existential Philosophy*. New York: E. P. Dutton and Co., 1962.

Saporta, Sol, ed. *Psycholinguistics: A Book of Readings*. New York: Holt, Rinehart and Winston, 1961.

Sartre, Jean Paul. *Existentialism and Human Emotions*. New York: Philosophical Library, Book Sales, Inc., 1957.

Schachter, Stanley. *The Psychology of Affiliation: Experimental Studies of the Sources of Gregariousness*. Stanford, Calif.: Stanford University Press, 1959.

Scherer, George A., and Michael Wertheimer. *A Psycholinguistic Experiment in Foreign-Language Teaching*. New York: McGraw-Hill, 1964.

Schlaifer, R. *Probability and Statistics for Business Decisions*. New York: McGraw-Hill, 1959.

Schneiders, Alexander A. *Counseling the Adolescent*. San Francisco: Chandler Publishing Co., 1967.

Schofield, William. *Psychotherapy—The Purchase of Friendship*. Englewood Cliffs, N. J.: Prentice-Hall, 1964.

Selye, Hans. *The Stress of Life*. New York: McGraw-Hill, 1956.

Shands, Harley C. *Thinking and Psychotherapy: An Inquiry into the Process of Communication*. Cambridge: Harvard University Press, 1960.

Shepherd, Clovis R. *Small Groups: Some Sociological Perspectives*. San Francisco: Chandler Publishing Co., 1964.

Shipley, Thorne, ed. *Classics in Psychology*. New York: Philosophical Library, 1961.

Skinner, B. F. "Teaching Machines," *Science*, 128, 1958.

———. *The Technology of Teaching*. New York: Appleton-Century-Crofts, 1967.

———. *Verbal Behavior*. New York: Appleton-Century-Crofts, 1957.

Smith, Karl, and William M. Smith. *Perception and Motion: An Analysis of Space Structured Behavior*. Philadelphia: W. B. Saunders Co., 1962.

Snyder, William. *Dependency in Psychotherapy: A Casebook*. New York: Macmillan Co., 1962.

————, and B. June. *The Psychotherapy Relationship.* New York: Macmillan Co., 1961.

Speers, Rex W., and Cornelius Lansing. *Group Therapy in Childhood Psychosis.* Chapel Hill: University of North Carolina Press, 1965.

Sperling, Melitta. "Fetishism in Children," *The Psychoanalytic Quarterly,* 32(3), 1963.

Stein, Morris I., and Shirley J. Heinze. *Creativity and the Individual: Summaries of Selected Literature in Psychology and Psychiatry.* Glencoe, Ill.: The Free Press of Glencoe, 1960.

Steiner, George. *Language and Silence: Essays on Language, Literature and the Inhuman.* New York: Atheneum Press, 1967.

Sullivan, Harry S. *The Interpersonal Theory of Psychiatry.* New York: W. W. Norton Co., 1953.

Szasz, Thomas. *The Myth of Mental Illness.* New York: Hoeber-Harper, 1960.

Teilhard de Chardin, Pierre. *The Phenomenon of Man.* Trans. by Bernard Wall. New York: Harper Torchbooks, Harper and Row, 1961.

Tennent, S. Foreward to Willa Cather's *On Writing.* New York: Alfred A. Knopf, 1949.

Tillich, Paul. *The Courage To Be.* New Haven: Yale University Press, 1952.

————. "The Impact of Psychotherapy on Theological Thought," *Pastoral Psychology,* February 1960.

Tournier, Paul. *The Meaning of Persons.* New York: Harper and Brothers, 1957.

Tranel, Daniel D. "Teaching Latin with the Chromacord," *Classical Journal,* 63(4), January 1960.

Tuchman, Barbara W. *The Proud Tower.* New York: Macmillan Co., 1962.

Tukey, J. W. "The Future of Data Analysis," *Annals of Mathematical Statistics,* 33, January 1967.

Vanderpool, James A. "Self-Concept Differences in the Alcoholic Under Varying Conditions of Drinking and Sobriety." Unpublished Doctoral Dissertation, Department of Psychology, Loyola University, 1967.

Van Kaam, Adrian L. "Assumptions in Psychology," *Journal of Individual Psychology,* 14, 1958.

————. "Clinical Implications of Heidegger's Concepts of Will, Decision and Responsibility," *Review of Existential Psychology and Psychiatry*, Fall, 1961.

――――. Commentary on "Freedom and Responsibility Examined," *Behavioral Science and Guidance: Proposals and Perspectives*. Ed. by E. Lloyd-Jones and E. M. Westervelt, Bureau of Publications, Teachers College, Columbia University, New York, 1963.

――――. "Counseling and Existential Psychology, *Harvard Educational Review*, Fall, 1962.

――――. "Counseling and Psychotherapy from the Viewpoint of Existential Psychology," *Counseling and Psychotherapy: An Overview*. Ed. by D. S. Arbuckle. New York: McGraw-Hill, 1967.

――――. *Existential Foundations of Psychology*. Pittsburgh: Duquesne University Press, 1966.

――――. "Existential Psychology as a Theory of Personality," *Review of Existential Psychology and Psychiatry*, Winter, 1963.

――――. "The Fantasy of Romantic Love," *Modern Myths and Popular Fancies*. Pittsburgh: Duquesne University Press, 1961.

――――. "Freud and Anthropological Psychology," *The Justice*, Brandeis University, May, 1959.

――――. "Humanistic Psychology and Culture," *Journal of Humanistic Psychology*, 1, Spring, 1961.

――――. *A Light to the Gentiles*. Detroit: Bruce Publishing Co., 1962.

――――. "Phenomenal Analysis: Exemplified by a Study of the Experience of 'Really Feeling Understood,'" *Journal of Individual Psychology*, 15, 1959.

Veatch, Henry. *Rational Man: A Modern Interpretation of Aristotelian Ethics*. Bloomington: Indiana University Press, 1964.

Vergote, A. *Problems in Psychoanalysis: A Symposium*. Baltimore: Helicon Press, 1961.

Von Domarus, E. "The Specific Laws of Logic in Schizophrenia," *Language and Thought in Schizophrenia*. Ed. by J. S. Kasanin. Berkeley: University of California Press, 1944.

Voth, H. M., R. Cancro and M. Kissen. "Choice of Defense," *Archives of General Psychiatry*, 18(1), January 1968.

Waldman, A., ed. "Programmed Instruction and Foreign Language Teaching," *Trends in Language Teaching*. New York: McGraw-Hill, 1966.

Weil, Simone. *The Need for Roots*. Boston: The Beacon Press, 1952.

Weitz, Henry. *Behavior Change Through Guidance.* New York: John Wiley and Sons, 1964.

Werner, Heinz, and Bernard Kaplan. *Symbol Formation.* New York: John Wiley and Sons, 1967.

Whatmough, J. *Language: A Modern Synthesis.* New York: The New American Library of World Literature, 1956.

Whyte, William H. *The Organization Man.* Garden City: Doubleday Anchor Books, Doubleday and Co., 1957.

Wilmer, Harry A. "Transference to a Medical Center," *California Medical,* 96, 1962.

Wilson, C. *Introduction to New Existentialism.* Boston: Houghton Mifflin, 1967.

Wilson, Roger H., and Seymour M. Farber, eds. *Man and Civilization: The Potential of Woman.* (A symposium.) University of California, San Francisco Medical Center, New York: McGraw-Hill, 1963.

Winnicott, D. W. *The Maturational Processes and the Facilitating Environment: Studies in the Theory of Emotional Development.* New York: International Universities Press, 1965.

Wolberg, Lewis. *Psycho-therapy and the Behavioral Sciences.* New York: Grune and Stratton, 1966.

Wolff, Harold. *Stress and Disease.* Springfield, Ill.: Charles C. Thomas Publishers, 1953.

Wylie, Ruth. *The Self Concept: A Critical Survey of Pertinent Research Literature.* Lincoln: University of Nebraska Press, 1961.

Young, Paul Thomas. *Motivation and Emotion: A Survey of the Determinants of Human and Animal Activity.* New York: John Wiley and Sons, 1961.

Zavalloni, Roberto. *Self Determination: The Psychology of Personal Freedom.* Trans. by Virgilio Biasiol and Carroll Tageson. Chicago: Forum Books, 1962.

Index

Adler, A., 107, 114, 134.
Affiliation, 85, 372-374.
Alcoholism, 110-111, 112.
Allport, G., 36.
Ampère, 36.
Anxiety, 76, 82, 96, 99, 108, 134, 184-185, 192, 228, 232, 299-300, 302, 339;
reduction of, 339-342.
Apparatus, teaching, 323, 324, 325-331, 332-338, 339-342, 347, 350.
Aquinas, St. Thomas, 45, 104, 107, 128, 130, 210.
Arbuckle, D. S., 186-187.
Aristotle, 35, 69, 97, 102, 104, 106, 107.
Arnold, M. B., 159.
Auerbach, E., 50.
Augustine, St., 35, 37, 38, 39, 69, 71, 104, 128.
Austin, G. A., 368-370.
Authority, 205-206, 207.

Bailey, P., 117.
Bakan, D., 61, 186, 361.
Becker, E., 116.
Begin, Y., 317-318.
Bernard de Chartres, 42.
Berkson, J., 61.
Brachfeld, O., 314.
Brown, J., 343.

Brunner, J. S., 368-371.
Buber, M., 57.
Burns, B. D., 343.

Carmichael, L., 89-90.
Cartesian concepts, 51, 52, 54, 55, 56, 58, 59, 71, 91, 93, 116, 127, 186, 200, 339, 361, 371.
Carstairs, G. M., 116.
Chart-Maturity and Therapy of Limits, 227.
Chesterton, 58.
Choice, 149, 154, 155.
Clarification, process of, 6.
Cognitive process, 367-372.
Cole, C. W., 158.
Color coding, 325-331, 341-342, 344.
Commitment, 3, 20-22, 26, 29, 44, 74, 85, 128, 131, 133-134, 146, 315-316, 365-366.
Communication, 127, 130, 134, 136, 138, 145, 147, 168, 174, 179, 233-234, 235, 236, 238-239, 256, 298, 303-304, 360, 363.
Confrontation, 211-212, 213-215, 221, 252, 372-374.
Convalidation, 201, 253, 374-375.
Counseling, 3-5, 7, 9, 12, 20, 45-46, 66-68, 79, 80, 96, 103,

Nihil Obstat, Rt. Rev. Msgr. James T. Clarke, Censor Librorum; Imprimatur, ✠ J. Carroll McCormick, Bishop of Scranton; August 8, 1968.